PROTECTING THE RIGHT TO LEAVE IN AN ERA OF EXTERNALISED MIGRATION CONTROL

This book explores the human right to leave any country – including one's own – in international law, and its applicability to externalised migration control.

It develops a framework for interpreting the right and demonstrates how various externalisation measures violate it, leading to the international responsibility of states and international organisations.

Analysing the work of international and regional systems enshrining the right and examining global externalisation practices, it demonstrates the radical reform required by states and international organisations to comply with the right to leave. Implementing the author's recommendations would compel the dismantlement of many current externalisation strategies and a re-imagining of the global (im)mobility regime.

This book offers compelling insights for lawyers in the fields of international law, human rights and refugee law, as well as migration policymakers, practitioners and officials.

Volume 100 in the series Studies in International Law

Studies in International Law

Recent titles in this series

International Agreements between Non-State Actors
as a Source of International Law
Melissa Loja

Judicial Decisions in International Law Argumentation:
Between Entrapment and Creativity
Letizia Lo Giacco

South-South Migrations and the Law from Below:
Case Studies on China and Nigeria
Oreva Olakpe

Territorial Status in International Law
Jure Vidmar

Marine Bioprospecting, Biodiversity and Novel Uses of Ocean Resources:
New Approaches in International Law
Edited by Niels Krabbe and David Langlet

The Standard of Review Before the International Court of Justice:
Between Principle and Pragmatism
Felix Fouchard

Global Lawmaking and Social Change:
The Varieties of Customary International Law
Gregor Novak

The Effectiveness of the Inter-American Court of Human Rights:
The Case of Indigenous Territorial Rights
Gabriela CB Navarro

Individuals in International Humanitarian Law: A Historical Analysis
Sarina Landefeld

The Pathology of Plenty: Natural Resources in International Law
Lys Kulamadayil

The United Nations Security Council and the Authorisation of Force: Form,
Character and Nature
Marko Svicevic

Protecting the Right to Leave in an Era of Externalised Migration Control
Emilie McDonnell

For a complete list of titles in this series
see www.bloomsbury.com/uk/series/studies-in-international-law/

Protecting the Right to Leave in an Era of Externalised Migration Control

Emilie McDonnell

•HART•
OXFORD • LONDON • NEW YORK • NEW DELHI • SYDNEY

HART PUBLISHING

Bloomsbury Publishing Plc

Kemp House, Chawley Park, Cumnor Hill, Oxford, OX2 9PH, UK

1385 Broadway, New York, NY 10018, USA

Bloomsbury Publishing Ireland Limited, 29 Earlsfort Terrace, Dublin 2, D02 AY28, Ireland

HART PUBLISHING, the Hart/Stag logo, BLOOMSBURY and the Diana logo are trademarks of Bloomsbury Publishing Plc

First published in Great Britain 2026

1

A catalogue record for this book is available from the British Library.

A catalogue record for this book is available from the Library of Congress.

Library of Congress Control Number: 2025949171

ISBN: HB: 978-1-50998-227-1
ePDF: 978-1-50998-229-5
ePub: 978-1-50998-228-8

Typeset by Compuscript Ltd, Shannon

For product safety related questions contact productsafety@bloomsbury.com

To find out more about our authors and books visit www.hartpublishing.co.uk. Here you will find extracts, author information, details of forthcoming events and the option to sign up for our newsletters.

For my husband, Oudai, who is my greatest inspiration.

Foreword

THE RIGHT TO leave any country, including one's own, is easy to say, but hard to comprehend. For too long, commentators, activists and academics have been content with the inchoate version, seeing the right as more of a liberty waiting to be complemented by the exercise of a more or less absolute discretion by a 'sovereign' State allowing the individual to enter.

Dr McDonnell, however, upends the argument and many of the underlying assumptions. In her comprehensive analysis, she demonstrates how the right to leave is in fact much more than we think. All the while, her thesis remains rooted in the realities of the present day, as States work continuously to find ways to avoid their international responsibilities, in particular, by 'externalising' both their duties and the individuals to whom they would otherwise like to say 'no' (or perhaps might well find that they have to say 'yes'). In framing policy and practice, many States must also deal with their own courts, and with regional tribunals and treaty supervisory mechanisms, all of which are under increasing pressure and struggle to deal effectively with the claims of those affected.

Appropriate solutions, as always, reside in political will and in the recognition that migration – the movement of people between States – is an ongoing phenomenon. It will not be stopped or deterred by increasingly frequent instances of inhumane treatment, often inflicted by officials of third States, or by casually leaving women, children and men to die, shipwrecked on the high seas or adrift and deprived of food and water in deserts and the land between.

I share Dr McDonnell's view that, absent an epochal change of attitude among the Ministries of the North, unlikely at the present time, incremental measures in liberal democracies and regional institutions committed to particular values and the rule of law are more likely to see progress. The right to leave any country is not just about the refugee in search of asylum, but encompasses everyone else; it is an inseverable part of the right to freedom of movement and must be protected on that account alone. As she says, even if migration control is legitimate, it must be subsumed within the overall obligation of protection; a 'better balance' can and must be struck, which is consistent with the implementation in good faith of States' international legal obligations at large.

If things are to change, nationally or regionally, advocates at all levels must have the resources that enable them to persuade reviewing courts and policy makers that the right to leave has normative force. Part of the argument, as Dr McDonnell demonstrates, is that the right is not respected, protected, promoted or fulfilled by arrangements that attempt to pass on responsibility for implementation in individual cases to other States, with or without the assistance and intervention of international or non-governmental organisations. In the absence of effective international supervision, as she shows with copious examples from the Americas, Australasia, Africa and Europe, no amount of money or other incentives are likely to lead to results consistent with international law. Moreover, the net result more often than not is systemic exclusion, for underlying every policy and practice of externalisation, is fear of the other, of the foreigner, of he or she who can be discriminated against on account of their race, colour, ethnic origin, or religion.

Dr McDonnell provides the reader with a comprehensive account and lines of argument, drawing together the work of adjudicative bodies, including the International Court of Justice, UN treaty mechanisms, and those of regional systems, including the European Court of Human Rights, the Court of Justice of the European Union, the Inter-American Court and Commission of Human Rights, and the African Commission and Court on Human and Peoples' Rights, among others.

She also makes effective use of the consolidating approach of courts to questions of jurisdiction and attribution, which is particularly relevant to the juridical assessment of 'pullbacks' and 'pushbacks' and to increasing recourse to so-called contact-less interventions, wherever the effect is to frustrate the exercise of the right to leave. Dr McDonnell clearly lays out the basis of shared international legal responsibility, taking account of the variety of different acts of destination States, of those that may be called partner States, and finally of international organisations, such as the International Organisation for Migration, all of which can and do contribute to breaches of the right to leave. As States tend to engage in more hands-off approaches, courts will need to hone their understanding of jurisdiction to bridge the accountability gap, to accommodate comprehensive, multi-party operations, and to assess not only direct actions, but also the impact of 'influence' in real life and its place in complicity in wrongdoing.

This is an engaging and very well-written book, reflecting the author's excellent scholarship and her deep commitment to the issues as they impact on the lives and well-being of people on the move and the communities they touch in their journey. I strongly recommend it. States and international organisations can do better; they have the power to bring meaningful protection to those currently affected by restrictions on the right to leave, and they need to stop, listen and act.

Guy S. Goodwin-Gill
All Souls College
Oxford
30 October 2025

Preface

THIS BOOK REFLECTS the relevant law and practice, to the best of my knowledge, as they stood on 30 June 2025. Earlier versions of the author's arguments in some Sections of Chapters two, three, five and six were published in 'Challenging Externalisation Through the Lens of the Human Right to Leave' (2024) 71 *Netherlands International Law Review* 119.

Acknowledgements

This book is largely based on my doctoral thesis and reflects my long-standing interest in human rights and asylum and my deep commitment to making a difference to the lives of asylum seekers and refugees. Reaching this point would not have been possible without the support, guidance and encouragement of so many people throughout my DPhil journey and in the drafting of this book.

First and foremost, I express my sincere gratitude to my doctoral supervisors, Professor Cathryn Costello and Associate Professor Miles Jackson. Thank you for your invaluable guidance, immense knowledge and continuous support during my DPhil and MPhil studies, as well as for your help in publishing my thesis as a book. You have inspired and encouraged me to push myself beyond what I thought possible, academically, personally and professionally. I am deeply indebted to you both.

I am very grateful to my two doctoral examiners, Professor Guy S. Goodwin-Gill and Professor Vincent Chetail, for their thoughtful and instructive feedback during the viva voce; the book is stronger because of it. Particular thanks to my earlier examiners, Professor Elspeth Guild, Professor Lavanya Rajamani and Assistant Professor Efthymios (Akis) Papastavridis, for their insightful comments and guidance, which shaped and enriched my work.

Thank you to the many colleagues and friends at the University of Oxford Law Faculty and beyond, especially those involved in the Public International Law seminars and at the Bonavero Institute of Human Rights, for your generous support, for providing opportunities to showcase my research, and for your constructive feedback, insights and lively debates. My Oxford experience, both professionally and personally, was shaped by you, and many parts of this book are richer thanks to your engagement.

My studies in Oxford and this subsequent work would not have been possible without the generosity of the Rhodes Trust. I am especially thankful to the many Rhodes House staff for their constant support and kindness over the years. I also thank University College, Hertford College, the Law Faculty and the many librarians and administrative staff who helped me, whether academically, financially or personally. Special thanks to the University of Tasmania, its School of Law and the many brilliant professors and staff for supporting me on this journey since 2011.

I am deeply appreciative of the editors and staff at Hart for their assistance, patience and belief in this work, as well as to the anonymous reviewers for their constructive comments. I also extend my thanks to Erick Yuji Yamachi for his careful assistance with footnote and reference formatting.

Since finishing my doctorate, I have benefited greatly from many thought-provoking discussions and interactions at conferences, seminars and other events. My work with organisations, including the Australian Human Rights Commission and Human Rights Watch, has been instrumental in enabling me to engage with policy and practical issues concerning asylum, migration and refugee matters, and to hear firsthand the experiences, struggles and strength of refugees and asylum seekers. These experiences and exchanges have both inspired and informed this book.

Last but not least, my heartfelt thanks to my family, friends and husband. To my parents, Terry and Vivi McDonnell: thank you for your unwavering support, encouragement and love over the years; I could not have done it without you. To my sister, Dr Kristina McDonnell: thank you for instilling a strong work ethic in me from a young age and for inspiring me to pursue my dreams. To my friends, near and far: thank you for your friendship, laughter and support since day one. And to my husband, Dr Oudai Tozan: I am deeply grateful for everything you do for me and your daily love and care. Thank you for always believing in and encouraging me, especially when completing this book felt like an impossible feat.

Emilie Vivi McDonnell
Sydney, Australia
28 October 2025

Contents

PART II
EXTERNALISED MIGRATION CONTROLS

Table of Abbreviations

AC	Appeal Cases
ACHPR	African Commission on Human and Peoples' Rights
ACHR	American Convention on Human Rights
ACtHPR	African Court on Human and Peoples' Rights
ADHR	American Declaration of the Rights and Duties of Man
AFP	Australian Federal Police
AHRLR	African Human Rights Law Reports
All ER	All England Law Reports
ALO	Airline Liaison Officer
ARIO	Articles on the Responsibility of International Organisations
ARSIWA	Articles on Responsibility of States for Internationally Wrongful Acts
ASEAN	Association of Southeast Asian Nations
ASGI	Association for Juridical Studies on Immigration
AVR	Assisted Voluntary Return
ATV	Airport Transit Visa
CAT	Committee Against Torture
CEDAW	Convention on the Elimination of All Forms of Discrimination against Women
CEPS	Centre for European Policy Studies
CERD	Committee on the Elimination of Racial Discrimination
CFSP	Common Foreign and Security Policy
CHR	United Nations Commission on Human Rights

CIHRS	Cairo Institute for Human Rights Studies
CIS	Commonwealth of Independent States
CISA	Convention implementing the Schengen Agreement
CJEU	Court of Justice of the European Union
CLR	Commonwealth Law Reports
CMW	Committee on Migrant Workers
CoE	Council of Europe
CRC	Committee on the Rights of the Child
CRPD	Convention on the Rights of Persons with Disabilities
CUP	Cambridge University Press
DEMIG	Determinants of International Migration
DRC	Democratic Republic of the Congo
EACJ	East African Court of Justice
EBCG	European Border and Coast Guard Agency
EC	European Community
ECDPM	European Centre for Development Policy Management
ECHR	European Convention on Human Rights (Convention for the Protection of Human Rights and Fundamental Freedoms)
ECLI	European Case-Law Identifier
ECmHR	European Commission of Human Rights
ECOSOC	United Nations Economic and Social Council
ECOWAS	Economic Community of West African States
ECRE	European Council on Refugees and Exiles
ECtHR	European Court of Human Rights
EHRR	European Human Rights Reports
EJIL	European Journal of International Law
ETA	Electronic Travel Authorisation

ETIAS	European Travel Information and Authorization System
ETS	European Treaty Series
EU	European Union
EUBAM	European Union Border Assistance Mission
EUCFR	Charter of Fundamental Rights of the European Union
EUI	European University Institute
EUNAVFOR	European Union Naval Force
EWCA	England and Wales Court of Appeal
EWHC	England and Wales High Court
EXCOM	Executive Committee of the High Commissioner's Programme
FCA	Federal Court of Appeal
FMR	Forced Migration Review
FRA	European Union Agency for Fundamental Rights
GCM	Global Compact for Safe, Orderly and Regular Migration
GLAN	Global Legal Action Network
HRC	Human Rights Committee
HRW	Human Rights Watch
HUP	Harvard University Press
IACHR	Inter-American Commission on Human Rights
IACtHR	Inter-American Court of Human Rights
IBM	Integrated Border Management
ICAO	International Civil Aviation Organization
ICCPR	International Covenant on Civil and Political Rights
ICERD	International Convention on the Elimination of All Forms of Racial Discrimination
ICIBI	Independent Chief Inspector of Borders and Immigration

ICJ	International Court of Justice
ICJ Rep	International Court of Justice Reports
ICLQ	International and Comparative Law Quarterly
ICMPD	International Centre for Migration Policy Development
ICRMW	International Convention on the Protection of the Rights of All Migrant Workers and Members of their Families
IDP	Internally Displaced Person
IFC-IOR	Information Fusion Centre – Indian Ocean Region
IHR	International Health Regulations
IHRL	International Human Rights Law
IHRR	International Human Rights Report
ILC	International Law Commission
ILM	International Legal Materials
ILO	Immigration Liaison Officer
ILOR	Immigration Liaison Officer Regulation
IMI	International Migration Institute
IMO	International Maritime Organization
INA	Immigration and Nationality Act
IO	International Organisation
IOM	International Organization for Migration
IRPA	Immigration and Refugee Protection Act
IRPR	Immigration and Refugee Protection Regulations
JCWI	Joint Council for the Welfare of Immigrants
LBCG	Libyan Coast Guard
LSE	London School of Economics
MENA	Middle East and North Africa
MoU	Memorandum of Understanding
MPA	Maritime Powers Act

MPC	Migration Policy Centre
MPF	Migration Partnership Framework
MPI	Migration Policy Institute
MRCC	Maritime Rescue and Coordination Centre
NABA	Nationality and Borders Act
NAFSA	National Association of Foreign Student Advisers
NATO	North Atlantic Treaty Organization
NGO	Non-Governmental Organisation
NYIL	Netherlands Yearbook of International Law
NYU	New York University
OAS	Organization of American States
OAU	Organization of African Unity
OECD	Organisation for Economic Cooperation and Development
OHCHR	Office of the High Commissioner for Human Rights
OJ	Official Journal
OLAF	European Anti-Fraud Office
OPT	Occupied Palestinian Territory
OUP	Oxford University Press
PGSC	Papua New Guinea Supreme Court
PNG	Papua New Guinea
QIL	Questions of International Law
RCA	Regional Cooperation Agreement
RCP	Regional Consultative Processes on Migration
RLI	Refugee Law Initiative
RSC	Refugee Studies Centre
RSCAS	Robert Schuman Centre of Advanced Studies
RSO	Regional Support Office
SAR	Search and Rescue

SAR	International Convention on Maritime Search and Rescue
SCC	Supreme Court of Canada
SCR	Supreme Court Reports
SOLAS	International Convention for the Safety of Life at Sea
STC	Safe Third Country
SWD	European Commission Staff Working Document
TEU	Treaty on European Union
TFEU	Treaty on the Functioning of the European Union
UDHR	Universal Declaration of Human Rights
UK	United Kingdom
UKHL	United Kingdom House of Lords
UKSC	United Kingdom Supreme Court
UN	United Nations
UNCAT	Convention against Torture and Other Cruel, Inhuman or Degrading Treatment or Punishment
UNCLOS	United Nations Convention on the Law of the Sea
UNCRC	United Nations Convention on the Rights of the Child
UNGA	United Nations General Assembly
UNHCR	United Nations High Commissioner for Refugees
UNODC	United Nations Office on Drugs and Crime
UNSC	United Nations Security Council
UNTS	United Nations Treaty Series
US	United States
USC	United States Code
USSR	Union of Soviet Socialist Republics
UTS Law Review	University of Technology Sydney Law Review
VAC	Visa Application Centre

VCCR	Vienna Convention on Consular Relations
VCLT	Vienna Convention on the Law of Treaties
WHO	World Health Organization
WLR	Weekly Law Reports
YBILC	Yearbook of the International Law Commission
ZAWCHC	South Africa Western Cape High Court

Table of Cases

African Commission on Human and Peoples' Rights

African Court on Human and Peoples' Rights

Committee Against Torture

Committee on the Elimination of Racial Discrimination

Committee on the Rights of Persons with Disabilities

Committee on the Rights of the Child

Court of Justice of the European Union

East African Court of Justice

ECOWAS

European Commission/European Court of Human Rights

Human Rights Committee

Inter-American Commission on Human Rights

Inter-American Court of Human Rights

International Court of Justice

Australia

Canada

Papua New Guinea

South Africa

UK

US

1

Introduction

I. A WORLD OF EXTERNALISATION AND CONTAINMENT

THIS BOOK EXPLORES the remarkably underexplored right to leave any country, including one's own, in international law and its significance to the global phenomenon of externalised migration control. Across the Middle East, North Africa, Southeast Asia and more, millions of people are being denied their right to leave and subjected to a discriminatory and exclusionary mobility regime. Many States, especially in the Global North, are engaging in what has become known as '*externalised migration control*', deploying a wide range of measures and policies designed to contain migrants in countries of origin and transit, including nationals seeking to leave their own country, to prevent them from ever reaching their intended destination. Wealthier States have externalised their border controls by shifting responsibilities onto countries in the Global South and outsourcing to international organisations (IOs) and private companies – key features of migration governance today.

Greater human mobility in the twenty-first century, marked by large-scale, irregular movements of asylum seekers, refugees and other migrants, is considered one of the most pressing global issues today. Harmful, dehumanising and misleading narratives on migration permeate public and political discourses, often disregarding migration's proven benefits for societies and people worldwide. Instead of embracing a rights-based approach and genuine responsibility sharing, externalisation strategies continue to proliferate globally, as governments double down on curbing irregular migration and build ever-higher walls to keep certain migrants far away. Amidst this backdrop, examining how externalisation measures breach the right to leave under international law and the responsibility of different actors for their role in these harms has never been timelier.

For decades, wealthy Western democracies, such as Australia, Europe and the United States, have utilised various externalisation measures, sometimes unilaterally and often in collaboration.[1] This includes interceptions at sea, on

[1] See UNGA, 'Report of the Special Rapporteur on the Human Rights of Migrants, François Crépeau on Regional Study: Management of the External Borders of the European Union and its

land and near borders, such as pushbacks, as well as policies of non-assistance and the criminalisation of search and rescue organisations; visa requirements, carrier sanctions and pre-clearance measures; offshore detention and extra-territorial asylum processing; and safe country mechanisms. More recently, destination States have turned to States of origin and transit to stem irregular migration and contain (would-be) migrants on their behalf, including through pullbacks, the criminalisation of exit, and detention. In exchange, States of origin and transit are given funding, equipment and technical support, and incentivised with promises of visa liberalisation, trade concessions and development aid, or threatened with aid cuts, harsher visa requirements and tariffs.

States are supported by and act through the EU, particularly the EU's border and coastguard agency Frontex, the International Centre for Migration Policy Development (ICMPD), the International Organisation for Migration (IOM) and NATO. These all play essential roles in designing and implementing externalisation policies, and may contribute to rights violations. The involvement of IOM, a UN related organisation, in border management and externalisation is particularly problematic. It has rebranded itself as the 'UN Migration Agency' despite lacking any formal protection mandate and being highly deferential to States.[2] The ICMPD is an IO comprising 21 countries, the majority of which are EU Member States, which is mandated to develop and implement 'long-term strategies to cope with the migration phenomenon'.[3] Alongside this, the privatisation of border control has led to private companies, such as commercial airlines, ferry operators and visa companies, becoming the gatekeepers of movement.

Governments continue to focus on preventing and controlling migration at all costs. The EU has concluded new migration deals with countries such as Egypt,[4] Lebanon[5] and Tunisia[6] to halt departures to Europe, including citizens

Impact on the Human Rights of Migrants' (24 April 2013) UN Doc A/HRC/23/46, paras 55–68; UNGA, 'Report of the Special Rapporteur on the Human Rights of Migrants, Felipe González Morales on Means to Address the Human Rights Impact of Pushbacks of Migrants on Land and at Sea' (12 May 2021) UN Doc A/HRC/47/30, paras 67–71.

[2] M Bradley, *The International Organization for Migration: Challenges, Commitments, Complexities* (Abingdon/New York, Routledge, 2020).

[3] ICMPD, 'About ICMPD', www.icmpd.org/about-us/about-icmpd.

[4] European Commission, 'Joint Declaration on the Strategic and Comprehensive Partnership Between the Arab Republic of Egypt and the European Union' (17 March 2024) enlargement.ec.europa.eu/news/joint-declaration-strategic-and-comprehensive-partnership-between-arab-republic-egypt-and-european-2024-03-17_en.

[5] Commission, 'President Von Der Leyen Reaffirms EU's Strong Support for Lebanon and Its People and Announces a €1 Billion Package of EU Funding' (2 May 2024) enlargement.ec.europa.eu/news/president-von-der-leyen-reaffirms-eus-strong-support-lebanon-and-its-people-and-announces-eu1-2024-05-02_en.

[6] Commission, 'Memorandum of Understanding on a Strategic and Global Partnership Between the European Union and Tunisia' (16 July 2023) IP/24/1301.

of these countries.[7] This approach ignores the counterproductive nature of funding dictators, militias and authoritarian regimes with well-known track records of abuse against citizens and migrants.[8] Democracy, human rights, development and the need to tackle deep-rooted problems are sidelined, which only contributes to greater migration. We have seen the EU's infamous cooperation with the abusive Libyan Coast Guard as well as the bolstering of the Rapid Support Forces (RSF), a paramilitary group in Sudan, previously deployed as border guards and responsible for recent atrocities in Darfur. Pushbacks have been legalised in multiple European countries, while successive US administrations have summarily turned away asylum seekers at the southern border.[9]

Meanwhile, more countries are turning to offshoring and so-called 'safe country' arrangements, emulating Australia and the US. The UK-Rwanda asylum partnership foresaw asylum seekers being sent to Rwanda on a one-way ticket; however, the deal was struck down by the UK Supreme Court and abandoned following a change of government.[10] In November 2023, Italy and Albania signed an agreement allowing migrants intercepted in the Mediterranean Sea to be sent to Albania for offshore detention, but legal challenges saw all the men brought to Italy.[11] Italy has since repurposed the centres into repatriation hubs for rejected asylum seekers.[12] The European Commission has endorsed 'return hubs' outside the EU for rejected asylum seekers and proposed amending the 'safe third country' concept to allow Member States to send asylum seekers to countries with which they have no connection, opening the door to offshore processing.[13] The United Nations High Commissioner for Refugees (UNHCR) is developing proposals to process asylum claims regionally in safe third countries and inside the EU.[14] Both Trump administrations struck 'safe third country' agreements obliging other States to accept third-country nationals

[7] Council of the European Union, *The External Dimension of Migration. From a Reactive to a Preventive Model* (Discussion Paper 12990/1/23 REV 1, 2023).

[8] See M Bulman and others, 'Desert Dumps' (*Lighthouse Reports*, 21 May 2024) www.lighthousereports.com/investigation/desert-dumps/.

[9] See ch 6; Washington Office on Latin America (WOLA), 'Trump's Executive Orders and Latin America: Key Things to Know' (24 January 2025) www.wola.org/analysis/trumps-executive-orders-and-latin-america-key-things-to-know/.

[10] *R (on the application of AAA and others) v Secretary of State for the Home Department* [2023] UKSC 42, [2024] 1 All ER 1; E McDonnell, 'UK Supreme Court Finds UK-Rwanda Asylum Scheme Unlawful: Rwanda not a Safe Country to Send Asylum Seekers' (*HRW*, 15 November 2023) www.hrw.org/news/2023/11/15/uk-supreme-court-finds-uk-rwanda-asylum-scheme-unlawful.

[11] See A Pettrachin and M Bassoli, 'The Italy-Albania Migration Deal – a Policy Failure?' (*EUROPP*, 7 February 2025) blogs.lse.ac.uk/europpblog/2025/02/07/the-italy-albania-migration-deal-a-policy-failure/.

[12] See ECRE, 'Weekly Bulletin' (8 May 2025) mailchi.mp/ecre/ecre-weekly-bulletin-8-may-2025.

[13] Commission, 'Commission Proposes a New Common European System for Returns' (11 March 2025) www.ec.europa.eu/commission/presscorner/detail/en/ip_25_724; Commission, 'Commission Proposes to Facilitate the Application of the Safe Third Country Concept' (20 May 2025) www.ec.europa.eu/commission/presscorner/detail/en/ip_25_1224.

[14] F Grandi, 'Populist Politicians Will Never "Control" Immigration. Here Are the Humane Alternatives' (*The Guardian*, 14 August 2024) www.theguardian.com/commentisfree/article/2024/aug/14/populist-politicians-immigration-deportation-rwanda.

removed from the US, and in January 2025, President Trump ordered the expansion of the migrant detention facility at Guantánamo Bay.[15]

We are witnessing a global race to the bottom. As these practices become normalised and more States seek to shift and shirk their international obligations, a domino effect occurs. While the focus is often on how wealthy Western States copy and learn from one another,[16] these restrictive tactics have also been exported to and between Global South States. As Global North States close their doors and increase restrictions on movement, developing countries already disproportionately shouldering responsibility for the world's refugees are incentivised to do the same. States in Asia and the Americas have imposed stricter visa requirements and carrier sanctions on transport operators;[17] Middle Eastern countries such as Lebanon, Turkey and Iran push back refugees at their borders;[18] while North African countries have proactively criminalised and securitised migration, affecting citizens and foreigners alike, for their self-interest.[19] South Africa is increasingly adopting containment and externalisation policies. Asylum seekers entering irregularly have been summarily removed and denied entry based on 'safe country' concepts.[20]

Externalisation has *become* contemporary refugee policy, no longer exceptional and the containment of migrants embedded in the global regime. Imagine a young Sudanese man desperate to escape the conflict and rampant abuses in Sudan. As a national of an unstable, refugee-producing country, he is unlikely to be granted a visa. Moreover, embassies are closed, he has no passport, and airlines will not board undocumented travellers. He plans to flee to Egypt, but the authorities have tightened their entry requirements. Denied safe and legal

[15] US Department of Homeland Security, 'DHS Agreements with Guatemala, Honduras and El Salvador' (Fact Sheet, November 2019) https://www.dhs.gov/sites/default/files/publications/19_1028_opa_factsheet-northern-central-america-agreements_v2.pdf; M Davies, 'President Trump Sends First US Migrant Detainees to Guantanamo Bay' (*BBC News*, 5 February 2025) www.bbc.com/news/articles/cy0p1ykxyzjo.

[16] T Gammeltoft-Hansen and JC Hathaway, '*Non-Refoulement* in a World of Cooperative Deterrence' (2015) 53 *Columbia Journal of Transnational Law* 235; D Ghezelbash, *Refuge Lost: Asylum Law in an Interdependent World* (Cambridge, CUP, 2018); DS FitzGerald, *Refuge Beyond Reach: How Rich Democracies Repel Asylum Seekers* (Oxford, OUP, 2019) 13–15, 55–56.

[17] See ch 5.

[18] Amnesty International, '"They Don't Treat Us Like Humans": Unlawful Returns of Afghans from Turkey and Iran' (31 August 2022) www.amnesty.org/en/documents/ASA11/5897/2022/en/; HRW, *"I Can't Go Home, Stay Here, or Leave": Pushbacks and Pullbacks of Syrian Refugees from Cyprus and Lebanon* (New York, HRW, 2024).

[19] JP Cassarino, 'Beyond the Criminalisation of Migration: A Non-Western Perspective' (2018) 4 *International Journal of Migration and Border Studies* 397.

[20] See *Scalabrini Centre of Cape Town and Another v Minister of Home Affairs (8684/2024)* [2025] ZAWCHC 202; F Khan and N Rayn, 'Country Fiche South Africa' (*ASILE*, 2020) 2–3, 10–14, www.asileproject.eu/wp-content/uploads/2021/03/Country-Fiche_South-Africa_Final_Pub.pdf; South Africa Department of Home Affairs, 'Press Statement on the Release of the Final White Paper on Citizenship, Immigration and Refugee Protection: Towards a Complete Overhaul of the Migration System in South Africa' (18 April 2024) paras 32.22–32.23, www.dha.gov.za/index.php/statements-speeches/1771-press-statement-on-the-release-of-the-final-white-paper-on-citizenship-immigration-and-refugee-protection-towards-a-complete-overhaul-of-the-migration-system-in-south-africa.

routes, he crosses into Chad and then endures a dangerous journey through the inhospitable desert into Libya, where he is met with violence, abuse and exploitation. With few alternatives, he boards an overcrowded, unseaworthy boat to cross the Mediterranean towards Italy. The boat may capsize or be pulled back by the Libyan Coast Guard, aided by Frontex, which shared the boat's location with the Libyans. The man and others on board are taken to an EU-funded detention centre in Libya. Meanwhile, IOM is supporting Libyan border authorities to enhance their capacities.

This example represents only a snapshot of the myriad possible restrictions on movement a migrant will encounter throughout their journey, imposed by State and non-state actors, from the point of departure and well before reaching their potential destination. The result is a global web of externalisation that has especially harmful effects in collectively containing migrants worldwide. *Prima facie*, externalisation measures may interfere with and violate the right to leave.

II. THE RIGHT TO LEAVE ANY COUNTRY

> Everyone shall be free to leave any country, including his own
> (Article 12(2), ICCPR)

The right to leave any country, including one's own, is a fundamental element of one's liberty. It is well-established in international law and enshrined in almost all global and regional human rights instruments. In 1948, the right to leave was recognised as a fundamental right in the world's first global instrument on human rights, the Universal Declaration of Human Rights (UDHR).[21] It has since been recognised in the International Covenant on Civil and Political Rights (ICCPR),[22] other international treaties[23] and across African, American, Arab,

[21] Universal Declaration of Human Rights (adopted 10 December 1948 UNGA Res 217 A(III)) (UDHR).

[22] International Covenant on Civil and Political Rights (adopted 16 December 1966, entered into force 23 March 1976) 999 UNTS 171 (ICCPR), art 12(2).

[23] International Convention on the Elimination of All Forms of Racial Discrimination (adopted 21 December 1965, entered into force 4 January 1969) 660 UNTS 195 (ICERD), art 5(d)(ii); Convention on the Suppression and Punishment of the Crime of Apartheid (adopted 30 November 1973, entered into force 18 July 1976) 1015 UNTS 243, art 2(c); Convention on the Rights of the Child (adopted 20 November 1989, entered into force 2 September 1990) 1577 UNTS 3 (UNCRC), art 10(2); International Convention on the Protection of the Rights of All Migrant Workers and Members of their Families (adopted 19 December 1990, entered into force 1 July 2003) 2220 UNTS 3 (ICRMW), art 8(1); Convention on the Rights of Persons with Disabilities (adopted 13 December 2006, entered into force 3 May 2008) 2515 UNTS 3 (CRPD), art 18(1)(c). See also Convention on the Elimination of All Forms of Discrimination against Women (adopted 18 December 1979, entered into force 3 September 1981) 1249 UNTS 13 (CEDAW), art 15(4).

Asian, Eurasian and European instruments.[24] Its near-universal recognition and consistent State practice have meant it is generally accepted as a norm of customary international law (see chapter two).

The right to leave bears great historical importance and has come to be understood as essential in protecting people's search for freedom, safety and broader human rights. In the aftermath of World War II, during which the Nazis had severely curtailed movement and millions of refugees had fled their homes, States described freedom of movement as 'the sacred right of every human being … necessary to progress and to civilization' and a principle which 'had to be stressed at that moment when the war and the resulting upheavals had demonstrated to what point that principle could be trodden underfoot'.[25] During the Cold War, when restrictions on emigration were commonplace across Communist and authoritarian regimes, the right to leave garnered international attention. The right was characterised as one of 'personal self-determination' and 'an indispensable condition for the full enjoyment by all of other civil, political, economic, social and cultural rights'.[26] The ability to flee to seek asylum from persecution and to enable political dissidents to express their dissent against oppressive regimes lay at the heart of the right to leave. Thus, being able to 'vote with one's feet' is arguably the ultimate expression of personal liberty.[27]

However, the end of the Cold War saw the right to leave neglected both intellectually and jurisprudentially – no longer afforded the same attention it once received. Restrictions on the right are increasingly imposed by States in the Global North for migration control purposes, who once critiqued the Soviet Union and Soviet States for severely curtailing the right to leave.[28] Immigration control is assumed to be intrinsic to State sovereignty, granting

[24] Convention for the Protection of Human Rights and Fundamental Freedoms (European Convention on Human Rights, as amended) (ECHR), art 2(2) protocol 4; American Convention on Human Rights (Pact of San José) (entered into force 18 July 1978) OAS Treaty Series No 36 (1969) (ACHR), art 22(2) and (3); African Charter on Human and Peoples' Rights (adopted 27 June 1981, entered into force 21 October 1986) (1982) 21 ILM 58 (African Charter), art 12(2); Commonwealth of Independent States (CIS) Convention on Human Rights and Fundamental Freedoms (adopted 26 May 1995, entered into force 11 August 1998) 3 IHRR 1, 212 (CIS Convention), art 22(2) and (3); Arab Charter on Human Rights (adopted 22 May 2004, entered into force 15 March 2008) 12 IHRR 893 (Arab Charter), art 27.

[25] UNGA Third Committee (3rd session) '120th Meeting' (2 November 1948) UN Doc A/C.3/SR.120, 316 (Chilean delegate), 322 (Belgian delegate).

[26] United Nations Commission on Human Rights (CHR) (Sub-Commission), 'Study of Discrimination in Respect of the Right of Everyone to Leave any Country, including his Own, and to Return to his Country by Special Rapporteur José D Inglés' (1963) UN Doc E/CN.4/Sub.2/220/Rev.1 9, 65.

[27] H Hannum, *The Right to Leave and Return in International Law and Practice* (Dordrecht, Martinus Nijhoff, 1987) 4.

[28] E Guild, *The Right to Leave a Country* (Issue Paper, Council of Europe Commissioner for Human Rights, 2013) 11; D Kochenov, 'The Right to Leave Any Country Including Your Own in International Law' (2012) 28 *Connecticut Journal of International Law* 43, 57.

States a 'monopoly over the legal means of movement'.[29] We are all, some to a far greater extent than others, subject to a relatively invisible 'shifting border' of migration controls that selectively restrict our mobility well beyond the physical border of a country.[30] The 'seamless' articulation of exit and entry policies marks a shift from simply managing both ends to 'asserting control over movement'.[31]

It follows that the right to leave is an apt starting point in any account of migration and asylum. It signifies the beginning of a person's journey from their State of origin in search of refuge, opportunity or a better life. Although the right to leave protects everyone, it is indispensable in protecting the rights of migrants and would-be migrants. It is a precondition for seeking and securing international protection. To qualify as a 'refugee' under the 1951 Refugee Convention, a person must have left their country of origin and crossed an international border. As the next section explores, the right is also essential in advancing equal opportunity and mobility, especially for those from the Global South.

A. Global Inequalities of Movement – *Who is Dying on the Move*?

The current global mobility regime is plagued by inequality and discrimination. Race, colonial legacies and discrimination continue to shape *who* is denied access to safe movement and *by whom*. Between 2014 and 2023, more than 63,000 women, men and children died or went missing on migratory routes worldwide, as recorded by IOM.[32] In this period, the top 10 countries of origin for migrants who died were Afghanistan, Myanmar, Ethiopia, Syria, Mexico, Algeria, Morocco, Venezuela, Senegal and Guatemala (based on those who could be identified). More than 25,000 Africans were recorded to have died or are missing and presumed dead over these 10 years.[33]

People from developing, conflict-affected, post-colonial States in the Global South – often of colour and with diverse ethnic backgrounds – are disproportionately targeted and impacted by externalisation, many unable to leave their home or region through safe and regular routes or flee instability and violence

[29] J Torpey, *The Invention of the Passport: Surveillance, Citizenship, and the State*, 2nd edn (Cambridge, CUP, 2018) 220; Kochenov (n 28) 57; Guild (n 28) 11.

[30] A Shachar, *The Shifting Border: Legal Cartographies of Migration and Mobility. Ayelet Shachar in Dialogue* (Manchester, Manchester University Press, 2020) chs 1, 8.

[31] A Macklin, 'Exit Rights, Seamless Borders and the New Carceral State' (2024) 73 *International & Comparative Law Quarterly* 891, 907, 928.

[32] J Black, 'A Decade of Documenting Migrant Deaths: Data Analysis and Reflection on Deaths During Migration Documented by IOM's Missing Migrants Project, 2014-2023' (IOM, Global Migration Data Analysis Centre, 2024) 5, missingmigrants.iom.int/MMP10years.

[33] ibid 12.

rooted in Western colonialism. They face strict immigration controls and exclusion from political membership by their former colonisers. International law's deference to State sovereignty allows harmful, racialised border practices to persist. A growing number of authors are challenging the racialised, discriminatory foundations of present-day migration regimes.[34] Achiume reveals how migration controls entrench global inequalities, sustaining a system of 'racial privilege' where whiteness disproportionately enables international mobility.[35] In 1998, Chimni detailed the Global North's shifting refugee policy – from the neglect of 'Third World' refugees, to their Cold War instrumentalisation, to containment – marking a new phase post-decolonisation.[36] A global *(im)*mobility regime exists, which facilitates selective mobility along racial, nationality, religious, class and gender lines, being 'disproportionally white, disproportionally wealthy, and disproportionally male'.[37] People are stratified into two groups: the privileged, who enjoy easy and affordable travel, and the excluded, who face stringent visa rules, long queues and high costs.[38] Local activists and grassroots movements play key roles in resisting externalisation, advocating for free movement, and exposing border violence and the migrant struggle.[39]

As an Australian, my passport ranks seventh worldwide, allowing access to 189 countries visa-free.[40] I have lived and worked in London, benefiting from quick, cheap travel. In contrast, Afghanistan ranks last at 103rd, with Afghan nationals able to visit only 25 countries visa-free.

The swift international response to the mass displacement of people fleeing Ukraine – through the activation of temporary protection, visa waivers and regional cooperation – highlights stark disparities in mobility and refugee policies

[34] eg N El-Enany, *Bordering Britain* (Manchester, Manchester University Press, 2020); D Owen, 'Migration, Structural Injustice and Domination on "Race", Mobility and Transnational Positional Difference' (2020) 46 *Journal of Ethnic and Migration Studies* 2585; C Briddick and C Costello, 'Introduction to the Symposium on Undoing Discriminatory Borders' (2021) 115 *American Journal of International Law Unbound* 328.

[35] See ET Achiume, 'Racial Borders' (2022) 110 *The Georgetown Law Journal* 445.

[36] BS Chimni, 'The Geopolitics of Refugee Studies: A View from the South' (1998) 11 *Journal of Refugee Studies* 350.

[37] T Spijkerboer, 'The Global Mobility Infrastructure: Reconceptualising the Externalisation of Migration Control' (2018) 20 *European Journal of Migration and Law* 452, 463, 469.

[38] E Neumayer, 'Unequal Access to Foreign Spaces: How States Use Visa Restrictions to Regulate Mobility in a Globalised World' (2006) 31 *Transactions of the Institute of British Geographers* 72; S Mau and others, *Liberal States and the Freedom of Movement: Selective Borders, Unequal Mobility* (Hampshire, Palgrave Macmillan, 2012); Spijkerboer (n 37).

[39] See eg T Wertheimer and W Grant, 'Migrants March Through Mexico in Demand for Justice' (*BBC News*, 24 April 2023) www.bbc.com/news/world-latin-america-65370238; IMS Vammen, 'The Struggle Over Mobility Narratives: How Senegalese Activists Use Alternative Information Campaigns to Contest EU Externalization' (2024) *International Migration Review* 1; B Brennan and B Anderson, 'Communities of Resistance: Migrant Organizing and Transnational Campaigning Past and Future' in B Anderson (ed), *Rethinking Migration Challenging Borders, Citizenship and Race* (Bristol, Bristol University Press, 2025).

[40] Henley & Partners, 'Passport Index', www.henleyglobal.com/passport-index.

(see chapter five). Afghans, Syrians and Sudanese have limited safe pathways and face externalisation measures that push them into dangerous journeys. 2023 was the deadliest year for Afghan refugees.[41] The openness to Ukrainian refugees compared with the rejection of non-European, non-Christian refugees arguably reflects a return to Cold War ideological refugee policies.[42]

B. Re-Imagining a Liberal and Equal Global Mobility Regime

Global inequalities in movement have spurred calls for reform, from open borders to migration as reparation and decolonisation to arguments for a 'right to migrate' and a 'birthright privilege levy'.[43] The focus has, however, been mainly on entry, overlooking the denial of the right to leave and the harms of externalisation. As such, this book advocates for a radical re-imagining of the global *(im)*mobility regime, requiring States and IOs to uphold the right to leave in their migration control policies and practices. This will require the dismantling of many externalisation strategies and shifting away from containment towards migration policies that uphold international law, promote responsibility sharing, and foster a far more liberal and equal global mobility regime. The response to Ukraine should serve as a guiding model, ensuring safe routes and refuge for all people fleeing conflict and persecution, regardless of nationality or race. Making this a reality demands accountability for violations of the right to leave, particularly for individuals from the Global South who have been discriminated against.

Migrants should be seen first and foremost as individuals with human rights. State sovereignty should, therefore, not be prioritised above human rights, *even if* migration control is legitimate. As Peters has argued, sovereignty 'is not merely limited by human rights, but should be seen to exist only in function of humanity'.[44] Protecting the dignity of people on the move and their 'right to have rights' is crucial.[45] Understanding the right to leave is an essential first step.

[41] Migration Data Portal, 'Migrant Deaths and Disappearances' (2 April 2024) www.migrationdataportal.org/themes/migrant-deaths-and-disappearances.

[42] JO Kleist, 'The Return of "Cold War" Refugee Policy' (2022) *International Politics & Society Journal,* www.ips-journal.eu/topics/european-integration/the-return-of-cold-war-refugee-policy-5762/.

[43] See, respectively, JH Carens, *The Ethics of Immigration* (Oxford, OUP, 2013) chs 11–12; ET Achiume, 'Migration as Decolonisation' (2019) 71 *Stanford Law Review* 1509; JK Appleby, 'The United States, Europe, and the Global Compacts: Honoring the Right to Remain and the Right to Migrate' (2025) 13 *Journal on Migration and Human Security* 151; A Shachar, *The Birthright Lottery: Citizenship and Global Inequality* (Cambridge, HUP, 2009) ch 2.

[44] A Peters, 'Humanity as the A and Ω of Sovereignty' (2009) 20 *European Journal of International Law* 513, 513.

[45] H Arendt, *The Origins of Totalitarianism* (Harcourt, Brace and Company, 1951) ch 9.

III. OBJECTIVES AND STRUCTURE

There is a dearth of contemporary research on the right to leave, and the compatibility of externalisation measures with the right remains largely overlooked.[46] The existing research remains limited and piecemeal. The last general monograph on the right to leave and return was published by Hannum in 1987, examining these rights under Article 12 of the International Covenant on Civil and Political Rights (ICCPR) and State practice.[47] More recent works lack a comprehensive, global perspective or only briefly address lawful limitations on the right, focused on States of nationality or departure.[48]

Most scholarship focuses on how externalisation prevents migrants from entering State territory and accessing asylum through so-called '*non-entrée*' measures.[49] While some scholars briefly mention and engage with the right to leave and exit controls, their primary focus remains arrival, leaving the right to leave underexplored, especially compared with *non-refoulement* obligations. Even when the COVID-19 pandemic and border closures brought international mobility to a near standstill and prevented the usually privileged persons from travelling abroad, the focus remained on entry, not exit.[50]

Some scholars have explored distinct aspects of the right to leave and externalisation, but their analyses typically concentrate only on specific adjudicative bodies or on practices in one or two countries or regions.[51] They nonetheless raise vital questions about the opposability of the right to leave to destination States, and whether those States can infringe an individual's right to leave another State – especially now that exit is no longer only being obstructed by

[46] See E McDonnell, 'Challenging Externalisation Through the Lens of the Human Right to Leave' (2024) 71 *Netherlands International Law Review* 119.

[47] Hannum (n 27).

[48] See eg, G Liu, *The Right to Leave and Return and Chinese Migration Law* (Leiden, Martinus Nijhoff, 2007); Kochenov (n 28); V Chetail, *International Migration Law* (Oxford, OUP, 2019) 77–92; Macklin (n 31).

[49] See eg, JC Hathaway, 'The Emerging Politics of *Non-Entrée*' (1992) 91 *Refugees* 40; T Gammeltoft-Hansen, *Access to Asylum: International Refugee Law and the Globalisation of Migration Control* (Cambridge, CUP, 2011); M den Heijer, *Europe and Extraterritorial Asylum* (Oxford, Hart Publishing, 2012); V Moreno-Lax, *Accessing Asylum in Europe: Extraterritorial Border Controls and Refugee Rights under EU Law* (Oxford, OUP, 2017); FitzGerald (n 16). See further McDonnell, 'Challenging Externalisation' (n 46) s 2.

[50] See M Benton and others, *COVID-19 and the State of Global Mobility in 2021* (Geneva/Washington DC, Migration Policy Institute and IOM, 2022) 21, 27, 30, which makes some reference to exit restrictions; and exceptionally, R Jefferies and J McAdam, 'Locked in: Australia's COVID-19 Border Closures and the Right to Leave' (2023) 41 *Australian Year Book of International Law* 185.

[51] E Guild and V Stoyanova, 'The Human Right to Leave Any Country: A Right to Be Delivered' in W Benedek and others (eds), *European Yearbook on Human Rights 2018* (Plymouth, Intersentia, 2018).

States of departure.[52] Core scholarship on the human rights of migrants has also overlooked the significance of the right to leave for migrants.[53]

The primary aim of this work is to provide a comprehensive examination of the right to leave in international law and to demonstrate its applicability to externalised migration control, including its opposability to States of destination. First, it provides a general framework for interpreting the right, including its interplay with well-traversed rights and obligations under international human rights, refugee law and the law of the sea. Given the qualified nature of the right to leave, it scrutinises its key requirements to determine when restrictions are lawful. Second, the work will tackle complex questions surrounding the relationship between leaving versus entry and unpack how discrimination, racism and colonial inequalities manifest through externalisation strategies, affecting who can exercise their right to leave safely and regularly. Finally, building on the abundance of literature on jurisdiction and the general rules of international responsibility, it uncovers which States and IOs bear and share responsibility for violations of the right to leave.[54] In doing so, it addresses attempts to sever jurisdictional links, evade one's obligations, and blur lines of responsibility, particularly in extraterritorial contexts and regarding enlisting other entities.

The work explores three main questions. What is the scope of the right to leave in international law and the obligations it generates? When do externalisation practices violate the right to leave? When do destination States, States of origin and transit, and IOs bear international responsibility for violating the right to leave, whether directly, for failing to uphold positive obligations, or through aid and assistance or direction and control over another? It emphasises moving beyond the dominant lens of entry, access to asylum and *non-refoulement* to capturing the myriad ways States impede movement throughout the migrant trajectory and their overarching goal of containment. The work challenges the inherent legitimacy afforded to migration control, interrogating how States often disguise restrictive techniques as legitimate and revealing how international law reinforces discrimination, exclusion and border violence.

The work is divided into two main parts. Part I (chapters two to four) advances a general framework for assessing restrictions on the right to leave and also analysing how the right is and ought to be interpreted, its key requirements,

[52] ibid 375–77; V Stoyanova, 'The Right to Leave Any Country and the Interplay between Jurisdiction and Proportionality in Human Rights Law' (2020) 32 *International Journal of Refugee Law* 403, 405.

[53] C Costello, *The Human Rights of Migrants and Refugees in European Law* (Oxford, OUP, 2016); MB Dembour, *When Humans Become Migrants: Study of the European Court of Human Rights with an Inter-American Counterpoint* (Oxford, OUP, 2015).

[54] It does not address the responsibility of private actors. Rather, it assesses the responsibility of States and IOs for private conduct under the rules on attribution and positive obligations.

lawful limitations, and corresponding obligations and duty-bearers. While mainly focusing on State obligations, the right to leave also binds IOs. Part I begins by situating the right within the history of mobility and free movement, which has shaped the evolution of the right and informed current debates on immigration. Chapter two examines the right to leave in depth, including its scope, sources of the right in international law, and the jurisprudence of adjudicative bodies. Chapter three tackles the delicate relationship and supposed tension between the right to leave and the State's prerogative to control entry, often used as a justification for denying the right to leave. It challenges the traditional starting point that States possess a near-unfettered right to exclude non-nationals, arguing that States must admit migrants in certain circumstances, such as under obligations of *non-refoulement*, the right to family life, and free movement regimes. It provides the reader with a fuller understanding of the relationship between exit and entry, concluding that individuals have the right to leave independently of any right of entry elsewhere. Part I concludes with chapter four on the special importance of the right to leave for asylum seekers, who are often the primary target of externalisation. It explores how the right to seek asylum, the obligation of *non-refoulement*, and the prohibition on collective expulsion interact to create a '*right to leave to seek asylum*' and the related duties.

Part II examines the phenomenon of externalised migration control, building on Part I's analysis to determine when and how externalisation practices violate the right to leave and to allocate international responsibility among States and IOs. The introduction to Part II presents the general framework governing international responsibility. Chapter five examines visa regimes and carrier sanctions, and chapter six examines pushbacks and pullbacks at sea and on land, drawing on practices worldwide. These practices are highly prevalent and pervasive in migration governance today, making them ripe for analysis. Visas and carrier sanctions, two longstanding, widespread State practices, are often presumed to be immune from challenge and their role in constructing and contributing to precarious, deadly journeys largely ignored. Chapter five assesses whether visa refusals and denials of embarkation by carriers constitute an exercise of jurisdiction under human rights law and whether they are attributable to the destination State. It concludes that these measures can violate the right to leave, leading to shared responsibility among destination States, the territorial State and, as relevant, the EU and IOM. Chapter six tackles pushbacks and pullbacks at sea and on land, practices often viewed solely through the prism of *refoulement* and denial of entry.[55] It grapples with questions surrounding the lawfulness of States of origin and transit stemming migration out of their territories, including their humanitarian obligations under the law

[55] See for a discussion comparing the case law invoking *non-refoulement* and other obligations with the limited cases invoking the right to leave, McDonnell, 'Challenging Externalisation' (n 46) pts 4.1, 4.4, 4.5.

of the sea. It concludes that in most circumstances, pushbacks and pullbacks violate the right to leave, save when they qualify as genuine rescues with disembarkation to a place of safety. It demonstrates that destination States, States of origin and transit, and the EU (including Frontex), the ICMPD, IOM and NATO share international legal responsibility for violating the right to leave and for failing to fulfil their positive duties, including rescuing individuals in distress.

IV. DEFINING KEY CONCEPTS

A. Contested Meanings of Externalisation

'*Externalisation*' is a contested term with no definitive legal or single meaning, despite its widespread use. Scholars and policymakers define it in various ways, though it is often understood as an 'umbrella' concept.[56] Externalisation overlaps significantly with other common descriptors, such as deterrence, extraterritorialisation, extraterritorial asylum processing, non-entrée, offshoring and remote control, which can contribute to conceptual confusion. Additionally, several definitional questions emerge regarding the scope of the term. Does it refer to the externalisation of migration and border controls or, more specifically, to the externalisation of asylum? Is it limited to conduct undertaken entirely outside a State's territory, or does it include extraterritorial effects? What practices and policies count as externalisation? And are externalisation practices inherently unlawful for shirking or shifting a State's international obligations? Must there be a transfer, 'sharing' or outsourcing of responsibilities onto another State or actor, or can unilateral practices also constitute externalisation?

UNHCR, in its *Note on the "Externalisation" of International Protection*, defined externalisation as 'measures taken by States – unilaterally or in cooperation with other States – which are implemented or have effects outside their own territories, and which directly or indirectly prevent asylum-seekers and refugees from reaching a particular "destination" country or region, and/or from being able to claim or enjoy protection there'.[57] For UNHCR, externalisation is by definition unlawful, being 'distinct from lawful practices involving transfer of the responsibility for international protection, undertaken in accordance with international standards'. Legality depends on whether the measure

[56] NF Tan, 'Conceptualising Externalisation: Still Fit for Purpose?' (2021) 68 *Forced Migration Review* 8; D Cantor and others, 'Externalisation, Access to Territorial Asylum, and International Law' (2022) 34 *International Journal of Refugee Law* 120, 122.

[57] UNHCR, 'Note on the "Externalization" of International Protection' (28 May 2021) para 5. See also UNHCR, 'Annex to UNHCR Note on the "Externalization" of International Protection: Policies and Practices related to the Externalization of International Protection' (28 May 2021).

is designed or effectively serves to shift international protection responsibilities or avoid them altogether, contrary to the principles of international cooperation and solidarity. This includes pushbacks at borders, interceptions at sea and extraterritorial asylum processing. Other extraterritorial measures, such as resettlement, complementary pathways (ie, humanitarian visas) and regional disembarkation mechanisms, are not externalisation provided they are implemented in the spirit of responsibility sharing and adequate safeguards are in place that protect rights.[58] However, UNHCR's definition is limited to the externalisation of international protection and excludes the broader spectrum of measures that seek to obstruct movement and limit arrivals not just of asylum seekers but migrants writ large, including visas, carrier sanctions and pre-clearance regimes.

Most scholars adopt a broader definition of externalised migration control, which can also encompass the externalisation of international protection.[59] Frelick and others provide a helpful starting point, describing externalisation as 'extraterritorial state actions to prevent migrants, including asylum seekers, from entering the legal jurisdictions or territories of destination countries or regions or making them legally inadmissible without individually considering the merits of their protection claims', including direct and indirect practices and preventative policies, undertaken unilaterally, bilaterally or multilaterally with other States or involving private actors.[60] Accordingly, externalisation is often understood as encompassing, but not necessarily limited to, pushbacks and pullbacks, extraterritorial and offshore processing, visa requirements, carrier sanctions, posting of immigration officials abroad, and the funding, equipping and training of third countries to manage migration. Other measures are often more contentious, such as information campaigns to discourage irregular migration, external asylum processing, and removals under safe country arrangements like 'safe third country' and 'first country of asylum' concepts – which will be discussed in more detail in chapter three.

Considering the different understandings and complex conceptual landscape of this area, this book adopts a broad definition of externalised migration control while seeking to maintain clarity. It defines externalisation as the diverse set of migration control practices and policies, implemented either extraterritorially or

[58] UNHCR, 'Note' (n 57) para 6.

[59] See eg, M Lemberg-Pedersen, 'Manufacturing Displacement. Externalization and Postcoloniality in European Migration Control' (2019) 5 *Global Affairs* 247; Refugee Law Initiative, 'Declaration on Externalisation and Asylum' (2022) 34 *International Journal of Refugee Law* 114, paras 2–3; Cantor and others (n 56) 122–23; J Crisp, 'What Is Externalization and Why Is It a Threat to Refugees?' (*Chatham House*, 14 October 2020) www.chathamhouse.org/2020/10/what-externalization-and-why-it-threat-refugees.

[60] B Frelick, IM Kysel and J Podkul, 'The Impact of Externalization of Migration Controls on the Rights of Asylum Seekers and Other Migrants' (2016) 4 *Journal on Migration and Human Security* 190, 193.

with extraterritorial effects, which are designed to or have the effect of preventing or deterring migrants, including asylum seekers, from leaving the country or region they are in, reaching or entering their intended destination, and/or being able to claim or access protection there. It recognises that externalisation enables States to control not only entry but also departure and movement throughout the migration journey. This may be undertaken unilaterally, in partnership with States of origin and transit, and/or through outsourcing to IOs or private actors. Externalisation will be unlawful where the specific measure or policy violates a State's international obligations or serves to shift the State's international responsibilities towards asylum seekers and refugees elsewhere or to shirk them altogether, leaving their needs unmet.

B. Who is an Asylum Seeker, Refugee or Migrant?

This work refers to '*asylum seekers*', '*refugees*' and '*migrants*', and it is important to clarify how these terms are understood amid ongoing debate. Generally, these categories refer to people who have left their home country and crossed an international border. Who qualifies as a 'refugee' is defined in international law. A 'refugee', defined in the 1951 Refugee Convention, is someone who fears persecution due to race, religion, nationality, social group or political opinion, and who is outside their country and unable or unwilling to avail themselves of the protection of that country.[61] Regional instruments in Africa, the Americas and Asia have expanded the refugee definition to include people fleeing generalised violence, external aggression, occupation, internal conflicts, massive human rights violations, or other events seriously disturbing public order.[62] Importantly, refugee status is declaratory: a person is considered a refugee as soon as the criteria are met.

The term 'asylum seeker' describes a person seeking protection outside their home country who is awaiting determination of their claim or has not yet lodged one.[63] Nonetheless, States often exclude irregular migrants from this

[61] Convention relating to the Status of Refugees (adopted 28 July 1951, entered into force 22 April 1954) 189 UNTS 137 (Refugee Convention), art 1A(2); Protocol relating to the Status of Refugees (adopted 31 January 1967, entered into force 4 October 1967) 606 UNTS 267 (Protocol).

[62] OAU, Convention Governing the Specific Aspects of Refugee Problems in Africa (adopted 10 September 1969, entered into force 20 June 1974) 1001 UNTS 45 (OAU Convention), art I(2); Cartagena Declaration on Refugees (adopted 22 November 1984 by the Colloquium on the International Protection of Refugees in Central America, Mexico and Panama) (Cartagena Declaration) conclusion III(3); Bangkok Principles on the Status and Treatment of Refugees, 31 December 1966 (adopted 24 June 2001 by the Asian-African Legal Consultative Organization) (Bangkok Principles), art I(2). See also UNHCR, 'Persons in Need of International Protection' (June 2017) 1–2.

[63] UNHCR, 'Guidance Note on Safeguards Against Unlawful or Irregular Removal of Refugees and Asylum-Seekers' (Division of International Protection Geneva, 2014) fn 1.

label and limit 'refugees' to those officially granted refugee status. Terms such as '*unlawful*', '*illegal*', '*irregular*' or '*economic migrant*' are primarily constructed by States, being highly politicised and stigmatising, and they may vary by context and political interests. This work embraces the broader notion of '*international protection*', which extends beyond the refugee definition. It encompasses individuals who do not qualify as refugees but nonetheless face a real risk of serious harm if returned to their country of origin for example owing to armed conflict, gang violence, trafficking or climate-related disasters. Such persons may be eligible for complementary, subsidiary or temporary forms of protection under international law.[64] Chapter three discusses the institution of '*asylum*' and the right to enter State territory to access asylum procedures, including refugee status and complementary protection assessments.

There is no universally accepted legal definition of 'migrant', and debates persist over whether it includes refugees. The UN Department of Economic and Social Affairs states that 'most experts agree that an international migrant is someone who changes his or her country of usual residence, irrespective of the reason for migration or legal status'.[65] This reflects the inclusivist approach, where 'migrant' includes asylum seekers, refugees, foreign workers, students, trafficking victims and those moving for economic reasons.[66] Migrants are thus a broad category without prejudice to the specific protection refugees, stateless persons and other groups are entitled to under international law.[67] The residualist approach, by contrast, treats migrants as the residual category of people on the move who are not refugees, to preserve the special obligations owed to refugees.[68] This book adopts the inclusivist view, recognising that all people on the move may require protection and shift between categories at different stages in their migration journey. Accordingly, it refers throughout to asylum seekers, refugees and *other* migrants.

[64] European Parliament, 'Directive 2011/95/EU of the European Parliament and of the Council of 13 December 2011 on standards for the qualification of third-country nationals or stateless persons as beneficiaries of international protection, for a uniform status for refugees or for persons eligible for subsidiary protection, and for the content of the protection granted (recast)' [2011] OJ L 337/9 (Qualification Directive) art 2(f), 15, 18; J McAdam, *Complementary Protection in International Refugee Law* (Oxford, OUP, 2007); H Lambert, 'Temporary Refuge from War: Customary International Law and the Syrian Conflict' (2017) 66 *International & Comparative Law Quarterly* 723.

[65] UN, 'Refugees and Migrants, Definitions' refugeesmigrants.un.org/definitions.

[66] J Carling, 'The Meaning of Migrants', www.meaningofmigrants.org/. See IOM, 'Who Is a Migrant?', www.weblog.iom.int/who-migrant; OHCHR, 'Differentiation between Migrants and Refugees', www.ohchr.org/sites/default/files/Documents/Issues/Migration/GlobalCompactMigration/MigrantsAndRefugees.pdf.

[67] OHCHR (n 66).

[68] UNHCR, '"Refugees" and "Migrants" – Frequently Asked Questions (FAQs)' (16 March 2016) www.unhcr.org/us/news/stories/refugees-and-migrants-frequently-asked-questions-faqs.

C. States of Origin, Transit and Destination

Externalised migration control involves three main groups of States: '*countries of origin*', '*countries of transit*' and '*countries of destination*'. Country of origin refers to a migrant's State of nationality or habitual residence. Transit countries are those migrants pass through en route to their destination. States of origin and transit are often referred to as '*third States*', enlisted by destination States to perform migration control. States (or regions) migrants aim to reach are known as destination countries – typically associated with wealthier nations in the Global North, despite most refugees living in neighbouring countries.[69] The labels origin, transit and destination are not clear-cut or mutually exclusive, given the dynamic nature of mobility and the fact that a State's designation can evolve over time.[70] Indeed, the restrictions migrants encounter before reaching their potential destination generate onerous, 'fragmented journeys' and the very notion of transit States.[71] These States can also be '*departure States*', from where citizens and migrants exit. Chapter two discusses the history of mobility and the drafting of the right to leave, introducing a more historical phrase, '*State of sojourn*', meaning the temporary stay of a person in a State that is not their country of origin. '*State of residence*' represents the place a 'resident' lives permanently or longer-term.

Further terminological clarification is necessary considering the asymmetrical power dynamics at play during externalisation between States in the '*Global North*' influencing less developed '*Global South*' States. Rather than demarcating geographic lines, the Global North typically includes developed, wealthy (and often Western) States, mainly in North America, Europe and parts of the Asia-Pacific. In contrast, the Global South encompasses developing and underdeveloped countries, primarily located in Africa, Latin America and the Caribbean, Asia, and most of the Middle East, often characterised by significant economic and social inequalities. However, some countries do not fit neatly into the so-called Global North-South divide, which can oversimplify complex economic, political and cultural differences, risking inaccurate and outdated stereotyping.[72] Finally, this work uses '*refugee-producing*' and '*least developed*' to denote States regarded as such by UNHCR and ECOSOC, respectively.

[69] UNHCR, 'Refugee Data Finder', www.unhcr.org/refugee-statistics.

[70] See eg, F Düvell, 'Transit Migration: A Blurred and Politicised Concept' (2012) 18 *Population, Space and Place* 415; M Berriane, H de Haas and K Natter, 'Introduction: Revisiting Moroccan Migrations' (2015) 20 *The Journal of North African Studies* 503.

[71] M Collyer, 'Stranded Migrants and the Fragmented Journey' (2010) 23 *Journal of Refugee Studies* 273; UNGA, 'Situation of Migrants in Transit. Report of the Office of the United Nations High Commissioner for Human Rights' (27 January 2016) UN Doc A/HRC/31/35, para 12.

[72] See S Patrick and A Huggins, 'The Term "Global South" Is Surging. It Should Be Retired.' (*Carnegie Endowment for International Peace*, 15 August 2023) www.carnegieendowment.org/posts/2023/08/the-term-global-south-is-surging-it-should-be-retired?lang=en.

V. GEOGRAPHICAL REACH

Externalisation is not a new phenomenon, and States have adopted externalisation practices and policies in regions worldwide. Nonetheless, the focus has centred on the Global North, particularly Australia, European countries and the US. They have become the orthodox jurisdictions for analysis, viewed as the leading externalising States for spearheading specific practices and promulgating explicit externalisation strategies, such as interdiction at sea and offshore detention.[73] On the other hand, there is a paucity of research on the externalisation practices of the Global South, with so-called third States often sidelined.[74] There has been an increasing focus on the responsibility of third States enlisted by destination States to perform migration control, as well as their motivations, interests and agency.[75] However, research on how restrictive tactics spread to and among Global South States and their own externalisation strategies remains limited. This work helps address that gap. Chapter five explores how restrictive visa policies and carrier sanctions have diffused from Global North to Global South and among Global South States. Chapter six highlights the interception practices of countries such as Algeria, Iran, Guatemala and Trinidad and Tobago, shaped by domestic priorities and politics.

By applying a global lens that focuses on externalisation practices worldwide, rather than on individual jurisdictions, this work de-centres Northern-centric perspectives and offers a more nuanced understanding of how certain dynamics unfold globally. However, given Global North States remain the key externalising countries, their practices naturally receive greater attention. To broaden the study of the right to leave beyond the traditional focus on the ICCPR and European Convention on Human Rights (ECHR) and the Human Rights Committee and European Court of Human Rights (ECtHR or Strasbourg Court), this book examines the work of international and regional adjudicative bodies across Africa and the Americas. This includes

[73] See eg, Gammeltoft-Hansen (n 49); Gammeltoft-Hansen and Hathaway (n 16); Ghezelbash (n 16); FitzGerald (n 16); A Dastyari, A Nethery and A Hirsch (eds), *Refugee Externalisation Policies: Responsibility, Legitimacy and Accountability* (Abingdon/New York, Routledge, 2022).

[74] There is, however, a general focus on migration governance in the Global South eg, FB Adamson and G Tsourapas, 'The Migration State in the Global South: Nationalizing, Developmental, and Neoliberal Models of Migration Management' (2020) 54 *International Migration Review* 853; G Rayp, I Ruyssen and K Marchand (eds), *Regional Integration and Migration Governance in the Global South* (Cham, Springer, 2020); G Heck and others (eds), *Making Routes: Mobility and Politics of Migration in the Global South* (Cairo, The American University in Cairo Press, 2024). See also Tan (n 56).

[75] A Missbach and G Hoffstaedter, 'When Transit States Pursue Their Own Agenda' (2020) 3 *Migration and Society* 64; NF Tan and T Gammeltoft-Hansen, 'Topographical Approach to Accountability for Human Rights Violations in Migration Control' (2020) 21 *German Law Journal* 335; L Kandilige and T Yeboah, 'West African Migration Regimes and the Externalization of EU Migration Management Policies' in G Heck and others (eds), *Making Routes: Mobility and Politics of Migration in the Global South* (Cairo, The American University in Cairo Press, 2024).

the International Court of Justice (ICJ), UN treaty bodies and the regional human rights systems of Europe, Africa and the Americas.[76]

VI. A PRINCIPLED INTERPRETATION OF THE RIGHT

While the right to leave is enshrined in nearly all global and regional human rights instruments, it remains underspecified and seldom litigated, especially in externalisation contexts. As a first step, chapter two maps its legal foundation in international and regional treaties and as a norm of customary international law, without delving into domestic law except where this informs customary law. To set out a principled reading of the right and general framework for its interpretation, this work relies on the general rules of treaty interpretation as enshrined in Articles 31–33 of the Vienna Convention on the Law of Treaties (VCLT).[77] Following the standard process of treaty interpretation, this work begins by ascertaining the 'ordinary meaning' of the text on the right to leave, which is presumed to be the authentic expression of the parties' intentions, determined in the context of the treaty and its object and purpose.[78] By externalising their migration controls, States seek to avoid their international obligations towards migrants, making the principle of good faith in international law particularly relevant. Article 26 of the VCLT further provides that 'Every treaty in force is binding upon the parties to it and must be performed by them in good faith'.[79] This work also considers subsequent practice under Article 31(3)(b) to clarify the meaning of relevant treaty terms. However, even where widespread State practice exists, a specific measure, or parts thereof, can nonetheless be rendered unlawful as adjudicative bodies delimit and develop a right (such as unlawful deprivations of liberty or excessive detention).[80] Finally, where ambiguity persists, recourse is had to supplementary means of interpretation, including the treaty's preparatory work and the circumstances of its conclusion (Article 32).

Decisions of international and regional courts and UN treaty bodies, although subsidiary, constitute authoritative pronouncements on the meaning

[76] In the EU context, the analysis centres on the ECHR rather than EU law, because the right has been litigated extensively before the ECtHR and is not expressly enshrined in EU law.

[77] Vienna Convention on the Law of Treaties (adopted 23 May 1969, entered into force 27 January 1980) 1155 UNTS 331 (VCLT). Article 33(1) provides that when a treaty is authenticated in two or more languages, each version is equally authoritative unless the treaty or the parties agree which text prevails in case of divergence.

[78] See the VCLT *travaux preparatoires*: ILC, 'Draft Articles on the Law of Treaties with Commentaries' (1966) *YBILC* Vol II 187, UN Doc A/CN.4/SER.A/1966/Add.l, 218 para 2, 220–21 paras 11–12, 223 para 18. See also R Gardiner, *Treaty Interpretation*, 2nd edn (Oxford, OUP, 2015) ch 5.

[79] Where a treaty admits two interpretations, good faith and its object and purpose require choosing the one that gives the treaty appropriate effect: 'Draft Articles on the Law of Treaties with Commentaries', 219 para 6.

[80] See generally on subsequent practice Gardiner (n 78) 253–80.

of the law.[81] ILC commentaries, treaty body comments, UN special rapporteur reports, UNHCR and its Executive Committee's materials,[82] and soft law instruments adopted by expert bodies are particularly instructive supplementary means for reaching a principled interpretation of the right to leave.[83] Rather than seeking a singular reading of the right to leave, this work examines these diverse sources to develop a general interpretative framework that other bodies and decision-makers can apply and adapt beyond the situations in this monograph.

Understanding the right to leave requires situating it within its normative environment and in light of other treaties, so that it functions as part of a coherent and meaningful whole.[84] Accordingly, this work adopts a systemic reading, interpreting the right to leave consistently with related obligations, including the right to seek asylum, obligations of *non-refoulement*, prohibition on collective expulsion, right to an effective remedy, and search and rescue duties.[85] This approach is also essential for States and IOs to align their migration controls with international law. Moreover, human rights treaties should be read as 'living instruments', ensuring rights are 'practical and effective' and capable of evolution.[86] This book also seeks to stimulate progressive development of the right to leave, addressing lacunas and uncertainties while challenging State prerogatives. It nevertheless remains anchored in traditional interpretative approaches and the qualified right to leave, including standard legality and proportionality frameworks.

[81] Statute of the International Court of Justice (signed 26 June 1945, entered into force 24 October 1945) 33 UNTS 993, art 38. The separate and dissenting opinions of judges are also authoritative, belonging to the teachings of the most highly qualified publicists: A Pellet, 'Decisions of the ICJ as Sources of International Law?' in E Cannizzaro and others (eds), *Gaetano Morelli Lectures Series: Decisions of the ICJ as Sources of International Law?*, vol 2 (Rome, International and European Papers Publishing, 2018) 21–22.

[82] The Executive Committee is a subsidiary organ of the UN General Assembly. The UNHCR's materials, especially its Handbook and EXCOM conclusions, are regarded by many as highly persuasive authority.

[83] Such supplementary means vary in weight and may also provide evidence of 'law-making'. See *Ahmadou Sadio Diallo (Guinea v DRC)* (Merits) [2010] ICJ Rep 639, 663–64, para 66; M Kanetake and A Nollkaemper, 'The Application of Informal International Instruments Before Domestic Courts' (2014) 46 *George Washington International Law Review* 765; Gardiner (n 78) ch 8.

[84] VCLT, art 31(3)(c). See ILC, 'Report of the Study Group of the ILC on the Fragmentation of International Law: Difficulties Arising from the Diversification and Expansion of International Law' (13 April 2006) UN Doc A/CN.4/L.682, particularly paras 37–43, sect F; A Rachovitsa, 'The Principle of Systemic Integration in Human Rights Law' (2017) 66 *International & Comparative Law Quarterly* 557, 558–59.

[85] As set out in ICJ Statute, art 38(1).

[86] *Legal Consequences for States of the Continued Presence of South Africa in Namibia (South West Africa) notwithstanding Security Council Resolution 276* (Advisory Opinion) [1971] ICJ Rep 16, para 53; M Forowicz, *The Reception of International Law in the European Court of Human Rights* (Oxford, OUP, 2010) 11–14, ch 1; D Rietiker, 'The Principle of "Effectiveness" in the Recent Jurisprudence of the European Court of Human Rights: Its Different Dimensions and Its Consistency with Public International Law – No Need for the Concept of Treaty *Sui Generis*' (2010) 79 *Nordic Journal of International Law* 245.

VII. CONCLUSION

Prompted by the proliferation of externalisation policies and the ongoing disregard for the human right to leave any country, this work provides a general framework for that right that can be utilised by litigants, decision-makers, practitioners and scholars in migration contexts and beyond. It engages with highly contested issues, including policy responses to irregular migration, the limits of State sovereignty, racialised borders and unequal mobility. It clarifies how the right to leave limits the migration controls that States and IOs can lawfully impose, including extraterritorially, and demonstrates that these actors bear international responsibility for any ensuing violations despite flagrant attempts to evade their obligations.

This book illustrates that the right to leave is integral to taking the rights of people on the move seriously and tackling deadly journeys, broadening the focus beyond entry, *non-refoulement* and access to asylum to address the harms of externalisation throughout the migrant journey. It calls for significant and radical reform by States and IOs to uphold this right, which would compel the dismantling of many current externalisation strategies and a re-imagining of the global *(im)*mobility regime. Recommendations are provided on integrating the right to leave into migration regimes going forward, shifting away from containment and externalisation. Instead, policies and practices should be developed that uphold international law, promote responsibility sharing, and foster a more liberal and equal global mobility regime to replace the one currently plagued by exclusion, discrimination and violence.

PART I

A General Framework for the Right to Leave

PART I OF this book (chapters two to four) examines the right to leave in international law, including its scope, content and functioning, to offer a principled interpretation of the right. Key questions exist over lawful restrictions on departure and the right's applicability to destination States when externalising border controls and exercising extraterritorial jurisdiction over movement, discussed in chapter two. A major critique involves the complex relationship with the right to entry, leading some to dismiss the right to leave as meaningless since States are not generally obliged to admit non-nationals. Chapter three unpacks this tension, clarifying whether States can obstruct departure over doubts about admission. Chapter four explores the importance of the right to leave for asylum seekers and refugees, its interaction with key international protection obligations, and the duties imposed on States and IOs to ensure their migration laws and policies safeguard the right to leave to seek asylum. Together, these chapters provide a framework for applying the right to leave in contemporary contexts, (re)shaping both individual rights and the obligations incumbent on States and IOs.

I. BORDERS, MOBILITY AND IMMIGRATION CONTROL

Before discussing the right to leave in international law in chapters two to four, this section offers a brief history of borders, mobility and immigration control, situating the right within broader debates on free movement, sovereignty and bordering. While a detailed historical and theoretical account of migration and borders is beyond this book's scope, this section introduces key themes, debates and events that are revisited throughout.

Movement across borders has been a permanent feature of history, marked by a right of travel, sojourn and a duty of hospitality to allow entry to non-nationals.[1] The right to leave is implicit in mass migrations and displacements

[1] See JAR Nafziger, 'The General Admission of Aliens under International Law' (1983) 77 *American Journal of International Law* 804, 807–16; S Juss, 'Free Movement and the World Order' (2004) 16 *International Journal of Refugee Law* 289, 292, 297–302; V Chetail, 'Sovereignty and

through history, raising important questions too about the right to return to one's country.[2] Migration has shaped history but it has also been a source of conflict, discrimination and tension. From slavery, colonisation and racialised exclusion to current debates about immigration, border control and openness to refugees, mobility remains a highly contentious and politicised issue.

A. Free Movement and Sovereignty

Since early classical thought, the concept of 'personal liberty' has underpinned mobility, with the right to leave and return to one's country rooted in ancient philosophy and natural law.[3] Historically, free movement and State sovereignty were not seen as diametrically opposed. Today, however, the right to control entry is often regarded as one of the earliest State prerogatives, with free movement the exception. Writing against the traditional view, Chetail reveals 'an alternative story to the prevailing narrative of migration control' and shows that the emergence of State sovereignty did not correspond with immigration control; free movement remained the rule until the late nineteenth century.[4] Countries like the US and European nations had relatively open policies favouring white Europeans (especially men), while non-white workers like the Chinese and Indians were imported mainly for cheap labour.[5] Free movement and the promotion of emigration to the colonies and dominions thus underpinned imperialist trade expansion, colonisation and previous eras of globalisation.[6]

By the late nineteenth century, Anglo-American and South American countries imposed racially discriminatory laws targeting groups deemed 'undesirables'.[7]

Migration in the Doctrine of the Law of Nations: An Intellectual History of Hospitality from Vitoria to Vattel' (2016) 27 *European Journal of International Law* 901, 902–04, 907–09, 918–20, 922.

[2] United Nations Commission on Human Rights (Sub-Commission), 'Study of Discrimination in Respect of the Right of Everyone to Leave any Country, including his Own, and to Return to his Country by Special Rapporteur José D Inglés' (1963) UN Doc E/CN.4/Sub.2/220/Rev.1, 1.

[3] See ibid 3–4; H Hannum, *The Right to Leave and Return in International Law and Practice* (Martinus Nijhoff, 1987) 4; J McAdam, 'An Intellectual History of Freedom of Movement in International Law: The Right to Leave as a Personal Liberty' (2011) 12 *Melbourne Journal of International Law* 27.

[4] Chetail (n 1) 902. See also Juss (n 1).

[5] See McAdam (n 3) 14–15; J Torpey, *The Invention of the Passport: Surveillance, Citizenship, and the State*, 2nd edn (Cambridge, CUP, 2018) ch 4.

[6] See JF Hollifield, 'The Emerging Migration State' (2004) 38 *International Migration Review* 885, 889–90; AR Zolberg, 'The Exit Revolution' in NL Green and F Weil (eds), *Citizenship and Those Who Leave: The Politics of Emigration and Expatriation* (Champaign, University of Illinois Press, 2007) 33–35; Chetail (n 1) 903–06, 908; V Chetail, 'Demystifying Sovereignty: Totem and Taboo of Migration Control in International Law' (2024) 118 *American Journal of International Law Unbound* 193, 194–95.

[7] Torpey (n 5) 118–24; L Kai, 'Embracing the Chinese Exclusion Case: An International Law Approach to Racial Exclusions' (2018) 59 *William & Mary Law Review* 2617, 2645–47. For examples of restrictions throughout history, particularly on select groups, see McAdam (n 3) 17–18.

The US's Chinese Exclusion Act of 1882 was the first piece of legislation that explicitly discriminated against immigrants based on race and nationality, barring the entry of Chinese labourers.[8] World War I and the economic downturn saw temporary wartime restrictions, such as visas and passports, continue beyond the post-war period, paving the way for regulated movement.[9] As chapters two and three explore further, interrogating the idea that States possess an almost absolute right to exclude and the legitimacy of migration control, considering the racialised colonial legacies, is central to this book.

B. The Cold War and Voting with One's Feet

The right to leave as a personal liberty took on new meanings during the Cold War. Severe restrictions on emigration were a hallmark of the Communist era. The Soviet Union and Soviet Bloc States made leaving (legally) 'virtually impossible', except to other Communist countries, and violations were commonplace in apartheid-era South Africa, authoritarian Latin American States, and similar regimes.[10] Restrictions included the need to renounce nationality and obtain exit permits, which were often denied to particular groups, such as professionals, skilled workers and Jewish citizens. Coercive policies oscillated between 'forced immobilisation' and 'forced exit' for minorities depending on political, ideological and other drivers.[11] The Berlin Wall was synonymous with infringements of the right to leave, sealing individuals within State borders to prevent individuals 'voting with their feet' or seeking asylum. Unlike other historical walls, the Berlin Wall was not about fortification and enemy defence.[12] 'Foot voting' through international migration, as Somin terms it, allowed individuals to exercise political choice and express their dissent or rejection of a political jurisdiction.[13] Western States, seeking to emphasise Eastern Europe's ideological failings and atone for their own failure to protect countless refugees during World War II, opened their borders to refugees fleeing Communism – treating

[8] Kai (n 7).

[9] Chetail, 'Sovereignty and Migration' (n 1) 922; Torpey (n 5) 136–50; DS FitzGerald, *Refuge Beyond Reach: How Rich Democracies Repel Asylum Seekers* (Oxford, OUP, 2019) ch 2.

[10] A Dowty, *Closed Borders: The Contemporary Assault on Freedom of Movement* (New Haven, Yale University Press, 1987) chs 3, 4, 6; G Cornelisse, 'European Vessels, African Territorial Waters and "Illegal Emigrants": The Right to Leave and the Principle of (Il)Legality in a Global Regime of Mobility' (2008) *Challenge* 6–10; D Kochenov, 'The Right to Leave Any Country Including Your Own in International Law' (2012) 28 *Connecticut Journal of International Law* 43, 48, 50–51, 60, 62, 68–69.

[11] Inglés (n 2) 1 18–22, 25–29; Dowty (n 10) 118–20, 181–204.

[12] Inglés (n 2) 58; E Haddad, *The Refugee in International Society: Between Sovereigns* (Cambridge, CUP, 2008) 144–47. See also S Dehm, 'Contesting the Right to Leave in International Law: The Berlin Wall, the Third World Brain Drain and the Politics of Emigration in the 1960s' in M Craven, S Pahuja and G Simpson (eds), *International Law and the Cold War* (Cambridge, CUP, 2019).

[13] Dowty (n 10) 4–5; I Somin, *Free to Move: Foot Voting, Migration, and Political Freedom* (Oxford, OUP, 2020).

them as victims of the enemy rather than as threats.[14] The severe restrictions imposed by totalitarian and authoritarian regimes on their citizens constitute the 'archetypal' violation of the right to leave. While there are stark differences in the types of migration control measures that now infringe upon the right to leave, similarities endure.

C. The (A)symmetry between Exit and Entry

Against this backdrop, political theorists debate the idea of open borders and the (a)symmetry between the right to leave and right of entry, from open to hard borders.[15] Open border proponents view immigration controls as morally inconsistent with liberal values of freedom and equality, meaning national borders must be open (or 'fairly open'). Conversely, defenders of hard or closed borders justify the power to exclude as inherent to sovereignty and self-determination, thereby imbuing States with broad discretion to regulate immigration as they see fit. Where one falls on this spectrum influences migration and refugee regimes. A dissonance becomes apparent when comparing the free flow of goods, capital and services across borders in a globalised world, but not necessarily people.[16] As chapter five illustrates, migration is usually tightly regulated, including labour mobility and the selection of economically desirable migrants. The debate, however, focuses predominantly on entry restrictions, often overlooking how States curtail the right to leave. Chapters two and three move beyond the ethics of border controls and free movement to the legal relationship between exit and entry.

[14] Haddad (n 12) 137–43, 155–60.

[15] See eg, R Bauböck, 'Free Movement and the Asymmetry Between Exit and Entry' (2006) 4 *Ethics & Economics* 1; CH Wellman and P Cole, *Debating the Ethics of Immigration: Is There a Right to Exclude?* (Oxford, OUP, 2011); JH Carens, *The Ethics of Immigration* (Oxford, OUP, 2013) pt 2; S Fine and L Ypi (eds), *Migration in Political Theory: The Ethics of Movement and Membership* (Oxford, OUP, 2016) pt 1.

[16] See Hollifield (n 6).

2

The Right to Leave Any Country in International Law

I. INTRODUCTION

IN 1948, THE UDHR proclaimed the right to leave as a fundamental right deserving of universal protection. However, the end of the Cold War saw attention on the right to leave fade. Today, the right is often forgotten. It remains underexplored in contemporary literature and jurisprudence, particularly compared to the obligation of *non-refoulement*, which is widely regarded as the cornerstone of refugee protection.[1] The right to leave has been extensively studied in the past, primarily in terms of how States prevented their nationals from leaving because they held State secrets, owed public debts or were political dissidents. This chapter explores the right to leave in international law in depth,

[1] Notable exceptions include R Higgins, 'The Right in International Law of an Individual to Enter, Stay in and Leave a Country' (1973) 49 *International Affairs* 341; H Hannum, *The Right to Leave and Return in International Law and Practice* (Dordrecht, Martinus Nijhoff, 1987); GS Goodwin-Gill, 'The Right to Leave, the Right to Return and the Question of the Right to Remain' in V Gowlland-Debbas (ed), *The Problem of Refugees in the Light of Contemporary International Law Issues* (The Hague, Martinus Nijhoff, 1996); V Chetail, 'Freedom of Movement and Transnational Migrations: A Human Rights Perspective' in TA Aleinikoff and V Chetail (eds), *Migration and International Legal Norms* (The Hague, TMC Asser Press, 2003); C Harvey and RP Barnidge, 'Human Rights, Free Movement, and the Right to Leave in International Law' (2007) 19 *International Journal of Refugee Law* 1; G Cornelisse, 'European Vessels, African Territorial Waters and "Illegal Emigrants": The Right to Leave and the Principle of (Il)Legality in a Global Regime of Mobility' (2008) *Challenge*; J McAdam, 'An Intellectual History of Freedom of Movement in International Law: The Right to Leave as a Personal Liberty' (2011) 12 *Melbourne Journal of International Law* 27; D Kochenov, 'The Right to Leave Any Country Including Your Own in International Law' (2012) 28 *Connecticut Journal of International Law* 43; E Guild, *The Right to Leave a Country* (Issue Paper, Council of Europe Commissioner for Human Rights, 2013); N Markard, 'The Right to Leave by Sea: Legal Limits on EU Migration Control by Third Countries' (2016) 27 *European Journal of International Law* 591; M Zieck, 'Refugees and the Right to Freedom of Movement: From Flight to Return' (2018) 39 *Michigan Journal of International Law* 21; E Guild and V Stoyanova, 'The Human Right to Leave Any Country: A Right to Be Delivered' in W Benedek and others (eds), *European Yearbook on Human Rights 2018* (Plymouth, Intersentia, 2018); V Chetail, *International Migration Law* (Oxford, OUP, 2019) 77–92; V Stoyanova, 'The Right to Leave Any Country and the Interplay between Jurisdiction and Proportionality in Human Rights Law' (2020) 32 *International Journal of Refugee Law* 403; A Macklin, 'Exit Rights, Seamless Borders and the New Carceral State' (2024) 73 *International & Comparative Law Quarterly* 891.

building on the previous historical and theoretical discussion on movement and borders.

It addresses questions about the scope of the right, relevant duty-bearers and the corresponding obligations of States and IOs, clarifying how the right is and ought to be interpreted, key parameters and permissible limitations. Section II outlines the sources of the right to leave in international and regional instruments and explores its existence as a norm of customary international law, which is more contentious. It then addresses the complex issue of whether IOs are bound by the right to leave. Section II continues by charting the legal evolution of the right at the UN and through international initiatives, which has been shaped significantly by historical contexts such as Nazi Germany and the rise of Communism. Section III explores how international and regional adjudicative bodies have interpreted and applied the right to leave in practice, highlighting the remaining gaps. This includes the ICJ, UN treaty bodies, and regional human rights courts in Africa, the Americas and Europe. At this juncture, section IV introduces the notion of 'jurisdiction' and extraterritorial human rights obligations. Establishing that destination States owe duties under the right to leave when they obstruct departure from *third* States, such as through carrier sanctions or funding pullbacks, has been a major hurdle to securing accountability. Section V discusses the key requirements for assessing whether a measure complies with the right to leave, specifically interference with leaving, legality, proportionality and consistency with other rights. Section VI concludes by distilling the key contours of the right to leave as established in the jurisprudence, thereby informing a general framework for its interpretation and operationalisation.

II. THE RIGHT TO LEAVE IN INTERNATIONAL LAW

A. Legal Framework

It is worth beginning with the text of the right to leave and broader freedom of movement. Article 12 of the ICCPR provides:

1. Everyone lawfully within the territory of a State shall, within that territory, have the right to liberty of movement and freedom to choose his residence.
2. Everyone shall be free to leave any country, including his own.
3. The above-mentioned rights shall not be subject to any restrictions except those which are provided by law, are necessary to protect national security, public order (ordre public), public health or morals or the rights and freedoms of others, and are consistent with the other rights recognized in the present Covenant.
4. No one shall be arbitrarily deprived of the right to enter his own country.

Other international and regional instruments generally formulate the right in this way, with some minor exceptions highlighted as relevant. The right to leave falls within the broader right to freedom of movement, which is understood as encompassing three distinct rights: the right to move freely within a country and choose one's place of residence; the right to leave any country; and the right to enter and return to one's own country.[2] Together, they form 'an indispensable condition for the free development of a person'.[3] Their enjoyment can depend on the lawfulness of a person's presence within a State and the meaning of 'own country'.

The right to leave was first expressed in the wake of World War II in Article 13(2) of the UDHR, a non-binding but authoritative instrument. It provides that 'Everyone has the right to leave any country, including his own, and to return to his country.' The UDHR's drafting history offers helpful insight into how the right was understood at the time, justifications for its inclusion, and concerns. The draft outline included two provisions on freedom of movement. Article 9 covered internal movement, while Article 10 provided that 'The right of emigration and expatriation shall not be denied'.[4] These two rights were considered 'vital' because of the Nazi regime's curtailment of free movement and forced relocations during World War II.[5] During drafting, the USSR objected to including the right to leave because it would encourage emigration. It asserted that 'every sovereign State should have the right to establish whatever rules it considered necessary to regulate movement on its territory and across its borders', proposing any right to leave be 'in accordance with the laws of that country'.[6] This was resoundingly rejected, 24 votes to 7, because this would nullify the right.[7] This rejection is valuable evidence of the intention of State parties during drafting.

Several redrafts proposed making freedom of movement '[S]ubject to any general law adopted in the interest of national welfare and security'.[8] The UN Sub-Commission on Prevention of Discrimination and Protection of

[2] CHR (Sub-Commission), 'Study of Discrimination in Respect of the Right of Everyone to Leave any Country, including his Own, and to Return to his Country by Special Rapporteur José D Inglés' (1963) UN Doc E/CN.4/Sub.2/220/Rev.1, 14; McAdam (n 1) 4–5; Zieck (n 1) 21.

[3] Human Rights Committee (HRC), 'General Comment No 27: Article 12 (Freedom of Movement)' (2 November 1999) UN Doc CCPR/C/21/Rev.1/Add.9, para 1.

[4] CHR Drafting Committee (1st session), 'Draft Outline of International Bill of Rights' (4 June 1947) UN Doc E/CN.4/AC.1/3. See also McAdam (n 1) 21–28.

[5] CHR Drafting Committee (2nd Session), 'Summary Record of 36th Meeting' (19 May 1948) UN Doc E/CN.4/AC.1/SR.36, 14; CHR (3rd Session), 'Summary Record of 55th Meeting' (15 June 1948) UN Doc E/CN.4/SR.55, 6 (Indian delegate); UNGA Third Committee (3rd session), '90th Meeting' (1 October 1948) UN Doc A/C.3/SR.90, 43; UNGA Third Committee (3rd session), '120th Meeting' (2 November 1948) UN Doc A/C.3/SR.120, 322 (Belgian delegate).

[6] CHR, '55th Meeting' (n 5) 7–8. See A Dowty, *Closed Borders: The Contemporary Assault on Freedom of Movement* (New Haven, Yale University Press, 1987) 111–12.

[7] There were also 13 abstentions, UNGA, '120th Meeting' (n 5) 315–16, 325. See Dowty (n 6) 136–37.

[8] CHR Drafting Committee (1st session), 'International Bill of Rights' (20 June 1947) UN Doc E/CN.4/AC.1/W.2/Rev.2, art 13; CHR Drafting Committee (1st session), 'Report to Commission on Human Rights' (1 July 1947) UN Doc E/CN.4/21, annex F, art 13; CHR (Sub-Commission), 'Report by Rapporteur Joseph Nisot' (6 December 1947) UN Doc E/CN.4/52, art 13.

Minorities[9] expressed concern about how these exceptions could be interpreted and the need to avoid giving States a loophole through ill-defined interests.[10] Some delegations also invoked the UDHR's aspirational nature to justify limiting restrictions on freedom of movement.[11] Consequently, all limitations were removed, and the general limitations clause, Article 29, assuaged concerns.[12] It provides:

> (2) In the exercise of his rights and freedoms, everyone shall be subject only to such limitations as are determined by law solely for the purpose of securing due recognition and respect for the rights and freedoms of others and of meeting the just requirements of morality, public order and the general welfare in a democratic society.

Interestingly, the US, responding to Haiti's position that everyone should be able to move freely around the world, stated that economic considerations had forced certain countries to take measures restricting immigration, which 'were well known and generally accepted'.[13] This reflects the notion of immigration control as inherently legitimate.

The right to leave was then incorporated into Article 12 of the ICCPR, becoming a binding obligation for State parties. The right, set out above, is not absolute. While the limitations clause in Article 12(3) contains similar restrictions as Article 29(2) of the UDHR, the right to leave can further be restricted to protect national security or public health. Concerns were raised, as during the UDHR negotiations, that phrases such as 'national security', 'public order' and 'health' could lead to abuse or be too far-reaching.[14] The right must also be protected 'without distinction of any kind, such as race, colour, sex, language, religion, political or other opinion, national or social origin, property, birth or other status' (Article 2(1) ICCPR). Similarly formulated provisions on the right to leave are found in many other international conventions.[15]

At the regional level, Article 2(2) Protocol 4 of the ECHR provides that 'Everyone shall be free to leave any country, including his own'. Restrictions are permitted (Article 2(3)) where they are

[9] This was the main subsidiary body of the former Commission on Human Rights, now the Human Rights Council.

[10] CHR (Sub-Commission) (1st Session), 'Summary Record of 8th Meeting' (28 November 1947) UN Doc E/CN.4/Sub.2/SR/8, 19–21.

[11] CHR, '55th Meeting' (n 5) 6, 11; UNGA, '120th Meeting' (n 5) 316–17 (Chilean delegate), 317–18 (Haitian delegate), 322 (Belgian delegate), 323 (UK delegate).

[12] CHR, '55th Meeting' (n 5) 6.

[13] UNGA, '120th Meeting' (n 5) 317–19.

[14] UNGA (10th Session), 'Annotations on Draft International Covenants on Human Rights, prepared by the Secretary-General' (1 July 1955) UN Doc A/2929, 108–10, paras 50–56. See on Art 12(3), M Nowak, *UN Covenant on Civil and Political Rights: CCPR Commentary*, 2nd edn (Kehl, NP Engel 2005) 270–71, 276.

[15] ICERD, art 5(d)(ii); Apartheid Convention, art 2(c); UNCRC, art 10(2); ICRMW, art 8(1); CRPD, art 18(1)(c). See also CEDAW, art 15(4).

> in accordance with law and are necessary in a democratic society in the interests of national security or public safety, for the maintenance of *ordre public*, for the prevention of crime, for the protection of health or morals, or for the protection of the rights and freedoms of others.

The right must also be secured without discrimination (Article 14). While the ECHR binds members of the Council of Europe, the Charter of Fundamental Rights of the European Union (EUCFR) binds EU Member States (see ii below).[16] Regional conventions also protect the right to leave, notably Article 22(2) and (3) of the ACHR; Article 12(2) of the African Charter; Article 22(2) and (3) of the CIS Convention; and Article 27 of the Arab Charter. It has also been included in declarations across the Americas, Islamic countries and Southeast Asia.[17] In addition to lawful restrictions, the ICCPR, ECHR, ACHR and CIS Convention permit derogation from the right during a public emergency, provided certain criteria are met.[18] The right to leave also forms part of the right to free movement under regional treaties establishing economic communities. However, this is conceptually distinct from the right to leave under human rights law. The free movement guarantee in regional treaties grants the nationals of States within the relevant community the right to freely enter the territory of any member State, travel there, establish residence and leave.[19]

The personal scope of the right to leave is broad.[20] It applies to 'everyone' within any country, as is clear from the text across instruments. By comparison, the right to internal freedom of movement in Article 12(1) of the ICCPR is limited to people 'lawfully' within State territory. The right to leave in Article 12(2) contains no such limitation. Crucially, this means an individual's nationality or migration status has no bearing on their entitlement to the legal guarantee and their right to leave 'any country' including one's 'own'.[21] However, the lawfulness of presence is relevant to assessing permissible limitations.

[16] Charter of Fundamental Rights of the European Union (7 December 2000, entered into force 1 December 2009) [2012] OJ C 326/391.

[17] American Declaration of the Rights and Duties of Man, OAS Res XXX adopted by the Ninth International Conference of American States (1948) reprinted in Basic Documents Pertaining to Human Rights in the Inter-American System (1992) OEA/Ser L V/II.82 Doc 6 Rev 1 at 17, art VIII (ADHR); the Cairo Declaration on Human Rights in Islam (adopted 5 August 1990) English translation reproduced in Contribution of the Organisation of the Islamic Conference UN Doc A/CONF.157/PC/62/Add.18 (1993) art 12; ASEAN Human Rights Declaration (adopted on 18 November 2012) art 15.

[18] ICCPR, art 4; ECHR, art 15; ACHR, art 27; CIS Convention, art 35. cf Arab Charter, art 4(2).

[19] See *Falana v Republic of Benin* [2012] ECOWASCJ 44, para 42, 'reference to free movement under Article 12 of the said [African] Charter is not akin to freedom of movement under the Protocol of ECOWAS'; Chetail, *International Migration Law* (n 1) 97–119.

[20] Chetail, *International Migration Law* (n 1) 81.

[21] Nowak (n 14) 268. cf ADHR, art VIII, referring to 'every' person's right not to leave the State of which the person is a national except by their own will.

i. Customary Status

The preceding section shows that the right to leave any country is firmly grounded in treaty law. Its customary status is more contentious. Chetail has undertaken an extensive analysis demonstrating the high likelihood of the right having become customary international law. As evidence of widespread and consistent State practice and *opinio juris*, Chetail has emphasised the plethora of international and regional treaties, declarations and resolutions enshrining or reaffirming the right; their similarity in wording, widespread ratification (the ICCPR has 174 State parties and 74 signatories) and endorsement (including by traditional opponents – former Communist countries – who in 1975 began ending their persistent objections to the right), few reservations; and the fact no less than 116 domestic constitutions protect the right.[22] Endorsement of the right by States that previously opposed its recognition so vigorously provides strong evidence of its crystallisation as a customary norm. Moreover, most scholars accept it as customary international law.[23]

While there is near-universal recognition of the right to leave, in practice, States breach the right – as this book seeks to demonstrate further. However, regular violations do not negate its customary character or other consistent State practice and enduring *opinio juris*. First, States often confirm the rule by asserting the lawfulness of their restrictions, as the cases on the right to leave in section III demonstrate. Second, it cannot easily be asserted that the right is any more violated than other customary norms, such as on torture, inhuman and degrading treatment or non-discrimination.[24] Third, exit controls are now increasingly imposed by destination States seeking to externalise their migration controls, or on their behalf, who were once the most vocal critics of the Soviet bloc's curtailment of movement. It could be queried whether, through subsequent practice, these States now conform to the Soviet view that exit is primarily a matter of State sovereignty, undermining arguments for the right to leave's customary status. Recall, however, that countries such as Australia, Greece, the Netherlands, UK and US, explicitly rejected this view during the UDHR's drafting.[25] Given the clear intention of these State parties during drafting, the better interpretation is that subsequent practice does not reflect a changed position on the right to leave. Instead, such practice should be understood within the context of an underdeveloped right to leave, with the jurisprudence focusing predominantly on departure States and yet to sufficiently explain how externalising States obstructing departure from third States

[22] V Chetail, 'The Transnational Movement of Persons Under General International Law: Mapping the Customary Law Foundations of International Migration Law' in V Chetail and C Bauloz (eds), *Research Handbook on International Law and Migration* (Cheltenham, Edward Elgar Publishing, 2014) 9–27; Chetail, *International Migration Law* (n 1) 76–92.

[23] Chetail, 'Transnational Movement' (n 22) 24–25 including footnotes.

[24] ibid 25–26.

[25] See UNGA, '120th Meeting' (n 5) 318–19, 323–25; Kochenov (n 1) 50–51.

properly falls within the scope of the right.[26] Analysing Chetail's cogent argumentation and the vast breadth of recognition of the right, this book endorses the right to leave as a customary norm. Questions, of course, remain regarding its precise scope.

ii. International Organisations

Whether the right to leave constitutes a binding obligation on IOs is complex. It is now beyond doubt IOs possess a distinct legal personality, can bear international rights and obligations, and may incur responsibility for breaches.[27] The relevant IOs in this work are the EU, ICMPD, IOM and NATO, whose responsibility is governed by ARIO.[28]

While IOs are not bound by human rights treaties (except the EU, which is party to the CRPD), there is consensus IOs must uphold at least some, if not all, human rights.[29] However, scholars differ on the source and scope of these obligations. Some conclude that IOs 'succeed' to the obligations of the States that create them.[30] Similarly, under the 'IOs-as-vehicle' view, IOs are subject to human rights law as the agents of State parties to treaties. Otherwise, States could evade their obligations through IOs.[31] The preponderant – yet still controversial – position is that norms of customary law, including many of the rights in the UDHR and ICCPR, are incumbent on IOs.[32]

[26] See Guild and Stoyanova (n 1) 374.

[27] See *Reparation for Injuries Suffered in the Service of the United' Nations* (Advisory Opinion) [1949] ICJ Rep 174, 179; *Interpretation of the Agreement of 25 March 1951 between the WHO and Egypt* (Advisory Opinion) [1980] ICJ Rep 73, para 37; ILC, 'Draft Articles on the Responsibility of International Organizations' (2011) *YBILC* Vol II(2) UN Doc A/RES/66/100 (ARIO) art 2(a).

[28] On the legal personality of the EU, see TEU, art 47; on NATO, N David, *The International Responsibility of NATO and Its Personnel during Military Operations* (Boston, Brill Nijhoff, 2017) ch 5; on IOM, V Chetail, 'The International Organization for Migration and the Duty to Protect Migrants: Revisiting the Law of International Organizations' in J Klabbers (ed), *The Cambridge Companion to International Organizations Law* (Cambridge, CUP, 2022).

[29] J Wouters and others, 'Accountability for Human Rights Violations by International Organisations: Introductory Remarks' in J Wouters and others (eds), *Accountability for Human Rights Violations by International Organisations* (Plymouth, Intersentia, 2010) 5–10; J Klabbers, *Advanced Introduction to the Law of International Organizations* (Cheltenham, Edward Elgar Publishing, 2015) 89–96; K Daugirdas, 'How and Why International Law Binds International Organizations' (2016) 57 *Harvard International Law Journal* 325; C Ferstman, *International Organizations and the Fight for Accountability* (Oxford, OUP, 2017) ch 2.

[30] See A Reinisch, 'Securing the Accountability of International Organizations' in J Klabbers (ed), *International Organizations* (Abingdon/New York, Routledge, 2016) 137–38; HG Schermers and NM Blokker, *International Institutional Law: Unity within Diversity*, 6th edn (Boston, Brill Nijhoff, 2018) 1037. See for the EU: *Air Transport Association of America v Secretary of State for Energy and Climate Change*, Case C-366/10, EU:C:2011:864, [2011] ECR I-13755 paras 50–51, 101, 107.

[31] See G Kent, 'The Human Rights Obligations of Intergovernmental Organizations' (2005) 42 *UN Chronicle* 32, 33; Daugirdas (n 29) 345–57; FL Bordin, *The Analogy between States and International Organizations* (Cambridge, CUP, 2019) 82–85, pt 1 generally.

[32] See O De Schutter, 'Human Rights and the Rise of International Organisations: The Logic of Sliding Scales in the Law of International Responsibility' in J Wouters and others (eds), *Accountability for Human Rights Violations by International Organisations* (Plymouth, Intersentia,

The EU is straightforward. EU institutions, agencies and Member States must respect the EUCFR when implementing EU law.[33] Although the right to leave is not expressly enshrined in Article 45 on free movement and residence, it is binding as a general principle of EU law and has been recognised by the CJEU.[34] Frontex, as an EU agency enjoying legal personality and capable of being liable under EU law, is also bound to uphold the EUCFR and general principles.[35] The ICMPD, although substantially funded by the European Commission, is not an EU agency and therefore not bound by EU law.[36] Leading scholars have shown that IOM is subject to a range of legal obligations, correcting earlier misconceptions that IOM has no obligations towards migrants.[37]

Unlike UNHCR, IOM is not a specialised UN agency or subsidiary organ, but a related organisation.[38] Its obligations derive from its internal law, which has evolved to include the protection of migrants as an implied power, reinforced by subsequent practice; its 2016 binding agreement with the UN; and the general rules of international law.[39] IOM's 2016 agreement includes a formal endorsement of duties to protect migrants, where it committed to act in accordance with the principles and policies of the UN, including the Charter, and other relevant international migration, refugee and human rights instruments.[40] Clarifying the source and scope of IO's obligations is beyond this work. It accepts that IOs are bound by most human rights, especially customary norms such as the right to leave, which is vital to establishing the shared responsibility of States and IOs during externalisation and avoiding responsibility vacuums. While issues may

2010) 62–64, 72–73; Daugirdas (n 29) 331–35, 357–72; Reinisch (n 30) 134–36; Ferstman (n 29) 28–42; Schermers and Blokker (n 30) 1046–47. See further on the doctrinal debate J Alvarez, 'Review of Dan Sarooshi, International Organizations and their Exercise of Sovereign Powers' (2007) 101 *American Journal of International Law* 674, 677–78; J Klabbers, 'Sources of International Organizations' Law: Reflections on Accountability' in J d'Aspremont and S Besson (eds), *Oxford Handbook of the Sources of International Law* (Oxford, OUP, 2017) 993–1000.

33 EUCFR, art 51(1).

34 Treaty on European Union (TEU), art 6(3); EUCFR, preamble, art 52(3); *Schmidberger v Austria*, Case C-112/00, EU:C:2003:333 [2003] ECR I-5659, paras 71–73; *Hristo Gaydarov*, Case C-430/10, EU:C:2011:749 [2011] ECR I-11637, paras 24–26; E Hancox, 'The Relationship Between the Charter and General Principles: Looking Back and Looking Forward' (2020) 22 *Cambridge Yearbook of European Legal Studies* 233.

35 Regulation (EU) 2019/1896 of the European Parliament and of the Council of 13 November 2019 on the European Border and Coast Guard and repealing Regulations (EU) No 1052/2013 and (EU) 2016/1624 [2019] OJ L 295/1, preamble 103, arts 5(4), 48(1), 80(1), 93(1).

36 ICMPD, 'Annual Report 2024' (*ICMPD*, 7 May 2025) 92–93, www.icmpd.org/file/download/64168/file/ICMPD%2520Annual%2520Report%25202024.pdf.

37 See Chetail, 'International Organization for Migration' (n 28); M Bradley, C Costello and A Sherwood (eds), *IOM Unbound? Obligations and Accountability of the International Organization for Migration in an Era of Expansion* (Cambridge, CUP, 2023).

38 See on UN agencies and UNHCR, G Verdirame, *The UN and Human Rights: Who Guards the Guardians?* (Cambridge, CUP, 2011) chs 1–3; N Kinchin, 'The Implied Human Rights Obligations of UNHCR' (2016) 28 *International Journal of Refugee Law* 251.

39 Chetail, 'International Organization for Migration' (n 28).

40 UN-IOM Agreement, art 2(5). See also IOM, 'Policy on Protection' (7 September 2015) C/106/INF/9.

arise vis-à-vis immunities and lack of fora, responsibility is not contingent on the existence of judicial remedies.[41]

B. The Evolution of the Right

Following the proclamation of the right to leave in the UDHR, UN bodies were tasked with giving meaning and substance to its scope and functioning. In 1953, the UN Sub-Commission on Prevention of Discrimination and Protection of Minorities asked ECOSOC to study discrimination in emigration and immigration.[42] Five years later, Judge José Inglés was appointed Special Rapporteur and completed his report and draft principles in 1963.[43] However, political obstacles delayed any substantive debate on Inglés's report until 1973.[44] Countries with discriminatory immigration policies, notably the US, pushed to exclude immigration from the study's scope, while the Soviet Union actively sought to block further discussion of the right.[45]

Amidst the erection of the Berlin Wall, Inglés warned 'that an ancient and basic right of the human being was in jeopardy'.[46] His report established the initial framework for the right's functioning, seeking to make the right to leave a reality.[47] Inglés distilled Article 13(2) of the UDHR into three interrelated rights, distinguishing between nationals and non-nationals: the right of a national to leave their country; the right to return to their country; and the right of a foreigner to leave the country of their sojourn.[48] The draft principles provided that every national is entitled, without distinction, to leave their country temporarily or permanently, which can only be limited as determined by law to meet specific legitimate aims.[49] Every foreigner, without distinction, has the right to leave the country of their sojourn. Foreigners lawfully present were to be accorded at least the same rights as nationals, while every foreigner has the right to leave the country of sojourn without arbitrary restriction.[50] Inglés recognised that discrimination against non-nationals attempting to leave had a greater impact than on nationals, for they experience not only the inconvenience inflicted upon nationals but are also precluded from returning to their own country.[51] However, Inglés noted that, in practice, non-nationals

[41] See generally SØ Johansen, *The Human Rights Accountability Mechanisms of International Organizations* (Cambridge, CUP, 2020).
[42] Hannum (n 1) 13–14.
[43] Nisot (n 8).
[44] Hannum (n 1) 14.
[45] Dowty (n 6) 131–41; Kochenov (n 1) 50–51.
[46] Inglés (n 2) 4.
[47] Kochenov (n 1) 53.
[48] Inglés (n 2) 14.
[49] ibid annex VI, art I.
[50] ibid annex VI, arts III(b), (c).
[51] ibid 14–15.

were hardly ever refused permission to leave the country of sojourn, unlike citizens.[52]

Inglés regarded the right as 'indispensable … for the full enjoyment by all of other civil, political, economic, social and cultural rights', including relating to family life, education, work, seeking asylum and changing nationality.[53] Inglés recognised the legal and practical necessity of passports and other travel documentation, highlighting the inextricable link between the right to leave (or return) and ability to obtain a passport and visa.[54] He called for coordinated action to facilitate international travel, stating that enjoyment of the right to leave 'would be meaningless … if a person has nowhere to go due to legal or artificial barriers to entering another State'.[55] Although Inglés' study did not alter the practice of Soviet States, his conclusions had an enduring influence on essential aspects of the right.

In response to the lack of UN action and persistent breaches, experts at the Uppsala Colloquium in 1972 met to examine Article 13(2) of the UDHR and adopted a 'Declaration on the Right to Leave and the Right to Return', using Inglés' draft principles as a springboard.[56] This renewed momentum prompted the Commission on Human Rights to finally debate Inglés' report in 1973. In the 1980s, following the ICCPR's entry into force, the UN Sub-Commission renewed its interest in addressing violations of the right to leave and return, requesting an update on Inglés' study.[57] Special Rapporteur Chama LC Mubanga-Chipoya completed his report in 1988, accompanied by a draft declaration, which addressed brain drain and permissible restrictions under Article 12(3) of the ICCPR.[58] This was expanded upon in 1997 by Volodymyr Boutkevitch.[59]

Outside of the UN, independent experts met in Strasbourg in 1986 to examine the right to leave and return under the UDHR and ICCPR,

[52] ibid 19.

[53] ibid 65.

[54] ibid 13, 45–46, 60–63.

[55] ibid 63.

[56] 'The Right to Leave and the Right to Return: A Declaration Adopted by the Uppsala Colloquium, Sweden, June 21, 1972' (1973) 7 *International Migration Review* 62 (Uppsala Declaration). See also K Vasak and S Liskofsky (eds), *The Right to Leave and to Return: Papers and Recommendations of the International Colloquium Held in Uppsala, Sweden, 19–20 June 1972* (New York, The American Jewish Committee, 1976).

[57] See Hannum (n 1) 14–15.

[58] CHR (Sub-Commission), 'Analysis of Current Trends and Developments in respect of the Right of Everyone to Leave Any Country including His Own and to Return to His Country, and Some Other Rights or Considerations Arising Therefrom, Final Report by Special Rapporteur Chama LC Mubanga-Chipoya' (20 June 1988) UN Doc E/CN.4/Sub.2/1988/35; CHR (Sub-Commission), 'Draft Declaration on Freedom and Non-Discrimination in Respect of the Right of Everyone to Leave any Country, including his Own and to Return to his Country' (15 June 1988) UN Doc E/CN.4/Sub.2/1988/35/Add.1 (Draft Declaration).

[59] CHR (Sub-Commission), 'Working Paper on the Right to Freedom of Movement and Related Issues Prepared by Volodymyr Boutkevitch' (29 July 1997) UN Doc E/CN.4/Sub.2/1997/22. See Dowty (n 6) 218–21; Kochenov (n 1) 53, who critiqued the rigour and ambition of the updates.

drawing on previous initiatives, emerging jurisprudence and State practice.[60] The Strasbourg Declaration made several advances to Inglés' original framework, detailing the narrow grounds for restriction and defining the meaning of permissible limitations under Article 12(3) of the ICCPR. It declared that restrictions must be narrowly construed and subject to international scrutiny, with the burden on States to justify restrictions.[61] The Declaration also underscored the importance of obtaining travel documents to exercise one's right to leave through procedural safeguards.[62] Notably, Article 10(c) provides that 'No state shall refuse to issue the documents referred to in Article 9 or shall otherwise impede the exercise of the right to leave, on the ground of the applicant's inability to present authorisation to enter another country'. The notion of the right to leave as 'self-standing' and exercisable irrespective of any right of entry is central to this work and will be returned to. Finally, in 1999, the Human Rights Committee adopted General Comment Number 27, providing the first authoritative interpretation of the right to freedom of movement under the ICCPR – what Inglés and other experts had sought to do since the 1960s to bring to life the right to leave and return.[63] This General Comment is discussed in detail in the following section.

III. INTERPRETING THE RIGHT: ADJUDICATIVE BODIES

The jurisprudence of international and regional bodies has been instrumental in elaborating the scope of the right to leave, lawful limitations and States' obligations. Cases have gone some way in resolving questions surrounding the practical operation of the right by providing real-life situations. Nonetheless, not all interpretative questions have been answered, which the remainder of this work seeks to address.

This section explores global and regional jurisprudence on the right to leave. It opens with the ICJ as the principal judicial organ of the UN, followed by UN treaty bodies, and then turns to regional systems, including the European Court of Human Rights, the Inter-American Commission and Court, and the African Commission and Court on Human and Peoples' Rights. It endeavours to cover every international or regional decision that substantively engages with the right to leave (even when discussed without reference to a specific legal provision). Cases from regional bodies, such as the CJEU, ECOWAS Court and East African

[60] H Hannum, 'The Strasbourg Declaration on the Right to Leave and Return' (1987) 81 *American Journal of International Law* 432, 433–34 (Strasbourg Declaration).
[61] Strasbourg Declaration, art 4.
[62] ibid arts 9 and 10. See also Uppsala Declaration, arts 13–16.
[63] HRC, 'General Comment No 27' (n 3). See Kochenov (n 1) 53.

Court of Justice, are only discussed where their rulings raise human rights issues related to the right to leave.

A. International Court of Justice

The ICJ's jurisprudence related to the right to leave falls into three broad categories: diplomatic protection and asylum; racial discrimination; and movement restrictions against an occupied population. However, in half the cases, the Court does not explicitly mention the right to leave, and where it does, the right is not explored in depth.

i. Diplomatic Protection and Asylum

In *Armed Activities on the Territory of the Congo (Democratic Republic of the Congo v Uganda* (2005), the Court held that the Ugandan armed forces had perpetrated widespread human rights violations against the Congolese civilian population during Uganda's unlawful military intervention in the DRC.[64] Concerning Uganda's counterclaim, the Court found that the maltreatment inflicted upon Ugandan diplomats by the Congolese armed forces at Congo's international airport as they attempted to leave the country violated the DRC's obligations under the Vienna Convention on Diplomatic Relations. However, the claim concerning the maltreatment of civilians without diplomatic status trying to evacuate the armed conflict was declared inadmissible as Uganda provided no proof of nationality.[65] Judge Simma's separate opinion powerfully articulated that the 17 victims attacked at the airport nonetheless remained protected by international human rights and humanitarian law, which the majority failed to recognise in only focusing on diplomatic protection. In his view, the DRC's conduct would have violated, *inter alia*, the right to leave in the ICCPR and African Charter.[66]

In the 1980 *Iranian Hostages Case*, the ICJ, invoking the diplomatic entitlement for embassy and consular staff to freedom of movement and travel within a territory, ordered Iran to ensure the American hostages had the necessary means to leave the country.[67] The right to leave was not raised by the US or the Court. The Court did, however, stress that deprivation of the individuals' freedom was manifestly incompatible with the fundamental principles of the UDHR.[68] And in the 1950 *Asylum Case*, which concerned Colombia's grant of

[64] *Armed Activities on the Territory of the Congo (Democratic Republic of the Congo v Uganda)* (Judgment) [2005] ICJ Rep 168.

[65] ibid paras 332–40.

[66] ibid paras 16–18, 30–32 (Separate Opinion Simma J).

[67] *United States Diplomatic and Consular Staff in Tehran (USA v Iran)* (Judgment) [1980] ICJ Rep 3, paras 61–62, 77, 95.

[68] ibid para 91.

diplomatic asylum to a prominent Peruvian political leader, the analysis centred on the Havana Convention on Asylum and whether Peru was bound to allow him to leave the country safely.[69] The right to leave was not invoked, which is unsurprising given the *lex specialis*. These cases demonstrate that even where the right to leave could apply, it will not be raised if a more specific treaty or legal regime governs.

ii. Racial Discrimination

Several cases have been brought under ICERD, invoking racial discrimination regarding restrictions on movement, including (explicitly or implicitly) the right to leave. However, the issue has never been examined because the State bringing the proceedings failed to establish that the measures amounted to racial discrimination under ICERD.

Following Russia's annexation of Crimea and intervention in eastern Ukraine since 2014, Ukraine brought a case against Russia under ICERD, arguing that Russia's actions amounted to racial discrimination against Crimean Tatars and ethnic Ukrainians.[70] Ukraine argued Russia had failed to uphold Article 5 on freedom of movement, residence and the right to leave by restricting the movement of Crimean Tatar leaders, banning them from entering Crimea and preventing them from leaving.[71] However, these restrictions were not addressed because the Court found Ukraine had not proven the leaders were targeted based on their ethnicity.

In a case brought against the UAE, Qatar argued that the UAE's imposition of a series of discriminatory measures directed at Qataris based on their national origin since June 2017 violated ICERD.[72] This diplomatic crisis between Qatar and the Arab League amounted to a de facto blockade on the country, with the UAE expelling all Qataris within its territory, prohibiting Qataris from entering or passing through the UAE, closure of UAE airspace and seaports for all Qataris, and banning all Qatari means of transportation from crossing, entering or leaving the UAE. These travel restrictions significantly impacted the rights of Qataris, other Gulf nationals, and migrant workers, including to leave and return.[73] In a controversial decision discussed in chapter five on

[69] *Colombian-Peruvian Asylum Case* (Judgment) [1950] ICJ Rep 266, 278–79.

[70] *Application of the International Convention for the Suppression of the Financing of Terrorism and of the International Convention on the Elimination of All Forms of Racial Discrimination (Ukraine v Russian Federation)* (Judgment) [2024] ICJ Rep 78.

[71] ibid paras 132–33.

[72] *Application of the International Convention on the Elimination of All Forms of Racial Discrimination (Qatar v UAE)* (Preliminary Objections) [2021] ICJ Rep 71.

[73] D Dudley, 'A Winner Emerges from the Qatar Crisis: Oman's National Airline' (*Forbes*, 8 June 2017) www.forbes.com/sites/dominicdudley/2017/06/08/oman-air-takes-advantage-of-qatar-crisis/; HRW, 'Qatar: Isolation Causing Rights Abuses' (12 July 2017) www.hrw.org/news/2017/07/12/qatar-isolation-causing-rights-abuses.

discriminatory visa policies, the ICJ held it had no jurisdiction to hear the case, on the basis that 'national origin' under Article 1(1) of ICERD excludes present nationality.

In the case of *Armenia v Azerbaijan*, the ICJ ordered provisional measures requiring Azerbaijan to ensure the 'unimpeded movement of persons, vehicles and cargo along the Lachin Corridor' – which connects ethnic Armenians in Nagorno-Karabakh with Armenia and the outside world.[74] By explicitly invoking the right to leave under Article 5(d)(ii) of ICERD in response to the blockade, Armenia has given the Court a crucial opportunity to engage substantively with the right and its intersection with racial discrimination, underscoring its importance in enabling people to flee confinement and conflict.[75]

iii. Freedom of Movement under Occupation

In the Occupied Palestinian Territory (OPT), Israel subjects millions of Palestinians to severe and longstanding restrictions on their freedom of movement and ability to leave the occupied territory. In its 2004 *Wall* advisory opinion, the ICJ found that Israel's separation wall in the West Bank violated Article 12(1) of the ICCPR by obstructing the rights of Palestinians to move freely within the OPT and choose their residence and violated their rights to work, health, education and an adequate standard of living.[76] In its landmark 2024 advisory opinion, the Court went further, holding that Israel's whole regime restricting the movement of Palestinians amounted to prohibited discrimination; contributed to forcible transfers in breach of the Fourth Geneva Convention; helped maintain a near-complete separation between settler and Palestinian communities contrary to Article 3 of ICERD (racial segregation and apartheid); and violated the Palestinian people's right to self-determination.[77]

In both opinions, the Court demonstrated how freedom of movement and restrictions imposed on its exercise hamper the enjoyment of other fundamental rights. Yet neither mentions the right to leave, even though Palestinians in the OPT are routinely prevented by Israel from travelling abroad. In its *Wall* opinion, the ICJ confirmed that Israel is bound by the ICCPR and other human

[74] *Application of the International Convention on the Elimination of All Forms of Racial Discrimination (Armenia v Azerbaijan)* (Provisional Measures) Order 22 February 2023 [2023] ICJ Rep 14, paras 36–39, 67. See also *Application of the International Convention on the Elimination of All Forms of Racial Discrimination (Armenia v Azerbaijan)* (Provisional Measures) Order 17 November 2023 [2023] ICJ Rep 619, paras 40, 57, 69.

[75] Order 22 February 2023, paras 29, 31.

[76] *Legal Consequences of the Construction of a Wall in the Occupied Palestinian Territory (Advisory Opinion)* [2004] ICJ Rep 136, paras 128–36. The ICJ in its 2024 advisory opinion also found a breach of family life.

[77] *Legal Consequences arising from the Policies and Practices of Israel in the Occupied Palestinian Territory, including East Jerusalem* (Advisory Opinion) General List No 186, 19 July 2024, paras 147, 198–206, 223–29, 239, 242–43.

rights treaties in the OPT (which it reaffirmed in 2024), but only found Israel to have violated Article 12(1) of the ICCPR on internal movement.[78] It was thus not contentious that Palestinians possess the right to leave, and a violation could have been found, especially since the Court has recognised Israel's control over the OPT and land, sea and air borders in Gaza.[79] It is not clear why the Court did not consider the right to leave, and its omission is particularly striking given UNGA's 2022 request for an advisory opinion explicitly asked the Court to address freedom of movement within the Palestinian territory, into and out of Gaza, and to and from the outside world.[80] As will be shown, at times other adjudicative bodies also overlook the right to leave.

B. UN Treaty Bodies

All UN treaty bodies whose constituent treaty enshrines the right to leave have addressed the right or restrictions on departure to some degree. The Human Rights Committee provides a generalised framework for understanding the right to leave, while the UN committees working to protect the rights of children, ethnic minorities, migrant workers, people with disabilities, and women provide valuable insight into how States should implement the right for specific groups and rectify discriminatory restrictions.

i. Human Rights Committee

The Human Rights Committee, as the authoritative UN body for interpreting the ICCPR, has played an eminent role in determining the scope of the right to leave and States' obligations under Article 12(2) through its General Comments and Individual Communications. Its views and guidance have also been instructive for the reasoning of other adjudicative bodies.

The Committee first touched on the right to leave in its 1986 General Comment on the Position of Aliens, stating that:

> Once an alien is lawfully within a territory, their freedom of movement within the territory and right to leave that territory may only be restricted in accordance with article 12, paragraph 3. Differences in treatment in this regard between aliens and nationals, or between different categories of aliens, need to be justified under article 12, paragraph 3.[81]

[78] *Wall* opinion (n 76) paras 107–13; 2024 opinion (n 77) paras 100, 194.

[79] *Wall* opinion (n 76) paras 112, 139; 2024 opinion (n 77) 89–94.

[80] UNGA, 'Resolution Adopted by the General Assembly on 30 December 2022, Israeli Practices Affecting the Human Rights of the Palestinian People in the Occupied Palestinian Territory, including East Jerusalem' (9 January 2023) UN Doc A/RES/77/247.

[81] HRC, 'General Comment No 15: The Position of Aliens Under the Covenant' (11 April 1986) UN Doc CCPR/A/41/40, paras 5, 7–8.

The Committee was clear that the burden lies on the State to prove that any differential treatment between different groups of non-nationals is strictly necessary. Yet, as Part II of this book scrutinises, the imposition of migration controls on some nationalities and racial groups but not others is often done without justification or is not based on legitimate grounds.

As mentioned, in 1999 the Committee issued General Comment No 27 on freedom of movement, providing guidance on applying the right in practice. This decades-old document remains the most comprehensive commentary on the right to leave of any adjudicative body. The parts of the Comment dedicated to the right to leave and non-discrimination were based largely on Judge Inglés' draft principles, and begin by affirming the importance of free movement as 'an indispensable condition for the free development of a person'.[82] The Comment makes several significant contributions to the right to leave framework. It provides that:

> Freedom to leave the territory of a State may not be made dependent on any specific purpose or on the period of time the individual chooses to stay outside the country ... Likewise, the right of the individual to determine the State of destination is part of the legal guarantee. As the scope of article 12, paragraph 2, is not restricted to persons lawfully within the territory of a State, an alien being legally expelled from the country is likewise entitled to elect the State of destination, subject to the agreement of that State.[83]

Individuals, therefore, are entitled to exercise their right to leave for an array of purposes, regardless of the duration they will be abroad. This clearly encompasses tourism, work, family, education, seeking asylum, and many more purposes. Individuals can also choose their desired destination State (of course, this does not mean they will be granted entry). The Comment forgoes any distinction Inglés made between nationals and non-nationals in assessing the lawfulness of a restriction on departure, more closely aligning with the text of Article 12(2). Against the backdrop of sweeping restrictions on movement by States, the Comment stresses that,

> The law itself has to establish the conditions under which the rights may be limited. State reports should therefore specify the legal norms upon which restrictions are founded ...
>
> States should always be guided by the principle that the restrictions must not impair the essence of the right ...; the relation between right and restriction, between norm and exception, must not be reversed. The laws authorising the application of restrictions should use precise criteria and may not confer unfettered discretion on those charged with their execution.
>
> ... it is not sufficient that the restrictions serve the permissible purposes; they must also be necessary to protect them. Restrictive measures must conform to the principle

[82] HRC, 'General Comment No 27' (n 3) 1.
[83] ibid para 8.

> of proportionality; they must be appropriate to achieve their protective function; they must be the least intrusive instrument amongst those which might achieve the desired result; and they must be proportionate to the interest to be protected.[84]

Any restriction on the right to leave must, therefore, be based on clear legal grounds and meet the tests of necessity and proportionality, which Inglés' study had not explored in depth.

Restrictions must also be consistent with other rights in the Covenant and the fundamental principles of equality and non-discrimination. Even where a restriction would otherwise be permissible under Article 12(3), it would be a clear violation of the ICCPR if the measure restricting departure involved discrimination based on a prohibited ground, such as race, colour, sex, religion or other status.[85]

The Committee further highlighted its major concern with the numerous legal and bureaucratic obstacles imposed by States that make it difficult for people, especially their own nationals, to leave the country, such as repatriation deposits, high passport fees, and harassment of applicants.[86] The Committee emphasised the utmost importance of State parties reporting on all legal and practical restrictions they apply on leaving both to nationals and foreigners so it can assess compliance with the requirements under the right. In particular, it called on States to include information on carrier sanctions for transporting people without the required travel documents.[87] The explicit reference already in 1999 by the Committee to carrier sanctions as a measure that can affect the right to leave is important in many respects, and will be returned to when considering carrier sanctions in depth (see chapter five). It implies that the right to leave is not dependent on any right of entry elsewhere and can be violated even if admission is unlikely. It also signifies that the right must be secured not only by departure States but also by destination States when exercising extra-territorial jurisdiction through measures that affect individuals leaving another country.

a. Communications

The Committee has considered very few communications on the merits concerning the right to leave under Article 12(2).[88] The decisions span from the 1980s to 2025 and are predominantly against former Soviet republics, as well as North African and South American States.

[84] ibid paras 12–14.
[85] ibid para 18.
[86] ibid para 17.
[87] ibid para 10.
[88] It is sometimes unclear whether cases concern internal movement, the right to leave or both eg *Karker v France*, Communication No 833/1998 (26 October 2000) UN Doc CCPR/C/70/D/ 833/1998.

In *Loubna El Ghar v Libya*, a Libyan citizen residing in Morocco applied for a Libyan passport in 1999 at the Libyan Consulate to allow her to continue her university studies in France.[89] More than three years later, the Libyan authorities indicated without any explanation that she could only be given a *laissez-passer* travel document to return to Libya. The author had yet to obtain a Libyan passport by the decision date in 2004. The Committee found that Libya had violated Article 12(2) in denying her a passport 'without any valid justification and subjected to an unreasonable delay' and, as a result, prevented her from travelling abroad to continue her studies.[90] The Committee considered that a *laissez-passer* 'cannot be considered a satisfactory substitute for a valid Libyan passport that would enable the author to travel abroad', highlighting the importance of passports in ensuring one's right to leave can be exercised.[91] The Committee had previously established the obligation of States to issue passports to their nationals living abroad concerning violations of the right to leave in the context of political dissidents. In the 'passport cases' of the early 1980s, the Committee found that the Uruguayan military government had violated the right to leave by refusing passports to Uruguayan nationals living abroad.[92] These decisions demonstrate that States owe obligations under Article 12(2) to nationals within their territory as well as nationals residing abroad, confirming the right's opposability to States exercising extraterritorial jurisdiction. The right protects an individual's right to leave a State of which they are not a national but merely a resident or which they are just passing through. Accordingly, States of nationality, residence and sojourn can all owe obligations to individuals under the right.[93] States must, therefore, secure the right for their nationals even when they are in another State's territory or want to sojourn or reside elsewhere, with travel documents representing a prerequisite for exercising one's right to leave.

In a second case against Libya, a Libyan national who was a member of the Muslim Brotherhood was in Egypt when he was warned that security personnel had been at his home in Libya seeking to arrest him.[94] Unable to return to Libya because of the risk of political persecution, he was separated from his wife and six children. He was granted asylum in Switzerland and approved family

[89] *Loubna El Ghar v Libya*, Communication No 1107/2002 (15 November 2004) UN Doc CCPR/C/82/D/1107/2002.

[90] ibid para 8.

[91] ibid paras 7.2–7.3. cf *Bwalya v Zambia*, Communication No 314/1988 (27 July 1993) UN Doc CCPR/C/48/D/314/1988, para 6.5 on art 12(1).

[92] *Sophie Vidal Martins v Uruguay*, Communication No R13/57 (23 March 1982) UN Doc Supp No 40 A/37/40, para 7; *Mabel Pereira Montero v Uruguay*, Communication No 106/1981 (31 March 1983) UN Doc CCPR/C/OP/2, para 9.4; *Samuel Lichtensztejn v Uruguay*, Communication No 77/1980 (31 March 1983) UN Doc CCPR/C/OP/2, para 8.30; *Carlos Varela Núñez v Uruguay*, Communication No 108/1981 (22 July 1983) UN Doc CCPR/C/OP/2, paras 6.1, 9.3.

[93] See Nowak (n 14) 268–69.

[94] *Farag El Dernawi v Libya*, Communication No 1143/2002 (20 July 2007) UN Doc CCPR/C/90/D/1143/2002.

reunification. His wife and three youngest children sought to leave Libya to join him, but they were stopped at the Libyan-Tunisian border and officials confiscated the family passport, which they refused to return. The Committee found that there had been a violation of Article 12(2) as Libya had failed to advance any justification in terms of national security, public order, etc, and such a basis was not apparent on the evidence before it.[95] In 2006, Colonel Gaddafi invited opponents in exile to return to Libya. This led a dissident holding political asylum in Switzerland to return to Libya after being granted a passport by the Libyan embassy and assured he would not be persecuted. Upon arrival, security agents confiscated his passport and refused to return it, preventing him from leaving and returning to Switzerland.[96] He ended up in secret detention and tortured. In the absence of any arguments justifying the confiscation of his passport, Libya was found to have breached the right to leave (among other violations).

In *Moses Solo Tarlue v Canada*, the Committee provided important guidance regarding the lawfulness of an individual's presence in relation to the right to leave, despite the claim being deemed inadmissible, which warrants its discussion.[97] It concerned Canada's refusal to return a Liberian national's passport to allow him to travel to Japan for business and then to the US to join his family after entering Canada on a false passport, being issued a deportation order, and having his valid Liberian passport seized. His claim for refugee status was refused because of his involvement in war crimes and crimes against humanity. The Committee found the author had failed to substantiate his claim that restricting his departure was unlawful, given Canada had explained that his passport was seized to execute a lawful removal.[98] While non-nationals are guaranteed the right to leave, the Committee's reasoning demonstrates that States are entitled to retain or confiscate a passport to effect lawful deportations. The lawfulness of an individual's presence is, therefore, relevant in considering legitimate aims and proportionality.

On another occasion, the Human Rights Committee considered that it may be justifiable on national security and public order grounds to restrict leaving for people awaiting judicial proceedings. However, where the proceedings are unduly delayed, the restriction will not be justified, as was the case for a Peruvian citizen who had been prevented from leaving Peru for seven years because of a pending arrest warrant.[99] It follows that if there is an unreasonable delay during other administrative or immigration proceedings, passport

[95] ibid para 6.2.

[96] *Aboufaied v Libya*, Communication No 1782/2008 (21 March 2012) UN Doc CCPR/C/104/D/1782/2008, para 7.8.

[97] *Moses Solo Tarlue v Canada*, Communication No 1551/2007 (27 March 2009) UN Doc CCPR/C/95/D/1551/2007.

[98] ibid para 7.7.

[99] *Gonzalez del Rio v Peru*, Communication No 263/1987 (2 November 1992) UN Doc CCPR/C/46/D/263/1987, para 5.3.

retention that amounts in effect to a lengthy travel ban will not be lawful. A measure initially appearing legitimate may nonetheless be unlawful if imposed prematurely. For example, two Belgian nationals brought a communication alleging a violation of Article 12(2) for a travel ban following their UN Security Council's sanctions listing for involvement in a charitable organisation that was suspected of financing Al-Qaida.[100] Considering it was Belgium that proposed their names to the Sanctions Committee only weeks after the criminal investigation had opened in Belgium, and that Belgium had subsequently requested that they be removed from the list, the Committee found the restriction on the Belgian nationals' right to leave was not necessary to protect national security or public order.

The Committee has further accepted that a State may refuse a passport to nationals or impose other 'reasonable' restrictions as are provided by law, who have failed to complete their compulsory military service for the protection of national security and public order, as supported by the ICCPR's *travaux préparatoires*.[101] However, a travel ban imposed on nationals who have legitimately exercised their right of conscientious objection to military service will violate the right to leave, for instance, in the case of a conscientious objector who was banned from leaving Greece for 14 years.[102]

As the Committee emphasised in its General Comment No 27, the burden is on the State to justify the necessity of its measure in protecting a legitimate aim. In a case against Uzbekistan, the author brought a communication on behalf of her father, a citizen of Uzbekistan who was the manager of a public company and held deputy roles with regional and state councils.[103] After returning from Turkmenistan on an official business trip, he was arrested and sentenced to five years' imprisonment for illegally crossing the Uzbek–Turkmen border with an expired exit visa and failing to obtain consent. The author argued that her father's conviction for travelling abroad on business, which did not constitute a threat to any legitimate aims, violated his right to leave. The Committee agreed, finding Uzbekistan had provided no information or justification that would support its necessity or proportionality.[104] The Committee has rendered several other decisions that relate more to the State's failure to defend its practices rather than providing useful guidance on the right's operation.[105]

[100] *Sayadi and Vinck v Belgium*, Communication No 1472/2006 (22 October 2008) UN Doc CCPR/C/94/D/1472/2006, paras 10.5–10.8.

[101] *Peltonen v Finland*, Communication No 492/1992 (26 July 1994) UN Doc CCPR/C/51/D/492/1992, paras 8.2–8.4.

[102] *Lazaros Petromelidis v Greece*, Communication No 3065/2017 (2 July 2021) UN Doc CCPR/C/132/D/3065/2017, para 9.9.

[103] *Zoolfia v Uzbekistan*, Communication No 1585/2007 (30 July 2009) UN Doc CCPR/C/96/D/1585/2007.

[104] ibid para 8.3.

[105] See *Oló Bahamonde v Equatorial Guinea*, Communication No 468/1991 (20 October 1993) UN Doc CCPR/C/49/D/468/1991, paras 8.2, 9.3; *Cholpon Djakupova and Narynbek Idinov v Kyrgyzstan*, Communication No 3195/2018 (14 March 2025) UN Doc CCPR/C/143/D/3195/2018, paras 7.9–7.11.

For instance, Turkmenistan was found to have violated Article 12(2) in the absence of any information provided by the State explaining why it had prevented its nationals from leaving.[106]

The Committee's decisions establish several key principles for how the right is to be interpreted and applied in practice. First, States of nationality, residence and sojourn are all duty-bearers who must respect individuals' right to leave the territory. This means that individuals possess the right to leave a State in which they reside or only pass through. States must secure the right for their nationals abroad and are obliged to issue them with travel documents. Therefore, the right to leave covers movement from one's home country to another country and vice versa, and between countries. Second, interferences with the right include refusals to issue travel documents and their confiscation or retention, prosecution and imprisonment for illegal departure, arrest warrants and travel bans. Third, the burden is on the State to explain the legitimacy, necessity and proportionality of the restriction. Fourth, while the right to leave protects everyone, lawfulness of presence is relevant at the limitations stage, which is pertinent concerning externalisation measures that seek to obstruct the departure of irregular migrants. Finally, great emphasis is placed on travel documents as the *sine qua non* for exercising the right to leave.

ii. Committee on the Elimination of Racial Discrimination

The Committee on the Elimination of Racial Discrimination (CERD) has engaged with the right to leave under Article 5(d)(ii) of ICERD on a limited basis. It has, for instance, urged States to abolish the requirement for migrant workers to have an exit permit from their employer to leave the country.[107] In its general comments concerning discrimination against non-citizens and refugees, the Committee has highlighted the right to freely return to their country of origin under conditions of safety and the need to ensure laws concerning expulsion and deportation do not discriminate among non-citizens, but failed to mention the right to leave any country.[108] In 2024, the Committee published the findings of the ad hoc Conciliation Commission established under ICERD

cf *Essono Mika Miha v Equatorial Guinea*, Communication No 414/1990 (10 August 1994) UN Doc CCPR/C/51/D/414/1990, para 6.6.

[106] *Orazova v Turkmenistan*, Communication No 1883/2009 (20 March 2012) UN Doc CCPR/C/104/D/1883/2009, para 7.4; *Geldy Kyarizov v Turkmenistan*, Communication No 3097/2018 (15 July 2016) UN Doc CCPR/C/141/D/3097/2018, para 3.4.

[107] See CERD, 'Concluding Observations on the Combined Twenty-second and Twenty-third Periodic Reports of Qatar' (23 May 2024) UN Doc CERD/C/QAT/CO/22-23, paras 18–19.

[108] CERD, 'General Recommendation XXII on Article 5 of the Convention on Refugees and Displaced Persons' (1996) UN Doc A/51/18, para 2; CERD, 'General Recommendation 30, Discrimination against Non-citizens' (2004) UN Doc CERD/C/64/Misc.11/rev.3, part 6.

to decide on the inter-State complaint initiated by Palestine against Israel.[109] While it is not per se a decision of the Committee, it warrants inclusion because the Commission, comprised solely of CERD members, explicitly made a finding on the right to leave. It highlighted that no investigations or fact-finding activities under Article 5(d)(ii) on this issue had been carried out by UN agencies and bodies and found that the blockade of Gaza has direct negative consequences on the rights of Palestinians to leave and return to their own country, including the ability to leave the area for medical treatment.[110]

iii. Committee on the Rights of the Child

The Committee on the Rights of the Child has underscored the obligation of States to facilitate family reunification by respecting freedom of movement and the right to leave under Article 10(2) of the Convention on the Rights of the Child (UNCRC). It has reminded States that applications by a child or their parents to enter or leave a State for family reunification purposes must be dealt with 'in a positive, humane and expeditious manner' and that States of origin must respect the rights of the child and their parents to leave any country, including that country of origin.[111] In two crucial decisions against France and Finland, the Committee was called upon to consider the dire situation for foreign children living in camps in northeast Syria, whose parents were alleged to have collaborated with Da'esh, and who were deprived of their liberty as their home countries had refused to repatriate them.[112] The authors argued that both States violated numerous articles under the UNCRC by failing to assist the children, who were French and Finnish nationals, leave the camps where their life, health and development were at risk, and repatriate them to France and Finland. Both States were urged to take urgent measures to repatriate the children or provide other consular responses, given their capability and power to protect the children's rights.[113] Although the authors did not invoke Article 10(2) on the right to leave (or return), the Committee's decisions underscore the potential obligation on States to take positive, protective measures to facilitate the exercise of the right to leave by children within their jurisdiction.

[109] See CERD, 'Report of the Ad Hoc Conciliation Commission on the inter-State communication submitted by the State of Palestine against Israel under Article 11 of the International Convention on the Elimination of All Forms of Racial Discrimination' (21 August 2024) UN Doc CERD/C/113/3/Add.2.

[110] ibid paras 27, 44.

[111] CRC, 'General Comment No. 6 (2005): Treatment of Unaccompanied and Separated Children Outside Their Country of Origin' (1 September 2005) UN Doc RC/GC/2005/6, para 83.

[112] *PN, KK and OM v Finland*, Communication No 100/2019 (12 September 2022) UN Doc CRC/C/91/D/100/2019; *FB and DA v France*, Communications No 77/2019, 79/2019 and 109/2019 (8 February 2022) UN Docs CRC/C/89/D/77/2019, CRC/C/89/D/79/2019 and CRC/C/89/D/109/2019.

[113] *PN* (n 112) paras 11.3, 13; *FB and DA* (n 112) paras 6.4, 6.6, 6.9, 8.

iv. Committee on Migrant Workers

The Committee on Migrant Workers is charged with protecting the rights of migrant workers through its oversight of the International Convention on the Rights of Migrant Workers (ICRMW). The Committee has not engaged with the right to leave in Article 8(1) of the ICRMW in depth, which is understandable in part because the mechanisms for individual and inter-State complaints are not yet in force. Nonetheless, in its General Comments and Concluding Observations on States, the Committee has raised the right to leave of migrant workers, going further than most adjudicative bodies in bringing attention to harmful externalisation practices and setting out the duties owed to regular and irregular migrant workers. Notably, only 60 States have ratified the Convention, all from the Global South and *none* from the Global North, where vast numbers of migrant workers reside.

In General Comment No 1, the Committee addressed the widespread practice of employers withholding passports, which restricts the movement of migrant workers both out of the house and the country.[114] It recommended that States should ensure that migrant workers retain possession of travel and identity documents.[115] States should also repeal sex-specific bans and discriminatory restrictions requiring women to obtain permission from their spouse or male guardian to obtain a passport or to travel.[116] It has also focused on the increasing criminalisation of migration and detention of migrants, reiterating that irregular entry, stay or exit should never be considered criminal offences, highlighting that criminalisation is often the result of political strategies seeking to deter irregular migration in a manner that is overwhelmingly inconsistent with States' obligations under the Convention.[117] It stresses that 'Migration irregularity is not the result of a decision of the migrant, but of restrictive policies of the State that prevent the exercise of the right to freedom of movement'.[118] In its most recent General Comment, the Committee affirmed the right of migrant workers and their families to leave their country of origin for destination and host countries, warning that greater vulnerability in their home makes them less able to exercise their right to leave safely and regularly, driving irregular, dangerous journeys.[119]

In concluding observations, the Committee has recommended to States such as Indonesia and Algeria that they decriminalise irregular exit and guarantee the right of both regular and undocumented migrant workers to leave

[114] CMW, 'General Comment No. 1 on Migrant Domestic Workers' (23 February 2011) UN Doc CMW/C/GC/1, para 12.

[115] ibid paras 13(d), 39. See ICRMW, art 21.

[116] ibid para 61.

[117] ibid.

[118] ibid para 36.

[119] CMW, 'General Comment No. 6 (2024) on the Convergent Protection of the Rights of Migrant Workers and Members of Their Families Through the Convention and the Global Compact for Safe, Orderly and Regular Migration' (2 January 2025) UN Doc CMW/C/GC/6, paras 41–433.

any country.[120] It has recommended that Honduras refrain from using military forces to prevent migrant workers and their families from leaving, as had been reported.[121] It has also drawn attention to exit bans and migrants being prevented from leaving until the execution of administrative penalties or because they cannot pay fines for irregular entry or stay, which may not comply with the permissible limitations under the right to leave.[122] Significantly, the Committee has urged Libya to end the pullback of migrants at sea, which it pronounced as a violation of the right of migrant workers and their families to leave the country.[123] It is notable that the Committee made this recommendation to Libya, one of the EU's vital migration control partners. It cannot make recommendations directly to responsible European countries because they are yet to support the Convention. Once the complaints mechanisms are in force, this Committee will have a crucial role in promoting respect for the right to leave and ensuring that externalising and partner States implement human rights-based migration policies.

v. Committee on the Rights of Persons with Disabilities

The Committee on the Rights of Persons with Disabilities has provided valuable guidance to States regarding their obligations under the right to leave in several concluding observations, urging them to abolish restrictions preventing people with disabilities from leaving the country (Article 18(1)(c) of the Convention on the Rights of Persons with Disabilities (CRPD)). For instance, the Committee raised its concerns about El Salvador's recent migration and passport laws that enforce legal impediments on leaving the country for people with hearing impairments and intellectual or psychosocial disabilities.[124] It urged El Salvador to review and reform its legislation to eliminate discriminatory restrictions and ensure that all people with disabilities who wish to leave or enter the country have access to procedures on an equal basis with others. It has also recommended that States take all necessary measures, in law and practice, to ensure that women with disabilities can exercise their right to liberty of movement without needing permission from a guardian, including for travel

[120] CMW, 'Concluding Observations on the Initial Report of Indonesia' (19 October 2017) UN Doc CMW/C/IDN/CO/1, para 31; CMW, 'Concluding Observations on the Second Periodic Report of Algeria' (25 May 2018) UN Doc CMW/C/DZA/CO/2, paras 39(b), 40(b).

[121] CMW, 'Concluding Observations on the Initial Report of Honduras' (13 October 2016) UN Doc CMW/C/HND/CO/1, paras 58–59.

[122] CMW, 'Concluding Observations on the 3rd Periodic Report of Azerbaijan' (2 November 2021) UN Doc CMW/C/AZE/CO/3, paras 31–32; CMW, 'Concluding Observations on the Combined Initial to Third Periodic Reports of Cabo Verde' (2 June 2022) UN Doc CMW/C/CPV/CO/1-3, paras 33–34.

[123] CMW, 'Concluding Observations on the Initial Report of Libya' (8 May 2019) UN Doc CMW/C/LBY/CO/1, paras 32–33.

[124] CRPD, 'Concluding Observations on the Combined Second and Third Periodic Reports of El Salvador' (1 October 2019) UN Doc CRPD/C/SAU/CO/1, paras 36–37.

abroad.[125] Similarly, it has urged States to abolish discriminatory requirements that prevent people with disabilities from travelling outside their territory, specifically requiring people with physical disabilities to provide medical reports as a pre-condition for air travel and people with intellectual or psychosocial disabilities to have approval from their guardians to travel abroad.[126]

Notably, the Committee has also made several significant statements on how States should uphold the right to leave of migrants with disabilities. It has urged Bangladesh to take effective measures to ensure the freedom of movement of persons with disabilities, particularly Rohingya refugees with disabilities and enable them to seek medical rehabilitation outside camps or abroad.[127] Against the backdrop of a migrant 'crisis' and the precarious situation for people with disabilities at its border, it recommended that Slovakia ensure people with disabilities are permitted free movement across its borders on an equal basis with others.[128] In response to reports of violence by border officials against asylum seekers, including those with disabilities, it urged Belarus to eliminate all forms of border violence and safeguard their freedom of movement.[129] It has also highlighted the limited protections in the EU for migrants with disabilities against denial of access to territory and pushbacks.[130] In guiding States in discharging their obligations, the Committee has highlighted the multiple and intersectional discrimination involved in violations of the right to leave, including against people with disabilities, women, ethnic minorities, and refugees.

vi. Committee on the Elimination of Discrimination against Women

The Committee on the Elimination of Discrimination against Women has also made several pronouncements relating to the right of women to leave any country, which is implicitly protected under Article 15(4) on freedom of movement of the Convention on the Elimination of All Forms of Discrimination against Women (CEDAW). The Committee has drawn attention to complete bans and restrictions on women travelling abroad or migrating, especially in Middle Eastern and North African countries, and requirements that women

[125] CRPD, 'Concluding Observations on the Initial Report of Saudi Arabia' (13 May 2019) UN Doc CRPD/C/SAU/CO/1, paras 33–34.

[126] CRPD, 'Concluding Observations on the Initial Report of Turkey' (1 October 2019) UN Doc CRPD/C/TUR/CO/1, paras 40–41; CRPD, 'Concluding Observations on the Initial Report of the Sudan' (10 April 2018) UN Doc CRPD/C/SDN/CO/1, paras 37–38.

[127] CRPD, 'Concluding Observations on the Initial Report of Bangladesh' (22 May 2017) UN Doc CRPD/C/BGD/CO/1, paras 37–38.

[128] CRPD, 'Concluding Observations on the Initial Report of Slovakia' (17 May 2016) UN Doc CRPD/C/SVK/CO/1, paras 53–54.

[129] CRPD, 'Concluding Observations on the Initial Report of Belarus' (26 September 2024) UN Doc CRPD/C/BLR/CO/1, paras 35–36.

[130] CRPD, Concluding Observations on the Combined Second and Third Periodic Reports of the European Union' (21 March 2025) UN Doc CRPD/C/EU/CO/2-3, paras 46–47.

must have written permission from male relatives to obtain a passport or to travel.[131] The Committee has further expressed concern regarding restraints on a woman's right to choose her domicile, which can prevent her from leaving a country freely and in her own right, and rules preventing women from travelling abroad, including with their children, without authorisation from the husband, father or guardian.[132] The Committee has repeatedly called for the repeal of such sex-specific bans and discriminatory restrictions. The Committee has also drawn attention to how women and girls are frequently impeded from leaving regions that are at high risk of disaster or after extreme climate events due to gender-based stereotypes, household responsibilities, discriminatory laws, lack of resources, and limited access to social capital, as well as subject to discriminatory migration and asylum policies that limit movement during flight from crises and conflict zones.[133]

C. European Court of Human Rights

The European Court of Human Rights has considered numerous cases concerning the right to leave any country enshrined in Article 2(2) Protocol 4 of the ECHR. Protocol 4 has been ratified by all Council of Europe Members except Greece, Switzerland, Turkey and the UK. The Court's jurisprudence overwhelmingly involves impediments imposed by former Soviet bloc States on their citizens' right to leave, such as travel bans and the seizure and denial of passports. Though many restrictions were dismantled following the end of the Cold War, the first cases were only decided in the 2000s. Nonetheless, the Court continues to hear cases concerning alleged violations of the right to leave by former Soviet States.[134]

The issues before the Court often concern whether the restriction was 'in accordance with law' and necessary. The 2012 case of *Stamose v Bulgaria* is

[131] CEDAW, 'General Recommendation No. 26 on Women Migrant Workers' (5 December 2008) UN Doc CEDAW/C/2009/WP.1/R, paras 10, 24 (a); CEDAW, 'Concluding Observations on the Combined Second and Third Periodic Reports of Oman' (22 November 2017) UN Doc CEDAW/C/OMN/CO/2-3, para 51.

[132] CEDAW, 'General Recommendation 21 (Thirteenth Session): Equality in Marriage and Family Relations' (12 April 1994) UN Doc A/49/38, para 9; CEDAW, 'Concluding Observations on the Initial Report of Qatar' (10 March 2014) UN Doc CEDAW/C/QAT/CO/1, para 41; CEDAW, 'Concluding Observations on the Second Periodic Report of the Syrian Arab Republic' (4 July 2014) UN Doc CEDAW/C/SYR/CO/2, paras 45–46.

[133] CEDAW, 'General Recommendation No. 37 (2018) on the Gender-related Dimensions of Disaster Risk Reduction in the Context of Climate Change' (13 March 2018) UN Doc CEDAW/C/GC/37, para 76; CEDAW, 'General Recommendation No. 38' (2020) on Trafficking in Women and Girls in the Context of Global Migration' (20 November 2020) UN Doc CEDAW/C/GC/38, para 24.

[134] eg, *Stetsov v Ukraine*, App no 5170/15 (ECtHR, 11 May 2021); *Case of Democracy and Human Rights Resource Centre and Mustafayev v Azerbaijan*, Apps nos 74288/14 and 64568/16 (ECtHR, 28 February 2022).

the leading decision of the Court on the right to leave.[135] Notably, it concerned externalised migration control, where, for the first time, the Court considered a travel ban designed to prevent breaches of a foreign State's immigration laws. The applicant, a Bulgarian national, was deported to Bulgaria for breaching the conditions of his student visa while in the US. The Bulgarian authorities imposed a two-year travel ban on the applicant and ordered the surrender of his passport. The Bulgarian Government submitted that the ban had been prompted by a letter from the US embassy. The applicant argued that the ban on him leaving Bulgaria for two years breached his right to leave and to family life under Article 8 of the Convention as he could not travel to the US to see his mother and brother, who lived there. He argued that the travel ban was 'unjustified and disproportionate'. Bulgaria argued that the domestic law providing the basis for travel bans was 'designed to discourage and prevent breaches of the immigration laws of other states' and reduce the likelihood of States refusing entry to or toughening visa requirements for Bulgarians.[136]

The Court found that the applicant's right to leave had been breached. It held that even if it were prepared to accept that the interference with leaving pursued the legitimate aims of maintenance of *ordre public* or the protection of the rights of others, the ban failed the 'necessary in a democratic society' test.[137] A blanket and indiscriminate measure preventing 'the applicant from travelling to any and every foreign country on account of his having committed a breach of the immigration laws of one particular country' could not be considered proportionate.[138] It was 'quite draconian' for Bulgaria to impose such a ban despite not being directly affected by the applicant's conduct.[139] The Court noted that while it 'may in certain compelling situations' accept that restrictions to prevent breaches of foreign immigration laws are justified, measures will not be characterised as necessary when they are automatic and disregard individual circumstances.[140]

The Court had previously found a violation of the right where the measure in question was of such a general nature that it would prevent nearly entire groups from leaving. In *Streletz, Kessler and Krenz v Germany*, which concerned the GDR's border-policing regime at the Berlin Wall to prevent East Germans escaping to West Germany, the Court declared that 'a general measure preventing almost the entire population of a State from leaving' cannot be deemed necessary to protect security or other aims.[141]

The *Stamose* decision is an important ruling that raises questions about whether States of origin and transit preventing irregular migration to and on

[135] *Stamose v Bulgaria*, App no 29713/05 (ECtHR, 27 November 2012).
[136] ibid paras 24, 32.
[137] ibid para 32.
[138] ibid paras 33–34.
[139] ibid para 34.
[140] ibid para 36.
[141] *Streletz, Kessler and Krenz v Germany* (2001) 33 EHRR 31, paras 98–101.

behalf of destination States is a compelling enough situation to justify interference with the right to leave. In another externalisation case from 2023, the Court ruled that North Macedonia had unlawfully discriminated against and violated the right to leave of Roma individuals who were subjected to racial profiling at the border and not allowed to leave the country.[142] Two of the individuals were stopped by border officials at Skopje Airport and denied travel to Germany, while the others were refused permission to cross via van into Serbia, headed for a traditional wedding ceremony in Kosovo. Despite having valid passports and visa-free access, the applicants argued that they were refused permission to leave because of their Roma ethnicity and that they would likely seek asylum in the EU. Border officials recorded that they had posed a threat to public policy and the relations of North Macedonia with an EU Member State and did not have sufficient financial means and letters of sponsorship to cover their stay abroad. The government had previously sent an internal alert to border affairs bodies stating that an increasing number of nationals were applying for asylum in the EU and Schengen Member States, thus abusing the visa-free regime.[143] North Macedonia had previously entered into an agreement with EU Member States, undertaking to cooperate in the fields of visas, border control, asylum and migration. The Court restated the compelling situations test from *Stamose* but proceeded to find that imposing such measures without any regard to the individual circumstances of the applicants cannot be characterised as necessary in a democratic society.[144]

Many cases before the Court concern travel bans or restrictions on individuals awaiting criminal trial whose presence was required for ongoing enforcement proceedings or for failing to pay outstanding debts to obtain a new passport. It bears mentioning that the Court has relied upon the work of the Human Rights Committee, notably General Comment No 27, given that Article 12 of the ICCPR served as the basis for Article 2 of Protocol No 4 of the ECHR.[145] In considering the lawfulness of such travel bans and restrictions, the Court has undertaken a balancing act, holding that any interference with leaving must strike a fair balance between the public interest and the individual's right.[146] Restrictions on leaving will only be justified if there are clear indications of a genuine public interest capable of outweighing the individual's

[142] *Memedova v North Macedonia*, Apps nos 42429/16 and 2 others (ECtHR, 24 October 2023).
[143] ibid paras 8, 83, 84, 90.
[144] ibid para 73.
[145] *Bartik v Russia*, App no 55565/00 (ECtHR, 23 February 2000) paras 36, 46, 49; *Riener v Bulgaria*, App no 46343/99 (ECtHR, 23 May 2006) paras 81–84.
[146] *Riener* (n 145) para 109; *Földes and Földesné Hajlik v Hungary*, App no 41463/02 (ECtHR, 26 March 2007) para 32; *Bessenyei v Hungary*, App no 37509/06 (ECtHR, 21 October 2008) para 21; *Makedonski v Bulgaria* App no 36036/04 (ECtHR, 20 January 2011) para 42; *Prescher v Bulgaria*, App no 6767/04 (ECtHR, 7 June 2011) para 44; *Popoviciu v Romania*, App no 52942/09 (ECtHR, 1 March 2016) para 83. Being prevented from leaving one's place of residence may also prevent travel abroad: *Hajibeyli v Azerbaijan*, App no 16528/05 (ECtHR, 10 July 2008) paras 16, 63.

right to freedom of movement.[147] A fair balance will not be struck where the restriction is an automatic measure without regard to individual circumstances or is indefinite.[148] In a case concerning a prohibition on leaving for a French national awaiting trial in Poland, the Court stated that the situation 'cannot be compared to a restriction on an applicant's freedom of movement imposed on him or her in his or her own country', giving considerable weight to family, friends and business ties and the availability of medical care back in France.[149] This suggests that the proportionality test will be stricter when non-nationals are prevented from leaving, especially to return home.

While measures may initially be justified, authorities must ensure they remain proportionate from the outset and for their duration by undertaking periodic reassessments of their justification, preferably through the courts.[150] The absence of review and other procedural safeguards can also raise issues with the measure's legality and whether it is 'in accordance with law'. For instance, the refusal to issue a passport over several years because of a failure to repay a debt was unlawful because the duration of the ban on obtaining a passport had not been specified, its proportionality had not been reviewed at any stage, and there was an absence of procedural safeguards to prevent arbitrariness on the part of the authorities.[151] A breach of the right to leave can be established without examining the necessity of a measure if it has no legal basis or the law lacks precision and foreseeability (discussed below in section V).[152]

Akin to the Human Rights Committee, the Strasbourg Court (also known as the ECtHR) has stressed the individual's right to elect their destination. In a recent case, the Court reiterated that Article 2(2) Protocol 4

> implies a right to leave for *any* country of the person's choice to which he may be admitted. Any measure by means of which an individual is denied the use of a

[147] *Makedonski* (n 146) para 36; *Miazdzyk v Poland*, App no 23592/07 (ECtHR, 24 January 2012) para 35. See also *Nalbant v Turkey*, App no 5991416 (ECtHR, 3 May 2022) para 65.

[148] *Földes* (n 146) paras 35–36; *Riener* (n 145) paras 127–30; *Battista v Italy*, App no 43978/09 (ECtHR, 2 December 2014) para 47; *Stamose* (n 135) paras 33–36. The CJEU has similarly held that a prohibition on leaving violates EU law if adopted automatically without considering the individual's conduct or imposed for an unlimited period: *Aladzhov*, Case C-434/10, EU:C:2011:750, para 43; *Hristo Byanko*, Case C-249/11, EU:C:2012:608, paras 29–30.

[149] *Miazdzyk* (n 147) para 39. See also *Riener* (n 145) para 126; *Prescher* (n 146) para 50 on the Court's consideration of impacts on family life.

[150] *Bessenyei* (n 146) para 23; *AE v Poland*, App no 14480/04 (ECtHR, 30 June 2009) para 49; *Ignatov v Ukraine*, App no 40583/15 (ECtHR, 15 December 2016), paras 36–37; *Gochev v Bulgaria*, App no 34383/03 (ECtHR, 26 February 2010) paras 49–50; *Makedonski* (n 146) para 45; *Pfeifer v Austria*, App no 12556/03 (ECtHR, 15 November 2007) paras 56–57; *Ivanov v Russia*, App no 57884/19 and 21 others (ECtHR, 25 May 2023) para 37; *Sarkizov v Bulgaria*, Apps no 37981/06, 38022/06, 39122/06 and 44278/06 (ECtHR, 17 April 2012) para 69; *Rotaru v Moldova*, App no 26764/12 (ECtHR, 8 December 2020).

[151] *Rotaru* (n 150) paras 27–35.

[152] *Sissanis v Romania*, App no 23468/02 (ECtHR, 25 January 2007) paras 66–79; *Dzhaksybergenov v Ukraine*, App no 12343/10 (ECtHR, 10 February 2011) paras 59–62; *Zabelin and Zabelina v Russia*, App no 55382/07 (ECtHR, 4 October 2016) paras 16–21.

> document which, had he so wished, would have permitted him to leave the country, amounts to an interference.[153]

However, this framing has left some confusion as the Court has not explicitly clarified the meaning of 'to which he may be admitted' and its bearing on the right to leave. Does it mean exercise of the right is always conditional upon the country of choice's willingness to admit the person? Or does it affirm the self-standing and independent nature of the right to leave? As chapter three discusses extensively, the right to leave is well-understood in terms of the latter, being exercisable irrespective of whether entry will be granted elsewhere.[154] Notably, the text of Article 2(2) does not contain any requirement that persons must first prove they will be admitted elsewhere to be able to leave. The Court's use of 'may', rather than 'will', expresses possibility rather than certainty while emphasising the individual's freedom to choose their destination.[155] Logically, leaving and admission must be distinct so individuals can set sail for the high seas as they have done for centuries.[156] Individuals, particularly asylum seekers, may not have a specific country in mind when they attempt to leave or move. As Weinzierl and Lisson aptly argue, when a migrant leaves by sea or is denied a passport, the destination State is not easily identifiable and the theoretical impossibility of securing entry on arrival to any such destination cannot justifiably play a role in any decision to forestall departure.[157] The Court itself has not taken this theoretical impossibility into account when finding that passport refusals and travel bans violate the right to leave.[158] For instance, in a recent case, a Syrian man granted refugee status in Serbia was refused a travel document for seven years, which 'curtailed his right to leave Serbia freely to such an extent as to impair its very essence and deprive it of its effectiveness'.[159] The Court reiterated the importance of being able to obtain a travel document to ensure the right to leave was practical and effective.[160] Whether the right to leave can be made dependent on securing admission elsewhere, such as obtaining

[153] *Berkovich v Russia*, Apps nos 5871/07 and 9 others (ECtHR, 27 June 2018) para 78 (emphasis added). See also *Baumann v France*, App no 33592/06 (ECtHR, 22 August 2001) para 61.

[154] See eg, Harvey and Barnidge (n 1) 20; M den Heijer, *Europe and Extraterritorial Asylum* (Oxford, Hart Publishing, 2012) 156–59; Guild and Stoyanova (n 1) 381–82, 385; Chetail, *International Migration Law* (n 1) 92; GS Goodwin-Gill and J McAdam, *The Refugee in International Law,* 4th edn (Oxford, OUP, 2021) 429–30; E McDonnell, 'Challenging Externalisation Through the Lens of the Human Right to Leave' (2024) 71 *Netherlands International Law Review* 119.

[155] Stoyanova (n 1) 414, including fn 60. cf V Moreno-Lax, *Accessing Asylum in Europe: Extraterritorial Border Controls and Refugee Rights Under EU Law* (Oxford, OUP, 2017) 358–359; V Moreno-Lax, 'Intersectionality, Forced Migration, and the Jus-Generation of the Right to Flee: Theorising A Composite Entitlement to Leave to Escape Irreversible Harm' in B Çalı, L Bianku, I Motoc (eds), *Migration and the European Convention on Human Rights* (Oxford, OUP, 2021) 43–83, 52 and 76–77.

[156] Guild (n 1) 9; Guild and Stoyanova (n 1) 381–82.

[157] R Weinzierl and U Lisson, *Border Management and Human Rights: A Study of EU Law and the Law of the Sea* (Berlin, German Institute for Human Rights, 2007) 68.

[158] *Baumann* (n 153); *Stamose* (n 135); *Berkovich* (n 153).

[159] *SE v Serbia*, App no 61365/16 (ECtHR, 11 July 2023) para 88.

[160] ibid para 47. See also *LB v Lithuania*, App no 38121/20 (ECtHR, 14 June 2022) paras 59–60.

a visa before departure, is a fundamental issue this work addresses in depth in chapters three and five.

The jurisprudence of the Court establishes several general principles that guide its assessment of violations of the right to leave. The Court has affirmed, in line with the text of the right, that the right protects nationals and non-nationals, including refugees.[161] Restrictions imposed against non-nationals can also warrant a stricter application of the proportionality test, given the more severe implications for them in being unable to leave or return home, such as the deprivation of family contact. Accordingly, in certain situations, greater weight should be afforded to the non-national's interests than the State's in assessing whether a fair balance has been struck. This is particularly relevant for asylum seekers stuck in transit, unable to return to their own country due to the risk of serious harm, and subject to migration control measures preventing them from leaving for another State. Second, interferences with the right often involve the seizure and retention of passports, the refusal to issue travel documents, and travel bans. Third, the measure must have a legal basis, which must be precise, foreseeable and accompanied by adequate procedural safeguards to protect against abuse. Fourth, regarding the necessity and proportionality of a measure, restrictions will be disproportionate when automatic, indefinite and disregard individual circumstances. Blanket and indiscriminate measures will always violate the right to leave. Only a clear indication that the public interest outweighs the individual's right to leave will satisfy the Court. The authorities must conduct periodic reviews of measures to ensure they remain proportionate throughout, as any restriction can only be justified so long as it serves its aim. It remains unclear what compelling situations may justify restricting the right to leave to prevent breaches of another country's immigration laws; it did not arise when Roma individuals were denied leaving by a non-EU State to ensure compliance with EU laws.

D. Inter-American System

The Inter-American Commission on Human Rights and Inter-American Court of Human Rights have heard several petitions concerning the right to leave any country enshrined in Article VIII of the ADHR and Article 22(2) of the ACHR. The decisions of the Commission regarding the right of asylum seekers to exercise their right to leave go noticeably further than other human rights courts and bodies. As Dembour has argued in her seminal text, the Inter-American system treats migrants first and foremost as humans and only secondly as foreigners (if they are).[162]

[161] It also protects people considered stateless: *Mogoş v Romania*, App no 20420/02 (ECtHR, 13 October 2005).

[162] MB Dembour, *When Humans Become Migrants: Study of the European Court of Human Rights with an Inter-American Counterpoint* (Oxford, OUP, 2015).

i. Inter-American Commission on Human Rights

On 13 July 1994, 72 men, women and children attempted to flee the Castro dictatorship in Cuba to the US aboard an old tugboat, the *13 de Marzo*. The boat was intercepted and attacked by Cuban State boats, causing the boat to sink seven miles off Havana. Forty-one people died, including 10 children. In *Victims of the Tugboat '13 de Marzo' v Cuba*, the Commission found that Cuba had violated the right of movement, alongside the rights to life and a fair trial, because the acts that caused the sinking prevented the 72 people on board from freely leaving Cuba.[163] The Commission considered that the method used by the Cuban nationals to leave was irrelevant 'as the laws in force, the ruling political system and the critical situation of human rights in that country forced them to take desperate measures to achieve their main objective: to flee Cuba'.[164] It restated the doctrine of the Commission that 'the right of every person to live in his own homeland, to leave it and to return to it when he so desires is a basic right recognized by all international instruments for the protection of human rights'.[165] The Commission's decision is laudable, promulgating the right of individuals to leave by any means to seek refuge in recognition that migrants are often forced to take desperate journeys. It also supports the right to leave as independent of any right of entry.

A year later, the Commission heard a major case challenging the US' interdiction of Haitians at sea.[166] In the 1990s, the US authorities forcibly returned thousands of asylum seekers to Haiti and detained Haitians in Guantánamo Bay following the interdiction of their vessels on the high seas by the US coastguard. The petitioners argued that the interdiction program violated their right to leave in Article 22(2) of the ACHR.[167] However, the Commission did not make a finding on the right to leave. As the US had not ratified the Convention, the Commission relied upon the ADHR, and the petitioners had not invoked Article VIII enshrining the right to leave. It instead found that the US violated the right of the Haitians to seek and receive asylum under the ADHR and the obligation of *non-refoulement* under Article 33 of the Refugee Convention (the opposite conclusion to the widely critiqued decision of the US Supreme Court in *Sale*).[168]

The Commission has continued to affirm the rights of nationals and migrants to leave, seek, and be granted asylum. While it has recognised the State's sovereign right to determine its immigration policy, it has made clear

[163] *Victims of the Tugboat '13 de Marzo' v Cuba*, Case 11.436 Report No. 47/96 (16 October 1996) OEA/Ser.L/V/II.95 Doc 7 Rev at 127.

[164] ibid para 91.

[165] ibid para 90.

[166] *The Haitian Centre for Human Rights v US*, IACHR, Case 10.675, Report No 51/96 (13 March 1997) OEA/Ser.L/V/II.95 Doc. 7 Rev at 550.

[167] See IACHR, *Decision of the Commission as to the Admissibility*, Case 10.675, Report No. 28/93 (13 October 1993) paras 9, 13.

[168] *Haitian Centre* (n 166) paras 151–63.

that such a 'policy cannot affect the right of nationals to leave and enter the country' nor result in cruel, inhuman or degrading treatment or discrimination for reasons of race, colour, religion or sex.[169] Amidst the recent forced migration of people from Central American countries, 'migrant caravans' headed to Mexico and the US have been subjected to numerous restrictions and the use of force when attempting to leave their country of origin and enter another. The Commission urged States to guarantee the right of migrants and refugees to leave their territories in accordance with Article 22(2) of the ACHR and refrain from criminalising migration, recognising that being unable to leave may also deny one's right to seek and receive asylum.[170]

Accordingly, the right to leave may be violated when force or intimidation is involved. This was the case when a Guatemalan national, who had been targeted for his union and social activities, was intercepted on his way to Chicago for medical treatment and detained at the airport by Guatemalan customs agents asserting his travel documents were false.[171] Only through the insistence of his accompanying doctor was he allowed to board the plane. The Commission found that this constituted a clear attempt to prevent him from exercising his right to leave, and given the agents never initiated an investigation to bring charges for falsified documents, was an act of intimidation and a violation of his right to leave.[172] Though not explicitly stated, this meant there was no legitimate aim or rational connection between the means and the end. This bears significance for externalised migration controls, given the abuse migrants face when attempting to flee places like Libya and Tunisia and the failure to assess individual circumstances or any threat a particular person may pose.

In a case from the 1980s, a woman and her child were denied permission to leave Cuba to reunite with her husband, who had entered the Peruvian embassy and left for the US, because she had a university degree and did not fall within the categories of persons allowed to emigrate.[173] The Commission found this to violate her rights to protection of the family, work and asylum under the ADHR. Although the right to leave was not explicitly considered, the decision underscores its fundamental importance in that restrictions on departure often give rise to other violations. A similar finding was reached in another case

[169] *Haitian and Haitian-Origin Dominican Persons in the Dominican Republic* (Provisional Measures Requested by the IACHR) IACtHR, Order of 18 August 2000, para 11(a).

[170] IACHR, 'IACHR Urges Honduras and Guatemala to Guarantee the Rights of People in the Migrant and Refugee Caravan', Press Release 37/19 (19 February 2019) www.oas.org/en/iachr/media_center/PReleases/2019/037.asp; IACHR, 'IACHR Urges El Salvador, Guatemala, Honduras, and Mexico to Guarantee the Rights of Migrants and Refugees Traveling Through the Region', Press Release 027/20 (7 February 2020) www.oas.org/en/iachr/media_center/PReleases/2020/027.asp.

[171] *Gómez López v Guatemala*, IACHR, Case 11.303, Report No 29/96 (16 October 1996) OEA/Ser.L/V/II.95 Doc 7 Rev at 425.

[172] ibid paras 58, 98.

[173] *Calvar Rivero v Cuba*, IACHR, Case 7602, Report No 6/82 (8 March 1982) OEA/Ser.L/V/II.57 Doc 6 Rev 1.

concerning Cuba's arbitrary arrest and refusal to allow an individual to leave the country.[174] The omission of the right to leave in these cases remains unclear. Perhaps it was because the matters predominantly concerned family reunification, or due to the lack of attention afforded to the right until the 1990s.

The Commission has also indirectly touched on the right to leave in the context of Indigenous Peoples. In 2010, the Commission considered a case against Ecuador concerning the grant of a permit to a private oil company to carry out oil exploration and exploitation activities in the territory of the Kichwa Indigenous People of Sarayaku in the 1990s, without consulting them and without their consent.[175] The Commission found that the Sarayaku People's inability to move freely within and leave their territory, all with the acquiescence and involvement of State agents, violated the right to freedom of movement under Article 22.[176] Ecuador was fully aware of the situation but did not offer or implement necessary or sufficient measures of protection to remedy it. It also prevented the movement and travel of the Sarayaku People by setting up military outposts.[177] While the Commission did not engage with the right to leave any country *per se*, given the case concerned territory within Ecuador, it was nonetheless the ancestral territory of the Sarayaku People, which its members could not leave. They may have been prevented from leaving Ecuador altogether.[178]

In 2019, the Commission adopted the Inter-American Principles on the Human Rights of All Migrants, Refugees, Stateless Persons and Victims of Human Trafficking.[179] Principle 52 covers the right to leave and enshrines, in nearly identical terms to the Human Rights Committee's General Comment No 27, that the right shall not be conditional upon any specific purpose or period that the individual chooses to stay out of the country, and the right to determine the State of the migrant's destination is part of the guarantee. Throughout its 2024 annual report, the Commission drew attention to restrictions on individuals leaving the country by Cuba, Nicaragua, Paraguay and Venezuela.[180]

[174] See *Alvarez Hernández v Cuba*, IACHR, Case 7898, Report No 11/82 (8 March 1982) OEA/Ser.L/V/II.57 Doc 6 Rev 1.

[175] *Application of the IACHR to the IACtHR against Ecuador, Kichwa Indigenous Peoples of Sarayaku and its members*, Case 12.465 (26 April 2010).

[176] ibid para 189.

[177] ibid para 186.

[178] Before the IACtHR, the victims' representatives argued that restrictions preventing Sarayaku members from travelling by river meant they had to fly to leave Sarayaku, a costly option only suitable for urgent matters, yet the Court found insufficient evidence to support this: *Case of the Kichwa Indigenous People of Sarayaku*, IACtHR, Series C No 245 (27 June 2012) fn 356.

[179] IACHR, 'Inter-American Principles on the Human Rights of All Migrants, Refugees, Stateless Persons and Victims of Human Trafficking' (7 December 2019) Resolution 04/19, www.oas.org/en/iachr/decisions/pdf/Resolution-4-19-en.pdf.

[180] *Annual Report of the IACHR 2024* (26 March 2025) OEA/Ser.L/V/II. Doc 39 Rev 2.

ii. Inter-American Court of Human Rights

The Inter-American Court of Human Rights has considered violations of the right to leave under the ACHR several times. It has recognised that freedom of movement is an essential condition to the free development of the individual.[181] Nearly all of them concern former politicians or political figures. In one case, a presidential candidate in Paraguay was charged, sentenced and prohibited from leaving the country except in exceptional circumstances because of statements he had made during electoral debates against a fellow candidate concerning business dealings.[182] For over eight years, the petitioner was prohibited from leaving as a precautionary measure to ensure he did not evade criminal proceedings should the sentence be executed.[183] The Court concluded Paraguay had violated his right to leave under Articles 22(2). The Court endorsed General Comment No 27 of the Human Rights Committee and stated that the right to leave may be restricted under Articles 22(3) and 30, provided the restrictions meet the requirements of legality, necessity and proportionality to the extent necessary in a democratic society.[184] The Court found that Paraguay had failed to observe the requirements of legality, necessity and proportionality. First, its criminal code did not authorise such a prohibition as a precautionary measure.[185] The Court emphasised the importance of the exercise of the principle of legality in establishing a restriction on the right, given the significant impact this restriction has on the exercise of personal freedom and outlined the need for the law to possess certain qualities:

> The State should define precisely and clearly by law, the exceptional circumstances under which a measure such as the restriction to leave the country is admissible … its regulation should lack any ambiguity so that it does not create doubts in those charged with applying the restriction, or the opportunity for them to act arbitrarily and discretionally, interpreting the restriction broadly.[186]

It further held that, with time, the restriction had become unnecessary because the petitioner had been granted permission to leave during the eight years and always returned. It was also disproportionate, as less restrictive measures were available to ensure the petitioner did not abscond.[187] Notably, the Court recognised that the restriction on the petitioner leaving the country indirectly restricted his freedom of thought and expression, in violation of his right of expression.[188]

[181] *Carrión v Nicaragua*, IACtHR, Series C No 550 (25 November 2024) para 146.
[182] *Ricardo Canese v Paraguay*, IACtHR, Series C No 111 (31 August 2004).
[183] ibid paras 115, 119–20.
[184] ibid paras 115–17, 123.
[185] ibid paras 128.
[186] ibid paras 125.
[187] ibid paras 131, 133–34.
[188] ibid para 107.

In another case, a former Minister of Suriname was charged with forgery and prevented from leaving the country for a four-day personal trip while the criminal proceedings were underway.[189] While at the departure gate at the airport, military police informed him that they had been ordered to ensure he did not leave the country. The Court found a violation of his right to leave because the legal basis relied upon by Suriname did not clearly and precisely define the exceptional circumstances that would permit such a restriction on leaving.[190]

The Court has also recognised the interrelated nature of the right to personal liberty and freedom of movement in the ACHR.[191] In a case concerning a Bolivian Mayor who was subject to a precautionary measure preventing her from leaving without authorisation pending criminal proceedings, the Court reiterated that the State can only impose such restrictions if they are necessary to prevent criminal offences, to protect national security or public order, or one of the other aims in Article 22(3).[192] It found that Bolivia had violated the Mayor's right to leave because there was excessive delay in the proceedings, and the length of the measures without periodic review meant they were disproportionate to the purposes that they sought to achieve, which also had not been duly substantiated.[193] The Court provided that measures restricting leaving must be expressly established in domestic law, and the judicial authorities, before issuing such measures, must consider whether the purpose is compatible with the Convention and weigh, based on objective evidence, procedural risks. The authorities must also ensure the measure is strictly necessary and proportionate to achieving the desired objective and periodically reviewed to ensure the risk subsists.[194] The Court has applied these principles in the case of a Venezuelan journalist who was prohibited from leaving the country as a precautionary measure during criminal proceedings for defamation after publishing on matters of public interest in Venezuela.[195]

The jurisprudence of the Inter-American Commission and Court demonstrates significant alignment with the principles promulgated by the Human Rights Committee and European Court of Human Rights. It indicates that restrictions on the right to leave must comply with the legality requirement, be strictly necessary and proportionate to achieving the specified purpose(s) throughout, and be periodically reviewed. Both bodies have affirmed that the

[189] *Liakat Ali Alibux v Suriname*, IACtHR, Series C No 276 (30 January 2014) para 130.
[190] ibid paras 133–36.
[191] *Andrade Salmón v Bolivia*, IACtHR, Series C No 330 (1 December 2016) para 142.
[192] ibid para 140.
[193] ibid paras 138–41, 146, 148–49, 150.
[194] ibid paras 141, 146–49.
[195] *Álvarez Ramos v Venezuela*, IACtHR, Series C No 380 (30 August 2019) paras 161–79. See also *Tulio Alberto Álvarez v Venezuela*, IACHR, Case 12.663, Report No. 4/17 (26 January 2017) OEA/Ser.L/V/II.150 (26 January 2017) paras 114–20.

right guarantees the right to leave any country freely.[196] The Commission explicitly recognised the right's applicability to refugees and migrants and, crucially, its importance for people seeking asylum *by any means*. It is pertinent that attacking a migrant boat was found to interfere with and violate the right to leave. Many types of measures may therefore interfere with the right to travel, beyond travel bans and passport restrictions. Various findings and statements also suggest that restrictions on leaving should be consistent with other rights, including the right to seek asylum, prohibition on cruel, inhuman, or degrading treatment, and obligation of non-discrimination.

E. African System

The African Commission on Human and Peoples' Rights (ACHPR) has played an important role in interpreting and applying the right to leave under Article 12(2) of the African Charter. The African Court on Human and Peoples' Rights appears to have decided only one case concerning this right.

i. African Commission on Human and Peoples' Rights

In July 1994, the Gambian Government was overthrown in a military coup. The complainant, the ousted President of The Gambia, brought a case to the Commission arguing that the incumbent military government had violated multiple articles of the African Charter, including by banning political parties and ministers of the former civilian government from taking part in any political activity and restricting their freedom of movement, killing soldiers, and arresting and detaining people incommunicado. The Commission held that the restrictions imposed on former ministers and members of parliament preventing them from travelling out of the country, with a maximum sentence of three years for non-compliance, violated the right to leave under Article 12(2).[197] As this case shows and those discussed in this section, the Commission often finds violations of the right to leave without detailed reasoning.

Similarly, the Commission considered another case in 2001 concerning a series of human violations committed in Burkina Faso since the days of the revolutionary government.[198] In 1995, the Secretary General of a political party was prevented from leaving the country following a publication by that party on the situation in the country. The Commission stated there was no information before it to suggest the journey or the Secretary General threatened public

[196] See *Canese* (n 182) para 114; *Gómez López* (n 171) para 98.
[197] *Sir Dawda K Jawara v The Gambia* (2000) AHRLR 107 (ACHPR 2000) para 70.
[198] *Movement Burkinabé des Droits de l'Homme et des Peuples v Burkina Faso* (2001) AHRLR 51 (ACHPR 2001) paras 46–47.

security or morality, concluding there was a violation of Article 12(2).[199] As other adjudicative bodies have held, the burden is on the State to justify the restrictions it imposes on leaving, with the Commission having cautioned in an earlier case against a too easy resort to limitations clauses in the African Charter, and that it must not be used to give credence to violations of the express provisions of the Charter.[200]

The right to leave has gained prominence in relation to the denial of nationality. In one case, the complainant had been denied Botswana nationality by ancestry.[201] He was deported four times to South Africa, which the complainant alleged was because of his political activities that made him an 'undesirable immigrant' for Botswana. Despite being born in South Africa, he was never accepted as a citizen and following each deportation, he was rejected by South Africa and forced to live for years in the defunct 'homeland' of Bophuthatswana and then in a 'No Man's Land' border strip between Bophuthatswana and Botswana. The Commission found that the deportations greatly jeopardised the complainant's right to freedom of movement as a citizen of Botswana and violated the right to leave and return to his country.[202]

The right to leave and freedom of movement have also been essential grounds for groups discriminated against because of their ethnicity and religion in obtaining identity and travel documents, rendering them stateless and unable to enjoy many rights and freedoms. In 2015, the Commission decided a case concerning the Nubian community in Kenya, a group comprising descendants of Sudanese soldiers forcibly conscripted and brought to Kenya by the British colonial government to serve in the King's African Rifles regiments in the 1900s.[203] The Nubians were never granted British citizenship and for a long period following Kenyan independence were consistently treated by the Kenyan Government as aliens and denied Kenyan passports and identity cards. The Commission held that the discrimination suffered by the Nubians left many of them stateless, depriving them of their nationality and violating a range of human rights including Article 12(2).[204] That same year, the Commission found that Cote d'Ivoire violated the right to leave and return of 'Dioulas', a predominantly Muslim ethnic group.[205] Owing to the discriminatory denial of Ivorian nationality, most Dioulas could not obtain a passport and were prevented from leaving the country. Those who had emigrated elsewhere had their requests for renewal of their travel documents denied, preventing them from travelling,

[199] ibid para 47.
[200] See *Amnesty International v Zambia* (2000) AHRLR 325 (ACHPR 1999) para 50.
[201] *Modise v Botswana*, ACHPR Communication 97 of 1993 [2000] ACHPR 25 (6 November 2000).
[202] ibid paras 91, 93.
[203] *The Nubian Community in Kenya v The Republic of Kenya*, ACHPR Communication No 317/06 (28 February 2015) para 5.
[204] ibid paras 7, 104, 132, 167–68, 170.
[205] *Open Society Justice Initiative v Côte d'Ivoire*, ACHPR Communication No 318/06 (27 May 2016) paras 159–61.

including returning to Cote d'Ivoire to visit family, also violating the right to family protection.[206]

In 2019, the ACHPR adopted a General Comment on the right to freedom of movement and residence in Article 12(1) of the Charter.[207] Though not covering the right to leave, several statements are relevant to its interpretation and inform its functioning. The Comment noted that 'every individual' (also in Article 12(2)) encompasses everyone legally and irregularly in the State.[208] The Comment further outlines that limitations should never render rights illusory, must serve a legitimate aim, be proportionate and absolutely necessary in a free and democratic society, construed with due respect for other Charter rights, cannot be exercised indiscriminately or stigmatise a particular group, and the legal basis must be unambiguous and limit the room for discretion. Rights can also be restricted for Article 27(2) purposes: 'due regard to the rights of others, collective security, morality and common interest'.[209]

In 2023, the Commission adopted the African Guiding Principles on the Human Rights of Migrants, Refugees and Asylum Seekers, which explicitly cover the right to leave any country for migrants and non-nationals.[210] The Preamble noted with concern 'the human rights violations of migrants in and out of Africa'. It recognised 'the need for a human rights approach towards migrants and their families', urging African States to safeguard the human rights of migrants and incorporate and implement these minimum standards into domestic law and practice. The 38 Guiding Principles are based on African regional treaty law, case law, standards and resolutions of the Commission, international law, and the experience of other world regions. Principle 17 provides that 'Every migrant shall have the right to leave any country including their own' and that States shall issue travel documents to migrants so they can leave their territory, unless there are compelling reasons of national security or public order. Principle 4 on the right to life provides that 'lethal force may never be used for the purpose of arresting or detaining migrants, including in the event of flight from ports of entry, to prevent the exercise of the right to leave any country, including their own, to prevent irregular entry into a State's territory or for suspicion of violation of migration laws'. These landmark principles for migrants promote freedom of movement on the African continent and strengthen the protections afforded to people moving across international borders. This should inform future cases before the Commission and Court on

[206] ibid paras 71, 179.

[207] ACHPR, 'General Comment No. 5 on the African Charter on Human and Peoples' Rights: The Right to Freedom of Movement and Residence (Article 12(1))' (10 November 2019).

[208] ibid para 8.

[209] ibid paras 14–17. See on limitations, Frans Viljoen, *International Human Rights Law in Africa*, 2nd edn (Oxford, OUP, 2012) 329–32.

[210] ACHPR, 'African Guiding Principles on the Human Rights of All Migrants, Refugees and Asylum Seekers' (2023) achpr.au.int/index.php/en/soft-law/african-guiding-principles-human-rights-all-migrants-refugees.

the right to leave, especially concerning externalised migration controls. To date, none of the cases decided by the Commission (or Court) have concerned the obstruction of leaving carried out by States such as Libya, Niger and Tunisia when implementing the EU's externalisation strategy by criminalising and thwarting irregular migration (see chapter six).

ii. The African Court on Human and Peoples' Rights

The African Court has heard a case concerning the arbitrary revocation of the passports of Rwandan nationals living abroad, who only found out their passports had been revoked when one of them was applying for a visa to travel to the US.[211] The African Court held that Rwanda ought to have demonstrated how revoking the applicant's passports pursued one of the purposes set out in Article 12(2) and (3) of the Charter and Article 12(2) and (3) of the ICCPR – which it notes are similar to the Charter – but Rwanda failed to provide any explanation.[212] This was the case notwithstanding that two of the applicants were alleged to have been convicted of genocide-related crimes and crimes of threatening state security.[213] Accordingly, Rwanda deprived them of their travel documents, preventing them from travelling to other countries and returning to their own country, thus violating their freedom of movement under Article 12(2).[214] The Court further held that revoking the passport of nationals living abroad impeded their full and effective enjoyment of their civic and citizenship rights.[215] While the Court did not invoke the views of the Human Rights Committee in General Comment No 27 in finding a violation of the right to leave, it did so for the right to return.[216] Accordingly, the Court accepts some, and possibly all, authoritative views of the Committee on freedom of movement. Other cases raising the right to leave more squarely fall within internal freedom of movement, as they concern imprisonment.[217]

iii. Regional Free Movement Bodies

The ECOWAS Court of Justice has heard several cases concerning the right to leave on human rights grounds and its findings align broadly with that of the African Commission. Most recently, the Court found that preventing a former Senegalese Minister from boarding a flight violated his right to leave under Article 12(2) of the African Charter in the absence of any justification from Senegal, affirming that restrictions must satisfy conditions of legality, necessity

[211] *Kennedy Gihana v Republic of Rwanda* [2019] AfCHPR 95.
[212] ibid paras 89–92.
[213] ibid para 48.
[214] ibid paras 108–09.
[215] ibid para 97.
[216] ibid paras 106.
[217] *Kalonge v United Republic of Tanzania* [2024] AfCHPR 28, 30.

and proportionality, and cannot be discriminatory.[218] However, the Court has sometimes focused only on subregional free movement rules despite the cases raising the same human rights issues and measures.[219] For instance, the ECOWAS Court considered a travel ban imposed against former Senegalese ministers and froze their assets at the preliminary stage of a criminal inquiry into corruption.[220] The applicants argued that the travel ban was made without any legal basis or notification and was therefore arbitrary, in violation of the UDHR, ICCPR and African Charter.[221] The Court ordered the removal of the travel ban because it was 'legally unfounded' and not based on any court decision.[222] Furthermore, nothing would justify the ban because the applicants, who had not been sued or charged, were not disrupting public order or national security, much less, public health or morality and Senegal had failed to bring any evidence to suggest otherwise in imposing the ban.[223] Though focusing on entry, the Court has also held that border closures between ECOWAS States violated the right to free movement guaranteed by the UDHR, African Charter and ECOWAS treaty and protocol on free movement.[224] The Court has also endorsed statements on the right to leave enabling individuals to escape political systems that deny basic freedoms.[225]

However, in another case concerning border closures and barriers to travel across West Africa, the focus was primarily on the protocol on free movement. The Court found that closing the Togolese border due to the presidential election was justified within the terms of the protocol.[226] Similarly, in another case, a Nigerian national was detained and his passport seized as he was stopped for a routine check by Benin police officers at the border with Togo on his return to Nigeria.[227] Although he argued a violation of Article 12(2) under the African Charter and the ECOWAS treaty and free movement protocol, the Court instead found a violation of his right to property. It stated that 'detention for purposes of calming down or obtaining travel documents' is not within the protocol's purview, without considering the Charter.[228]

The East African Court of Justice has also considered a travel ban following the prosecution and disbarment by the Burundi Bar Association of the Burundi

[218] *Lat Diop v Republic of Senegal* [2025] ECOWASCJ 23, paras 54–80.

[219] See LR Helfer, 'Subregional Courts in Africa: Litigating the Hybrid Right to Free Movement of Persons' (2018) 16 *I-CON: International Journal of Constitutional Law* 235.

[220] *Abdoulaye Baldé v Republic of Senegal* (22 February 2013) ECW/CCJ/APP/22/12.

[221] ibid para 30.

[222] ibid paras 56–61, 77.

[223] ibid paras 58, 61.

[224] *Chief Sunday Adeyemo (Aka Sunday Igboho) v Benin* [2023] ECOWASCJ 7, paras 14–15, 21. See also *Afolabi v Nigeria* (27 April 2004) ECW/CCJ/APP/01/03, but the Court lacked jurisdiction.

[225] *Amnesty International Senegal Section v Republic of Senegal* [2022] ECOWASCJ 16, para 136.

[226] *Falana* (n 19) paras 33, 42–43. See Helfer (n 219) 251.

[227] *Okomba v Republic of Benin* [2017] ECOWASCJ 5.

[228] ibid 17.

President, who was charged with corruption.[229] However, it failed to make a finding on the right to leave. Instead, the Court held that the restriction on him leaving, although imposed by a Burundian court, was imposed without due process and therefore violated the rule of law enshrined in the Treaty for the Establishment of the East African Community.[230]

F. Conclusion

There is substantial convergence on the scope of the right to leave and how the right is interpreted and applied across the jurisprudence of global and regional courts and bodies. The right to leave appears to have developed rather harmoniously, which allows us to speak of 'a' right to leave under customary international law and treaty. Adjudicative bodies have established a number of key principles for determining how the right to leave operates and functions in practice for different groups of people as well as with respect to different types of measures hampering departure. This does not, however, mean that States understand or are implementing their obligations accordingly. The international jurisprudence on the right to leave can be summarised in a single chapter, in stark contrast to the extensive case law on *non-refoulement*.[231] Only a handful of decisions have addressed externalisation as a breach of the right to leave, specifically travel bans to prevent breaches of foreign immigration laws, interceptions at sea and racial profiling at the border. This is leading to gaps in protection, especially for asylum seekers and other migrants prevented from departing their own country or transit States. As chapter six explores, several recent cases have been brought arguing that harmful externalisation measures are breaching the right to leave.

To begin to address these gaps and develop an extensive framework for understanding and applying the right, the key requirements to be considered in assessing whether a violation of the right has occurred will be discussed in turn (section V). First, however, the concept of 'extraterritorial jurisdiction' is introduced, as it is central to discussions on when States owe duties under the right to leave to individuals, particularly when they act outside their borders or their acts have effects beyond their borders.

IV. INTRODUCING EXTRATERRITORIAL JURISDICTION

Given the abundance of literature on the meaning of jurisdiction under human rights law, this section will only briefly outline the settled but ever-evolving

[229] *East Africa Law Society v Attorney General of Burundi* [2015] EACJ 92.
[230] ibid para 96.
[231] McDonnell (n 154).

tests on jurisdiction.[232] Jurisdiction has become a hotly debated issue, not least because of the increase in States impairing the rights of migrants well beyond their territory. As Sassen has argued, State authority is now often detached from territory and exercised also by non-state actors.[233] Attempts by States to sever jurisdictional links and evade legal responsibility for violations make this focus on jurisdiction essential to the analysis of international responsibility in later chapters on visa regimes and interceptions.

Under human rights law, whether a State has the obligation to uphold human rights typically depends on whether that State exercises jurisdiction in the given context.[234] Most human rights treaties include a jurisdictional clause requiring State parties to secure the rights of individuals within or subject to their jurisdiction (ie, Article 1 ECHR, Article 2(1) ICCPR, Article 1(1) ACHR). Other instruments such as the ADHR and African Charter contain no jurisdiction clause limiting their scope of application. Nevertheless, there is considerable convergence as to the scope of applicability and extraterritorial application of these treaties.

States are usually considered to exercise jurisdiction within their territory.[235] There is also widespread agreement that States can exercise jurisdiction over individuals outside their borders, affirming that States must comply with their human rights obligations in many externalisation contexts.[236] Extraterritorial jurisdiction is generally understood to arise whenever a State exercises effective control over territory or individuals.[237] Several interpretations of the effective control test and avenues for establishing jurisdiction with respect to individuals outside a State's territory have emerged, including in response to new practices, existing uncertainties and gaps. However, treaty bodies and the

[232] See on the EU: L Bartels, 'The EU's Human Rights Obligations in Relation to Policies with Extraterritorial Effects' (2015) 25 *European Journal of International Law* 1071; K da Costa, *The Extraterritorial Application of Selected Human Rights Treaties* (Leiden, Martinus Nijhoff, 2013).

[233] S Sassen, *Territory, Authority, Rights: From Medieval to Global Assemblages* (Princeton, Princeton University Press, 2008).

[234] S Besson, 'The Extraterritoriality of the European Convention on Human Rights: Why Human Rights Depend on Jurisdiction and What Jurisdiction Amounts to' (2012) 25 *Leiden Journal of International Law* 857, 862–64; den Heijer (n 154) 24; M Milanovic, *Extraterritorial Application of Human Rights Treaties: Law, Principles, and Policy* (Oxford, OUP, 2011) 19; T Gammeltoft-Hansen, 'International Cooperation on Migration Control: Towards a Research Agenda for Refugee Law' (2018) 20 *European Journal of Migration and Law* 107–12.

[235] See eg *Banković v Belgium* (2007) 44 EHRR SE5, para 59; den Heijer (n 154) 24; Milanovic (n 234) 22, 58–61; Gammeltoft-Hansen (n 234) 56.

[236] D Cantor and others, 'Externalisation, Access to Territorial Asylum, and International Law' (2022) 34 *International Journal of Refugee Law* 120, 123–29.

[237] See eg T Meron, 'Extraterritoriality of Human Rights Treaties' (1995) 89 *American Journal of International Law* 78, 79–82; CM Cerna, 'The Extraterritorial Scope of Human Rights Treaties: The American Convention on Human Rights' in F Coomans and MT Kamminga (eds), *Extraterritorial Application of Human Rights Treaties* (Plymouth, Intersentia, 2004) 141; Gammeltoft-Hansen (n 234) 84–85, 100; Milanovic (n 234) 53, 127–219; Da Costa (n 232) chs 1–2.

Inter-American and African bodies adopt a much more expansive understanding of jurisdiction than Strasbourg, detached from territorial notions.[238]

Article 2(1) of the ICCPR provides that every State Party 'undertakes to respect and to ensure to all individuals within its territory and subject to its jurisdiction the rights recognized in the present Covenant'. The Human Rights Committee has held that the Covenant applies to anyone within the power or effective control of a State, even if not situated within the territory of that State,[239] which the ICJ has affirmed.[240] The Committee in General Comment No 36 predicates jurisdiction as the exercise of control over an individual's rights, looking at the direct and foreseeable harm caused to an individual by the State's conduct:

> [A]ll persons subject to its jurisdiction, that is, all persons *over whose enjoyment of the right to life it exercises power or effective control*. This include persons located outside any territory effectively controlled by the State, whose right to life is nonetheless impacted by its military or other activities in *a direct and reasonably foreseeable manner*.[241]

The Committee has also adopted a functional approach, holding that the reference to jurisdiction is 'not to the place where the violation occurred, but rather to the relationship between the individual and the State in relation to a violation of any of the rights'.[242] The Committee has clearly recognised the extraterritorial application of the right to leave in the Uruguayan passport cases.

Similarly, the Inter-American Commission and Court recognise the extraterritorial reach of the ADHR and ACHR, holding that States are obliged to uphold the rights of individuals within their authority and control, which generally arises through the actions of State agents abroad such as interdictions

[238] See Y Shany, 'Taking Universality Seriously: A Functional Approach to Extraterritoriality in International Human Rights Law' (2013) 7 *Law & Ethics of Human Rights* 47, 51–52; D Cassel, 'Extraterritorial Application of Inter-American Human Rights Instruments' in F Coomans and MT Kamminga (eds), *Extraterritorial Application of Human Rights Treaties* (Antwerp, Intersentia, 2004) 181; A Oloo and W Vanderhole, 'Enforcement of Extraterritorial Human Rights Obligations in the African Human Rights System' in M Gibney and others, *The Routledge Handbook on Extraterritorial Human Rights Obligations* (Abingdon, Routledge, 2021).

[239] See eg *Delia Saldias de Lopez v Uruguay*, Communication No 52/1979 (29 July 1981) UN Doc CCPR/C/OP/1, paras 12.1–12.3; *Nabhari v Australia*, Communication No 3663/2019 (25 October 2024) UN Doc CCPR /C/142/D/3663/2019, para 7.5; HRC, 'General Comment No 31: The Nature of the General Legal Obligation imposed on States Parties' (26 May 2004) UN Doc CCPR/C/21/Rev.1/Add.13, para 10.

[240] *Wall* opinion (n 76) paras 109–11; *DRC* (n 64) para 216.

[241] HRC, 'General Comment No 36 (2018) on Article 6 of the International Covenant on Civil and Political Rights, on the Right to Life' (30 October 2018) UN Doc CCPR/C/GC/36, para 63 (emphasis added). Applied in *AS, DI, OI and GD v Italy*, Communication No 3042/2017 (27 January 2021) UN Doc CCPR/C/130/D/3042/2017, paras 7.5, 7.8.

[242] *Lilian Celiberti de Casariego v Uruguay*, Communication No 56/1979 (29 July 1981) UN Doc CCPR/C/13/D/56/1979, para 10.2; *Lopez Burgos v Uruguay*, Communication No 52/1979 (29 July 1981) UN Doc CCPR/C/13/D/52/1979, para 12.2. See Gammeltoft-Hansen (n 234) 101, 124–25, 150–57.

at sea.[243] Under certain circumstances, the State will also be responsible for the acts and omissions of its agents that produce *effects* outside its territory.[244] This includes the exercise of effective control over activities causing trans-boundary violations where the State is in a position to prevent the harms.[245] The African Commission has also recognised the extraterritorial obligations of African States to respect and protect the rights in the African Charter.[246] In its General Comment No 3, the Commission stipulates that the State shall respect the right to life of individuals outside its territory and has certain obligations to protect their right to life. The nature of these obligations depends

> on the extent that the State has jurisdiction or otherwise exercises effective authority, power, or control over either the perpetrator or the victim (or the victim's rights), or exercises effective control over the territory on which the victim's rights are affected, or whether the State engages in conduct which could reasonably be foreseen to result in an unlawful deprivation of life.[247]

Article 1 of the ECHR provides that 'Contracting Parties shall secure to everyone within their jurisdiction the rights and freedoms' in the Convention. Despite there being no reference to territory, the European Court on Human Rights has taken the most restrictive approach to extraterritorial jurisdiction.[248] It has, however, moved away from its infamous *Banković* decision,[249] consistently holding that extraterritorial jurisdiction arises first, where the State exercises effective control over an area and second, where State agents exercise authority and control over individuals.[250] Effective control over persons has

[243] See eg *Haitian Centre* (n 166); *Saldaño v Argentina*, IACHR, Report No 38/99 (11 March 1999) OEA/Ser.L/V/II.95 Doc 7 Rev at 289, paras 15–20; *Armando Alejandre Jr v Cuba*, IACHR, Case 11.589, Report No 86/99 (29 September 1999) OEA/Ser.L/V/II.106 Doc 3 Rev at 586, paras 23–25; *Coard v US*, IACHR, Case 10.951 Report No 109/99 (29 September 1999) OEA/Ser.L./V/II.106 Doc 3 Rev at 1283, para 37.

[244] See *Saldaño* (n 243) para 17; *Armando* (n 243) para 25.

[245] *Advisory Opinion on the Environment and Human Rights (State obligations in Relation to the Environment in the Context of the Protection and Guarantee of the Rights to Life and to Personal Integrity – Interpretation and Scope of Articles 4(1) and 5(1) of the American Convention on Human Rights)*, IACtHR, OC-23/17 (15 November 2017) paras 36, 71–82, 101–04.

[246] BT Soboka and L Chenwi, *Extraterritoriality in the African Regional Human Rights System from a Comparative Perspective* (Cambridge, Intersentia, 2018). See further *DRC v Burundi, Rwanda and Uganda* [2003] ACHPR 41; *Mohammed Abdullah Saleh Al-Asad v Djibouti*, ACHPR, Communication 383/2010 (12 May 2014) para 134–36.

[247] ACHPR 'General Comment No. 3 on the African Charter on Human and Peoples' Rights: The Right to Life (Article 4)' (12 December 2015) para 14. See also Oloo and Vanderhole (n 238).

[248] See M Jackson, 'Freeing *Soering*: The ECHR, State Complicity in Torture and Jurisdiction' (2016) 27 *European Journal of International Law* 817, 820.

[249] *Banković* (n 235), where aerial bombing by NATO forces outside their States' borders did not amount to jurisdiction.

[250] *Loizidou v Turkey* (1996) 23 EHRR 513, para 62; *Cyprus v Turkey* (2002) 35 EHRR 731, paras 76–77; *Issa v Turkey* (2005) 41 EHRR 27, paras 68–71; *Öcalan v Turkey* (2005) 41 EHRR 18, para 91; *Al-Jedda v UK* (2011) 53 EHRR 23, para 85; *Al-Skeini v UK* (2011) 53 EHRR 18, paras 133–42; *Hirsi Jamaa v Italy* (2012) 55 EHRR 21, paras 71–75; *Jaloud v Netherlands* (2015) 60 EHRR 29, paras 139, 152.

arisen through the exercise of physical power and control, including arrest, detention or custody,[251] unlawful killings[252] and abduction.[253] Jurisdiction can arise through the exercise of *de jure* control, for instance under exclusive flag State jurisdiction[254] as well as *de facto* control over individuals during interceptions,[255] or when boarding and towing a vessel[256] The Court's underlying normative position for Article 1 is that States cannot be allowed 'perpetrate violations of the Convention on the territory of another state, which it could not perpetrate on its own territory'.[257]

The Court does not always require physical or effective control.[258] It has consistently held that 'acts of the Contracting States performed, or *producing effects*, outside their territories can constitute an exercise of jurisdiction' – a cause and effect approach.[259] What is required is a 'direct and immediate' link between the State conduct and harm, which has arisen for 'isolated and specific acts' involving proximity.[260] The Court has also developed a test based on decisive influence in a series of cases in which Transdniestria was found to be 'under the decisive influence, of the Russian Federation, and … survives by virtue of the military, economic, financial and political support given to it by the Russian Federation'.[261] However, there are many controversial cases where extraterritorial jurisdiction has not been found to arise when individuals have been directly and adversely affected by a State's actions.[262] Understanding the fundamental

[251] *Al-Skeini* (n 250) para 149; *Al-Saadoon and Mufdhi v UK* (2010) 51 EHRR 9, paras 86–89; *Öcalan* (n 250) para 91; *Al-Jedda* (n 250) paras 80–86; *Hassan v UK*, App no 29750/09 (ECtHR, 16 September 2014) paras 76–80.

[252] *Isaak v Turkey*, App no 44587/98 (ECtHR, 28 September 2006) (admissibility) 20–21; *Pad v Turkey*, App no 60167/00 (28 June 2007) para 54; *Andreou v Turkey*, App no 45653/99 (3 June 2008) (admissibility) 9–11; *Solomou v Turkey*, App no 36832/97 (ECtHR, 24 June 2008) paras 44–45, 51; *Andreou v Turkey*, App no 45653/99 (ECtHR, 27 October 2009) (judgment) para 25.

[253] See above: *de Lopez* (n 239) para 10; *de Casariego* (n 242) para 10.1; *Lopez Burgos* (n 242) para 12.1.

[254] *Banković* (n 235) para 73; *Medvedyev v France* (2010) 51 EHRR 39, para 65; *Hirsi* (n 250) paras 75, 77.

[255] *Hirsi* (n 250) para 81.

[256] *Medvedyev* (n 254) paras 63–67.

[257] *Issa* (n 250) para 71, citing *de Casariego* and *Lopez Burgos* (n 242).

[258] Den Heijer (n 154) 45–49.

[259] See *Hirsi* (n 250) paras 71–72 (emphasis added).

[260] *Andreou v Turkey*, App no 45653/99 (2008) admissibility, 10–11, (2009) judgment, para 25. See also *Ilaşcu v Moldova and Russia* (2005) 40 EHRR 1030, para 317; *Isaak v Turkey* (n 252) paras 19–21; *Pad* (n 252) para 54; *Solomou* (n 252) paras 44, 48–51; *Panayi v Turkey*, App no 45388/99 (ECtHR, 27 October 2009) para 27; *Nada v Switzerland* (2013) 56 EHRR 18, paras 121–22; *Big Brother Watch v UK*, App nos 58170/13, 62322/14 and 24960/15 (ECtHR, 13 September 2018) para 271; *Georgia v Russia (II)*, App no 38263/08 (ECtHR, 21 January 2021) paras 131–33.

[261] See eg, *Ilaşcu* (n 260) paras 392–93; *Ivanţoc v Moldova and Russia*, App no 23687/05 (ECtHR, 15 November 2011) paras 115–20; *Catan v Moldova and Russia*, App nos 43370/04, 8252/05 and 18454/06 (ECtHR, 19 October 2012) para 122; *Mozer v Moldova and Russia*, App no 11138/10 (ECtHR, 23 February 2016) para 110; *Turturica and Casian v Moldova and Russia*, App nos 28648/06 and 18832/07 (ECtHR, 30 August 2016) para 30.

[262] See *Georgia v Russia (II)*, App no 38263/08 (ECtHR, 21 January 2021) reviving *Banković* (n 235) paras 133–44; *MN v Belgium*, App no 3599/18 (ECtHR, 5 March 2020).

rules of jurisdiction allows us to examine the right to leave and its extraterritorial applicability in greater detail.

V. REQUIREMENTS UNDER THE RIGHT TO LEAVE

Five key requirements are to be considered in determining whether a measure complies with the right to leave any country, under the relevant limitation's clause (see Article 12(3) ICCPR, Article 2(3) Protocol 4 ECHR, Article 22(3) ACHR, Article 12(2) African Charter; Article 22(3) CIS Convention; Article 27 Arab Charter).

1. The restriction amounts to an *interference* with the right to leave;
2. is provided by or in accordance with *law*;
3. is in pursuit of one of the *legitimate aims*;
4. is *proportionate* to achieving that aim; and
5. is *consistent* with other rights (a somewhat unique addition under the ICCPR).

It is generally accepted that limitations on a right should be strictly construed and that restrictions must not destroy the essence of the right.[263]

A. Interference

Adjudicative bodies rarely engage with the interference stage. They generally accept that the impugned measure interferes with the right because it is not disputed or is evident on the facts, such as travel bans or passport refusals.[264] Cases concerning externalisation are notable exceptions to this and raise important questions regarding the definitional scope of the right, in other words, whether the right to leave is infringed in the first place.

[263] See among many *Klass v Germany* (1979) 2 EHRR 214, para 42; *Jalloh v Germany* (2007) 44 EHRR 32, para 97; CHR, 'The Siracusa Principles on the Limitation and Derogation Provisions in the International Covenant on Civil and Political Rights' (28 September 1984) UN Doc E/CN.4/1985/4 (Siracusa Principles) pt 1; HRC, 'General Comment No 27' (n 3) para 16; ACHPR, 'General Comment No.5 on the African Charter on Human and Peoples' Rights: The Right to Freedom of Movement and Residence (Article 12(1))' (10 November 2019) para 14; *Salmón* (n 191) para 141; ACHPR, 'Guiding Principles' (n 210) principle 38.

[264] For HRC see: *Peltonen* (n 101) para 8.4; *Farag El Dernawi* (n 94) para 6.2; *Zoolfia* (n 103) para 8.2; *Orazova* (n 106) para 7.2. For ECtHR see: *Baumann* (n 153) para 62; *Napijalo v Croatia*, App no 66485/01 (ECtHR, 13 February 2004) para 69; *Földes* (n 146) para 33; *Diamante and Pelliccioni v San Marino*, App no 32250/08 (ECtHR, 27 September 2011) para 211; *Sarkizov* (n 150) (ECtHR, 17 April 2012) para 66; *Khlyustov v Russia*, App no 28975/05 (ECtHR, 11 July 2013) para 65; *Navalnyy v Russia*, Apps nos 29580/12 and others (ECtHR, 15 May 2018) para 17.

In 1997, the Italian and Albanian authorities took several joint measures to prevent Albanians leaving Albania and entering Italy by boat. The case of *Xhavara v Italy and Albania* before the Strasbourg Court concerned an incident that took place 35 nautical miles from the Italian coast when an Italian warship intercepted and collided with a boat of Albanians causing the Albanian boat to sink and the death of nearly 60 people.[265] The Court found that the right to leave in Article 2(2) Protocol 4 did not apply because the measures were not aimed at preventing people *leaving* Albania but rather they aimed to prevent them from *entering* Italy. The decisive factor appeared to be that it was Italy acting, leaving it open whether an interference would have been found if Albania was acting alone or alongside Italy.[266] The Court's conclusion is difficult to support. If the reasoning in *Xhavara* were applied more broadly, no pre-border control measures that seek to prevent entry and irregular migration to destination States, would not trigger the right to leave.[267] As Nessel and Brouwer have argued, the measures were clearly exit controls. A bilateral agreement was entered into authorising Italy to intercept Albanian boats and establish a naval blockade in international and Albanian waters precisely to prevent irregular migration out of Albania.[268]

The State's intention in imposing a measure should not be considered relevant to demarcating the threshold of a right, but rather to ascertaining whether it pursues a legitimate aim and is proportionate in the circumstances.[269] The decisive factor at the interference stage should be the measure's effect: whether it prevents departure, even if simultaneously preventing entry.[270] When unilateral acts are involved, such as the Cuban authorities attacking Cubans fleeing by boat or the border policing regime at the Berlin Wall, it is easier to establish that a measure is directed at exit. However, various migration controls are designed to forestall exit and hence entry (see chapters five and six), as Cornelisse aptly describes: 'By portraying these practices as measures that are necessary to protect the external borders of the Member States, the fact that they entail emigration control is conveniently obscured.'[271] Indeed, if States were successful

[265] *Xhavara v Italy and Albania*, App no 39473/98 (ECtHR, 11 January 2001).

[266] Markard (n 1) 605.

[267] Den Heijer (n 154) 160.

[268] LA Nessel, 'Externalized Borders and the Invisible Refugee' (2009) 40 *Columbia Human Rights Law Review* 625, 675; E Brouwer, 'Extraterritorial Migration Control and Human Rights: Preserving the Responsibility of the EU and its Member States' in B Ryan and V Mitsilegas (eds), *Extraterritorial Immigration Control: Legal Challenges* (Leiden, Martinus Nijhoff, 2010) 225.

[269] Den Heijer (n 154) 160.

[270] T Rodenhäuser, 'Another Brick in the Wall: Carrier Sanctions and the Privatisation of Immigration Control' (2014) 26 *International Journal of Refugee Law* 223, 236. cf Zieck (n 1) 41–44.

[271] Cornelisse (n 1) 23. See also Markard (n 1) 616; M Giuffré and V Moreno-Lax, 'The Rise of Consensual Containment: From "Contactless Control" to "Contactless Responsibility" for Forced Migration Flows' in SS Juss (ed), *Research Handbook on International Refugee Law* (Cheltenham, Edward Elgar Publishing, 2019) 84–85; Guild and Stoyanova (n 1) 375.

in fully controlling exit, they would avoid altogether having to control the entry of irregular migrants.[272]

Stoyanova argues that the closer to the departure State, the easier it may be to show an interference, viewing the finding in *Xhavara* as persuasive because the individuals were far from Albania and the interception did not prevent them leaving.[273] However, the judgment does not specify whether the collision occurred in international or Albanian waters. Nonetheless, such a territorialised reading of 'leaving' renders the right impractical and ineffective. As chapter three explores, while entry and exit are distinct, a sharp line cannot always be drawn, particularly for air travel or at land borders. This reading presumes that the right has no 'existence of its own in regard of destination countries', for instance, during the implementation of extraterritorial border controls.[274] Ignoring the dual effect of measures and adopting a strictly territorialised approach allows destination States to evade their obligations under the right to leave.

Nevertheless, in the 2006 case of *Consorts Demir v France*, the applicants complained following the death of their family member (their father and husband) that France's refusal to issue an entry visa so he could travel there for medical treatment breached Article 2(2) Protocol No 4. Strasbourg declared this part of the case inadmissible for being incompatible *ratione materiae*, holding that the right to leave does not confer a right for individuals to obtain a visa to stay in a State.[275] However, the Court did not provide sufficient reasoning as to why visa refusals could not engage the right to leave (nor is it clear how the applicants framed it as an interference with leaving). Decisions ignoring the potential applicability of the right to leave when States exercise extraterritorial jurisdiction are inconsistent with early authoritative statements. In 1988, Special Rapporteur Mubanga-Chipoya concluded that a limitation on entry may also constitute a restriction on leaving.[276] Also, recall that in 1999, the Human Rights Committee explicitly recognised that carrier sanctions can interfere with the right to leave. It should therefore not be presumed without robust reasoning that pre-entry controls do not interfere with the right to leave, given the right's opposability to destination States exercising extraterritorial jurisdiction (as unpacked further in Part II).

A related issue is whether the right to leave a country applies when a person is only restricted from travelling to one specific State. The jurisprudence

[272] See Weinzierl and Lisson (n 157) 70, 79; Markard (n 1) 616 on emigration controls and non-departure measures in third States.

[273] Stoyanova (n 1) 415–16.

[274] V Moreno-Lax, 'Must EU Borders have Doors for Refugees? On the Compatibility of Schengen Visas and Carriers' Sanctions with EU Member States' Obligations to Provide International Protection to Refugees' (2008) 10 *European Journal of International Law* 315, 353–54. See also Weinzierl and Lisson (n 157) 67–68; Guild and Stoyanova (n 1) 386–87; Moreno-Lax, 'Intersectionality' (n 155) 77.

[275] *Consorts Demir v France*, App no 3041/02 (ECtHR, 4 April 2006) para 23.

[276] Mubanga-Chipoya (n 58) 65, para 321.

makes clear that there does not need to be a complete inability to leave for all States.[277] UN and regional adjudicative bodies have determined that preventing an individual from travelling beyond a particular region or group of countries (for example, the Schengen Area or only neighbouring countries) constitutes an interference with the right, hampering their ability to travel to countries of their choice outside this region, as well as finding violations when individuals could not leave for the specific country they desired.[278] Most of the adjudicative bodies have stated that the right protects the freedom of individuals to leave for the State of their choice (with admission distinct). Nor do the cases suggest that individuals have no other way to leave. The right to return to one's own country also cannot be used to deny leaving for other states, given the freedom to choose.[279] Stoyanova has asserted that 'The expected level of protection that migrants can avail themselves of in any alternative destination is a relevant factor in assessing whether their right to leave is infringed'. Though she adds that, given the definitional scope of qualified rights is typically interpreted broadly, it will be relatively easy to find an interference.[280] However, the availability of alternatives should not affect whether the right applies in the first place. The interests it protects are harmed regardless of how many countries are closed-off. Instead, any alternatives should be addressed under proportionality.

B. Provided by or in Accordance with Law

The second requirement is that restrictions must be provided by or in accordance with law. If they are not, the measure will already breach the right to leave at this stage, though adjudicative bodies often go on to consider necessity and proportionality. The adjudicative bodies have established several general principles, outlined above, regarding when restrictions on the right to leave will not meet the legality test. Only key points will be reiterated here. First, the measure must have an express legal basis and second, it must meet quality of law requirements.[281] In cases not concerning the right to leave, the Strasbourg Court

[277] Markard (n 1) 596.

[278] See *Peltonen* (n 101); *Victims of Tugboat* (n 163); *Soltysyak v Russia*, App no 4663/05 (ECtHR, 10 February 2011) para 37; *LB* (n 160) para 81. The HRC has also found a violation of art 12(2) where an individual was unable to travel to the specific country they wanted to: *El Ghar* (n 89). See further Stoyanova (n 1) 406–07, 413.

[279] Stoyanova (n 1) 406–07.

[280] ibid 406–14.

[281] *Canese* (n 182) para 125, 128; *Riener* (n 145) para 112; *Gochev* (n 150) paras 46–47; *Soltysyak* (n 278) paras 40–43; *Stamose* (n 135) para 26; *Khlyustov* (n 264) paras 68–77; *Battista* (n 148) paras 38–39; HRC, 'General Comment No 27' (n 3) paras 12–13; ACHPR, 'General Comment No 5' (n 207) paras 16–17.

has clarified that statute, common law and sources of international law can provide a sufficient legal basis.[282]

On the other hand, administrative orders, instructions, guidelines or sources that are 'neither legally binding nor … directly publicly accessible' will usually be insufficient.[283] The legal basis must be clear, accessible to the people concerned, and foreseeable as to its effects, which requires the law to use precise criteria so people can regulate their conduct and not confer unfettered discretion on the authorities.[284] Procedural safeguards, including regular oversight, and clearly demarcated discretionary powers must be in place to protect against arbitrariness and the abuse of rights.[285] Review of a restriction should be done by the courts at least in the first instance.[286] In the case law, restrictions on the right to leave did not meet the legality test where the relevant basis was vague, imprecise and lacking adequate safeguards;[287] where the basis was not clear or foreseeable;[288] where it was based on an incorrect interpretation and application of domestic law;[289] or where the State did not cite a basis or there was no legal basis at all.[290] Strasbourg has also found travel bans to be disproportionate where the domestic court merely verified the lawfulness of the ban without assessing proportionality or taking into account the individual's specific situation.[291]

At this juncture, it is worth pointing out that restrictions on freedom of movement are distinct from a deprivation of liberty involving confinement in a 'particular restricted space', the difference turning on degree and intensity.[292]

[282] *Sunday Times v UK*, App no 6538/74 (ECtHR, 26 April 1979) para 47; *Silver v UK*, Apps nos 5947/72 and others (ECtHR, 25 March 1983) para 86; *Malone v UK*, App no 8691/79 (ECtHR, 2 August 1984) para 66; *Kruslin v France*, App no 11801/85 (ECtHR, 24 April 1990) para 29; *Perry v UK* (2004) 39 EHRR 3, para 47; *Medvedyev* (n 254) paras 79, 96; *Toniolo v San Marino and Italy*, App no 44853/10 (ECtHR, 26 June 2012) para 46.

[283] *Khan v UK* (2000) 31 EHRR 1016, para 27. See also *Golder v UK* (1979) 1 EHRR 524, paras 17, 45; *Silver* (n 282) paras 86–89; *Leander v Sweden*, App no 9248/81 (ECtHR, 26 March 1987) para 51; *Shimovolos v Russia* App no 30194/09 (ECtHR, 21 June 2011), paras 68–69; *Medvedyev* (n 254). See Nowak (n 14) 272–73.

[284] *De Groot v Netherlands*, Communication No 578/1994 (14 July 1995) UN Doc CCPR/C/54/D/578/1994, para 4.3; HRC, 'General Comment No 27' (n 3) paras 12–13; *Canese* (n 182).

[285] *De Tommaso v Italy*, App no 43395/09 (ECtHR, 23 February 2017) paras 106–27.

[286] *Sissanis* (n 152) para 70; *Gochev* (n 150) para 50; *Timofeyev v Russia*, App no 58263/00 (ECtHR, 23 October 2003).

[287] *Sissanis* (n 152) paras 66–79; *Rotaru* (n 150) paras 27–35. See also *Khlyustov* (n 264) paras 70, 74.

[288] *Dzhaksybergenov* (n 152) paras 59–62.

[289] *Kerimli v Azerbaijan* App no 3967/09 (ECtHR, 16 July 2015) para 48; *Cherepanov v Russia* (2016) ECHR 398, para 45.

[290] *Canese* (n 182) para 128; *Shioshvili v Russia*, App no 19356/07 (ECtHR, 20 December 2016), para 60; *Orazova* (n 106) para 7.2; *Zabelin* (n 152) paras 16–21; *Mursaliyev v Azerbaijan*, Apps nos 66650/13, 24749/16, 43327/16 and others (ECtHR, 13 December 2018) paras 32–36.

[291] eg, *Gochev* (n 150) paras 50, 57; *Navalnyy* (n 264) paras 22–23; *Komolov v Russia*, App no 32811/17 (ECtHR, 25 February 2020), paras 28–35. See also *LB* (n 160) paras 95–96.

[292] *Guzzardi v Italy* (1980) 3 EHRR 333, para 93; *Storck v Germany* (2005) 43 EHRR 96, para 74.

Nonetheless, restrictions can significantly impact people and their right to liberty of movement.[293] This is not just the case where preventing departure would amount to severe confinement, such as on small islands like Nauru. Strasbourg has established that where an interference with a human right is especially serious, the law should be exact with detailed guidelines and independent oversight.[294] Given physical liberty and security are often at stake when people are attempting to leave, these principles will provide helpful guidance. The more severe the restriction, such as a ban on leaving for many States or obstructing someone's search or asylum, the more precision and safeguarding should be required.

C. Proportionality

Restrictions on the right to leave must be necessary to achieve a specified aim; in other words, they must comply with proportionality. Measures must (i) pursue a legitimate aim; (ii) be rationally connected to that aim; (iii) be strictly necessary, meaning the least intrusive means; and (iv) strike a fair balance between the individual's right and aims pursued. A measure that destroys the essence of the right – reversing the relationship between norm and exception – is plainly disproportionate and unlawful. The above principles will not be reiterated here, but it is worth examining the meaning of specific legitimate aims.

i. Interpreting Legitimate Aims and Deference to the State

International and regional human rights treaties outline an exhaustive list of legitimate aims that would justify limiting the right to leave. Though the articles can use slightly different language, they generally cover the pursuit of *national security*, *public order*, the *protection of health or morals*, and *the protection of the rights and freedoms of others*. As mentioned, national security, public order and health generated much controversy while drafting the UDHR and ICCPR, with drafters emphasising how such phrases could lead to abuse and overreach.[295] States frequently invoke these aims in imposing migration controls. However, a great deal of deference is typically afforded to the State when it asserts national security or public order concerns. As a result, most scrutiny focuses on the proportionality of a measure.

a. National Security

'National security' is a key example of a term whose meaning is elusive. National security is defined in the Oxford English Dictionary as 'The safety

[293] *De Tommaso* (n 285) para 111.
[294] *Kruslin* (n 282) para 33; *Kopp v Switzerland* (1999) 27 EHRR 91, para 72; *Medvedyev* (n 254) para 80; *Big Brother Watch* (n 260) paras 304–20, 387–88.
[295] Nowak (n 14).

of a nation and its people, institutions, etc., esp. from military threat or from espionage, terrorism, etc'.[296] According to Hannum, even though national security has become a term of the art, the constituent parts of the phrase retain their ordinary meaning. Accordingly, national security denotes a threat to the existence of the State itself, such as the use of external force against the State.[297] This is confirmed by the drafters of the ICCPR, who had military interests and vital security in mind.[298] Similarly, a 1983 UN study revealed that States understood national security within the UDHR and ICCPR as measures safeguarding territorial integrity and national independence against external threats, covering any activity prejudicial to the State's existence.[299]

Special Rapporteur Inglés observed that national security can be understood as limited to national defence, or broadly as covering anything affecting public safety or the internal or external security of the state.[300] However, other supplementary means of interpretation confirm the narrower interpretation of the term. The Siracusa Principles on the Limitation and Derogation Provisions in the ICCPR adopted by eminent international lawyers in 1985 specify that national security can only be invoked 'to protect the existence of the nation or its territorial integrity or political independence against force or threat of force', not for 'local or relatively isolated threats to law and order'.[301] Special Rapporteur Mubanga-Chipoya's report and declaration on the right to leave and return endorses this interpretation.[302] Similarly, in the Strasbourg Declaration on the Right to Leave and Return, national security encompasses a 'clear, imminent and serious danger to the state'.[303] National security, therefore, appears limited to grave military, territorial, or other threats to the whole State.[304]

Possession of State secrets,[305] conscription[306] and implementing Security Council sanctions against terrorism[307] have been deemed legitimate national security aims. Pending arrest warrants or criminal proceedings *may*, under

[296] Oxford English Dictionary, 'National security' (OUP) www.oed.com/dictionary/national-security_n.

[297] Hannum (n 1) 27–29.

[298] Mubanga-Chipoya (n 58) 51.

[299] UN, 'The Individual's Duties to the Community and the Limitations on Human Rights and Freedoms Under Article 29 of the Universal Declaration of Human Rights: A Contribution to the Freedom of the Individual Under Law: Study prepared by Erica-Irene A. Daes, Special Rapporteur of the Sub-Commission on Prevention of Discrimination and Protection of Minorities' (1983) UN Doc E/CN.4/Sub.2/432/Rev.2, 88-89, 177, 187.

[300] Inglés (n 2) 39. See also G Liu, *The Right to Leave and Return and Chinese Migration Law* (Leiden, Martinus Nijhoff, 2007) 62–64.

[301] Siracusa Principles, paras 29–32.

[302] Draft Declaration, art 7(d); Mubanga-Chipoya (n 58) 51–52.

[303] Strasbourg Declaration, art 4(d).

[304] Nowak (n 14) 276.

[305] *Bartik* (n 145) paras 42–43; *Soltysyak* (n 278) paras 44–45; *Berkovich* (n 153) paras 84–85. See also HRC, 'General Comment No 27' (n 3) para 16.

[306] *Peltonen* (n 101) para 8.4; *Peltonen v Finland*, App no 19583/92 (Commission Decision, 20 February 1995), which also deem conscription legitimate to maintain public order.

[307] *Sayadi and Vinck* (n 100) paras 8.2, 10.7.

certain circumstances, justify restrictions on leaving on national security grounds.[308] Given the potential breadth of national security, many matters, such as border security, could fall within scope.[309] The African Commission, for instance, has held that national security encompasses external biosecurity risks to human health that threaten the physical integrity of a State's citizens.[310]

In many countries, government rhetoric frames migration as an existential threat to the State and its people.[311] States, invoking their 'near-absolute' sovereign power to control immigration, routinely justify imposing egregious measures based on far-reaching and vague assertions of national security. This should not be accepted, given the term's narrow meaning and the importance of ensuring that national security is not used as a pretext for imposing arbitrary restrictions on the exercise of human rights.[312] Further, as Mubanga-Chipoya argues, States can misuse 'national security' as a cover for different reasons they do not wish to disclose.[313] We need to be alive to this as most States, though not all, are unlikely to explicitly declare that they are obstructing asylum and migration from 'unwanted' nationalities as their goal.

b. Public Order

While the English text of Article 12(3) of the ICCPR refers to 'public order (*ordre public*)', the French and Spanish texts refer only to '*l'ordre public*' and '*el orden público*' respectively. Article 2(3) Protocol 4 ECHR refers to 'maintenance of *ordre public*'. The meaning of these terms is far from clear, open to several interpretations, and differs across legal systems.[314] While drafting Article 12, the drafters had difficulty finding an exact English translation for the French concept of *ordre public*. 'Public order' was deemed unsatisfactory, not equivalent to the French or Spanish concepts.[315] 'Public order' in

[308] *Gonzalez del Rio* (n 99) para 5.3.

[309] *Streletz* (n 141) para 100. See also *ND and NT v Spain*, Apps nos 8675/15 and 8697/15 (ECtHR, 13 February 2020) para 168.

[310] *Sudan Human Rights Organisation & Centre on Housing Rights and Evictions (COHRE) v Sudan*, ACHPR Communication 279/03-296/05 (27 May 2009) para 174.

[311] See CMW, 'Concluding Observations on the Second Periodic Report of Peru' (23 January 2025) UN Doc CMW/C/PER/CO/2, para 35; CMW, 'Concluding Observations on Nigeria in the Absence of a Report' (23 May 2017) UN Doc CMW/C/NGA/CO/1-2, para 26.

[312] Daes (n 299) 178.

[313] Mubanga-Chipoya (n 58) 52.

[314] Inglés (n 2) annex IV, 91–92; AC Kiss, 'Permissible Limitations on Rights' in L Henkin (ed), *The International Bill of Rights: The Covenant on Civil and Political Rights* (New York, Columbia University Press, 1981) 299–301; BB Lockwood, J Finn and G Jubinsky, 'Working Paper for the Committee of Experts on Limitation Provisions' (1985) 7 *Human Rights Quarterly* 35, 56–59; MJ Bossuyt, *Guide to the "Travaux Préparatoires" of the International Covenant on Civil and Political Rights* (Dordrecht, Martinus Nijhoff, 1987) 258–59.

[315] UNGA Third Committee (14th session), 'Draft International Covenants on Human Rights' (3 December 1959) UN Doc A/4299, paras 15–16.

common law countries is generally understood as the absence of disorder. In French private law, *ordre public* coincides largely with the common law concept of public policy, while in French public law it denotes the sum of principles on which a society is founded.[316] The Strasbourg Declaration and Mubanga-Chipoya's Draft Declaration define public order (*ordre public*) as the 'universally accepted fundamental principles, consistent with respect for human rights, on which a democratic society is based'.[317] Accordingly, public order can be construed narrowly as concerning the absence of disorder or broadly as referring to the French notion of regulating society based on fundamental principles.

The *travaux préparatoires* resolved the apparent tension, demonstrating that the drafters of the ICCPR and ECHR intended public order and *ordre public* to represent the broader French meaning.[318] Accordingly, limitations on the right to leave are permissible when necessary to ensure the functioning of society based on fundamental principles. The breadth of what States may deem 'fundamental principles' makes the aim inherently vague and far-reaching, especially when adopting an evolutionary interpretation.[319]

A significant point of contention concerns whether public order covers only domestic concerns or the international public order.[320] Can a State assert that public order covers the protection of *another* State or the international community's public order? Do measures induced by international obligations, such as measures to combat people trafficking and smuggling, justify restricting the right to leave? Can third States thwart departures to prevent irregular migration to destination States? Relying on the ICCPR's *travaux préparatoires*, Zieck argues that public order does not extend beyond domestic concerns. Like national security, which focuses on threats to the State itself, public order is also geared at protecting the interests of the state invoking the restriction.[321] In contrast, Mubanga-Chipoya specifies that under the generally recognised interpretation, restrictions based on public order can be applied to individuals posing a danger for the State to which they intend to travel.[322]

[316] UNGA Third Committee (5th session), '288th Meeting' (18 October 1950) UN Doc A/C.3/SR.288, paras 17–18 (UK delegate); UNGA Third Committee (14th session), '956th Meeting' (13 November 1959) UN Doc A/C.3/SR.956, para 12 (Belgian delegate), para 13 (Philippines delegate), para 25 (UK delegate); Inglés (n 2) 36–37; Lockwood, Finn and Jubinsky (n 314) 58–59.

[317] Strasbourg Declaration, art 4(e); Siracusa Principles, para 22. See also Draft Declaration, art 7(e); Mubanga-Chipoya (n 58) 11; Nowak (n 14) 277; Daes (n 299) 175–76.

[318] UNGA, '956th Meeting' (n 316) paras 5, 25; Council of Europe, 'Explanatory Report to Protocol No. 4 to the ECHR (1963) ETS No 46, para 16; Zieck (n 1) 30. See also Kiss (n 314) 300–02; Lockwood, Finn and Jubinsky (n 314) 57, 59–60. cf Inglés (n 2) 37.

[319] See Hannum (n 1) 30–41; Cornelisse (n 1) 16; E Bjorge, *The Evolutionary Interpretation of Treaties* (Oxford, OUP, 2014).

[320] See Zieck (n 1) 29.

[321] ibid 30–31.

[322] Mubanga-Chipoya (n 58) 54.

The jurisprudence of adjudicative bodies shows that the right can be restricted on grounds of public order, including to secure availability at trial,[323] financial obligations[324] and criminal sentences;[325] to prevent convicted but not yet rehabilitated offenders from travelling abroad[326] or to prevent child abduction;[327] or to implement UNSC sanctions.[328] Several of these areas indicate that public order can encompass international interests. The case of *Jipa v Romania* before the CJEU provides helpful guidance.[329] It involved a travel ban prohibiting a Romanian citizen from travelling to Belgium for up to three years, after he had been deported to Romania for 'illegal residence' in Belgium. The Court held that restrictions on the freedom of movement that citizens of the EU are entitled to under community law must be based on public policy considerations concerning the State imposing the measure and not exclusively on another Member State. However, the latter can be considered.[330] The Strasbourg Court has left open whether protecting the immigration laws of another state is justified.[331] Notably, during the ICCPR negotiations, the UK proposed restricting the right to emigrate to help neighbouring States control 'illegal' immigration and prevent 'primitive or unsophisticated communities from exploitation abroad'; but this suggestion ultimately did not make the final text.[332]

Against the backdrop of shared migration control initiatives, anti-smuggling and trafficking commitments under the Palermo Protocols and other global interests accepted in the jurisprudence like counter-terrorism, it seems incongruous to deny an international public order.[333] These speak to general interests that

[323] ECtHR: *Földes* (n 146) para 33; *Bessenyei* (n 146) para 22; *AE* (n 146) para 47; *Prescher* (n 146) para 46; *Miazdzyk* (n 147) para 31; *Popoviciu* (n 146) para 87. ECOWAS Court of Justice: *Baldé* (n 220) paras 58, 61; HRC: *Gonzalez del Rio* (n 99) para 5.3; IACtHR: *Salmón* (n 191) para 140.

[324] *Napijalo* (n 264) paras 78–82; *Riener* (n 145) para 116.

[325] *Pfeifer* (n 150) para 54; *Kerimli* (n 289) para 49.

[326] *Vlasov v Russia*, App no 78146/01 (ECtHR, 12 June 2008) para 31; *Sarkizov* (n 150) para 66; *Salmón* (n 191) para 140; *Navalnyy* (n 264) para 18; *Kostov v Bulgaria*, Apps nos 66581/12 and 25054/15 (ECtHR, 14 May 2020) para 16; *Nalbant* (n 147) paras 63, 65; *Ivanov* (n 150) paras 36–37.

[327] *Teixeira de Castro v Portugal*, App no 25829/94 (ECtHR, 9 June 1998) 5; *Diamante* (n 264) para 213.

[328] *Sayadi* (n 100) para 10.7.

[329] *Jipa v Romania*, Case C-33/07, EU:C:2008:396, [2008] ECR I-5157.

[330] ibid paras 25–27.

[331] *Stamose* (n 135).

[332] CHR, 'Report of the Third Session of the Commission on Human Rights' (28 June 1948) UN Doc E/800, Annex B, 26 (art 11); Bossuyt (n 314) 252, 256.

[333] Protocol to Prevent, Suppress and Punish Trafficking in Persons, especially Women and Children, Supplementing the United Nations Convention Against Transnational Organized Crime (adopted 15 November 2000, entered into force 25 December 2003) 2237 UNTS 319 (Trafficking Protocol); Protocol against the Smuggling of Migrants by Land, Sea and Air, Supplementing the United Nations Convention against Transnational Organized Crime (adopted 12 December 2000, entered into force 28 January 2004) 2241 UNTS 507 (Smuggling Protocol) (Palermo Protocols). cf University of Michigan, 'The Michigan Guidelines on Refugee Freedom of Movement' (2018) 39 *Michigan Journal of International Law* 5, para 7.

transcend bilateralism – supporting an international public order that extends beyond domestic concerns.[334] However, do States, other than the destination State, have an interest in preventing irregular migration? Can States generate a legitimate aim merely because they owe cooperative obligations to one another or have deemed their actions to pursue shared interests? Notably, Wolman shows that historical attempts to establish a duty on departure States to combat irregular emigration have been largely unsuccessful and fail to amount to a customary norm.[335]

A normative valuation of the aims asserted by the State should be required. It can hardly be legitimate to restrict the right to leave if this destroys the possibility of seeking asylum, thus undermining fundamental norms and violating the principle of good faith.[336] The Strasbourg Court supports this proposition, holding that confinement in an international zone is acceptable only to enable States 'to prevent unlawful immigration while complying with their international obligations' particularly under the Refugee Convention and ECHR. 'States' legitimate concern to foil the increasingly frequent attempts to circumvent immigration restrictions must not deprive asylum-seekers of the protection afforded by these conventions'.[337] It follows that public order interests should not be accepted as legitimate where they prejudice other rights and obligations. This requires adjudicative bodies to refrain from simply invoking the State's right to control entry and instead challenge 'hidden' motives. Too often, States use the language of humanitarianism to justify externalisation and obstruct movement. The Strasbourg Court is, however, particularly hesitant to declare aims illegitimate.[338] The lawfulness of States obstructing departure to fulfil humanitarian duties to rescue people in distress at sea and combat people smuggling and trafficking is a central issue returned to in chapter six.

c. Public Health

The Covid-19 pandemic brought global attention to the critical importance of protecting public health. It resulted in enormous mobility issues as governments imposed restrictive immigration policies aimed at curbing its spread, while also weaponising public health fears to justify harsh measures targeting

[334] B Simma, 'From Bilateralism to Community Interest in International Law' (1994) 250 Recueil des Cours (Collected Courses of the Hague Academy of International Law) 217, 233–34.

[335] A Wolman, 'The Role of Departure States in Combating Irregular Emigration in International Law: An Historical Perspective' (2019) 31 *International Journal of Refugee Law* 30.

[336] See Weinzierl and Lisson (n 157) 68; E McDonnell, 'Externalisation as a Breach of the Good Faith Principle' (*Externalizing Asylum*, 2024) externalizingasylum.info/externalisation-as-a-breach-of-the-good-faith-principle/.

[337] *Amuur v France* (1996) 22 EHRR 533, para 43.

[338] Guild and Stoyanova (n 1) 388; Macklin (n 1) 910–15.

asylum seekers.[339] Most treaties enshrining the right to leave refer to 'public health' (ie, ICCPR, ACHR, African Charter), while Article 2(3) Protocol of the ECHR refers broadly to 'health'. Notably, 'public health' was not subject to controversy during the drafting of the ICCPR.[340] The International Health Regulations were adopted by the World Health Organisation (WHO) 'to prevent, protect against, control and provide a public health response to the international spread of disease in ways that are commensurate with and restricted to public health risks, and which avoid unnecessary interference with international traffic and trade'.[341] The Regulations further specify that health measures must be implemented with respect for human rights and fundamental freedoms.[342] Mubanga-Chipoya's Draft Declaration and the Siracusa Principles provide that public health may be invoked to address a 'serious threat to the health of the population or individual members of the population'.[343] Measures 'must be specifically aimed at preventing disease or injury or providing care for the sick and injured', and due regard must be paid to the International Health Regulations.[344] Accordingly, States can temporarily restrict departure to prevent the spread of disease or infection, provided the remaining right to leave requirements are satisfied. Public health covers the community at large.[345] This includes migrants whom the State is obliged to protect, ensuring their safety and wellbeing when they fall within its jurisdiction.

D. Consistency with Other Rights

Finally, restrictions on the right to leave must be consistent with other rights. Only Article 12(3) of the ICCPR incorporates this additional test; however, the requirement that restrictions be necessary '*in a democratic society*' included in the ECHR and ACHR can largely be considered the equivalent of the consistency requirement. It is difficult to see how a restriction otherwise satisfying the right to leave's limitations clause could be inconsistent with other rights.[346] Further, the jurisprudence of various adjudicative bodies suggests limitations on leaving should be consistent with other rights, including the right to seek asylum, prohibition of inhuman treatment, and obligation of

[339] See H Damon-Feng, 'Refoulement as Pandemic Policy' (2022) 31 *Washington International Law Journal* 186.

[340] Hannum (n 1) 41.

[341] International Health Regulations (adopted 23 May 2005, entered into force 14 June 2007) 2509 UNTS 79 (as amended) (IHR), art 2. See historically Mubanga-Chipoya (n 58) 55.

[342] IHR, arts 3(1), 32.

[343] Siracusa Principles, para 25; Draft Declaration, art 7(f); Nowak (n 14) 280.

[344] Siracusa Principles, paras 25–26.

[345] Daes (n 299) 127, 177.

[346] A Grahl-Madsen, *The Status of Refugees in International Law: Asylum, Entry and Sojourn*, vol 2 (Leiden, AW Sijthoff, 1972) 107; Lockwood, Finn and Jubinsky (n 314) 43; Hannum (n 1) 43–44.

non-discrimination. The Human Rights Committee has not clarified whether the consistency test involves a comprehensive assessment of the potential infringement of the other right or a less stringent one, where *prima facie* inconsistency is sufficient.[347]

The obligation of non-discrimination is particularly relevant here.[348] The UN Sub-Commission mandated both Inglés and Mubanga-Chipoya to study discrimination with respect to the right to leave and drew attention to discriminatory practices, including discrimination that may force people to leave to escape it.[349] At the time of these studies, exercising one's right to leave often depended on one's identity or sovereign affiliation.[350] As outlined above, the Human Rights Committee has stated there will be a clear violation of the right to leave if restrictions make distinctions of any kind based on a prohibited ground.[351] Thus, a measure satisfying all other requirements will nonetheless violate the right when applied or operating in a discriminatory manner, impairing the enjoyment or exercise of the right for particular individuals or groups on an equal footing.

Serious questions exist about whether externalisation measures comply with the right to leave and are consistent with the obligation of non-discrimination, especially on the basis of race, nationality, sex and migration status. Both the Inter-American Commission and the African Commission's guiding principles on the human rights of migrants emphasise the right of all migrants to equal treatment and the prohibition of discrimination of any type and on any ground, including their status.[352] Council of Europe Commissioners for Human Rights have repeatedly called for the right to leave to be applied without discrimination.[353]

Each UN treaty body explored in section III called for eliminating discriminatory migration control measures.[354] This work is dedicated to demonstrating how millions worldwide do not enjoy their right to leave or the opportunity to move equally or safely, depriving them of a range of other fundamental rights such as their right to life and freedom from inhuman treatment. As Inglés

[347] eg *Gonzalez del Rio* (n 99) para 5.3. See Nowak (n 14) 274 supporting the latter.

[348] See UNGA, 'Annotations on Draft' (n 14) para 54; HRC, 'General Comment No 15' (n 81) para 7; Guild (n 1) 37–40; Chetail, *International Migration Law* (n 1) 145–63.

[349] Inglés (n 2) 14–35; Mubanga-Chipoya (n 58) 27–33, 47.

[350] Cornelisse (n 1) 13; Kochenov (n 1) 61–62.

[351] HRC, 'General Comment No 27' (n 3) para 18. See also Nowak (n 14) 274; Zieck (n 1) 27–28.

[352] IACHR (n 179) principle 12; ACHPR (n 210) 12, principle 3.

[353] Guild (n 1); T Hammargberg, 'The Right to Leave One's Country Should Be Applied Without Discrimination' (Council of Europe Commissioner for Human Rights Comment, 22 November 2011) www.coe.int/en/web/commissioner/-/the-right-to-leave-one-s-country-should-be-applied-without-discriminati-1.

[354] See CMW and CRC, 'Joint General Comment No. 3 (2017) of the Committee on the Protection of the Rights of All Migrant Workers and Members of Their Families and No. 22 (2017) of the Committee on the Rights of the Child on the General Principles Regarding the Human Rights of Children in the context of International Migration' (16 November 2017) UN Doc CMW/C/GC/3-CRC/C/GC/22, paras 21–26.

declared, the right is indispensable to fully enjoying all other rights.[355] Ensuring the consistency of States' migration policies and laws with the right to leave is thus critical to promoting equality and non-discrimination for all people.

VI. CONCLUSION

This chapter affirms that the right to leave any country is well-established in international law and of fundamental importance. It is closely interlinked to the exercise of other fundamental rights, including to seek asylum, the right to life and family life, and is essential to advancing non-discrimination and equality regardless of one's identity or migration status. However, there has been a wax and wane of attention afforded to the right: it attracted international concern amidst severe restrictions on movement during World War II and the Cold War, only to fade as States adopted modern migration controls. Authoritarian regimes once sealed individuals within borders to prevent 'foot voting', drawing vocal opposition from Western States. Today, those very same States employ measures to obstruct the departure and arrival of migrants. Despite this shift, the right to leave remains largely overlooked, with its content and value underexplored and underdeveloped.

Nevertheless, there is broad convergence in international and regional jurisprudence across the Americas, Africa, Europe and beyond, helping to inform a general framework for the right's functioning and implementation. The right to leave protects everyone regardless of nationality or migration status, including refugees, asylum seekers, stateless people and 'irregular' migrants. Individuals have the right to leave any country, which must be secured by the State of departure and nationality if abroad, for a destination country of their choice. The jurisprudence supported the right to leave being independent of any right of entry elsewhere, although the legality of conditioning exit on admission elsewhere remains hotly contested. All States must refrain from unlawfully blocking departure from their territory and issue travel documents to their nationals abroad, confirming the right's applicability to States exercising extraterritorial jurisdiction, and confirming that both departure and destination States can infringe the right to leave. Nevertheless, much will depend on whether courts will adopt an expansive approach to jurisdiction to hold States responsible for externalisation measures such as pullbacks and carrier sanctions.

Finally, blanket, indefinite or automatic restrictions that ignore individual circumstances; those without a legal basis or lacking clarity, foreseeability and procedural safeguards; and measures inconsistent with other rights are incompatible with the right to leave. The Inter-American Commission champions the

[355] Inglés (n 2) 9–11, 65. See also HRC, 'General Comment No 27' (n 3) para 1.

right of asylum seekers to flee by any means, whereas the Strasbourg Court has ruled that intercepting migrant boats attempting to leave does not interfere with the right. Whether States can lawfully restrict departure to protect another State's immigration laws or interests remains unsettled. Anti-trafficking and smuggling efforts must nonetheless uphold all other rights and obligations. We must therefore interrogate States' asserted 'legitimate' aims to ensure they do not serve as pretexts for denying asylum or discriminating against migrants.

3

The State's Right to Control Entry and Obligations to Admit: The Relationship between Entry and Exit

I. INTRODUCTION

At the core of the right to leave is the principle that everyone is free to exit any State without unlawful restriction. Conversely, the general starting point is that States have the right to exclude non-nationals from their territory under international law. Individuals may, therefore, be able to leave a country but unable to find another one willing to admit them, stuck in limbo and unable to reach their destination or return home if at risk of serious harm. Accordingly, the right to leave is often viewed as 'incomplete' since its full realisation depends on securing a corresponding right to enter another country.

This chapter challenges the dominant view that States possess a nearly unfettered right to exclude non-nationals, which is often invoked to assert an incomplete right to leave and to deny exit. Scholars such as Goodwin-Gill and Nafziger have long contested traditional presumptions of an absolute sovereign prerogative to exclude or expel non-nationals.[1] Chetail has uncovered that the narrative of immigration control as an attribute of sovereignty is a myth and historically inaccurate. Historically, free movement and State sovereignty were not perceived as incompatible.[2] This chapter provides a much more comprehensive understanding of the right to leave and migrant trajectory, fleshing out

[1] GS Goodwin-Gill, *International Law and the Movement of Persons Between States* (Oxford, Clarendon Press, 1978); JAR Nafziger, 'The General Admission of Aliens under International Law' (1983) 77 *American Journal of International Law* 804. See also, A Shachar and J Ramji-Nogales (eds), 'Unsettling the Sovereign "Right to Exclude"' (2024) 118 *American Journal of International Law* 187.

[2] V Chetail, 'Sovereignty and Migration in the Doctrine of the Law of Nations: An Intellectual History of Hospitality from Vitoria to Vattel' (2016) 27 *European Journal of International Law* 901; V Chetail, 'Demystifying Sovereignty: Totem and Taboo of Migration Control in International Law' (2024) 118 *American Journal of International Law Unbound* 193.

the obligation on States to admit migrants in certain contexts and the complex relationship between entry and exit.

The chapter begins by exploring the State's prerogative to control entry, unpacking the exclusionary nature of international law and the inherent legitimacy afforded to migration control. It then discusses how the right to *seek* asylum generally does not equate to a right *to* asylum. Nonetheless, while there is no universal right to admission, certain categories of non-nationals enjoy a right of entry stemming from entitlements under international and regional treaties and customary international law. It demonstrates how the obligation of *non-refoulement* and prohibition on collective expulsion impose a procedural duty on States to admit migrants so migrants can access asylum procedures and exercise their right to an effective remedy before removal. The right to family life can also generate a positive obligation on a State to admit certain family members to its territory for family reunification, while regional free movement regimes provide a significant legal basis for non-nationals to secure entry and move freely within specific regions. The chapter then considers how 'safe country' concepts operate as an exception to the duty to grant asylum seekers entry to access asylum procedures. It concludes by exploring how exit and entry are distinct, albeit interrelated, rights and argues that the right to leave is an 'independent' – not incomplete – right, which cannot be restricted over doubts as to whether admission will be granted by the destination State.

II. THE RIGHT TO CONTROL ENTRY: EXCLUSION IN INTERNATIONAL LAW

It is well-established in international law that States have the right to control the admission of non-nationals onto their territory.[3] In 1892, the US Supreme Court in *Nishimura Ekiu* asserted,

> It is an accepted maxim of international law that every sovereign nation has the power, as inherent in sovereignty, and essential to self-preservation, to forbid the entrance of foreigners within its dominions, or to admit them only in such cases and upon such conditions as it may see fit to prescribe.[4]

State powers of immigration control have been deemed quintessential to State sovereignty. Hence, non-nationals have no general right to enter another State. Entry is reserved for nationals, who possess the right to return to and enter

[3] See eg L Oppenheim and H Lauterpacht, *International Law: A Treatise*, 8th edn (New York, Longmans, 1955) 692; Goodwin-Gill (n 1) 3–4, 51, 96, 160, 203; R Jennings and A Watts, *Oppenheim's International Law: Volume 1 Peace*, 9th edn (New York, Longman, 1992) 897–98, 901–02; S Sassen, *Losing Control? Sovereignty in an Age of Globalisation* (New York, Columbia University Press, 2015) ch 3.

[4] *Nishimura Ekiu v US* [1892] 142 US 651, 659.

their 'own country' (and this right often extends to long-term or permanent residents).[5] Border controls are therefore premised on belonging to a nation. Yet, already in 1983, Nafziger wrote about the trend of limited exclusion in State practice and how States have customarily admitted non-nationals unless there were legitimate reasons for exclusion in individual cases based on a serious danger to public safety, security, general welfare or essential institutions.[6] Admission was the norm, and exclusion the exception.

The right to exclude is now firmly ingrained in the jurisprudence. The Strasbourg Court declares that as a matter of well-established international law, States have the right to control the entry, residence and expulsion of aliens, *subject to their treaty obligations*.[7] Dembour has characterised the choice of the Court to begin with the State's right to exclude as the 'Strasbourg reversal' to 'stress the incongruous nature of a human rights reasoning which starts with a prerogative which neither serves to affirm human rights nor is inscribed in the text'.[8] As Costello has argued, a 'statist assumption' exists where States appear to have the right to exclude without justification, a strange notion in an era of human rights.[9] And in many ways, 'States have not relinquished sovereign territorial prerogative – they have employed international law to enhance rather than to impede it'.[10] Sovereignty has endowed racial discrimination with an air of legitimacy, allowing discriminatory policies and practices to be justified as objective and facially-neutral.[11] As Chimni argues, 'International law is playing a crucial role in helping legitimise and sustain the unequal structures and processes that manifest themselves in the growing north-south divide'.[12]

[5] ICCPR, art 12(4); HRC, 'General Comment No 27: Article 12 (Freedom of Movement)' (2 November 1999) UN Doc CCPR/C/21/Rev.1/Add.9, para 20: 'own country' denotes 'special ties to or claims in relation to a given country'. cf *Stewart v Canada*, Communication No 538/1993 (1 November 1996) UN Doc CCPR/C/58/D/538/1993, paras 12.4–12.9; *Nystrom v Australia*, Communication No 1557/2007 (18 July 2011) UN Doc CCPR/C/102/D/1557/2007, paras 7.4–7.5.

[6] Nafziger (n 1) 804–05, 832.

[7] *Abdulaziz, Cabales and Balkandali v UK* (1985) 7 EHRR 471, para 67; *Moustaquim v Belgium* (1991) 13 EHRR 802, para 43; *Vilvarajah v UK* (1991) 14 EHRR 248, para 102; *Amuur v France* (1996) 22 EHRR 533, para 41; *Boujlifa v France* (1997) 25 EHRR 686, para 42; *Hirsi Jamaa v Italy* (2012) 55 EHRR 21, para 113. See also *Samuel Lichtensztejn v Uruguay*, Communication No 77/1980 (31 March 1983) UN Doc CCPR/C/OP/2, para 8.3; *Carlos Varela Núñez v Uruguay*, Communication No 108/1981 (22 July 1983) UN Doc A/38/40, para 9.3; *R v Immigration Officer at Prague Airport, ex p European Roma Rights Centre* [2004] UKHL 55, [2005] 2 AC 1, paras 15, 19.

[8] MB Dembour, *When Humans Become Migrants: Study of the European Court of Human Rights with an Inter-American Counterpoint* (Oxford, OUP, 2015) 4, 507.

[9] C Costello, *The Human Rights of Migrants and Refugees in European Law* (Oxford, OUP, 2016) 10.

[10] C Thomas, 'What Does the Emerging International Law of Migration Mean for Sovereignty' (2013) 14 *Melbourne Journal of International Law* 392, 432.

[11] See ET Achiume, 'Racial Borders' (2022) 110 *The Georgetown Law Journal* 445, 458–59, 488–94.

[12] BS Chimni, 'Third World Approaches to International Law: A Manifesto' (2006) 8 *International Community Law Review* 3, 3.

Against this backdrop, the right to leave is characterised as incomplete.[13] Individuals have the right to leave any country, but this does not correspond with a right to enter. This asymmetry reflects an in-built limitation to how human rights law treats migration control, and demonstrating that a State has violated one's right to leave will not guarantee entry elsewhere.[14] Notwithstanding, as the proceeding sections demonstrate, the State's prerogative is constrained by its international obligations. As Chetail has powerfully articulated, sovereignty should be understood as a relative notion and not an absolute power, allowing migration control to be 'decoupled from sovereignty as a basic tenet of international law'.[15]

III. A RIGHT TO RECEIVE ASYLUM OR ONLY TO SEEK IT?

The apparent tension between the right to leave and the right to control entry begs the question of whether people fleeing to seek asylum possess a right to enter as an exception to the State's migration control prerogative. Answering this first involves determining whether a right to asylum exists.

The concept of 'asylum' has been conceived in differing ways, referring to the traditional right of the *State* to grant asylum, the right of the *individual* to *seek* asylum, and the *individual's* right to be *granted* asylum.[16] Asylum in the first sense is a discretionary right belonging to the State, allowing it to grant protection within its territory or diplomatic premises to individuals seeking refuge.[17] Traditionally, asylum involved admission to residence and lasting protection against persecution and the jurisdiction of another State.[18] Today, however, asylum is generally understood as constituting the broad institution of protection against a violation of fundamental rights, not only the narrow sense of a durable or permanent solution.[19]

[13] M Paz, 'The Incomplete Right to Freedom of Movement' (2017) 111 *American Journal of International Law* 514; GS Goodwin-Gill and J McAdam, *The Refugee in International Law,* 4th edn (Oxford, OUP, 2021) 430–31.

[14] C Harvey and RP Barnidge, 'Human Rights, Free Movement, and the Right to Leave in International Law' (2007) 19 *International Journal of Refugee Law* 1, 20; C Costello and I Mann, 'Border Justice: Migration and Accountability for Human Rights Violations' (2020) 21 *German Law Journal* 311, 313.

[15] Chetail, 'Demystifying Sovereignty' (n 2) 197.

[16] A Grahl-Madsen, *Territorial Asylum* (Stockholm, Almqvist & Wiksell International, 1980) 2; R Boed, 'The State of the Right of Asylum in International Law' (1994) 5 *Duke Journal of Comparative & International Law* 1, 2–16; A Grahl-Madsen, 'The Case for a Uniform Aliens Law in Western Europe' in P Macalister-Smith and G Alfredsson (eds), *The Land Beyond: Collected Essays on Refugee Law and Policy* (The Hague, Martinus Nijhoff, 2001) 69.

[17] Institute of International Law, 'Asylum in Public International Law' (5th Commission, Resolutions Adopted at its Bath Session, September 1950) arts 1–3; A Grahl-Madsen, *The Status of Refugees in International Law: Asylum, Entry and Sojourn*, vol 2 (Leiden, AW Sijthoff, 1972) 285.

[18] Goodwin-Gill and McAdam (n 13) 400–15.

[19] ibid 298–300, 401–03. See also MT Gil-Bazo, 'Asylum as a General Principle of International Law' (2015) 27 *International Journal of Refugee Law* 3, 3–4; GS Goodwin-Gill, '*Non-Refoulement*,

Asylum as a right of the individual was proclaimed in Article 14(1) of the UDHR, which guarantees the 'right to seek and to enjoy in other countries asylum from persecution'. The initial draft referred to the right 'to be granted' asylum, but this was replaced by 'to enjoy' after Australia, Saudi Arabia and the UK opposed any text obliging States to grant asylum.[20] Grahl-Madsen considered Article 14(1)'s final formulation to be no more than a moral obligation, not going much further than the right to leave in Article 13(2).[21] Similarly, Lauterpacht questioned whether States even intended to assume a moral obligation as Article 14(1) was 'artificial to the point of flippancy'.[22] In 1967, the UN General Assembly adopted the Declaration on Territorial Asylum, with the principle of *non-refoulement* at its core.[23] The Declaration placed only a moral duty on States not to reject asylum seekers at the frontier and stated: 'It shall rest with the State granting asylum to evaluate the grounds for the grant of asylum'.[24] This reflects the continued reluctance of States to accept a right of individuals to be granted asylum. The ICCPR and ECHR are silent on asylum altogether. As Haddad puts it, 'The right to flee the source of persecution is acknowledged, while the right to offer protection from the persecution remains a state prerogative' with the refugee bringing to the forefront 'the clash between sovereign rights and human rights'.[25] Accordingly, it is generally accepted that States do not have an obligation to grant asylum and individuals do not have a right to receive it, only to seek it.[26]

Over time, regional human rights treaties in the Americas, Africa and the EU have recognised the right to seek and *receive* asylum. The 1969 ACHR recognised the right of the individual 'to seek and be granted asylum in a foreign territory, in accordance with the legislation of the state and international conventions', as was earlier enshrined in the ADHR.[27] Although the ADHR and ACHR specify that asylum is to be granted in accordance with domestic law, both the Inter-American Commission and Court have affirmed that these provisions amount to an obligation to grant asylum to any person who objectively satisfies the refugee definition or qualifies for protection from *refoulement*

Temporary Refuge, and the "New" Asylum Seekers' in DJ Cantor and JF Durieux (eds), *Refuge from Inhumanity? War Refugees and International Humanitarian Law* (Leiden, Brill Nijhoff, 2014).

[20] P Weis, 'The Right of Asylum in the Context of the Protection of Human Rights in Regional and Municipal Law' (1966) 6 *International Review of the Red Cross* 470; Boed (n 16) 9–11.

[21] Grahl-Madsen, *Status of Refugees* (n 17) 101–02, 196.

[22] H Lauterpacht, *International Law and Human Rights* (London, Stevens & Sons, 1950) 421–22.

[23] Declaration on Territorial Asylum (adopted 14 December 1967, UNGA Res 2312 (XXII)).

[24] ibid arts 1(3), 3(1).

[25] E Haddad, *The Refugee in International Society: Between Sovereigns* (Cambridge, CUP, 2008) 95.

[26] See eg *Minister for Immigration and Multicultural Affairs v Khawar* (2002) 210 CLR 1, para 42; Grahl-Madsen, 'Uniform Aliens Law' (n 16) 69; E Lauterpacht and D Bethlehem, 'The Scope and Content of the Principle of *Non-Refoulement*: Opinion' in E Feller, V Türk and F Nicholson (eds), *Refugee Protection in International Law: UNHCR's Global Consultations on International Protection* (Cambridge, CUP, 2003) 112–13; S Behrman, 'Refugee Law as a Means of Control' (2019) 32 *Journal of Refugee Studies* 42 43–44; Goodwin-Gill and McAdam (n 13) ch 8.

[27] ADHR, art XXVII; ACHR, art 22(7).

under international law. It is not a matter of State discretion, as refugee status 'is recognised by the state rather than conferred by it'.[28] Similarly, the African Charter provides that 'Every individual shall have the right, when persecuted, to seek and obtain asylum in other countries in accordance with the law of those countries and international conventions' – an obligation reflected in the open-door refugee policy of some African States.[29] Article 18 of the EU Charter of Fundamental Rights also guarantees a right to asylum:

> The right to asylum shall be guaranteed with due respect for the rules of the Geneva Convention of 28 July 1951 and the Protocol of 31 January 1967 relating to the status of refugees and in accordance with the Treaty on European Union and the Treaty on the Functioning of the European Union.

Although some scholars argue that Article 18 only restates the generally accepted right to seek asylum,[30] most scholars conclude it does establish a right to be granted asylum when the criteria are met.[31]

Regional recognition of a right to asylum and State practice has led some scholars to assert the existence of a right to asylum as a general principle of international law or as customary international law.[32] Nevertheless, while asylum seekers do not have the right to be granted asylum, they do have the right to seek it. Although the Refugee Convention does not enshrine a right to asylum, the right to seek asylum is implicit, for the very existence of refugees depends on it.[33] As chapter four explores, denial of the right to seek asylum can frustrate the object and purpose of the Convention because if people cannot seek asylum, they cannot receive refugee status.

[28] IACHR, 'Report on the Situation of Human Rights of Asylum-Seekers within the Canadian Refugee Determination System' (2000) OEA/Ser.L/V/II.106/Doc 40 Rev, paras 60, 70; IACHR, 'Report on Terrorism and Human Rights' (2002) OEA/Ser.L/V/II.116 Doc 5 Rev 1 corr, paras 394, 405; *Pacheco Tineo Family v Bolivia*, IACtHR, Series C No 272 (25 November 2013) paras 139–40, 151, 153–55; *Advisory Opinion on the Institution of Asylum and its Recognition as a Human Right in the Inter-American System of Protection*, IACtHR, OC-25/18 (30 May 2018) paras 123, 131–32 but cf on diplomatic asylum, paras 155–56, 163. See Cantor and Durieux (n 19).

[29] Art 12(3). See also Arab Charter, art 28; D Drewski and J Gerhards, *Pan-African Solidarity and International Reputation: Uganda's Policy of Open Doors Toward Refugees* (Oxford, OUP, 2024) ch 7.

[30] See H Battjes, *European Asylum Law and International Law* (Leiden, Martinus Nijhoff, 2006) 113–14; Goodwin-Gill and McAdam (n 13) 413–15; K Hailbronner, 'Introduction into the EU Immigration and Asylum Law' in K Hailbronner (ed), *EU Immigration and Asylum Law: Commentary* (Munich, CH Beck, 2010) 19–20; Behrman (n 26) 44.

[31] See eg MT Gil-Bazo, 'The Charter of Fundamental Rights of the European Union and the Right to be Granted Asylum in the Union's Law' (2008) 27 *Refugee Survey Quarterly* 33; M den Heijer, 'Article 18 – Right to Asylum' in S Peers and others (eds), *The EU Charter of Fundamental Rights: A Commentary* (Oxford, Hart Publishing, 2014) 530–31; SF Nicolosi, 'Going Unnoticed? Diagnosing the Right to Asylum in the Charter of Fundamental Rights of the European Union' (2017) 23 *European Law Journal* 94; Costello, *Human Rights* (n 9); M Moraru, 'The EU Fundamental Right to Asylum: In Search of Its Legal Meaning and Effects' in S Iglesias Sánchez and M González Pascual (eds), *Fundamental Rights in the EU Area of Freedom, Security and Justice* (Cambridge, CUP, 2021).

[32] Gil-Bazo, 'Asylum' (n 19) 17, 28.

[33] A Edwards, 'Human Rights, Refugees, and the Right "to Enjoy" Asylum' (2005) 17 *International Journal of Refugee Law* 293, 296, 301; Goodwin-Gill and McAdam (n 13) ch 8 fn 53.

Article 14 of the UDHR has been described as an empty right because individuals have the right to leave and seek asylum but there is no corresponding duty upon a State to admit them.[34] However, as the next section demonstrates, there are various circumstances in which migrants enjoy a right of entry, including to apply for asylum and access asylum procedures.

IV. STATE DUTIES TO ADMIT TO TERRITORY

The traditionally broad competence of States to control their borders and evaluate the grounds for asylum is today necessarily constrained by the protections afforded to individuals under international human rights, refugee law and custom, as well as free movement regimes.[35] In 2018, 164 UN Member States adopted the Global Compact for Migration, the first inter-governmental agreement on a common approach to international migration, which 'reaffirms the sovereign right of States to determine their national migration policy … in conformity with international law'.[36] In 1986, the Human Rights Committee specified that while the ICCPR does not recognise the right of aliens to enter or reside in the territory of a State party, in certain circumstances, an alien may enjoy protection in relation to entry or residence when considerations of non-discrimination, inhuman treatment and respect for family life arise.[37] This section demonstrates that while there is no universal right of asylum, a right of temporary entry stems from the obligation of *non-refoulement* and prohibition on collective expulsion to allow individuals access to asylum procedures and procedural safeguards prior to any removal. Migrants may also enjoy a right of entry stemming from the right to family reunification and regional free movement regimes.

A. Obligations of *Non-refoulement*

On its widest meaning, the obligation of *non-refoulement* stipulates that no person shall be returned, extradited or expelled by a State to any place where

[34] See S Kneebone, *Refugees, Asylum Seekers and the Rule of Law: Comparative Perspectives* (Cambridge, CUP, 2009) 10.

[35] Goodwin-Gill, *International Law* (n 1) 3–4, 21–23, 136-47, 160–96, 204–05; LB Sohn and T Buergenthal, *The Movement of Persons Across Borders* (Washington DC, American Society of International Law, 1992) 1, 49, 52.

[36] UNGA, 'Global Compact for Safe, Orderly and Regular Migration' (11 January 2019) UN Doc A/RES/73/195, paras 7, 11, 15(c); V Chetail, 'The Global Compact for Safe, Orderly and Regular Migration: A Kaleidoscope of International Law' (2020) 16 *International Journal of Law in Context* 253, 254–55; F Capone, 'The Alleged Tension between the Global Compact for Safe, Orderly and Regular Migration and State Sovereignty: "Much Ado about Nothing"?' (2020) 33 *Leiden Journal of International Law* 713.

[37] HRC, 'General Comment No 15: The Position of Aliens Under the Covenant' (11 April 1986) UN Doc CCPR/A/41/40, para 5.

they are likely to face persecution, torture, inhuman, degrading treatment or punishment, or other serious harms.[38] Under Article 33 of the Refugee Convention, refugees are guaranteed protection from being returned 'in any manner whatsoever to the frontiers of territories where his life or freedom would be threatened on account of his race, religion, nationality, membership of a particular social group or political opinion', subject to narrowly defined exceptions. Article 33 is recognised as extending to asylum seekers and not only people formally recognised as refugees.[39] It also covers protection from direct and indirect *refoulement*,[40] and is widely accepted to encompass rejection at the frontier.[41]

The principle of *non-refoulement* now extends well beyond the Refugee Convention, being complemented by *non-refoulement* obligations under international human rights law and generally considered a norm of customary international law.[42] Therefore, even if a person is not facing persecution within the meaning of the Refugee Convention, their removal or return may still be precluded when at risk of other serious harms as a beneficiary of complementary protection.[43] *Refoulement* to 'another State where there are substantial grounds for believing that he would be in danger of being subjected to torture' is explicitly proscribed by Article 3 of CAT,[44] and implicitly proscribed for torture, inhuman or degrading treatment or punishment under Article 7 of the ICCPR.[45]

[38] Goodwin-Gill and McAdam (n 13) 241, ch 7.

[39] EXCOM, 'No 6 (XXVIII) Non-Refoulement' (1977) UN Doc A/32/12/Add.1, (c); Lauterpacht and Bethlehem (n 26) paras 89–99; JC Hathaway, *The Rights of Refugees under International Law* (Cambridge, CUP, 2005) 158–60, 303–04; Goodwin-Gill and McAdam (n 13) 265–66.

[40] UNHCR, 'Note on the Principle of Non-Refoulement' (November 1997); Lauterpacht and Bethlehem (n 26) para 121. In human rights treaties, see eg *TI v UK*, App no 43844/98 (ECtHR, 7 March 2000) 14; *Hirsi Jamaa* (n 7) para 147; CAT, 'General Comment No 4 (2017) on the Implementation of Article 3 of the Convention in the Context of Article 22' (4 September 2018) UN Doc CAT/C/GC/4, para 12.

[41] EXCOM, 'No. 22 (XXXII) Protection of Asylum-Seekers in Situations of Large-Scale Influx' (1981) UN Doc A/36/12/Add.1, sect II; EXCOM, 'No. 99 (LV) General Conclusion on International Protection' (2004) UN Doc A/AC.96/1003, (l). See also Lauterpacht and Bethlehem (n 26) paras 76–86; Hathaway (n 39) 315–17; G Noll, 'Seeking Asylum at Embassies: A Right to Entry under International Law?' (2005) 17 *International Journal of Refugee Law* 542, 549; Goodwin-Gill and McAdam (n 13) 245–48.

[42] See eg GS Goodwin-Gill, *The Refugee in International Law*, 2nd edn (Oxford, Clarendon Press, 1996) 66–79, 167–71; J Allain, 'The *Jus Cogens* Nature of *Non-refoulement*' (2001) 13 *International Journal of Refugee Law* 533, 538; Lauterpacht and Bethlehem (n 26) paras 193–253; C Costello and M Foster, 'Non-refoulement as Custom and *Jus Cogens*? Putting the Prohibition to the Test' in M den Heijer and H van der Wilt (eds), *NYIL 2015: Jus Cogens: Quo Vadis?* (The Hague, TMC Asser Press, 2016) 282–306; Goodwin-Gill and McAdam (n 13) 300–06. cf Hathaway (n 39) 363–67.

[43] J McAdam, *Complementary Protection in International Refugee Law* (Oxford, OUP, 2007).

[44] Convention against Torture and Other Cruel, Inhuman or Degrading Treatment or Punishment (adopted 10 December 1984, entered into force on 26 June 1987) 1465 UNTS 85 (UNCAT).

[45] See HRC, 'General Comment No 20: Article 7 (Prohibition of Torture, or Other Cruel, Inhuman or Degrading Treatment or Punishment)' (10 March 1992) UN Doc HRI/GEN/1/Rev.1 at 30, para 9; HRC, 'General Comment No 31: The Nature of the General Legal Obligation imposed on States Parties' (26 May 2004) UN Doc CCPR/C/21/Rev.1/Add.13, para 12.

Regional instruments also prohibit *refoulement*.[46] This means that States must not return any person to a country where they would face a real risk of arbitrary deprivation of life, torture or other forms of ill-treatment, and even egregious breaches of the right to a fair trial.[47] *Non-refoulement* under human rights law is absolute and may never be permissibly limited, representing the principal source of protection beyond Convention grounds.

To fulfil their protective duty, States are obliged to assess the risk of harm of returning someone to a third country and examine their protection claim, which has significant implications for admission to the territory of a potential State of refuge. Neither the UDHR nor the Refugee Convention expressly require entry so individuals can claim asylum.[48] Nonetheless, the UNHCR, its Executive Committee and scholars conclude that the obligation of *non-refoulement*, underpinned by the right to seek asylum, imposes a *procedural duty* on States to grant individuals at least temporary entry to access asylum procedures.[49] Although not amounting to a general right of entry, non-rejection at the border can be interpreted as amounting to a procedural duty on States to admit individuals pending status determination.[50] As Edwards notes, it would be nonsensical in light of the Refugee Convention if entry was not intended at least for status determination, especially where that person has reached State territory. The right to apply for asylum and access asylum procedures is an implied right under the Convention because without it *refoulement* might occur.[51]

[46] *Soering v UK* (1989) 11 EHRR 439, paras 86–87. The prohibition extends to all forms of art 3 ill-treatment: *Chahal v UK* (1996) 23 EHRR 413, paras 74, 79–80 and all types of removal: *Cruz Varas v Sweden* (1991) 14 EHRR 1, para 70; *Vilvarajah* (n 7) paras 73–74, 79–81; OAU Convention, art II(3); ACHR, art 22(8); Cartagena Declaration, conclusion III(5); African Charter, art 12(4); Bangkok Principles, art III; EUCFR, art 19(2). For ADHR: *The Haitian Centre for Human Rights v US*, IACHR, Case 10.675 Report No 51/96 (13 March 1997) OEA/Ser.L/V/II.95 Doc 7 Rev at 550, paras 164–71.

[47] For an extensive analysis see C Costello, 'The Search for the Outer Edges of *Non-refoulement* in Europe: Exceptionality and Flagrant Breaches' in B Burson and DJ Cantor (eds), *Human Rights and the Refugee Definition: Comparative Legal Practice and Theory* (Leiden, Brill Nijhoff, 2016). See on climate change and the right to life *Teitiota v New Zealand*, Communication No 2728/2016 (24 October 2019) UN Doc CCPR/C/127/D/2728/2016, para 9.11.

[48] C Dauvergne, 'Sovereignty, Migration and the Rule of Law in Global Times' (2004) 67 *Modern Law Review* 588, 601; K Ogg, 'Protection Closer to Home? A Legal Case for Claiming Asylum at Embassies and Consulates' (2014) 33 *Refugee Survey Quarterly* 81, 84.

[49] EXCOM, 'No. 85 (XLIX) Conclusion on International Protection' (1998) A/53/12/Add.1, (q); UNHCR, 'Background Note on the Protection of Asylum-Seekers and Refugees Rescued at Sea' (Geneva, 2002), para 25; Grahl-Madsen, *Status of Refugees* (n 17) 11; Edwards (n 33) 301; Hathaway (n 39) 301; R Weinzierl and U Lisson, *Border Management and Human Rights: A Study of EU Law and the Law of the Sea* (Berlin, German Institute for Human Rights, 2007) 15; V Stoyanova, 'The Principle of *Non-Refoulement* and the Right of Asylum-Seekers to Enter State Territory' (2008) 3 *Interdisciplinary Journal of Human Rights Law* 1, 4–6; AL Hirsch and N Bell, 'The Right to Have Rights as a Right to Enter: Addressing a Lacuna in the International Refugee Protection Regime' (2017) 18 *Human Rights Review* 417, 427–28; Goodwin-Gill and McAdam (n 13) 254, 404, 428–32.

[50] Goodwin-Gill and McAdam (n 13) 254.

[51] Edwards (n 33) 301–02.

However, as discussed in section IV.E, returning or transferring asylum seekers to a safe third country may be lawful.

In contrast, Noll and Gammeltoft-Hansen argue that neither in theory nor in practice do *non-refoulement* obligations amount to a right of admission.[52] According to Noll, 'neither a homogeneous State practice nor a corresponding *opinio juris* can be made out to support a right to access territory in order to seek asylum'.[53] '*Non-refoulement* is about being admitted to the state community, although in a minimalist form of non-removal' being no more than a right to 'transgress an administrative border', something quite different from transgressing the territorial border.[54] Noll's arguments were made over twenty years ago and are largely based on customary international law, despite support for the right to temporary admission being predominantly based on treaty (while also setting a rather high standard for State practice). Gammeltoft-Hansen posits that the fact States grant admission to instigate asylum procedures does not equal a *right* to admission.[55] It was envisioned that where a State is unwilling to grant admission or asylum, they must adopt a course of action that does not amount to *refoulement* or collective expulsion, such as safe third country policies or extraterritorial asylum processing.[56] This, he concludes, reveals a space 'between the negative responsibility not to return a refugee to persecution and positive obligation of allowing entry'.[57]

However, admission to territory is usually the only way to prevent exposure to risk.[58] Securing an individual's right to seek asylum and ascertaining whether they face risk on return is *near* impossible without conducting a fair and effective asylum procedure where the individual can present their case. As the UK House of Lords held in the *Roma Rights* case,

> There would appear to be general acceptance of the principle that a person who leaves the state of his nationality and applies to the authorities of another state for asylum, whether at the frontier of the second state or from within it, should not be rejected or returned to the first state without appropriate enquiry into the persecution of which he claims to have a well-founded fear.[59]

[52] G Noll, *Negotiating Asylum: The EU Acquis, Extraterritorial Protection and the Common Market of Deflection* (The Hague, Martinus Nijhoff, 2000) 387; T Gammeltoft-Hansen, *Access to Asylum: International Refugee Law and the Globalisation of Migration Control* (Cambridge, CUP, 2011) 63–64.

[53] Noll, 'Seeking Asylum' (n 41) 547.

[54] ibid 548.

[55] Gammeltoft-Hansen (n 52) 64.

[56] ibid. See also Lauterpacht and Bethlehem (n 26) para 76.

[57] Gammeltoft-Hansen (n 52) 64.

[58] Hathaway (n 39) 300–01; Stoyanova (n 49) 4–6; V Chetail, 'The Transnational Movement of Persons Under General International Law: Mapping the Customary Law Foundations of International Migration Law' in V Chetail and C Bauloz (eds), *Research Handbook on International Law and Migration* (Cheltenham, Edward Elgar Publishing, 2014) 40.

[59] *Roma Rights* (n 7) para 26.

Discharging the obligation of *non-refoulement* and ensuring individuals can access an effective remedy before any removal requires minimum procedural safeguards to be in place. Adjudicative bodies have established several fundamental safeguards that must be met before an asylum seeker can be returned or expelled to another country. As the Strasbourg Court held in *MK v Poland*, States cannot deny access to their territory to a person presenting themselves at the border who alleges they would face a risk of ill-treatment if forced to remain in the neighbouring State.[60] In such situations, the State is obliged to allow the individual to remain within the State's jurisdiction pending examination of their asylum claim and assess the risk of any ill-treatment prior to sending them back to a third country.[61] The Court has made clear in various pushback cases that individuals are entitled to have their claims examined on the merits, ensuring 'sufficient information to enable them to gain effective access to the relevant procedures and to substantiate their complaints', 'close scrutiny by a national authority, independent and rigorous scrutiny of any claim', and the right of appeal before an independent, impartial body.[62] Legal remedies must be accessible in practice and have suspensive effect, enabling applicants who have been denied entry or had their asylum claim rejected to stay in the territory pending decision on the appeal.[63] Such obligations apply even in transit and international zones at land borders or airports, making any distinction between the administrative and physical border a legal fiction.[64] Additionally, asylum seekers need to be given access to a lawyer and interpreters, protection from unlawful detention, and a reasoned decision in writing from trained asylum experts (not border or coastguard officials).[65] While the case law does not explicitly provide that migrants intercepted at sea or before

[60] *MK v Poland*, Apps nos 40503/17, 42902/17 and 43643/17 (ECtHR, 23 July 2020) para 179.

[61] ibid para 178. See also *Sherov v Poland*, Apps nos 54029/17 and 3 others (ECtHR, 4 April 2024).

[62] *MSS v Belgium and Greece* (2011) 53 EHRR 2, para 293, 387; *Hirsi Jamaa* (n 7) paras 198, 201–05, 72 (Separate Opinion Albuquerque J); *Kebe v Ukraine*, App no 12552/12 (ECtHR, 12 January 2017) paras 100, 107; *AEA v Greece*, App no 39034/12 (ECtHR, 15 March 2018) paras 69–79. See also *Pacheco Tineo* (n 28) paras 152–53, 159; UNHCR, 'Global Consultations on International Protection/ Third Track: Asylum Processes (Fair and Efficient Asylum Procedures)' (31 May 2001) UN Doc EC/GC/01/12, para 43; CAT, 'General Comment No 4' (n 40) para 13; *MA and ZR v Cyprus*, App no 39090/20 (ECtHR, 8 October 2024) paras 82–96.

[63] See *MSS* (n 62) paras 293, 301–18; *Hirsi Jamaa* (n 7) para 200; *Sharifi v Italy and Greece*, App no 16643/09 (ECtHR, 21 October 2014) para 167; Weinzierl and Lisson (n 49) 16, 50–54; *Ilias and Ahmed v Hungary*, App no 47287/15 (ECtHR, 21 November 2019); *DA v Poland*, App no 51246/1 (ECtHR, 8 July 2021) paras 38–40.

[64] See *Amuur* (n 7) paras 43, 52–54; *Ilias* (n 63) paras 63, 213, 215; *ZA v Russia*, App nos 61411/15 and 3 others (ECtHR, 21 November 2019), paras 156, 164–71; *RR v Hungary*, App no 36037/17 (ECtHR, 2 March 2021).

[65] *Amuur* (n 7) para 43; *MSS* (n 62) para 301; *Sharifi* (n 63) paras 175–78; UNHCR, 'Global Consultations' (n 62) para 43; UNHCR, 'Maritime Interception Operations and the Processing of International Protection Claims: Legal Standards and Policy Considerations with Respect to Extraterritorial Processing' (Division of International Protection Geneva, 2010) para 58. See A Dastyari and D Ghezelbash, 'Asylum at Sea: The Legality of Shipboard Refugee Status Determination Procedures' (2020) 32 *International Journal of Refugee Law* 1, 8–16.

approaching the border are to be brought to the State's territory, the UNHCR and numerous scholars have concluded that providing fair and effective asylum procedures extraterritorially is difficult, if not impossible, particularly onboard maritime vessels.[66] Nevertheless, it remains possible to lawfully conduct other extraterritorial arrangements, as evidenced by resettlement, visa processing, and embassy procedures.[67]

Accordingly, the procedural limb of *non-refoulement* should be understood as amounting to a de facto right of entry to State territory to access asylum procedures under both the Refugee Convention and human rights treaties.[68] This must be observed wherever the State exercises jurisdiction.[69] Where individuals have reached the frontier or come within the State's effective control after exercising their right to leave and seek asylum, entry should be granted, save in exceptional circumstances (ie, the use of safe country mechanisms). Article 31 of the Refugee Convention prohibits penalising refugees and asylum seekers for 'illegal entry or presence', in recognition that the reality of refugee flight may lead people to resort to irregular journeys.[70] As Goodwin-Gill and McAdam argue, Article 31 supports the right to temporary admission and due process read alongside the obligation of *non-refoulement* and the right to leave and seek asylum.[71]

The normative weight of the principle of *non-refoulement* – widely regarded as the cornerstone of refugee protection – therefore mitigates against the general absence of a right to asylum and right of entry. Nevertheless, as Hathaway observes, *non-refoulement* under Article 33 of the Refugee Convention only obliges States not to return individuals to a place where they will face persecution, following admission to avoid exposure to risk, and not to receive refugees.[72] *Non-refoulement* acts as a 'trump card' to the State's prerogative but does not call into question its right to regulate admission.[73] Furthermore, because entry

[66] UNHCR, 'Maritime Interception' (n 65) paras 55–59; Hirsch and Bell (n 49) 428; Dastyari and Ghezelbash (n 65) 25–26. See also ch 6.

[67] See *R (Bashir) v Secretary of State for the Home Department* [2018] UKSC 45, [2019] AC 484, paras 73–89 on entry to *metropolitan territory from* dependent territories.

[68] Supported by Grahl-Madsen, *Status of Refugees* (n 17) 11; Hathaway (n 39) 301; Hirsch and Bell (n 49) 427.

[69] On the extraterritorial nature of non-refoulement, *Haitian Centre* (n 46) paras 156–57, 171; *Hirsi Jamaa* (n 7) paras 74, 81; HRC, 'General Comment No 31' (n 45) para 10; Lauterpacht and Bethlehem (n 26) paras 62–67; Hathaway (n 39) 169, 339; Goodwin-Gill and McAdam (n 13) 307–28. cf *Sale v Haitian Centres Council* 509 US 155 (1993); Noll 'Seeking Asylum' (n 41) 55. But note evolution: US Department of State, 'Fourth Periodic Report of the United States of America to the United Nations Committee on Human Rights Concerning the ICCPR' (30 December 2011) UN Doc CCPR/C/USA/4, paras 504–05.

[70] C Costello, Y Ioffe and T Büchsel, 'Article 31 of the 1951 Convention Relating to the Status of Refugees' (Legal and Protection Policy Research Series, UNHCR, 2017) 14–23, 30–32.

[71] Goodwin-Gill and McAdam (n 13) 432. See also Hirsch and Bell (n 49) 429.

[72] Hathaway (n 39) 300–01.

[73] Allain (n 42) 557–58; ibid; Gammeltoft-Hansen (n 52) 14; Costello and Foster (n 42) 306–10. See also *Roma Rights* (n 7) para 19.

under *non-refoulement* obligations stems entirely from risk, individuals could be returned if that risk dissipates.[74]

B. The Prohibition on Collective Expulsion

The conclusion that States have a procedural obligation to grant individuals entry while they assess *refoulement* risks can also be reached for the prohibition on the collective or mass expulsions of aliens enshrined in Article 4 Protocol 4 of the ECHR, Article 22(9) of the ACHR, Article 12(5) of the African Charter, and other regional treaties.[75] While neither the ICCPR nor CAT explicitly prohibit collective expulsion, their respective Committees have found the prohibition is implied.[76] Collective expulsion is defined as:

> [A]ny measure of the competent authority compelling aliens as a group to leave the country, except where such a measure is taken after and on the basis of a reasonable and objective examination of the particular cases of each individual alien of the group.[77]

Article 12(5) of the African Charter further defines mass expulsions as being aimed at national, racial, ethnic or religious groups. In contrast to *non-refoulement* – the removal of a single alien to a place of risk – collective expulsion involves the indiscriminate removal of a group of aliens.[78] It applies irrespective of whether the non-nationals are lawfully present or not. The purpose of the prohibition is to 'prevent States from being able to remove certain aliens without examining their personal circumstances and, consequently, without enabling them to put forward their arguments against the measure'.[79] Accordingly, it mandates a procedural duty to examine all relevant individual circumstances, including *refoulement* risks.

In the groundbreaking case of *Hirsi Jamaa v Italy*, the Strasbourg Court found Italy, in intercepting Somali and Eritrean migrants on the high seas and

[74] Grahl-Madsen, 'Uniform Aliens Law' (n 16) 58, 69; Hathaway (n 39) 302; A Nollkaemper and others, *The Practice of Shared Responsibility in International Law* (Cambridge, CUP, 2017) 492–93. See also JF Durieux, 'Three Asylum Paradigms' (2013) 20 *International Journal on Minority and Group Rights* 147, 155–56.

[75] African Charter, art 12(5); CIS Convention, art 25(4); EUCFR, art 19(1); Arab Charter, art 26(2).

[76] HRC, 'General Comment No 15' (n 37) para 10; CAT, 'General Comment No 4' (n 40) para 13; HRC, 'Concluding Observations on the Dominican Republic' (26 April 2001) CCPR/CO/71/DOM, paras 16. See also ICRMW, art 22(1); CERD, 'General Recommendation 30 Discrimination against Non-citizens' (2004) UN Doc CERD/C/64/Misc.11/rev.3, para 26.

[77] *Henning Becker v Denmark* (1975) 4 DR 215, 235; *Hirsi Jamaa* (n 7) para 166. See also *Nadege Dorzema v Dominican Republic*, IACtHR, Series C No 251 (24 October 2012) para 171; ILC, 'Third Report on the Expulsion of Aliens, by Mr Maurice Kamto, Special Rapporteur' (19 April 2007) UN Doc A/CN.4/581, para 107.

[78] *Georgia v Russia (I)*, App no 13255/07 (ECtHR, 3 July 2014) paras 170–78; *Sharifi* (n 63) paras 210, 223; *Khlaifia v Italy*, App no 16483/12 (ECtHR, 1 September 2015) para 245.

[79] *Hirsi Jamaa* (n 7) para 177; *Khlaifia* (n 78) para 238.

returning them to Libya, violated Articles 3, 13 and Article 4 Protocol 4 of the ECHR. Strasbourg confirmed the extraterritorial application of the prohibition on collective expulsion, holding that it applies to the collective expulsion of aliens on State territory, non-admission at the frontier, and removals performed during the exercise of extraterritorial jurisdiction so long as individuals are 'drive[n] away'.[80] Each person is entitled to an individualised assessment and a thorough and rigorous assessment of their protection request before a removal measure is enforced, accompanied by the procedural safeguards outlined above to protect against *refoulement*.[81] Despite differing in scope from the obligation of *non-refoulement*, it can similarly be concluded that the prohibition on collective expulsion requires States to admit non-nationals to their territory to examine their individual circumstances.

However, in recent cases involving collective expulsion before the Strasbourg Court, it has adopted a restrictive and exclusionary approach. In the 2016 case of *Khlaifia v Italy*, which concerned the expulsion of Tunisian nationals who had been intercepted at sea by Italy, the Court held that the prohibition on collective expulsion does not guarantee an individual interview in all circumstances, so long as each alien has a genuine and effective possibility to submit arguments against their expulsion.[82] Judge Serghides, in his dissent, highlighted the indispensable nature of personal interviews and the importance of procedural safeguards that do not depend on State discretion.[83] Nonetheless, *Asady v Slovakia* affirmed *Khlaifia*, deeming ten-minute interviews sufficient to allow the applicants to have their individual circumstances sufficiently considered.[84]

In 2020, the Grand Chamber issued a highly controversial decision in *ND and NT v Spain*, reversing the Chamber's previous decision and finding no violation of the prohibition on collective expulsion.[85] The case concerned the expulsion of two sub-Saharan nationals to Morocco who were part of a group of several hundred migrants attempting to climb the border fence at Melilla, a Spanish enclave. The Court held that the applicant's 'own culpable conduct' was relevant to assessing the protection afforded by Article 4 of Protocol No 4, setting out an exception in 'situations in which the conduct of persons who cross

[80] *Hirsi Jamaa* (n 7) paras 174, 177–78, 185. See also *Khlaifia* (n 78) para 243; *Medvedyev v France* (2010) 51 EHRR 39, para 67; *Sharifi* (n 63) para 212; *ND and NT v Spain*, Apps nos 8675/15 and 8697/15 (ECtHR, 13 February 2020), paras 178–87.

[81] See eg *Hirsi Jamaa* (n 7) paras 185–86, 201–06; *Nadege Dorzema* (n 77) paras 156–78; *MK* (n 60) paras 144, 220; *MD v Hungary*, App no 60778/19 (ECtHR, 19 September 2024) 60–67. See *Rencontre Africaine pour la Défense des Droits de l'Homme v Zambia* [1996] ACHPR 8 and *Union Inter-Africaine des Droits de l'Homme v Angola* [1997] ACHPR 6, where the African Commission found violations of Article 12(5) in cases of mass expulsions without any opportunity to challenge deportation.

[82] *Khlaifia* (n 78) para 248, on suspensive effect paras 279–81.

[83] ibid paras 7, 10–1, 21. See *Čonka v Belgium* (2002) 34 EHRR 54, paras 62–63.

[84] *Asady v Slovakia*, App no 24917/15 (ECtHR, 24 March 2020) 63–71.

[85] *ND and NT* (n 80).

a land border in an unauthorised manner, deliberately take advantage of their large numbers and use force, is such as to create a clearly disruptive situation which is difficult to control and endangers public safety'.[86] The Court added that in such contexts, it would take into account whether the State provided genuine and effective access to means of legal entry and, if it did, whether there were cogent reasons why the individual did not make use of these means that were based on objective facts for which the State was responsible.[87]

It concluded that in the present case the lack of individualised decisions or remedy against removal was attributable to the applicants having participated 'in the storming of the Melilla border fences', 'taking advantage of the group's large numbers and using force'. They also failed to make use of the existing procedures for gaining lawful entry to Spanish territory.[88] Crucially though, the Court specified that its finding *does not* call into question the obligation on States to protect their borders in a manner compliant with the obligation of *non-refoulement* under Article 3 (the Chamber having previously excluded *refoulement* risks for the applicants) nor the conclusion in *Hirsi* on the illegality of pushbacks at sea.[89] This judgment has been widely criticised for legalising the rapid expulsion of migrants and punishing them for the situation created by European border policies. It has also drawn criticism for overlooking the violent conduct of the authorities, the racialised assumptions made, and the substantial evidence showing the practical impossibility of sub-Saharan Africans securing legal entry to Spain.[90]

Later cases have referred to the 'own culpable conduct' test established in *ND and NT*, explicitly considering the conditions it laid down and concluding that they were not fulfilled.[91] In *Asady*, the joint dissenting opinion highlighted that *ND and NT* 'must be confined to its proper context in order to avoid depriving the right secured by Article 4 of Protocol No. 4 of its very essence'.[92] However, in *AA v North Macedonia*, concerning the summary return of more than 1,500 migrants from North Macedonia to Greece in 2016, the Court

[86] ibid paras 200–01.

[87] ibid.

[88] ibid paras 211–12, 218–20, 231, 242.

[89] ibid paras 187, 206, 232.

[90] S Carrera, 'The Strasbourg Court Judgement *N.D. and N.T. v Spain*: A *Carte Blanche* to Push Backs at EU External Borders?' (2020) EUI Working Paper RSCAS 2020/21, https://hdl.handle.net/1814/66629; M Provera, *The Detention of Asylum Seekers in the European Union and Australia: A Comparative Analysis* (Nijmegen, Wolf Legal Publishers, 2013); A Gündoğdu, 'From the Colony to the Border: The Lawful Lawlessness of Racial Violence' in S Benhabib and A Shachar (eds) *Lawless Zones, Rightless Subjects: Migration, Asylum, and Shifting Borders* (Cambridge, CUP, 2025).

[91] *MK* (n 60) paras 203, 207, 210; *Shahzad v Hungary*, App no 12625/17 (ECtHR, 8 July 2021) paras 59–64; *MH v Croatia*, App no 15670/18 and 43115/18 (ECtHR, 18 November 2021) 294–304; *AI v Poland*, App no 39028/17 (ECtHR, 30 June 2022) para 55; *MA and ZRV v Cyprus*, App no 39090/20 (ECtHR, 8 October 2024) paras 116–19; *Sherov* (n 61) para 60.

[92] *Asady* (n 84) paras 15–25 (Joint Dissenting Opinion Lemmens, Keller and Schembri Orland JJ). See also para 62.

extended the test. It concluded that despite the group not using any force, there was no collective expulsion because the group had circumvented genuine and effective procedures for legal entry, including the ability to claim asylum at the border, despite evidence to the contrary.[93] Importantly, in the 2024 case of *MA and ZR v Cyprus*, which concerned the summary return of Syrians to Lebanon after their interception at sea in Cypriot waters, the Court rejected Cyprus' arguments that the applicants could have applied for an entry visa, noting that 'the nature of an entry visa, subject to financial and other requirements, could not constitute a genuine and effective possibility for the present applicants to submit their reasons (asylum) against expulsion'.[94]

Nevertheless, the precedent set in *ND and NT* does not nullify the duty of States to grant temporary entry under the prohibition on collective expulsion. The Court affirmed that individuals remain protected from *refoulement* regardless of any culpable conduct and, as such, pushbacks remain unlawful. To avoid exposing migrants to serious harm and uphold both *non-refoulement* and collective expulsion obligations, the State *must first* undertake individualised procedures on its territory to ascertain the existence of any protection needs, which the applicants in ND and NT were denied.[95] It does not matter that *refoulement* risks are excluded *later* in court, as they were for ND and NT. What matters is that this assessment is done prior to any expulsion. Of course, collective expulsion may not always be connected to credible *non-refoulement* claims. But allowing States to exclude migrants *en masse* who may have potential protection needs from accessing the territory to make and substantiate such a claim only serves to normalise racialised border violence and the denial of fundamental rights.

C. The Right to Family Reunification

The right to family reunification can generate a positive obligation on States to provide entry to their territory to ensure the family unity of migrants. International human rights law recognises that 'the family is the natural and fundamental group unit of society and is entitled to protection by society and the State',[96] and guarantees the right to family life.[97] Adjudicative bodies have recognised that refusing to allow a family member to enter a State's territory

[93] *AA v North Macedonia*, App no 55798 (ECtHR, 5 April 2022) paras 114–23; 7, 27, 88.

[94] ibid para 118.

[95] *ND and NT* (n 80) para 209; C Hruschka, 'Hot Returns Remain Contrary to the ECHR: *ND & NT* before the ECHR' (*EU Migration Law Blog*, 28 February 2020) www.eumigrationlawblog.eu/hot-returns-remain-contrary-to-the-echr-nd-nt-before-the-echr/.

[96] UDHR, art 18(3); ICCPR, art 23(1).

[97] See ADHR, arts V, VI; ECHR, art 8; ICCPR, art 17; ACHR, arts 11(2), 17(1); African Charter, art 18(1); UNCRC, arts 10(1), 16(1); CIS Convention, arts 9, 13(3); ICRMW, art 44; EUCFR, arts 7, 33(1); Arab Charter, arts 21, 33(2).

may amount to an arbitrary or unlawful interference with family life and States have a positive obligation, in certain circumstances, to admit to their territory the relatives of migrants residing there.[98] Unlike other treaties, the Convention on the Rights of the Child explicitly provides that States should deal with applications by a child or their parents to enter for family reunification in a positive, humane and expeditious manner.[99] While the 1951 Refugee Convention does not confer a right to family reunification on refugees, the UNHCR Executive Committee has stated that, in upholding the right to family unity and family life, every effort should be made to ensure the reunification of separated refugee families.[100]

In this sense, the right of migrants to family reunification is an exception to the States' migration control prerogative, in which adjudicative bodies seek to strike a balance between the two.[101] Under Article 8 of the ECHR on the right to family life, the Strasbourg Court has clarified that securing entry is only available when one family member is present in a Contracting State. A State is not obligated to allow aliens entry to pursue a private life.[102] Applicants must show that reunion is the 'most adequate' way to family life.[103] Both the Court and Human Rights Committee have found violations of the right to family life where the State has refused to issue residence permits to allow family members to reunite in its territory.[104] Differences in treatment between certain categories of nationals as well as between categories of non-nationals (ie, refugees compared with students or workers) under family reunification rules, for example on the

[98] eg *Abdulaziz* (n 7) paras 67–68; *Gül v Switzerland* (1996) 22 EHRR 93; *Şen v Netherlands* (2001) 36 EHRR 81, para 31; *Tuquabo-Tekle v Netherlands*, App no 60665/00 (ECtHR, 1 December 2005); *Rodrigues da Silva v Netherlands* (2006) 44 EHRR 729, para 39; HRC, 'General Comment No 15' (n 37) paras 5, 7; HRC, 'General Comment No 19: Article 23 (The Family) Protection of the Family, the Right to Marriage and Equality of the Spouses' (27 July 1990) UN Doc HRI/GEN/1/Rev.9, para 5; CMW and CRC, 'Joint General Comment No 4 (2017) of the Committee on the Protection of the Rights of All Migrant Workers and Members of Their Families and No 23 (2017) of the Committee on the Rights of the Child on State Obligations regarding the Human Rights of Children in the Context of International Migration in Countries of Origin, Transit, Destination and Return' (16 November 2017) UN Doc CMW/C/GC/4-CRC/C/GC/23, paras 27–28, 32; IACHR, 'Inter-American Principles on the Human Rights of All Migrants, Refugees, Stateless Persons and Victims of Human Trafficking' (7 December 2019) Resolution 04/19, principle 33, www.oas.org/en/iachr/decisions/pdf/Resolution-4-19-en.pdf; ACHPR, 'African Guiding Principles on the Human Rights of All Migrants, Refugees and Asylum Seekers' (20 October 2023) principle 31, achpr.au.int/index.php/en/soft-law/african-guiding-principles-humanrights-all-migrants-refugees. See also V Chetail, *International Migration Law* (Oxford, OUP, 2019) 124–32; C Costello, K Groenendijk and LH Storgaard, *Realising the Right to Family Reunification of Refugees in Europe* (Issue Paper, Council of Europe Commissioner for Human Rights, 2017).

[99] Art 10(1). See Costello, Ioffe and Büchsel (n 70) also on art 9.

[100] EXCOM, 'No. 24 (XXXII) on Family Reunification' (1981) UN Doc A/36/12/Add.1, para 1.

[101] Dembour (n 8) 119; A Desmond, 'The Private Life of Family Matters: Curtailing Human Rights Protection for Migrants under Article 8 of the ECHR?' (2018) 29 *European Journal of International Law* 261, 265; Costello, Groenendijk and Storgaard (n 98) 6, 21.

[102] *Khan v UK* App no 11987/11 (ECtHR, 28 January 2014), para 27.

[103] *Tuquabo-Tekle* (n 98); *Jeunesse v the Netherlands*, App no 12738/10 (ECtHR, 3 October 2014).

[104] See *Şen v Netherlands* (n 98) para 40; *Tuquabo-Tekle* (n 98) 52; *Gonzales v Guyana*, Communication No 1246/2004 (2010) UN Doc CCPR/C/98/D/1246/2004, para 14.3.

grounds of race, sexual orientation or sex, have amounted to unlawful discrimination read together with the right to family life.[105]

The extent of the State's obligation to admit relatives of settled migrants, as opposed to those with temporary status, varies according to the particular circumstances of the family members involved and considerations such as family ties, obstacles to living in the State of origin, and prior immigration breaches.[106] In the case of refugees, reunification is generally appreciated as the only way to protect the right to family life given the impossibility of refugees returning to their country of origin.[107] In the case of children separated (or potentially being separated) from their family across borders, the child's best interests are paramount.[108] The Committee on the Rights of the Child has affirmed that only the child's best interests could impede family reunification for an unaccompanied or separated child and non-rights-based arguments such as the State's interest in controlling migration cannot override best interests considerations.[109]

The right to family reunification, obligation of *non-refoulement* and prohibition on collective expulsion provide strong protections for migrants, circumscribing who States can lawfully reject and allowing migrants to assert a right of entry to the territory. Despite stemming largely from negative obligations, adjudicative bodies have imposed a positive duty on States to admit migrants to preserve family unity as well as allow migrants at least temporary entry to the territory to access individualised asylum procedures. This is significant because it reveals 'immigration control prerogatives encompass *the power to admit*, as much as to exclude'.[110]

D. Free Movement Regimes

Regional free movement regimes provide a significant legal basis for non-nationals to secure entry and move freely within specific regions. The paradigmatic

[105] *Abdulaziz* (n 7) paras 70–89; *Pajić v Croatia*, App no 68453/13 (ECtHR, 23 February 2016) para 64; *Biao v Denmark*, App no 38590/10 (ECtHR, 24 May 2016); *Hode and Abdi v the United Kingdom*. cf *MA v Denmark*, App no 6697/18 (ECtHR, 9 July 2021) paras 140, 145, 197 and *MT v Sweden,* App no 22105/18 (ECtHR, 20 October 2022) para 111, where the Court does not appear to consider differences in family reunification rights between people with refugee status and subsidiary protection beneficiaries as unlawful.

[106] See *Abdulaziz* (n 7) paras 67–68; *Gül* (n 98) paras 38–39; *da Silva* (n 98) para 39.

[107] See *Farag El Dernawi v Libya*, Communication No 1143/2002 (20 July 2007) UN Doc CCPR/C/90/D/1143/2002 para 6.3; *Tanda-Muzinga v France*, App no 2260/10 (ECtHR, 10 July 2014); *Mugenzi v France*, App no 52701/09 (ECtHR, 10 July 2014); Costello, *Human Rights* (n 9) 21–22.

[108] See *Bakhtiyari v Australia*, Communication No 1069/2002 (29 October 2003) UN Doc CCPR/C/79/D/1069/2002, paras 9.6–9.7; *Mohamed El-Hichou v Denmark*, Communication No 1554/2007 (22 July 2010) UN Doc CCPR/C/99/D/1554/2007, paras 7.3, 7.5; Costello, *Human Rights* (n 9) 22–23.

[109] CRC, 'General Comment No 6: Treatment of unaccompanied and separated children outside their country of origin (1 September 2005) UN Doc CRC/GC/2005/6, paras 81, 86. See Costello, Ioffe and Büchsel (n 70) 228–32.

[110] Durieux (n 74) 156 (emphasis added).

example is that of the EU where EU citizens and their family members have the right to move freely, live, study, work and retire anywhere in the EU, which has led to the abolition of many internal border controls within the Schengen area.[111] However, States across Africa, Asia, the Americas and the Caribbean have also formed economic communities entailing the free movement of people within member States, guaranteeing community citizens the right to enter and move freely, establish residence, and work on an equal footing with nationals of that member State. The Free Move project maps the proliferation of free movement regimes globally and by January 2024 had identified the adoption of 33 bilateral and 22 multilateral regimes involving more than 110 countries across all continents.[112] As a result, the regionalisation of free movement represents perhaps the most significant restriction to States' sovereignty in the field of admission.[113] There is huge variation across regions on both the macro and micro levels: from more modest developments in the Asia-Pacific region, to differences regarding the scope and content of regional agreements, and varying degrees of implementation and effectiveness.[114] Africa, for instance, has a long history of sub-regional economic communities and free movement arrangements; however, making this a reality has been impacted by broader challenges of instability and conflict (at times leading to the intensification of border controls), resources and capacity.[115] In 2018, the African Union concluded a Protocol to the Treaty Establishing the African Economic Community Relating to Free Movement of Persons, Right of Residence and Right of Establishment, but it has not yet entered into force as only four States have ratified it.[116]

Nevertheless, only specific categories of individuals are entitled to mobility under regional free movement regimes. Similarly only certain migrants possess the right of entry under family reunification, *non-refoulement* and collective expulsion obligations. There remains no general right of entry, and even where States are obliged to admit certain migrants, many now engage in pushbacks,

[111] R Bauböck, 'Free Movement Regimes: Is the EU Experience Exportable?' in E Recchi and M Safi, *Handbook of Human Mobility and Migration* (Cheltenham, Edward Elgar Publishing, 2024).

[112] IP Chime and others, 'The AU Free Movement Protocol: Challenges in Its Implementation' (2023) 68 *Journal of African Law* 3; D Acosta and L van der Baaren, 'An Introduction to the Freemove Project' www.freemovehub.com; D Acosta, 'Free Movement Regimes: The New Normal at a Global Level?' (*Henley & Partners*, 2025) www.henleyglobal.com/publications/citizenship-program-index-2025/industry-insights/free-movement-regimes-new-normal-global-level.

[113] Chetail, *International Migration Law* (n 98) 98, see generally 92–119; D Acosta, *The National versus the Foreigner in South America: 200 Years of Migration and Citizenship Law* (Cambridge, CUP, 2018).

[114] V Chetail, 'Freedom of Movement and Transnational Migrations: A Human Rights Perspective' in TA Aleinikoff and V Chetail (eds), *Migration and International Legal Norms* (The Hague, TMC Asser Press, 2003) 91–100.

[115] See ACHPR, 'Guiding Principles' (n 98) 10–11, principle 19.

[116] Protocol to the Treaty Establishing the African Economic Community Relating to the Free Movement of Persons, Right of Residence and Right of Establishment (adopted 29 January 2018) arts 1, 6(1).

hot returns, build physical and virtual walls, or otherwise externalise their migration controls so these obligations never attach in the first place.

E. A Controversial Exception: The 'Safe Country' Concept

Safe country practices may be an exception to the conclusion that States are duty-bound to grant individuals entry to access asylum procedures. The primary responsibility for processing asylum claims and providing protection rests with the State where a person arrives and seeks protection.[117] However, destination States increasingly rely on arrangements predicated on the idea that asylum seekers may be returned or transferred to a country where they have already or could have sought protection. In an effort to stem the arrival of irregular migrants, they are denied access to the asylum system and/or the territory and returned to a so-called 'safe' third country through which they passed *en route* or possibly to an entirely different safe third country.

Broadly, the concept of a '*safe country*' refers to countries designated by destination States as either non-refugee-producing or where individuals can enjoy asylum without danger.[118] It encompasses '*safe countries of origin*' and '*safe countries of asylum*'. The latter allows asylum seekers to be returned to a State where they previously received protection ('*first country of asylum*') or to a place where protection should have been sought but was not ('*safe third country*' (STC)).[119] The distinction between the two has somewhat dissipated, and STC practices are becoming an increasingly prevalent tool of externalisation, and are being adapted to new contexts.[120]

Since the late 1970s, Global North States have engaged in 'protection elsewhere' practices, transferring asylum seekers to third countries for protection, underpinned by safe country concepts.[121] The EU's Dublin Regulation

[117] UNHCR, 'Legal Considerations Regarding Access to Protection and a Connection Between the Refugee and the Third Country in the Context of Return or Transfer to Safe Third Countries' (April 2018) para 2.

[118] UNHCR, 'Background Note on the Safe Country Concept and Refugee Status' (Geneva 1991) UN Doc EC/SCP/68, para 3.

[119] C Costello, 'The Asylum Procedures Directive and the Proliferation of Safe Country Practices: Deterrence, Deflection and the Dismantling of International Protection?' (2005) 7 *European Journal of Migration and Law* 35, 39. See the distinction drawn in EXCOM, 'No. 15 (XXX) Refugees Without an Asylum Country' (1979) UN Doc A/34/12/Add.1, s h(iv), (k); EXCOM, 'No. 58 (XL) Problem of Refugees and Asylum Seekers Who Move in an Irregular Manner from a Country in Which They Had Already Found Protection' (1989) UN Doc A/44/12/Add.1, (f).

[120] Costello, 'Asylum Procedures' (n 119) 39, 68; M Foster, 'Responsibility Sharing or Shifting? "Safe" Third Countries and International Law' (2008) 25 *Refuge* 64, 64–65. See UNHCR, 'Background Note' (n 118) paras 3, 11.

[121] M Foster, 'Protection Elsewhere: The Legal Implications of Requiring Refugees to Seek Protection in Another State' (2007) 28 *Michigan Journal of International Law* 223; BN Osso, 'Unpacking the Safe Third Country Concept in the European Union: Borders, Legal Spaces, and Asylum in the Shadow of Externalization' (2023) 35 *International Journal of Refugee Law* 272.

is based on the 'first country of asylum' concept, establishing a hierarchy of criteria for determining the Member State responsible for examining an asylum application, which allows asylum seekers to be sent back to the first safe EU country that they arrived in.[122] However, more recent agreements amount to an expansion and manipulation of the STC concept, seeking to remove asylum seekers to countries designated as 'safe' they have no connection whatsoever to and have never even transited through. For instance, Australia's offshore processing regime on Nauru and PNG, the UK's asylum deal with Rwanda, the US' asylum cooperative agreement with Guatemala, and Italy's offshore detention deal with Albania.[123]

It is well-established in international law and State practice that it is lawful to transfer asylum seekers to third States provided such arrangements afford individuals effective protection in line with the Refugee Convention and international standards and ensure adequate safeguards.[124] STC mechanisms will be unlawful where they fail to meet these standards or are aimed at, or effectively serve, to shift rather than share responsibility in the spirit of international cooperation and solidarity.[125] However, safe country concepts have been the site of much controversy.[126] In reality, STC arrangements nearly always shift responsibility from wealthy countries with greater capacity to provide effective protection to those with less capacity, leading to serious human rights violations. As I have argued elsewhere, States are resorting to STC and other externalisation measures to flagrantly disregard their international obligations

[122] Regulation (EU) No 604/2013 of the European Parliament and of the Council of 26 June 2013 establishing the criteria and mechanisms for determining the Member State responsible for examining an application for international protection lodged in one of the Member States by a third-country national or a stateless person (recast) [2013] OJ L 180/31, ch III.

[123] See eg *Migration Act 1958* (Cth) div 8 subdiv B; Agreement Between the Government of the United States of America and the Government of the Republic of Guatemala on Cooperation Regarding the Examination of Protection Claims (signed 26 July 2019, entered into force 15 November 2019) TIAS 19-1115. See M Gleeson, 'Protection Deficit: The Failure of Australia's Offshore Processing Arrangements to Guarantee "Protection Elsewhere" in the Pacific' (2019) 31 *International Journal of Refugee Law* 415.

[124] See EXCOM, 'No. 58' (n 119) (f), (g); UNHCR, 'Summary Conclusions on the Concept of "Effective Protection" in the Context of Secondary Movements of Refugees and Asylum-Seekers (Lisbon Expert Roundtable 9–10 December 2002)' (February 2003) para 15; UNHCR, 'Safe third Countries' (n 117) paras 3–5, 7–10; Lauterpacht and Bethlehem (n 26) para 76; Hathaway (n 39) 326–35; Foster, 'Responsibility Sharing' (n 120) 65–66; Goodwin-Gill and McAdam (n 13) 438–60. cf V Moreno-Lax, 'The Legality of the "Safe Third Country" Notion Contested: Insights from the Law of Treaties' in GS Goodwin-Gill and P Weckel (eds), *Migration & Refugee Protection in the 21st Century: Legal Aspects – The Hague Academy of International Law Centre for Research* (The Hague, Martinus Nijhoff, 2015) and literature at fns 21–22.

[125] UNHCR, 'Annex to UNHCR Note on the "Externalization" of International Protection: Policies and Practices related to the Externalization of International Protection' (28 May 2021) paras 1–2, 20–25.

[126] S Aiken and A Neve, 'Refugee "Responsibility Sharing" – Challenging the Status Quo' (2023) 7 *PKI Global Justice Journal* 7.

towards refugees and commitments to responsibility sharing, neither ensuring nor enhancing protection. This should be understood as a breach of the State's duty to implement its obligations in good faith, rendering such practices inherently unlawful.[127] Dublin, for instance, has always been at odds with free movement and fair and equitable responsibility sharing, designed to prevent 'asylum shopping' and disproportionately 'burdening' frontline EU States.[128]

Nevertheless, the status quo remains that safe country mechanisms are lawful in principle but unlawful in practice. While safe country practices may displace the right to be admitted temporarily to access asylum procedures, States must not remove an asylum seeker to a third country without first conducting an individualised assessment of whether that country is safe for a particular person and giving them the opportunity to rebut the presumption of safety.[129] It is highly dubious whether this could be done while fully respecting procedural guarantees unless individuals are first admitted to the State's territory. As chapter six explores, a pressing issue is whether third States can prevent people from leaving their territory so they do not reach or return to a destination State, such as along the Turkey–Greece or Mexico–US borders. Perhaps in the context of secondary refugee movements, the scope of the right to leave is exhausted when a person's protection needs are fully met. However, it remains the case all migrants possess the right to leave for other purposes, including family reunification and tourism, subject only to justifiable restrictions.

V. AN 'INCOMPLETE' RIGHT TO LEAVE OR INDEPENDENT RIGHT

The conclusion that certain migrants possess a right of entry flowing from specific obligations, rights and free movement regimes challenges the common conception of the right to leave as '*incomplete*'. In the absence of a general right of entry, the right to leave has at times been dismissed as effectively meaningless in practice. However, part of the conceptual problem stems from a lack of understanding of the 'outer edges' of the right to leave: where does the right to leave end and the issue of entry begin? Articulating this allows us to speak not of an incomplete right to leave but one that is '*independent*' of any right of entry, as supported by the jurisprudence in chapter two.

[127] E McDonnell, 'Externalisation as a Breach of the Good Faith Principle' (*Externalizing Asylum*, 2024) externalizingasylum.info/externalisation-as-a-breach-of-the-good-faith-principle/.

[128] See M Mouzourakis, '"We Need to Talk about Dublin": Responsibility under the Dublin System as a Blockage to Asylum Burden-sharing in the European Union' (2014) RSC Working Paper Series No 105, www.rsc.ox.ac.uk/publications/we-need-to-talk-about-dublin.

[129] See *Ilias* (n 63) paras 139–64.

Leaving and admission should be seen as distinct parts of the migrant trajectory. The right to leave protects the freedom to travel, including the freedom to leave and not know where one is going. As Chetail has articulated, 'despite the practical meddling between the two, departure and admission have been conceived and recognized by international law as two distinct legal spheres'.[130] Self-evidently, leaving in many contexts will result in a person reaching another State's territory to which they may be admitted. However, States are not under a duty to 'complete' the right to leave; rather, it is a right each State must guarantee.[131] This is a key strength of the right, whereby the inability to enter a State does not bar its activation.[132] Special Rapporteur Mubanga-Chipoya wrote in his report that the fact there is no right of entry 'does not imply that other States are free to prohibit their nationals from leaving the country on such a pretext or excuse'.[133] This is not unique to the right to leave. Rights can exist without the practical ability to exercise them and do not immediately correspond to identifiable duty-bearers (for instance, people possess the right to marry but they may not have a partner). Individuals are therefore entitled to leave to search for possible duty-bearers, in this case, a State to admit them, or otherwise attempt unlawful entry.[134] Framed differently, although the right is self-standing, the value of leaving is clearly strengthened for those granted entry, making human rights more effective and providing real opportunities for its fulfilment.[135] In this sense, full realisation of the right to leave by departure States could pressure destination States to ensure leaving one's country does not become an empty promise.[136]

Preserving the right to leave's independence suggests the right reaches its limit when a person seeks entry at the border. Accordingly, migration control measures would fall to be examined against the State's right to control entry. Den Heijer argues that to construe entry restrictions as interferences 'transforms the right to leave into a qualified right of entry'.[137] However, any right of

[130] Chetail, *International Migration Law* (n 98) 92. See also M den Heijer, *Europe and Extraterritorial Asylum* (Oxford, Hart Publishing, 2012) 158.

[131] Goodwin-Gill and McAdam (n 13) 430.

[132] E Guild and V Stoyanova, 'The Human Right to Leave Any Country: A Right to Be Delivered' in W Benedek and others (eds), *European Yearbook on Human Rights 2018* (Plymouth, Intersentia, 2018) 381, 392; V Stoyanova, 'The Right to Leave Any Country and the Interplay between Jurisdiction and Proportionality in Human Rights Law' (2020) 32 *International Journal of Refugee Law* 403, 414.

[133] CHR (Sub-Commission), 'Analysis of Current Trends and Developments in respect of the Right of Everyone to Leave Any Country including His Own and to Return to His Country, and Some Other Rights or Considerations Arising Therefrom, Final Report by Special Rapporteur Chama LC Mubanga-Chipoya' (20 June 1988) UN Doc E/CN.4/Sub.2/1988/35, 65.

[134] Den Heijer, *Europe* (n 130) 159; J Waldron, 'Duty-bearers for Positive Rights' (2014) NYU School of Law Public Law Research Paper No 14–58, papers.ssrn.com/sol3/papers.cfm?abstract_id=2510506.

[135] See *Amuur* (n 7) para 48; R Bauböck, 'Free Movement and the Asymmetry between Exit and Entry' (2006) 4 *Ethics & Economics* 1, 1–2, 5; den Heijer, *Europe* (n 130) 159; PT Lenard, 'Exit and the Duty to Admit' (2015) 8 *Ethics & Global Politics* 25975.

[136] Mubanga-Chipoya (n 133) para 321.

[137] Den Heijer, *Europe* (n 130) 159–61.

entry stems not from the right to leave but from obligations of *non-refoulement*, collective expulsion and the right to family reunification, for example. In reality, exit and entry cannot always be easily disentangled from one another, given the nature of movement and borders. Sometimes, exit in a particular direction may only be possible if entry is available. To establish whether an entry or pre-entry measure infringes the right to leave (and not only other more frequently invoked obligations) what matters is whether the measure has the (dual) effect of obstructing departure.

Conceptualising the right to leave as independent and exercisable irrespective of any right of entry elsewhere is not only normatively accurate but also reinforces the human rights of migrants above the State. Accordingly, States cannot restrict departure by asserting the right's *incompleteness* or that the destination will not grant entry.

VI. CONCLUSION

This chapter has outlined several normative foundations that challenge traditional assumptions surrounding the State's prerogative to control entry and the right to leave. International law operates to constrain, rather significantly, the sovereign power of States to control the entry of non-nationals onto their territory. Although there is no universal right to asylum or entry, the prohibitions on *refoulement* and collective expulsion impose an obligation on States to, at a minimum, grant temporary admission so individuals can access asylum procedures and procedural safeguards prior to return or removal. Migrants may also enjoy a right of entry for family reunification purposes or under free movement regimes. However, safe country concepts may (and often do) legitimise the transfer of asylum seekers from wealthy developed States to less developed countries before their claim is heard or entry granted. International law, therefore, not only limits who States can reject but also *institutionalises* exclusion (and discriminatory treatment) as the norm and admission as the exception.[138]

A proper understanding of the right to leave and its outer limits allows us to move away from the notion of an 'incomplete' right to one that is self-standing. It recognises that leaving and entry are distinct, albeit related, parts of the migratory process and States cannot obstruct departure over doubts about whether a person will be admitted to the destination. To do so would nevertheless be erroneous, given migrants enjoy a right of entry in certain circumstances, including to seek asylum. Of course, this is not always the case in practice, especially given the proliferation of externalisation.

[138] Costello, *Human Rights* (n 9) 10.

As subsequent chapters demonstrate through real-world examples, the right to leave thus provides an avenue to challenge the 'immobilisation' of migrants and unequal, discriminatory access to mobility when States assert the asymmetry between leaving and entry. The traditional primacy afforded to the States' right to exclude above human rights and belief in the inherent legitimacy of migration control should no longer be the norm. International law should regard the protection of human rights as primary and State sovereignty as a secondary norm *underpinned* by human rights.

4

The Right to Leave for Asylum Seekers and Refugees

I. INTRODUCTION

THE RIGHT TO leave in international law protects everyone irrespective of their identity or migration status. However, externalisation specifically targets asylum seekers and would-be refugees and seeks to obstruct access to protection, which warrants this dedicated chapter. Through visas, pullbacks, detention and other restrictions on movement, States seek to prevent asylum seekers, including a country's own nationals, from leaving and seeking asylum elsewhere (see chapters five and six). The ability of asylum seekers to flee persecution and irreversible harm in search of asylum hinges on the right to leave, as underscored in the jurisprudence outlined in chapter two. Denial of leaving can thus amount to a denial of the right to seek asylum and access to protection. The right to leave, therefore, bears special significance for asylum seekers and refugees and should be understood as a '*right to leave to seek asylum*'.

This chapter explores how fundamental protections owed to asylum seekers and refugees – specifically the right to seek asylum, the obligation of *non-refoulement*, and the prohibition on collective expulsion – inform the content and scope of the right to leave. It demonstrates that the right to leave is indispensable for asylum seekers and refugees, being a precondition for seeking and securing asylum and accessing protection from *refoulement* or expulsion. Together, these fundamental protections interact to create a 'right to leave to seek asylum'. In engaging with debates on whether the right to leave for asylum seekers becomes 'absolute' when *refoulement* risks are involved, and instead proposes a stricter test when assessing violations of the right for asylum seekers given their protection needs. The chapter concludes by exploring the duties generated by the right to leave to seek asylum on States and IOs bound by the right to leave – specifically duties to issue travel documents to asylum seekers and refugees, not to negate the flight of asylum seekers, and a general obligation to facilitate departure – which if implemented would have profound consequences for externalisation strategies.

A. The Relationship between the Right to Leave and Other Rights

It is worth briefly reiterating the importance of interpreting the right to leave consistently with the broader international obligations owed to asylum seekers and refugees. States and IOs should ensure a systemic interpretation of their duties towards asylum seekers and refugees – one which takes into account the relationship between the right to leave and other relevant rights and obligations. The situation of people attempting to leave in search of asylum necessitates an approach 'that apprehends the complexity of the position of refugees and recovers the indivisibility of human rights', which is fundamental to addressing the totality of their plight.[1]

Accordingly, restrictions on the right to leave should uphold – rather than hamper – the right to seek asylum, the obligation of *non-refoulement*, and other key international protection standards under refugee and human rights treaties. This is further reflected in the requirement that restrictions on the right to leave be consistent with other rights. Adopting a holistic and integrated approach will help guarantee that the right to leave is not interpreted in isolation but is properly understood in a manner that ensures the rights of asylum seekers and refugees are practical and effective throughout the migrant trajectory. This will have significant repercussions for States and IOs in ensuring their migration laws and policies are consistent with the right to leave and protection standards.

II. THE RIGHT TO LEAVE TO SEEK ASYLUM

This section explores the interplay between the right to leave any country and the right to seek asylum, the obligation of *non-refoulement*, and the prohibition on collective expulsion. It argues the right to leave for asylum seekers is best characterised as a 'right to leave to seek asylum', a notion supported by various scholars.[2] It represents the individual's entitlement to flee a harmful situation to seek asylum or a better life.[3] The notion of a right to leave to seek asylum can

[1] V Moreno-Lax, 'Intersectionality, Forced Migration, and the Jus-Generation of the Right to Flee: Theorising a Composite Entitlement to Leave to Escape Irreversible Harm' in B Çalı, L Bianku and I Motoc (eds), *Migration and the European Convention on Human Rights* (Oxford, OUP, 2021) 43, 47.

[2] See eg A Grahl-Madsen, 'Asylum, Territorial' in P Macalister-Smith and G Alfredsson (eds), *The Land Beyond: Collected Essays on Refugee Law and Policy* (The Hague, Martinus Nijhoff, 2001) 282; D Kanstroom, 'The "Right to Remain Here" as an Evolving Component of Global Refugee Protection: Current Initiatives and Critical Questions' (2017) 5 *Journal on Migration and Human Security* 614, 624; V Moreno-Lax, *Accessing Asylum in Europe: Extraterritorial Border Controls and Refugee Rights under EU Law* (Oxford, OUP, 2017) ch 9; GS Goodwin-Gill and J McAdam, *The Refugee in International Law*, 4th edn (Oxford, OUP, 2021) 416–17, 431.

[3] S Trevisanut, 'The Principle of Non-Refoulement and the De-Territorialization of Border Control at Sea' (2014) 27 *Leiden Journal of International Law* 661, 667; Moreno-Lax, *Accessing Asylum* (n 2) ch 9, 348–54; M Giuffré and V Moreno-Lax, 'The Rise of Consensual Containment: From "Contactless Control" to "Contactless Responsibility" for Forced Migration Flows' in SS Juss (ed), *Research Handbook on International Refugee Law* (Cheltenham, Edward Elgar Publishing, 2019) 94, 100.

be understood both as a precondition for seeking and securing asylum, including Convention refugee status, and triggering protection from *refoulement* and collective expulsion.

A. Precondition to Seeking and Securing Asylum

The right to leave and the right to seek asylum are *inherently* intertwined in the refugee context. They are two sides of the same coin.[4] The UDHR protects the right to seek and enjoy asylum from persecution, which is assisted by the right to leave any country (Articles 13(2) and 14(1)). As Goodwin-Gill and McAdam highlight, 'To have any meaning, the right to seek asylum implies not only a right to access asylum procedures, but also to be able to leave one's country in search of protection'.[5] 'No one is obliged to sit out his or her fate' even if there is no immediate remedy or universal right to asylum.[6]

At a foundational level, international refugee protection is contingent on mobility: the right to leave is a prerequisite for escaping persecution and accessing international protection.[7] Refugee status under the 1951 Convention is only available to people 'outside the country of his nationality' or 'country of his former habitual residence'. As Hannum puts it, 'To "seek" asylum, a refugee must be able to present himself before the appropriate authorities of the country of refuge; by definition, this requirement presupposes that he must be able to leave his own country'.[8] If destination States prevent people from leaving their country of origin, 'then refugees do not "exist" in the state's eyes or are not the responsibility of the state which has put the measures in place'.[9] People forced to flee their homes who have not crossed an international border do not qualify for refugee status but are considered internally displaced persons (IDPs), who nonetheless possess the right to leave.[10]

In practice, many asylum seekers face significant obstacles when attempting to flee a country and are unable to secure entry or asylum elsewhere *before* departure, as this work addresses. Denial of the right to leave will inevitably

[4] Grahl-Madsen (n 2) 282; A Edwards, 'Human Rights, Refugees, and the Right "to Enjoy" Asylum' (2005) 17 *International Journal of Refugee Law* 293, 301–02.

[5] Goodwin-Gill and McAdam (n 2) 428.

[6] GS Goodwin-Gill, 'The Extraterritorial Processing of Claims to Asylum or Protection: The Legal Responsibilities of States and International Organisations' (2007) 9 *UTS Law Review* 26, 30.

[7] K Long, 'In Search of Sanctuary: Border Closures, "Safe" Zones and Refugee Protection' (2013) 26 *Journal of Refugee Studies* 458, 458; M Zieck, 'Refugees and the Right to Freedom of Movement: From Flight to Return' (2018) 39 *Michigan Journal of International Law* 21, 21; Giuffré and Moreno-Lax (n 3) 100.

[8] H Hannum, *The Right to Leave and Return in International Law and Practice* (Dordrecht, Martinus Nijhoff, 1987) 50.

[9] E Guild, *The Right to Leave a Country* (Issue Paper, Council of Europe Commissioner for Human Rights 2013) 25–26.

[10] See UNHCR, 'Guiding Principles on Internal Displacement' (11 February 1998) UN Doc E/CN.4/1998/53/Add.2, principle 15.

undermine the right to seek and enjoy asylum – beyond asylum granted within the Refugee Convention's confines. The Inter-American Commission on Human Rights has recognised that 'the inability to leave your country may also imply a restriction to the right to seek and be granted asylum'.[11] Likewise, the European Court of Human Rights has subtly identified the linkage, stating that the 'applicant had been trying to leave Greece cannot be held against him' given he 'was attempting to find a solution to a situation the Court considers contrary to Article 3'.[12] In doing so, the Court recognised that leaving to seek protection, regularly or irregularly, is legitimate.[13] Indeed, under refugee law, people who have illegally exited their country and would face severe penalties upon return qualify as refugees if their reason for fleeing is related to a Convention ground.[14] Reading the right to leave and right to seek asylum harmoniously serves to ensure that the protections asylum seekers and refugees are legally entitled to are meaningful and effective.

B. Accessing Protection from *Refoulement* and Expulsion

The notion of a right to leave to seek asylum is also underpinned by the intersection of the right to leave with the prohibitions on *refoulement* and collective expulsion. Scholars have recognised that the right to leave – as a precondition for seeking asylum – complements the obligation of *non-refoulement*, and together, they form the basis of international protection.[15] UNHCR's Executive Committee has similarly affirmed *non-refoulement* as the 'logical complement to the right to seek and enjoy asylum', highlighting the inability of individuals to seek asylum because of physical and administrative barriers preventing their departure.[16]

The right to leave, right to seek and to enjoy asylum, and obligations of *non-refoulement* 'share a delicate but significant relationship'.[17] As Moreno-lax argues, this interaction reinforces the legal strength of the right to seek asylum.[18]

[11] IACHR, 'IACHR Urges Honduras and Guatemala to Guarantee the Rights of People in the Migrant and Refugee Caravan' (19 February 2019) www.oas.org/en/iachr/media_center/PReleases/2019/037.asp.

[12] *MSS v Belgium and Greece* (2011) 53 EHRR 2, para 315.

[13] Giuffré and Moreno-Lax (n 3) 100.

[14] UNHCR, 'Handbook on Procedures and Criteria for Determining Refugee Status and Guidelines on International Protection under the 1951 Convention and the 1967 Protocol relating to the Status of Refugees' (February 2019) UN Doc HCR/1P/4/ENG/REV.4 paras 61, 168–70.

[15] GS Goodwin-Gill, 'The Right to Seek Asylum: Interception at Sea and the Principle of *Non-Refoulement*' (2011) 23 *International Journal of Refugee Law* 443, 444; N Markard, 'The Right to Leave by Sea: Legal Limits on EU Migration Control by Third Countries' (2016) 27 *European Journal of International Law* 591, 596, 603.

[16] EXCOM, 'Note on International Protection' (4 June 2018) UN Doc EC/SC/69/CRP.8 paras 21–22.

[17] Goodwin-Gill and McAdam (n 2) 430.

[18] Moreno-Lax, *Accessing Asylum* (n 2) 349.

Recent complaints before to the Human Rights Committee have emphasised the interconnection between these rights and obligations, which 'renders the right to leave of vital importance to those fleeing irreversible harm'.[19] Chapter three contended that *non-refoulement* and collective expulsion obligations trigger a duty on States to temporarily admit asylum seekers so they can access asylum procedures. On the one hand, the right to leave protects the individual's right to flee and search for a State to admit them, and on the other, the right to protection from *refoulement* and expulsion affords asylum seekers *de facto* asylum, albeit narrowly confined and perhaps only temporarily.[20] Critically, to enjoy protection from *refoulement* or expulsion, asylum seekers must enter the territory or fall under the jurisdiction of the State. While there is no requirement under human rights treaties precluding *refoulement* for individuals to be outside their country of origin, if individuals cannot leave their country, they cannot access protection from *refoulement*.[21] In other words, to be protected from *refoulement* or collective expulsion, individuals must be able to bring themselves within the State's jurisdiction. The ability to leave ultimately allows individuals to escape harm and not be sent back to it, the denial of which can have irreversible consequences. Therefore, the right to leave is a fundamental precondition for the right to seek asylum and securing protection from *refoulement* and expulsion under human rights and refugee law.

C. An Absolute Right?

The interaction of the right to leave with the procedural dimension under the prohibition on *refoulement* and collective expulsion has led to a debate on whether the right to leave for asylum seekers becomes 'absolute' when *refoulement* risks are involved. Some scholars have contended that the right of entry to access asylum procedures should be understood as the procedural limb of the aggregate right to leave to seek asylum.[22] Consequently, the right would incorporate 'a substantive-procedural-physical entitlement' to flee to seek asylum accompanied by a right of entry to claim asylum.[23] However, this framing undermines the well-established independent nature of the right to leave. Instead of incorporating such a procedural entitlement *into* the right to leave, the migrant

[19] ASGI and CIHRS, 'Complaint to the UN Human Rights Committee Over the Role of Italy, Malta, and Libya in Violating the Right to Leave Libya, Resulting in Denial of the Rights of Asylum Seekers' (Press Release, 24 July 2020) www.statewatch.org/media/1267/un-asgi-cihrs-complaint-libya-pull-backs-pr-24-7-20.pdf; *SDG v Italy*, Communication to the HRC, 18 December 2019, paras 94, 98, www.glanlaw.org/_files/ugd/14ee1a_e0466b7845f941098730900ede1b51cb.pdf (declared inadmissible).

[20] Moreno-Lax, *Accessing Asylum* (n 2) 348–50.

[21] See S Kneebone, *Refugees, Asylum Seekers and the Rule of Law: Comparative Perspectives* (Cambridge, CUP, 2009) 9–10; Goodwin-Gill and McAdam (n 2) 427.

[22] Moreno-Lax, *Accessing Asylum* (n 2) 340–41, 474–75; Giuffré and Moreno-Lax (n 3) 100–01.

[23] Moreno-Lax, *Accessing Asylum* (n 2) 476.

trajectory should be understood as the exercise of one's right to leave in search of a State of asylum, followed by the prohibitions on *refoulement* and collective expulsion operating to secure a right of entry for those who do manage to make contact with the State or reach its frontier. As argued in chapter three, entry does not stem from the right to *leave*.

Some have gone so far as to argue that where restrictions on the right to leave involve a real risk of extraterritorial *refoulement*, which is prohibited in absolute terms under human rights law, the aggregate right to leave to seek asylum constitutes a *lex specialis* of absolute character to the qualified right to leave available to everyone. Moreno-Lax suggests that this disallows any proportionality reasoning and instead imposes a duty on States to actively avoid *refoulement*.[24] Den Heijer concludes that any restriction on leaving exposing individuals to *refoulement* should automatically be construed as disproportionate.[25]

However, the notion of an *absolute* right to leave to seek asylum is not legally sound.[26] The right to leave is clearly qualified in all treaties enshrining it. As Stoyanova argues, 'The interdependence between leaving and seeking asylum – understood as having access to a procedure to be protected from *refoulement* – does not transform the right to leave into an absolute right'.[27] It is far more defensible to assess whether restrictions are consistent with *non-refoulement* obligations in accordance with the right to leave's consistency and proportionality requirements. In fact, den Heijer recognises that construing restrictions on leaving which violate other rights as disproportionate corresponds Article 12(3) of the ICCPR that restrictions must be consistent with other rights.[28]

Additionally, a stricter test should be adopted when assessing violations of the right to leave for asylum seekers when these other rights and obligations are at play, given their protection needs. Moreno-Lax has herself suggested that the public order aim of controlling migration should play a much lesser role for asylum seekers as the underlying reasons for fleeing and *refoulement* risks must be given considerable weight (though she goes on to say they should be given no weight at all).[29] This is supported by *MSS v Belgium and Greece*, where the Strasbourg Court attached 'considerable importance to the applicant's status as an asylum seeker and … member of a particularly underprivileged

[24] ibid 354, 391–93, 475.

[25] M den Heijer, *Europe and Extraterritorial Asylum* (Oxford, Hart Publishing, 2012) 166.

[26] Goodwin-Gill and McAdam (n 2) ch 8 fn 198 are similarly of the view that this goes much too far.

[27] V Stoyanova, 'The Right to Leave Any Country and the Interplay between Jurisdiction and Proportionality in Human Rights Law' (2020) 32 *International Journal of Refugee Law* 403, 436.

[28] Den Heijer (n 25) 166.

[29] Moreno-Lax, *Accessing Asylum* (n 2) 349. See also E Guild and V Stoyanova, 'The Human Right to Leave Any Country: A Right to Be Delivered' in W Benedek and others (eds), *European Yearbook on Human Rights 2018* (Plymouth, Intersentia, 2018) 391–93, particularly fn 78.

and vulnerable population group in need of special protection' in determining whether his detention and living conditions amounted to inhuman and degrading treatment.[30] Even under Article 3 of the ECHR, the Court has considered general and competing interests in cases concerning the removal of seriously ill migrants. In determining the impact of removal and whether this would reach the minimum threshold for ill-treatment, the Court compares the compelling humanitarian considerations against expulsion.[31] Nevertheless, a measure negating the right to seek asylum and/or leading to *refoulement* will almost always fail the legitimacy, proportionality and consistency tests. However, this does not render the right to flee absolute nor eliminate the need to apply the textual requirements of the right to leave.

D. Who is Protected?

This work began by defining an asylum seeker as any person fleeing to seek international protection, encompassing a wide range of beneficiaries, and asylum as the broad institution of protection from harm. Accordingly, 'the right to leave to seek asylum' should protect all people escaping persecution or other serious harm. This broad characterisation is warranted because the reasons people flee are complex and compounding. New protection needs may emerge throughout their flight, and many people flee while uncertain of the protection status they are seeking or entitled to. Since this work adopts an inclusivist view of migrants, migrants with protection needs would also be captured by the right to leave to seek asylum. However, the right is unlikely to apply to refugees *sur place* – people who were not refugees when they left their country of origin but developed a well-founded fear due to events occurring after they left.

This *lex specialis* formulation should not be perceived as calling into question the universal protection of the right to leave, which applies to everyone irrespective of protection needs. However, from a legal standpoint, the purpose of departure matters. A person's status as an asylum seeker and entitlement to protection from *refoulement* may trump a State's restrictions on the right to leave when applying the right's proportionality and consistency limbs.[32] Together, these rights and obligations form the basis of international protection, intertwining to strengthen the protection afforded to asylum seekers and refugees.

[30] *MSS* (n 12) paras 232, 251.

[31] See *Paposhvili v Belgium*, App no 41738/10 (13 December 2016) paras 174, 177–78, 188; Stoyanova, 'Right to Leave' (n 27) 436–37.

[32] Zieck (n 7) 32, 35–36.

III. DUTIES OWED TO ASYLUM SEEKERS

It is well-established within human rights law that States must respect, protect and fulfil the rights of individuals within their jurisdiction. Rights can generate a multiplicity of duties, followed by successive waves of duties tailored to what is needed to realise and protect the right.[33] The general obligation to protect requires States (and IOs) to exercise due diligence and take all reasonable steps to prevent violations against individuals within their jurisdiction by State and non-State actors.[34] Accordingly, there are a range of possible obligations generated by the right to leave. It is clear from chapter two that States have a negative obligation to refrain from unjustifiably interfering with the right to leave and a positive obligation to facilitate the right by issuing travel documents to their nationals. Part II of this book identifies additional obligations and duties necessary to respect and realise the right to leave for migrants in the context of externalisation. This section focuses specifically on the duties that are or should be imposed on States to give effect to the right to leave to seek asylum, which may also be borne by IOs bound by the right to leave.

A. Duty to Issue Travel Documents

There has been increasing discussion on refugee travel documents to facilitate refugee mobility and support access to resettlement, complementary pathways and opportunities abroad.[35] However, this discussion has not focused on whether such a duty exists by virtue of the right to leave to seek asylum. The jurisprudence of adjudicative bodies, expert studies and declarations outlined in chapter two recognised the necessity of travel documents for the right to leave. The right to obtain a passport is clearly expressed by the Human Rights Committee in General Comment No 27:

> Since international travel usually requires appropriate documents, in particular a passport, the right to leave a country must include the right to obtain the necessary travel documents. The issuing of passports is normally incumbent on the State of nationality of the individual.[36]

[33] J Waldron, 'Rights in Conflict' (1989) 99 *Ethics* 503, 509–12; IE Koch, 'Dichotomies, Trichotomies or Waves of Duties?' (2005) 5 *Human Rights Law Review* 81.

[34] See RP Barnidge, 'The Due Diligence Principle under International Law' (2006) 8 *International Community Law Review* 81; M Hakimi, 'State Bystander Responsibility' (2010) 21 *European Journal of International Law* 341; V Stoyanova, *Positive Obligations under the European Convention on Human Rights: Within and Beyond Boundaries* (Oxford, OUP, 2023).

[35] See S Davidoff-Gore, 'The Mobility Key: Realizing the Potential of Refugee Travel Documents' (*Migration Policy Institute*, 2024) www.migrationpolicy.org/research/refugee-travel-documents. The term 'travel document' describes passports or other forms of identity documents facilitating travel across international borders and return to the issuing State.

[36] HRC, 'General Comment No 27: Article 12 (Freedom of Movement)' (2 November 1999) UN Doc CCPR/C/21/Rev.1/Add.9, para 9.

The jurisprudence demonstrated that the right to leave imposes obligations on States of nationality, residence and sojourn so individuals can exercise their right to leave. Most of the jurisprudence concerned issuing travel documents to nationals but more recently also recognised refugees and permanent residents previously granted protection. Whether States of sojourn are obliged to issue travel documents to irregular migrants within their territory has not yet been considered.[37] Historically, Special Rapporteur Inglés limited the duty to provide travel documentation under the right to nationals.[38] To date, the obligations of States of residence and sojourn have largely been equated with a negative duty to refrain from impeding departure out of their territory.[39] However, nothing in the jurisprudence or text of the right to leave limits the duties in this manner. On the contrary, the Human Rights Committee's statement recognised that the issuance of travel documents is 'normally', but not only, incumbent on the State of nationality. Given the right to leave's applicability to everyone and all States can bear obligations under the right, there is a sound legal basis for interpreting the right to leave to seek asylum as obliging States of sojourn to issue travel documents to asylum seekers and refugees, regardless of status.[40] This is supported by three main justifications.

First, such a duty accords with the principle of effectiveness and fundamental principles of equality and non-discrimination, ensuring the right to leave is practical and effective, not theoretical and illusory, for everyone, not just select groups. The Strasbourg Court has held that the right to leave cannot be considered to impose 'a general obligation to issue aliens residing on their territory with any particular document permitting them to travel abroad'.[41] However, where the host State refuses to issue a travel document to a non-national so as to allow that person to leave its territory in a lawful manner, in certain circumstances, the individual's right to leave would not be practical and effective, and a breach will have occurred.[42] The Court has found this to be the case for refugees and former subsidiary protection beneficiaries who cannot obtain documentation from their country of origin, which they fled fearing persecution or threats to their safety. Host States cannot bypass their own obligations by requiring

[37] This was proposed by U Brandl, 'The Human Right to Leave a Country: To Protect or Forget?' (Conflict and Compromise between Law and Politics in EU Migration and Asylum Policies conference, Brussels, February 2018).

[38] CHR (Sub-Commission), 'Study of Discrimination in Respect of the Right of Everyone to Leave any Country, including his Own, and to Return to his Country by Special Rapporteur José D Inglés' (1963) UN Doc E/CN.4/Sub.2/220/Rev.1, 66–67.

[39] See Goodwin-Gill and McAdam (n 2) 430; G Cornelisse, 'European Vessels, African Territorial Waters and "Illegal Emigrants": The Right to Leave and the Principle of (Il)legality in a Global Regime of Mobility' (2008) *Challenge*.

[40] JC Hathaway, *The Rights of Refugees under International Law* (Cambridge, CUP, 2005) 850–51; Zieck (n 7) 88–90.

[41] *LB v Lithuania*, App no 38121/20 (ECtHR, 14 June 2022) para 59.

[42] *SE v Serbia*, App no 61365/16 (ECtHR, 11 July 2023) paras 47–49, 88; ibid.

refugees to approach their country of origin or to naturalise to be able to leave the host State's territory.[43]

The Court's reasoning is important for present purposes in underscoring the duty of States under the right to ensure decisions regarding travel documents are justified and proportionate in the individual situation, which requires assessing whether obtaining such documentation from one's country of origin is accessible in practice. The Court was also clear that the 'economic wellbeing of the country' and lack of resources are not among the legitimate aims justifying restricting the right to leave and State inaction.[44] However, these decisions concerned people with refugee status and permanent residents lawfully within the territory, who were deprived of travel documents for several years. It is beyond question that States have an obligation to issue travel documents to refugees and stateless persons lawfully in their territory unless compelling reasons of national security or public order exist, in accordance with Article 28 of the Refugee Convention and the Convention relating to the Status of Stateless Persons.[45] The right to leave reinforces this and provides another avenue to enforce the international freedom of movement of refugees.[46]

This relates to the second justification: the issuance of travel documents is arguably inherent in the notion of international protection. As Vedsted-Hansen posits, the 'issuance of travel documents to refugees has been one of the most important aspects of international protection of their legal status'.[47] Asylum seekers and refugees are in a special position compared to other migrants, unable to apply to their State of origin for documentation due to fear of persecution or serious harm, or their papers may be destroyed, lost or confiscated during their journey.[48] A major implication of the Refugee Convention's cessation provisions in Article 1C is that refugees cannot apply to their State of origin for a passport as this risks cessation of their refugee status, as they may be seen as voluntarily re-availing themselves of the protection of their country of nationality. Third, the right to recognition as a person before the law is enshrined in numerous instruments, which also protect the right to leave.[49] Possessing a travel document provides asylum seekers and refugees with crucial recognition of their legal personhood and identity.[50]

[43] *LB* (n 41) paras 90–98; *SE* (n 42) 79–81.

[44] *SE* (n 42) para 87.

[45] See also OAU Convention, art VI; Qualification Directive, art 25.

[46] UNHCR, 'Amicus Curiae of the United Nations High Commissioner for Refugees (UNHCR) on the Interpretation and Application of Article 25, Article 27 and Article 28 of the 1951 Convention Relating to the Status of Refugees' (22 December 2016) paras 29–35.

[47] J Vedsted-Hansen, 'Article 28/Schedule' in A Zimmermann, J Dörschner and F Machts (eds), *The 1951 Convention Relating to the Status of Refugees and its 1967 Protocol: A Commentary* (Oxford, OUP, 2011) 1182 para 1, 1185 para 7, particularly fn 3.

[48] ibid.

[49] See ADHR, art XVII; UDHR, art 6; ICCPR, art 16; ACHR, art 3; African Charter, art 5; UNCRC, arts 7 and 8; ICRMW, art 24; Arab Charter, art 22; CRPD, art 12.

[50] GS Goodwin-Gill, *International Law and the Movement of Persons Between States* (Oxford, Clarendon Press, 1978) 43–44.

It is far less clear and more controversial that States of sojourn or first countries of asylum should be obliged to issue travel documents to asylum seekers and refugees irregularly present or residing there temporarily, which would represent an expansion of a State's duties under the right to leave. On the one hand, doing so would help rectify the plight of asylum seekers in recognition of their protection needs, lack of traditional travel documents and potential statelessness, and contribute to preventing irregular migration. Such a duty would enable people to seek asylum and longer-term solutions through safe and regular means if protection is unavailable where they are, for family reunification, resettlement, labour migration and other regular travel purposes.[51]

In principle, States are free to issue passports to whomever they choose.[52] The Refugee and Stateless Conventions contain a discretionary power to issue documents to any other refugee or stateless person therein, providing that States shall give 'sympathetic consideration' to those unable to obtain such documents from their country of lawful residence.[53] The African Commission's Guiding Principles provide that 'States shall issue travel documents to migrants, for the purpose of travel outside their territory, unless compelling reasons of national security or public order otherwise require' and that States shall facilitate the issuance of identity and other documents for migrants.[54] The Inter-American Commission has similarly concluded that every migrant, regardless of migration status, has the right to access and possess all documents necessary to exercise their rights, including passports and travel documents, and countries of transit and destination must facilitate the issuance of identity documents.[55]

This supports States of sojourn possessing negative duties under the right to leave and a positive duty to facilitate leaving for asylum seekers and refugees. This naturally raises issues surrounding practicality, resource, security and vetting, as well as public order considerations. States are likely to defend against issuing travel documents to asylum seekers who are irregularly present or hold temporary status but want to keep moving in search of greater protection or better opportunities, which some courts may accept as legitimate and necessary. However, a progressive approach would extend the duty to issue travel documents to all asylum seekers and refugees to secure their right to leave to seek

[51] See ICRMW, art 68(1): States 'shall collaborate with a view to preventing and eliminating illegal or clandestine movements and employment of migrant workers in an irregular situation'.

[52] Goodwin-Gill, *International Law* (n 50) 45–46; J Torpey, *The Invention of the Passport: Surveillance, Citizenship, and the State*, 2nd edn (Cambridge, CUP, 2018) 222–23. However, there are limits on whether accompanying rights are opposable to other States: *Nottebohm Case (Liechtenstein v Guatemala)* (Judgment) [1955] ICJ Rep 4.

[53] See also Refugee Convention, sch paras 6(3), 13(1); Convention relating to the Status of Stateless Persons (adopted 28 September 1954, entered into force 6 June 1960) 360 UNTS 117, sch paras 6(3), 13(1); OAU Convention, art VI(I).

[54] ACHPR, 'African Guiding Principles on the Human Rights of All Migrants, Refugees and Asylum Seekers' (2023) principles 17(2) and 7(5), achpr.au.int/index.php/en/soft-law/african-guiding-principles-humanrights-all-migrants-refugees. cf principle 7(4).

[55] IACHR, 'Inter-American Principles on the Human Rights of All Migrants, Refugees, Stateless Persons and Victims of Human Trafficking' (2019) principle 4, www.oas.org/en/iachr/decisions/pdf/Resolution-4-19-en.pdf.

asylum.[56] This would be particularly beneficial for asylum seekers and refugees falling outside Article 28 of the Refugee Convention, especially those trapped in transit and in protracted situations in the first country of asylum, given the almost-universal passport requirement for international travel.[57] With the existence of resettlement schemes, complementary pathways, and evacuation and relocation mechanisms out of places like Libya, Ukraine and hotspots in Greece, a global regime can be envisioned that supports refugee mobility. Such a regime would prioritise protection needs, access to solutions and regular travel opportunities, and individual agency, coordinated and supported by governments, donors and IOs.[58] UNHCR, IOM and the International Committee of the Red Cross (ICRC) already play a primary role in facilitating mobility, and the ICRC also issues travel documents. A duty on States to issue travel documents to refugees and asylum seekers regardless of status can be seen as a revival and expansion of the Nansen Passport, which was an identification and travel document created by States for refugees and stateless persons post-World War I, the success of which depended on States recognising its validity.[59]

Although many States want to reduce irregular migration, this proposal would have serious implications for State practice, which draws a sharp distinction between initial and secondary movement and attempts to suppress the latter through externalisation measures. As such, securing the political will of States on this remains idealistic. The provision of travel documents for recognised refugees is a need that already remains largely unmet in many countries around the world. Moreover, the benefit of recognising a duty on States to issue travel documents to refugees and asylum seekers beyond Convention Travel Documents and similar should not be overstated. As chapter five delves into, without an entry visa, a passport may be necessary but insufficient to secure exit, with departure often dependent on possessing a visa or visa-waiver for the destination. Nonetheless, creating an entitlement for all refugees and asylum seekers to receive travel documents would be one step closer to ensuring that the right to leave is effective and meaningful for all.

B. Duty Not to Obstruct the Right to Leave

The existence of a duty not to obstruct the right to leave for asylum seekers is clearer, though not without some opposition. Goodwin-Gill and McAdam

[56] See Hathaway (n 40) 840–51.

[57] See further S Dehm, 'Passport' in J Hohmann and D Joyce (eds), *International Law's Objects* (Oxford, OUP, 2018).

[58] See Davidoff-Gore (n 35) 2, 16–17.

[59] See Torpey (n 52) 157–60; UNHCR, 'Refugee travel documents', www.unhcr.org/what-we-do/build-better-futures/long-term-solutions/complementary-pathways-admission-third-4; UNHCR, 'Summary Conclusions – UNHCR Expert Roundtable on travel documents for persons in need of international protection and stateless persons' (22 October 2024). On gaps and weaknesses that would need to be overcome, see K Bengel, 'Understanding the Nansen Passport: A System of Manipulation' (2022) 29 *Indiana Journal of Global Legal Studies* 217.

have long argued that the right to leave to seek asylum imposes a duty on States not to frustrate the exercise of this right so as to expose individuals to persecution or other serious harms, in accordance with the principle of good faith.[60] To comply with the right to leave, States must implement and interpret their treaty obligations in good faith and, more specifically, Contracting Parties must refrain from acting against the object and purpose of the Refugee Convention, namely 'to extend the protection of the international community to refugees, and to assure to refugees "the widest possible exercise of … fundamental rights and freedoms"'.[61] The imposition of migration controls that systematically obstruct departure and block access to asylum procedures not only violates the right to leave but also demonstrates a lack of good faith in upholding the right to seek asylum and the obligation of *non-refoulement*.[62] Such measures may also constitute discrimination. A good faith interpretation requires States to organise their immigration controls so individuals can leave to seek asylum.[63] As chapter two demonstrated, the right to control entry operates *within* the confines of international law, and the right to leave should not be read as permitting obstructions of departure on the pretext that entry will not be granted.

In 1996, Hailbronner, responding to Goodwin-Gill, doubted the existence of any general duty on States to ensure individuals can effectively exercise their right to seek and enjoy asylum, arguing legal duties under *non-refoulement* only arise when individuals are within State territory or at the border.[64] However, as discussed, *non-refoulement* obligations are widely accepted as applying extra-territorially. More problematic are the decisions of UK courts. In the *Roma Rights* case, the House of Lords held that neither Article 33 of the Refugee Convention nor customary law requires States 'to abstain from controlling the movements of people outside its borders who wish to travel to it in order to claim asylum' nor those who presented themselves, save in a highly metaphorical

[60] Goodwin-Gill and McAdam (n 2) 403, 416–17, 431.

[61] See Refugee Convention, preamble; GS Goodwin-Gill, 'State Responsibility and the "Good Faith" Obligation in International Law' in M Fitzmaurice and D Sarooshi (eds), *Issues of State Responsibility before International Judicial Institutions: The Clifford Chance Lectures* (Oxford, Hart Publishing, 2004) 93; Goodwin-Gill and McAdam (n 2) 433–36.

[62] R Weinzierl and U Lisson, *Border Management and Human Rights: A Study of EU Law and the Law of the Sea* (Berlin, German Institute for Human Rights, 2007) 68; Goodwin-Gill and McAdam (n 2) 433–34. See also *AEA v Greece*, App no 39034/12 (ECtHR, 15 March 2018) paras 77–85; Moreno-Lax, *Accessing Asylum* (n 2) 354, 393–94.

[63] See HRC, 'General Comment No 36 (2018) on Article 6 of the International Covenant on Civil and Political Rights, on the Right to Life' (30 October 2018) UN Doc CCPR/C/GC/36, para 19; GS Goodwin-Gill, 'The Right to Leave, the Right to Return and the Question of the Right to Remain' in V Gowlland-Debbas, *The Problem of Refugees in the Light of Contemporary International Law Issues* (The Hague, Martinus Nijhoff, 1996); Moreno-Lax, *Accessing Asylum* (n 2) 349; Moreno-Lax, 'Intersectionality' (n 1) 76, 82.

[64] K Hailbronner, 'Comments on the Right to Leave, Return and Remain' in V Gowlland-Debbas (ed), *The Problem of Refugees in the Light of Contemporary International Law Issues* (The Hague, Martinus Nijhoff, 1996) 115–16.

sense, at the State's frontier.[65] The case concerned the interception of Czech nationals of Roma ethnicity by British authorities stationed at Prague airport implementing a pre-clearance programme targeting Roma asylum seekers. The Law Lords found that to argue such measures are incompatible with the Convention's object and purpose and principle of good faith 'is to argue for the enlargement of the obligations which are to be found in the Convention', which defines refugees as persons outside their country of origin and requires return to the State's frontiers.[66] Neither the Refugee Convention nor customary law supports the proposition that *non-refoulement* obligations extend to general deterrence measures denying would-be refugees the ability to leave their own State.[67] As a result, the applicants' appeal failed on Article 33 grounds because they were still in the Czech Republic.

Similarly, in the highly contentious cases brought in the UK against the proposed UK–Rwanda asylum deal, the High Court and Court of Appeal rejected the claimant's argument that deterring refugees from undertaking irregular journeys was inconsistent with the spirit and purpose of the Convention. The courts held that there is no implied limitation when making a removal decision requiring consideration of the person's irregular arrival, even where there were no available regular means, or the aim of deterrence.[68] The Supreme Court did not consider these arguments, but ultimately declared the scheme unlawful because Rwanda could not be considered a safe third country.

However, the decisions of one jurisdiction are not determinative, and moreover, these decisions relied only on narrow Convention grounds and failed to consider obligations under human rights law.[69] As I have highlighted elsewhere, none of the UK courts in the Rwanda litigation appear to have considered Lord Steyn's conclusion in *Roma Rights* that controlling the movement of asylum seekers outside a State's territory 'is not incompatible with the acceptance of the obligations *which arise when refugees have arrived in its territory*', despite the fact those earmarked for removal to Rwanda had already entered the UK.[70] The systematic frustration of the right to flee and the containment of asylum seekers in their States of origin and transit by destination States, with the express purpose of preventing their obligations from ever attaching, displays

[65] *R v Immigration Officer at Prague Airport, ex p European Roma Rights Centre* [2004] UKHL 55, [2005] 2 AC 1, paras 26, 64.

[66] ibid paras 18, 20, 63–64.

[67] Hathaway (n 40) 307; Goodwin-Gill and McAdam (n 2) 428.

[68] *R (on the application of AAA and others) v The Secretary of State for the Home Department* [2022] EWHC 3230 (Admin), para 121; *R (on the application of AAA and others) v Secretary of State for the Home Department* [2023] EWCA Civ 745, [2023] 4 All ER 253, paras 315(2), 316, 319.

[69] See GS Goodwin-Gill, 'R (ex parte European Roma Rights Centre et al) v Immigration Officer at Prague Airport and another (UNHCR intervening)' (2005) 17 *International Journal of Refugee Law* 427, paras 24–38.

[70] E McDonnell, 'Externalisation as a Breach of the Good Faith Principle' (*Externalizing Asylum*, 2024) externalizingasylum.info/externalisation-as-a-breach-of-the-good-faith-principle/ (emphasis added).

a clear lack of good faith.[71] The UNHCR has encapsulated this: a State lacks good faith 'when it seeks to avoid or to "divert" the obligation which it has accepted, or to do indirectly what it is not permitted to do directly'.[72]

This conclusion is further reinforced by the jurisprudence. In the landmark pushbacks case of *Hirsi Jamaa v Italy*, the Strasbourg Court held that problems 'managing migratory flows cannot justify having recourse to practices which are not compatible with the State's obligations' under the ECHR, which must be interpreted in good faith and in accordance with the principle of effectiveness.[73] The Inter-American Court of Human Rights has further recognised that States must not adopt measures to prevent individuals from seeking asylum nor hide behind legal fictions to avoid giving access to corresponding protection procedures.[74] The Committee Against Torture has stipulated that imposing obstacles against leaving clashes with the State's duty to take preventive measures against possible violations of *non-refoulement*.[75] Similarly, the UN Special Rapporteur on Torture and Other Cruel, Inhuman or Degrading Treatment or Punishment has concluded that States cannot engage in any activity or conclude agreements which would undermine or defeat the very object and purpose of the right not to be subjected to torture and ill-treatment or of 'any ancillary rights designed to give it effect in practice, such as the rights to leave any country or territory, to seek and enjoy asylum'.[76] Therefore, general deterrence measures imposed by States should be considered incompatible with the right to leave to seek asylum and obligations of *non-refoulement* for breaching the principle of good faith.

If refugee and asylum seeker rights are to be taken seriously, 'a reconsideration of the premise underpinning extraterritorial entry controls is necessary. The rights to asylum and to *non-refoulement* require that access to international protection be not unduly obstructed.'[77] To conclude otherwise upholds the protection gap resulting from the lack of a general right of entry, where individuals are only protected from *refoulement* or expulsion if within the State's jurisdiction but where they cannot access the State to begin with.[78] As Judge Cançado Trindade of the Inter-American Court has opined, the States that have perpetuated this gap have 'created more problems not only for numerous individuals directly affected but also, ultimately, for themselves, in contributing

[71] Goodwin-Gill and McAdam (n 2) 434. See also ibid.

[72] Goodwin-Gill, *International Law* (n 50) 93. See 'UNHCR Intervention Before the House of Lords in the Case of European Roma Rights Centre and Others v Immigration Officer at Prague Airport, Secretary of State for the Home Department' (28 September 2004) para 81.

[73] *Hirsi Jamaa v Italy* (2012) 55 EHRR 21, para 179.

[74] *Advisory Opinion on the Institution of Asylum and its Recognition as a Human Right in the Inter-American Protection System*, IACtHR, OC-25/18 (30 May 2018) para 122.

[75] CAT, 'General Comment No 4 (2017) on the Implementation of Article 3 of the Convention in the Context of Article 22' (4 September 2018) UN Doc CAT/C/GC/4, para 18.

[76] UNGA, 'Report of the Special Rapporteur on Torture and Other Cruel, Inhuman or Degrading Treatment or Punishment' (23 November 2018) UN Doc A/HRC/37/50, para 14.

[77] Moreno-Lax, *Accessing Asylum* (n 2) 467.

[78] AL Hirsch and N Bell, 'The Right to Have Rights as a Right to Enter: Addressing a Lacuna in the International Refugee Protection Regime' (2017) 18 *Human Rights Review* 417, 418.

indirectly' to irregular migration.[79] To comply with the duty not to obstruct the right to leave to seek asylum, States must ensure their restrictions do not defeat the object and purpose of fundamental rights and obligations nor make seeking asylum impossible.

C. General Duty to Facilitate Leaving

The right to leave is often made dependent on having permission to enter another State, alongside destination States requesting third States to prevent irregular migration on their behalf. This raises the question of whether the right to leave to seek asylum imposes a general duty requiring States to take steps to *facilitate* asylum seekers' exercise of their right to leave through regular and safe means, moving beyond the duty of non-obstruction to one of actual realisation. These situations also raise complex issues of international responsibility and the lawfulness of cooperative externalisation arrangements, explored in Part II.

Eminent scholars conclude that States do not have a duty to facilitate travel to their territories for asylum seekers, as *non-refoulement* is not equated with a duty to *receive* refugees.[80] In the case of *ND and NT v Spain*, the Strasbourg Court considered that although rights must be practical and effective, 'This does not, however, imply a general duty ... to bring persons who are under the jurisdiction of another State within its own jurisdiction'.[81] Nonetheless, the Court's conclusion was related to collective expulsion, without appreciation of the right to leave. The effectiveness of the right to leave for asylum seekers requires the right to be read in a comprehensive and systemic manner. All components of the migration trajectory – including departure, admission, and sojourn – are framed by international law, as chapters two and three demonstrated.[82]

Recognition of a general facilitative duty would ensure all surrounding rights and obligations are duly accounted for and fulfilled. Such a duty would be dynamic, variable and context-specific; for example, it would require intense cooperation amongst countries of origin, transit and destination and IOs, such as the EU, UNHCR and IOM, to ensure the safe departure to another country of asylum seekers and refugees who are trapped in precarious or protracted situations.[83] The duty-bearers of the right to leave are not limited to departure

[79] *Advisory Opinion on Juridical Condition and Rights of Undocumented Migrants*, IACtHR, OC-18/03 (17 September 2003) 12 para 32 (Concurring Opinion Cançado Trindade J).

[80] Hathaway (n 40) 301; Goodwin-Gill and McAdam (n 2) 434.

[81] ND and NT v Spain, Apps nos 8675/15 and 8697/15 (ECtHR, 13 February 2020) para 221. See also *European Roma Rights Centre v Immigration Officer at Prague Airport* [2003] EWCA Civ 666, [2003] 4 All ER 247, paras 37, 43; *Roma Rights* (n 65) paras 43, 64.

[82] V Chetail, *International Migration Law* (Oxford, OUP, 2019) 162–63.

[83] See V Chetail, 'Freedom of Movement and Transnational Migrations: A Human Rights Perspective' in TA Aleinikoff and V Chetail (eds), *Migration and International Legal Norms* (The Hague, TMC Asser Press, 2003) 59.

or States of nationality but can equally impose duties on destination States exercising extraterritorial control and IOs, as chapter two demonstrated. States have already committed to international solidarity and responsibility sharing so interpreting the right to leave to seek asylum as generating this facilitative duty is not far-fetched.[84] Proposing a facilitative duty of *departure* may sound akin to asserting a facilitative duty of *admission*, creating a potential incoherence with the right to leave as distinct from the right of entry. However, it is necessary to view the migration trajectory holistically and the interrelated nature of exit and entry. A State giving meaningful effect to an individual's right to leave by facilitating their departure will necessarily result in entry elsewhere following the agreement of that receiving State, but this does not deny their distinctiveness. Entry would continue to stem from other obligations or agreements such as States consenting to resettlement, complementary pathways and relocation schemes.

Nonetheless, accepting there is no general facilitative duty to facilitate asylum seekers' right to leave is unlikely to be overly problematic. This is where the strength of the right to leave shows. There is a fine line between the duty not to obstruct departure and the duty to create the conditions under which the right can be exercised. Measures appearing to require positive action to facilitate departure, such as granting visas or removing visa requirements altogether, can instead be viewed as an obstruction of the right to leave, such as refusing to issue a visa (chapter five).[85] Whether framed as a negative or positive duty, States must ensure the right to leave to seek asylum is upheld.

IV. CONCLUSION

This chapter demonstrated the vital importance of the right to leave for asylum seekers and refugees, fittingly characterised as a *right to leave to seek asylum*. The right to leave is an essential precondition for seeking and securing asylum. Ultimately, to be granted refugee status or to secure protection from *refoulement* and collective expulsion by triggering one's right of entry, asylum seekers must be able to leave the country they are in. It follows that a stricter test should be applied when assessing violations of the right to leave for asylum seekers and refugees, taking into account their protection needs and *refoulement* risks when applying the legitimacy, proportionality and consistency limbs. Several possible duties are generated by the right to leave to seek asylum, going beyond existing duties to strengthen the rights and protection of asylum seekers and refugees.

[84] See EXCOM, 'Note on International Protection' (16 June 2017) UN Doc EC/68/SC/CRP.12, pt II; UNGA, 'Report of the United Nations High Commissioner for Refugees: Part II Global Compact on Refugees' (2 August 2018) UN Doc A/73/12, paras 4–5; EXCOM, 'Note on International Protection' (10 July 2020) UN Doc A/AC.96/1200, paras 2–3.

[85] See den Heijer (n 25) 158.

However, their recognition would face significant pushback and controversy. First, it was argued States of sojourn possess a duty to issue travel documents to asylum seekers and refugees therein, regardless of their migration status. In coordination with IOs, this would help rectify the immobility of many asylum seekers and refugees trapped in transit and protracted situations, supporting their agency and access to regular travel opportunities enjoyed by non-refugees. Second, States must not negate the flight of asylum seekers. This requires States to organise their migration laws and policies to enable individuals to leave and seek asylum, giving due regard to the right to leave, *non-refoulement*, collective expulsion and non-discrimination obligations, and the performance of their obligations in good faith. Third, States and IOs may also be obliged more generally to proactively facilitate departure, by taking steps towards actual realisation of the right to leave to seek asylum.

Recognition of the duty not to obstruct departure and to allow asylum seekers to search for a State to admit them would have profound consequences for externalisation strategies and serve to limit the measures States and IOs can lawfully impose. The significance of the right to leave for asylum seekers has not yet been adequately appreciated by the Strasbourg Court, failing to address the 'compounded nature of the rights and realities of asylum seekers attempting to leave a country in search of international protection'.[86] A holistic and systemic interpretation of the right to leave, read alongside the fundamental protections owed to asylum seekers and refugees, is essential to safeguarding the ability of individuals to leave a country, seek protection without unnecessary barriers, and access asylum procedures in their destination.

[86] Moreno-Lax, 'Intersectionality' (n 1) 45–53; McDonnell (n 70).

PART II

Externalised Migration Controls

In Part II (chapters five and six), this book turns to the phenomenon of externalised migration control, applying the framework developed in Part I to assess whether, and under what circumstances, externalisation practices violate the right to leave and which actors bear responsibility for violations. It focuses on visa regimes and carrier sanctions (chapter five) and pushbacks and pullbacks at sea and on land (chapter six), while also drawing on other practices deployed to prevent departure such as offshore processing, safe country arrangements and detention. This section lays the groundwork for Part II by shifting focus beyond the Global North to the often-overlooked migration control policies of the Global South. It then introduces the law of international responsibility for States and IOs.

I. EXTERNALISATION AND THE GLOBAL SOUTH

Recent scholarship increasingly focuses on migration governance within the Global South, critiquing simplistic North-South binaries.[1] The literature highlights the interdependencies between Global South and North migration regimes, as well as the complicated power hierarchies within the South-South context.[2] Many countries in the Global South, which previously had open-door policies or long histories of daily migration, are emulating restrictive

[1] See eg, A Abass and F Ippolito (eds), *Regional Approaches to the Protection of Asylum Seekers: An International Legal Perspective* (Abingdon/New York, Routledge, 2016); I Stock, A Üstübici and SU Schultz, 'Externalization at Work: Responses to Migration Policies from the Global South' (2019) 7 *Comparative Migration Studies* 48; G Rayp, I Ruyssen and K Marchand (eds), *Regional Integration and Migration Governance in the Global South* (Cham, Springer, 2020); OG El-Taliawi, *The Politics of Refugee Policy in the Global South*, vol 15 (Montreal, McGill-Queen's University Press, 2024); P Rugunanan and XG Nomkhosi (eds), *Migration in Southern Africa: IMISCOE Regional Reader* (Cham, Springer, 2022); J Crush, A Chikanda and S Ramachandran (eds), *New Directions in South-South Migration* (Singapore, Springer Singapore, 2025); H Crawley and JK Teye (eds), *The Palgrave Handbook of South–South Migration and Inequality* (New York, Palgrave Macmillan, 2024); T Fakhoury and D Chatty (eds), *Refugee Governance in the Arab World: The International Refugee Regime and Global Politics* (London, Bloomsbury, 2025).

[2] See N Winters and C Mora Izaguirre, '*Es Cosa Suya*: Entanglements of Border Externalization and African Transit Migration in Northern Costa Rica' (2019) 7 *Comparative Migration Studies* 27; G Heck and others (eds), *Making Routes: Mobility and Politics of Migration in the Global South* (Cairo, The American University in Cairo Press, 2024).

measures. This can be driven by pressure or incentives from the Global North, or a unilateral response to increased migration and asylum seeking. There is growing recognition that 'partner' States are not merely passive recipients but active participants with their own interests and agency to both resist and reproduce externalisation strategies.[3] While Global North countries like Australia, EU Member States and the US routinely use political and economic leverage to outsource migration control, governments and local actors in countries such as Indonesia, Mexico and Turkey leverage their strategic position to advance their own agendas.[4] Nevertheless, there remains limited in-depth research on how Global South States implement externalisation measures and their impact on citizens and migrants.

II. INTERNATIONAL LEGAL RESPONSIBILITY

In international law, responsibility follows obligation: every breach by a State or IO of its international obligations entails international responsibility and triggers duties to cease the wrongful conduct and make reparation.[5] Establishing responsibility for violations, such as of the right to leave, requires recourse to the rules of international responsibility. These are codified in the ILC's Articles on Responsibility of States for Internationally Wrongful Acts (ARSIWA) and Articles on Responsibility of International Organisations (ARIO).[6]

[3] See A Üstübici, 'The Impact of Externalized Migration Governance on Turkey: Technocratic Migration Governance and the Production of Differentiated Legal Status' (2019) 7 *Comparative Migration Studies* 1; IMS Vammen, CR Signe and H Lucht, 'Borderwork in the Expanded EU-African Borderlands' (2022) 27 *Geopolitics* 1317; F Zanker, '"When There Is No Migration, the Whole Region Has a Problem": The Political Priorities of Migration Policies in West Africa' (2024) 10 *African Human Mobility Review* 9.

[4] See H de Haas and S Vezzoli, 'Leaving Matters: The Nature, Evolution and Effects of Emigration Policies' (International Migration Institute, 2011) Working Paper 34, www.migrationinstitute.org/publications/wp-34-11; W Vogt, 'Dirty Work, Dangerous Others: The Politics of Outsourced Immigration Enforcement in Mexico' (2020) 3 *Migration and Society* 50; M Lee, 'The Externalization of Border Control in the Global South: The Cases of Malaysia and Indonesia' (2022) 26 *Theoretical Criminology* 537.

[5] ILC, 'Draft Articles on Responsibility of States for Internationally Wrongful Acts' (2001) *YBILC* Vol II(2) UN Doc A/RES/56/83 (ARSIWA), arts 1, 30–31; ARIO, arts 3, 30–31. For a useful overview, see Refugee Law Initiative, 'Declaration on Externalisation and Asylum' (2022) 34 *International Journal of Refugee Law* 114 paras 4–10; D Cantor and others, 'Externalisation, Access to Territorial Asylum, and International Law' (2022) 34 *International Journal of Refugee Law* 120, 129–31.

[6] For authoritative interpretations of ARSIWA and ARIO see ILC, 'Draft Articles on Responsibility of States for Internationally Wrongful Acts, with Commentaries' (2001) *YBILC* Vol II(2) 31, UN Doc A/56/10 (ARSIWA Commentary); ILC, 'Draft Articles on the Responsibility of International Organizations, with Commentaries' (2011) *YBILC* Vol II(2) 46, UN Doc A/66/10 (ARIO Commentary). See generally, J Crawford and others, *The Law of International Responsibility* (Oxford, OUP, 2010); HP Aust, *Complicity and the Law of State Responsibility* (Cambridge, CUP, 2011); J Crawford, *State Responsibility: The General Part* (Cambridge, CUP, 2013); M Jackson, *Complicity in International Law* (Oxford, OUP, 2015).

An 'internationally wrongful act' is any act or omission attributable to a State or IO that breaches one of its international obligations.[7] Crucially, neither Articles distinguish between territorial and extraterritorial acts. As established in Chapter two, IOs are bound by core human rights, including the right to leave. States and IOs may invoke six 'circumstances precluding wrongfulness' to justify otherwise wrongful conduct.[8] However, domestic law cannot be invoked as a defence for failing to uphold international obligations.[9] A State may be directly responsible for wrongful conduct when cooperating with or delegating functions to other States, IOs or private actors. Conduct is attributable to a State if performed by its de jure or de facto organs, whether inside or outside its territory; private persons or entities empowered to exercise governmental authority, or under the direction or control of the State; or organs of another State placed at its exclusive disposal – even if *ultra vires*.[10] ARIO sets out similar rules for attributing conduct to an IO.[11] The law remains complex and evolving, with ongoing uncertainties explored in the forthcoming chapters.

When multiple States or IOs contribute to the same harmful outcome, this should lead to shared responsibility.[12] This can take various forms, but is not without complexity. Several actors may share responsibility when they commit separate breaches that contribute to a single injury (see below on positive duties). Multiple actors may share responsibility when they engage in a single course of conduct that is attributable to several actors or when they act in concert. Alternatively, a State or IO may incur indirect or derived responsibility by being implicated in the wrongful conduct of another, including by aiding and assisting, directing and controlling, or coercing another to commit a breach.[13] The essential principle is that 'a State should not be able to do through another what it could not do itself'.[14]

[7] ARSIWA, art 2; ARIO, art 4. See ARSIWA Commentary, arts 32–34, 54(1); ARIO Commentary, arts 53, 62–64.

[8] ARSIWA, arts 20–25; ARIO, arts 20–25 on consent, self-defence, countermeasures, *force majeure*, distress and necessity. See also art 26; ARSIWA Commentary, ch V; ARIO Commentary, 48–49(10), ch V.

[9] ARSIWA, art 3; ARSIWA Commentary, 36–38. See also ARIO, art 5; ARIO Commentary, 53–54.

[10] ARSIWA, arts 4–8; ARSIWA Commentary, ch II.

[11] ARIO, arts 6–9; ARIO Commentary, ch II.

[12] See ARSIWA, art 47; ARIO, art 48; ARSIWA Commentary, 44(3), 64–65 (2)–(8), 67 (10), 124–25; ARIO, Commentary, 50 (10), 53 (6), ch II 54 (4). See also Crawford (n 6) chs 10, 12; A Nollkaemper and I Plakokefalos, *Principles of Shared Responsibility in International Law: An Appraisal of the State of the Art* (Cambridge, CUP, 2014); A Nollkaemper and others, *The Practice of Shared Responsibility in International Law* (Cambridge, CUP, 2017); A Nollkaemper and others, 'Guiding Principles on Shared Responsibility in International Law' (2020) 31 *European Journal of International Law* 15.

[13] ARSIWA, arts 16–19; ARIO, arts 14–16, 19, 58–60, 63; ARIO, Commentary, ch IV; ARIO, Commentary, ch IV; Nollkaemper and others, 'Guiding Principles' (n 12). See also ARIO, arts 17, 61 on circumvention of obligations.

[14] ARSIWA Commentary, 69 (8).

However, as scholars have observed, adjudicative bodies often address cooperative conduct through positive obligations.[15] This enables States or IOs to be held responsible for failing to protect, prevent or respond reasonably, even for conduct not attributable to them, and without needing to meet the high thresholds for complicity, control or coercion.[16] Positive duties owed extraterritorially are commensurate with the degree of control and influence an actor exercises over potential victims, the specific context, and their capacity to prevent harm.[17] This enables shared responsibility between the primary violator and another whose failure to uphold positive duties contributes to the harm. Given the intense collaboration on migration control, it is essential for both ensuring accountability and preventing repeat violations that all layers of involvement are identified, and responsibility appropriately assigned.[18]

[15] See M den Heijer, 'Shared Responsibility Before the European Court of Human Rights' (2013) 60 *Netherlands International Law Review* 411; H Keller and R Walther, 'Evasion of the International Law of State Responsibility? The ECtHR's Jurisprudence on Positive and Preventive Obligations under Article 3' (2019) 24 *International Journal of Human Rights* 957; R Garciandia, 'State Responsibility and Positive Obligations in the European Court of Human Rights: The Contribution of the ICJ in Advancing towards More Judicial Integration' (2020) 33 *Leiden Journal of International Law* 177.

[16] See Aust (n 6) ch 8, 422–23; O Corten and P Klein, 'The Limits of Complicity as a Ground for Responsibility: Lessons Learned from the *Corfu Channel* Case' in K Bannelier, T Christakis and S Heathcote (eds), *The ICJ and the Evolution of International Law: The Enduring Impact of the Corfu Channel Case* (Abingdon/New York, Routledge, 2012).

[17] See eg, *Ilaşcu v Moldova and Russia* (2005) 40 EHRR 1030, paras 313–18, 331; *Application of the Convention on the Prevention and Punishment of the Crime of Genocide (Bosnia and Herzegovina v Serbia and Montenegro)* (Judgment) [2007] ICJ Rep 43, paras 430–31; M Hakimi, 'State Bystander Responsibility' (2010) 21 *European Journal of International Law* 341, 364–67, 371–79; M den Heijer, *Europe and Extraterritorial Asylum* (Oxford, Hart Publishing, 2012) 52–55, 83–90; V Stoyanova, *Positive Obligations under the European Convention on Human Rights: Within and Beyond Boundaries* (Oxford, OUP, 2023) ch 8.

[18] C Ferstman, *International Organizations and the Fight for Accountability* (Oxford, OUP, 2017) 66.

5

Visa Regimes and Carrier Sanctions

I. INTRODUCTION

VISAS AND CARRIER sanctions have long been used by States to proactively prevent migration and keep certain would-be migrants far from their physical borders. They serve as the primary means of 'remote control'.[1] Without a visa or access to visa-free travel, people cannot lawfully reach their destination, enforced by carrier sanctions and immigration officials posted abroad. Accordingly, people needing a visa may be unable to leave their home country or transit through others. Airlines and other transport operators will likely deny boarding if people attempt to travel without valid documentation. In a world of visas and carrier sanctions, individuals face limited choices: find another country willing to grant a visa, remain in potentially dangerous situations, or travel irregularly. These policies enable mobility for some but immobilise others.

This chapter examines the compatibility of visa regimes and carrier sanctions with the right to leave, arguing that visa refusals and denials of embarkation can violate the right to leave. This is a controversial topic, as their long-standing, widespread use has led to their normalisation and presumed lawfulness. The chapter begins with the history of visas and carrier sanctions, followed by an overview of various visa regimes, distilling key features including selectivity; delegation and outsourcing to carriers, private visa companies, IOM and ICMPD; and growing automation. It shows how pressure from the Global North and between Global South States has driven the global spread of restrictive visa regimes and carrier sanctions. It then demonstrates how visa refusals and denials of embarkation by carriers constitute an exercise of jurisdiction and are attributable to the destination State. It concludes that visa refusals and denials of embarkation can breach the right to leave. In many instances, they fail the legality and proportionality tests under the right and also impede several other fundamental rights. Visa regimes disproportionately

[1] AR Zolberg, 'The Archaeology of "Remote Control"' in A Fahrmeir, O Faron and P Weil (eds), *Migration Control in the North Atlantic World: The Evolution of State Practices in Europe and the United States from the French Revolution to the Inter-War Period* (New York, Berghahn Books, 2003); AR Zolberg, 'Managing a World on the Move' (2006) 32 *Population and Development Review* 222, 223–24.

impact asylum seekers and refugees by denying them visas and access to regular, safe travel options, thus undermining their ability to seek asylum. It scrutinises whether visa policies amount to unlawful discrimination, especially in light of stark differences in treatment based on nationality, race and religion, as illustrated by the divergent treatment of Ukrainian versus other refugees.[2] It then explores the shared responsibility of destination States, territorial States, the EU and IOM for their roles in obstructing the right to leave. The chapter concludes by critiquing the normalisation in the global refugee regime of practices that push migrants into irregularity and often deadly flight, which should not be legitimised under international law.

II. VISA POLICIES

A. History of Visas and Carrier Sanctions

Visa regimes push the border far away from the destination country, which serves to externalise migration control and obligations under international law. Visas have been a key instrument, alongside the passport, in controlling movement and migration by modern States since around World War I, although earlier versions date back to the early nineteenth century.[3] Immigration controls emerged primarily at the turn of the twentieth century, as noted earlier in this work. In traditional States of immigration and settlement, such as Australia, Canada and the US, visas have been a long-standing tool designed to control immigration, sift and sort migrants, and reduce the arrival of asylum seekers and refugees. In 1917, the US began requiring non-citizens to apply for visas at consular posts abroad as a temporary wartime measure, but by the 1920s, this became a permanent visa regime.[4] The events of 1938 and the growing number of refugees fleeing Nazi Germany led many States to tighten their visa requirements, with devastating consequences as many persecuted groups, mainly Jews, were unable to escape.[5] Increased migratory pressures following the fall of the Iron Curtain, unfolding civil wars, and greater availability of air travel led to preventing migration at the source becoming the chosen approach of many

[2] C Costello and M Foster, '(Some) Refugees Welcome: When Is Differentiating Between Refugees Unlawful Discrimination?' (2022) 22 *International Journal of Discrimination and the Law* 244, 245.

[3] See R Koslowski, 'The International Travel Regime' in R Koslowski (ed), *Global Mobility Regimes* (New York, Palgrave Macmillan, 2011); J Torpey, *The Invention of the Passport: Surveillance, Citizenship, and the State*, 2nd edn (Cambridge, CUP, 2018) chs 3–5; DS FitzGerald, *Refuge Beyond Reach: How Rich Democracies Repel Asylum Seekers* (Oxford, OUP, 2019) chs 2, 4.

[4] AR Zolberg, 'Global Movements, Global Walls: Responses to Migration, 1885–1925' in G Wang (ed), *Global History and Migrations* (Abingdon/New York, Routledge, 2018) particularly 298–300; Torpey (n 3) ch 4; FitzGerald (n 3) 59.

[5] B Ryan, 'Extraterritorial Immigration Control: What Role for Legal Guarantees?' in B Ryan and V Mitsilegas (eds), *Extraterritorial Immigration Control: Legal Challenges* (Leiden, Martinus Nijhoff, 2010) 4–5.

destination States in the 1980s and 1990s.[6] As Hathaway has described, visas are a classic, albeit relatively invisible, *non-entrée* measure to avert irregular migration.[7] Visa regimes allow States to target both specific nationalities and refugee-producing countries.

B. Selecting Who Can and Cannot Move

There are various types of visas worldwide, allowing States to regulate mobility and pre-select who can and cannot move.[8] Visa categories benefit different types of travellers and lengths of stay: the majority of visas are for temporary stays, including for family, tourism, work and study purposes, and minimal settlement routes since the end of settler societies and move towards hard-line immigration policies.[9] It is estimated that imposing a tourist visa requirement on a particular country decreases the number of inbound travellers from that country by about 70 per cent.[10] Visa waivers, on the other hand, enable and facilitate cross-border mobility. When it comes to economic migrants, points-based systems allow governments to select the most desirable and highly skilled migrants from the pool of applicants.[11] As will be explored further, a global (im)mobility regime exists, which stratifies individuals into two groups: the privileged, who can access safe, quick and cheap travel, and the excluded, who are subject to stringent visa checks, longer queues and high costs.[12] Visa-free travel, generally understood as permission to enter for 90 days without obtaining a visa in advance (also the standard length for short-term visas), is granted most

[6] G Lahav, 'Immigration and the State: The Devolution and Privatisation of Immigration Control in the EU' (1998) 24 *Journal of Ethnic and Migration* Studies 675; FitzGerald (n 3) 59–61, 164–66, 221–22. For a history, see AR Zolberg, 'The Exit Revolution' in NL Green and F Weil (eds), *Citizenship and Those Who Leave: The Politics of Emigration and Expatriation* (Urbana, University of Illinois Press, 2007).

[7] JC Hathaway, 'The Emerging Politics of *Non-Entrée*' (1992) 91 *Refugees* 40; T Gammeltoft-Hansen and JC Hathaway, '*Non-Refoulement* in a World of Cooperative Deterrence' (2015) 53 *Columbia Journal of Transnational Law* 235, 244–45.

[8] See H de Haas, K Natter and S Vezzoli, 'Growing Restrictiveness or Changing Selection? The Nature and Evolution of Migration Policies' (2018) 52 *International Migration Review* 324.

[9] C Dauvergne, *The New Politics of Immigration and the End of Settler Societies* (Cambridge, CUP, 2016).

[10] RA Lawson and S Roychoudhury, 'Do Travel Visa Requirements Impede Tourist Travel?' (2016) 40 *Journal of Economics and Finance* 817, 824.

[11] D Ghezelbash, 'Forces of Diffusion: What Drives the Transfer of Immigration Policy and Law Across Jurisdictions?' (2014) 1 *International Journal of Migration and Border Studies* 139, 145–47.

[12] See E Neumayer, 'Unequal Access to Foreign Spaces: How States Use Visa Restrictions to Regulate Mobility in a Globalised World' (2006) 31 *Transactions of the Institute of British Geographers* 72; S Mau and others, *Liberal States and the Freedom of Movement: Selective Borders, Unequal Mobility* (Hampshire, Palgrave Macmillan, 2012); T Spijkerboer, 'The Global Mobility Infrastructure: Reconceptualising the Externalisation of Migration Control' (2018) 20 *European Journal of Migration and Law* 452.

frequently to high-income, Western, democratic countries and less frequently to poor, unstable ones.[13]

i. State Practice and Diffusion of Visa Regimes

States worldwide impose visa requirements, which are tracked in the DEMIG visa database.[14] This shows the widespread diffusion of visas, evolving from a temporary wartime restriction to a global system of control over movement. Torpey, in his seminal work, asserts that the posture of the US 'played a crucial role in the shift toward more rigorous and bureaucratic mechanisms for regulating movement'.[15]

Australia is the only country in the world that imposes a universal visa requirement on all nationalities – a policy that has been in place since the 1970s.[16] All non-citizens, except New Zealanders, must be granted a visa prior to arrival. However, certain nationals, for example, from Canada, European countries, the US and selected Asian countries (developed and relatively high-income), can apply for an electronic travel authorisation (ETA) online with ease.[17] ETAs were introduced in the 1990s to facilitate travel for passengers from high-volume, low-risk areas, labelled a 'visa without a visa'.[18] The US Visa Waiver Program allows nationals of participating countries, such as Australia, most European States, Israel, Singapore and Qatar, to travel with an ETA, and there are special visa-free provisions for Bermudians, Canadians and Mexicans. All other nationalities require a visa and transit visa when passing through the US en route to another country.[19]

Within the Schengen Area, all EU Member States (except Ireland and previously the UK) and Iceland, Liechtenstein, Norway and Switzerland have adopted uniform visa requirements. The EU's common visa policy (the Visa Code) sets out harmonised and mandatory procedures and conditions for issuing a 'Schengen visa' to third-country nationals for transit or short-stays in the Area.[20] In contrast to Australia and the US, where nationality-based

[13] See empirical studies, eg B Whyte, 'Visa-Free Travel Privileges: An Exploratory Geographical Analysis' (2008) 10 *Tourism Geographies* 127; S Mau and others, 'The Global Mobility Divide: How Visa Policies Have Evolved over Time' (2015) 41 *Journal of Ethnic and Migration Studies* 1192; M Czaika, H de Haas and M Villares-Varela, 'The Global Evolution of Travel Visa Regimes' (2018) 44 *Population and Development Review* 589.

[14] DEMIG, 'DEMIG VISA Data', www.migrationinstitute.org/data/demig-data/demig-visa-data.

[15] Torpey (n 3) 114.

[16] Department of Home Affairs, *Administration of the Immigration and Citizenship Program*, 4th edn (2020) 3, 20.

[17] Migration Regulations 1994 (Cth) sch 2, subclasses 601, 651.

[18] BP Christian, 'Visa Policy, Inspection and Exit Controls: Transatlantic Perspectives on Migration Management' (1999) 14 *Georgetown Immigration Law Journal* 215, 226.

[19] See Immigration and Nationality Act of 1952, 8 USC ss 1182, 1187; US Department of State, 'Tourism & Visit', www.travel.state.gov/content/travel/en/us-visas/tourism-visit.html.

[20] Regulation (EC) No 810/2009 of the European Parliament and of the Council of 13 July 2009 establishing a Community Code on Visas (Visa Code) [2009] OJ L 243/1.

visa requirements are the rule rather than the exception, most EU States have historically imposed visas only on 'blacklisted' countries.[21] EU law designates the nationalities whose citizens must possess a visa (the so-called 'blacklist') and those that are exempt (the 'whitelist').[22] These lists have seen several iterations since their adoption in 1995 and 2001, respectively.[23] The current blacklist includes 101 countries covering every African country and most of the Middle East, Asia, the Caribbean and the Pacific. The current whitelist includes 61 countries, primarily in the Americas, Europe, Antipodes, some Pacific islands, and wealthy parts of Asia.[24] Additionally, nationals of 12 States deemed to produce large numbers of 'illegal immigrants' require an airport transit visa (ATV) for stopovers in Schengen airports.[25]

Though visa rules vary considerably across States, there is a growing convergence of visa policies within OECD States, meaning they increasingly exclude the same people and nationalities.[26] Analysing data until 2020, Gülzau and Mau concluded that the global mobility divide has only widened and been consolidated.[27] Half of all States can only enable visa-free travel for their citizens to no more than 30 countries. While States in Central America and Central Asia were able to increase their mobility opportunities due to regional integration processes, other regions, including Sub-Saharan Africa, South Asia, the Middle East and North Africa, hardly benefit from visa-free travel. High visa fees mean many people from these regions are excluded from regularised global travel.[28] The conditions for granting short-stay visas have also reached a level of standardisation globally.

ii. Beyond a North-South Divide

Nonetheless, the reality is more complex than a simplistic North-South mobility divide. Visa regimes reflect multi-polar and multi-layered geopolitical relations,

[21] See Christian (n 18) 219.

[22] See on the history, E Feller, 'Carrier Sanctions and International Law' (1989) 1 *International Journal of Refugee Law* 48, 50; V Moreno-Lax, *Accessing Asylum in Europe: Extraterritorial Border Controls and Refugee Rights under EU Law* (Oxford, OUP, 2017) 90–94.

[23] See E Guild, 'The Border Abroad: Visas and Border Controls' in K Groenendijk, E Guild and P Minderhoud (eds), *In Search of Europe's Borders* (Leiden, Kluwer Law International, 2003) 90–100; FitzGerald (n 3) 164–67.

[24] Regulation (EU) 2018/1806 of the European Parliament and of the Council of 14 November 2018 listing the third countries whose nationals must be in possession of visas when crossing the external borders and those whose nationals are exempt from that requirement [2018] OJ L 303/39 (as amended); European Council, 'EU Visa Policy' (3 June 2024) www.consilium.europa.eu/en/policies/eu-visa-policy/.

[25] Visa Code, art 3, annex IV.

[26] Mau and others, *Liberal States* (n 12) 78–80, 119; FitzGerald (n 3) 14–15; F Gülzau and S Mau, 'Visas and Border Infrastructures: What Makes Them Tighter or Looser?', *Handbook of Human Mobility and Migration* (Cheltenham, Edward Elgar Publishing, 2024).

[27] Gülzau and Mau (n 26).

[28] ibid 217.

comprising regional and sub-regional levels, alliances and ties, and the dissolution and formation of States and regional blocs.[29] Examining data between 1973 and 2013, Czaika, de Haas and Villares-Varela found that while European and North American countries impose restrictive visa controls on most African and Asian countries, these latter regions have the highest overall levels of entry restrictions. Developing states in sub-Saharan Africa and South and South-East Asia are among those with the highest levels of entry restrictions.[30] Visa restrictiveness has been consistently high in countries such as China, Cambodia, Laos, Myanmar, Nepal and Vietnam and has been increasing in India and Pakistan. Visa policies have remained rigid or tightened further in several Central Asian countries notably Turkmenistan and Uzbekistan.[31] While citizens of wealthy countries generally enjoy the greatest visa-free travel, this is best characterised as the freedom to travel to other OECD countries. Similarly, visa-free travel is more likely to be granted to nationals of geographically proximate States within regional blocs.[32] Increased levels of visa reciprocity mainly reflect the formation of regional blocs. In contrast, asymmetrical visa rules, where countries, especially in the OECD, secure visa-free access for their own citizens but do not lift restrictions in return, expose power asymmetries and inequalities.[33]

While visa regimes in the Global South often receive less attention, it is vital to understand them and the dynamics at play. Restrictive visa policies (and carrier sanctions) have spread from Global North to Global South States, including following pressure from the more powerful regional player on its neighbours and efforts to align visa lists in exchange for visa liberalisation and trade access, as discussed in section IV.A.iii.c. Historical and diplomatic tensions have led to Global South States imposing restrictive visa requirements on one another, such as those between India–Pakistan, Sudan–South Sudan, and Saudi Arabia–Qatar. Restrictions may also be introduced to curb irregular migration and asylum-seeking, partially driven by the externalisation strategies of the Global North that make certain routes more dangerous and costly, forcing migrants to seek alternative routes and destinations in the Global South.[34]

[29] Czaika, de Haas and Villares-Varela (n 13) 589–90.

[30] ibid.

[31] S Horák, 'Visa Regimes and Regulatory Documents as an Obstacle for Tourism Development in Central Asia' in K Kantarci, M Uysal and VP Magnini (eds), *Tourism in Central Asia: Cultural Potential and Challenges* (New Jersey, Apple Academic Press, 2014).

[32] Czaika, de Haas and Villares-Varela (n 13) 589, 606–12. See also Gülzau and Mau (n 26) 214–17.

[33] Czaika, de Haas and Villares-Varela (n 13) 594–99, 606. See also S Mau, 'Mobility Citizenship, Inequality, and the Liberal State: The Case of Visa Policies' (2010) 4 *International Political Sociology* 339, 49–354; Neumayer (n 12) 76–81.

[34] See eg ML Flahaux and H de Haas, 'African Migration: Trends, Patterns, Drivers' (2016) 4 *Comparative Migration Studies* 1, 18, 21–22; IMS Vammen, 'New Contested Borderlands: Senegalese Migrants En Route to Argentina' (2019) 7 *Comparative Migration Studies* 8; N Cintra, 'Visa Policies as Externalisation Practices in the Global South' (*E-International Relations*, 2 October 2021) www.e-ir.info/2021/10/02/visa-policies-as-externalisation-practices-in-the-global-south/.

For example, both Lebanon and Jordan ended pre-existing visa-waiver policies for Syrians in response to the civil war.[35]

In South America, Acosta has described how visa policies are generally consistent with those in Australia, Canada, Europe and the US (except in the case of Ecuador).[36] However, there are several notable differences, specifically general exemptions for South Africans, Russians and Turks, and Filipino, Thai and Indonesian nationals in certain South American States. US practices have significantly influenced South America's migration controls since the late nineteenth century through policy diffusion and emulation, including racial and other entry bans. Bureaucrats within Argentina, Brazil and Chile have also promoted and influenced the revocation of liberal policies and encouraged migrant selectivity.[37]

Such diffusion also exists between ASEAN States who agreed in 2002 to consult on visa waiver lists, share blacklists at visa-issuing offices and exchange airline passenger lists – some of whom had a long history of free and open migration but are now influenced by Australia's push for increased harmonisation of restrictive border policies across the region.[38] Despite existing free movement agreements, African States continue to require visas for most other African nationals. Political, security and other factors – such as xenophobia and anti-immigrant sentiment – often lead to the re-introduction of visa requirements.[39] There has also been a documented increase in restrictiveness towards nationals from non-African States since the 1970s, except for Southern Africa, which likely mirrors reciprocal visa requirements.[40] Countries in the Middle East and North Africa, such as Libya and Turkey, have also introduced visa requirements for nationalities that were previously welcome – often

[35] OG El-Taliawi, *The Politics of Refugee Policy in the Global South*, vol 15 (Montreal, McGill-Queen's University Press, 2024) chs 6, 8.

[36] D Acosta, *The National versus the Foreigner in South America: 200 Years of Migration and Citizenship Law* (Cambridge, CUP, 2018) 125. In 2008, Ecuador withdrew visa requirements for all countries worldwide, but these were later reinstated for several Asian and African countries amid increased irregular migration.

[37] DS FitzGerald and D Cook-Martín, *Culling the Masses: The Democratic Origins of Racist Immigration Policy in the Americas* (Cambridge, Harvard University Press, 2014) 22–27; Acosta (n 36) 87–101; MV Espinoza, 'Migration Governance in South America: Change and Continuity in Times of "Crisis"' in H Crawley and JK Teye (eds), *The Palgrave Handbook of South–South Migration and Inequality* (Cham, Palgrave Macmillan, 2024). See more recently, the White House, 'Fact Sheet: Fourth Ministerial Meeting on the Los Angeles Declaration on Migration and Protection' (26 September 2024) bidenwhitehouse.archives.gov/briefing-room/statements-releases/2024/09/26/fact-sheet-fourth-ministerial-meeting-on-the-los-angeles-declaration-on-migration-and-protection/.

[38] CC Low, 'Externalization of Border Control in ASEAN Countries' in AKMA Ullah, *Handbook of Migration, International Relations and Security in Asia* (Singapore, Springer Singapore, 2024) 12; M Lee, 'The Externalization of Border Control in the Global South: The Cases of Malaysia and Indonesia' (2022) 26 *Theoretical Criminology* 537, 543–44.

[39] Flahaux and de Haas (n 34); Gülzau and Mau (n 26) 215–17; African Development Bank Group, 'Africa Visa Openness Report 2024' (2024) www.au.int/en/documents/20250206/africa-visa-openness-report-2024.

[40] Flahaux and de Haas (n 34) 18–21.

pressured by the EU.[41] Conversely, Tunisia – a key destination and transit country – permits visa-free travel for several African nationalities (eg, Côte d'Ivoire, Mali, Niger); however, border officials have reportedly not always upheld this policy.[42] In the Maghreb, visa-free travel has ended for certain African nationalities despite long-standing relations, citing security concerns and increasing irregular migration to Europe.[43]

Visa policies thus reflect a State's broader economic, political and regional interests, serving as an instrument to facilitate the movement of desirable travellers while controlling risks, restricting spontaneous asylum seeking, and pre-emptively limiting the mobility of those deemed undesirable.

C. Delegation, Extraterritorialisation and Automation

In addition to the visa requirement, visa regimes involve various actors and processes. Border control is outsourced to private commercial carriers, while visa processing is partly delegated to private visa companies and, in some contexts, IOM. Destination States also post immigration officers and operate pre-clearance programmes in airports and ports abroad. Technology has been leveraged to issue online visas and automate decision-making.

i. Carrier Sanctions and Immigration Liaison Officers

Visa requirements are inextricably linked to carrier sanctions, the enforcement arm of visas. They penalise airlines, ferry and bus operators for carrying passengers without the required documentation, such as a visa or passport.[44] Though various forms have existed since the nineteenth and early twentieth centuries, modern-day carrier sanctions spread in the second half of the

[41] L Kandilige and T Yeboah, 'West African Migration Regimes and the Externalization of EU Migration Management Policies' in G Heck and others (eds), *Making Routes: Mobility and Politics of Migration in the Global South* (Cairo, The American University in Cairo Press, 2024) 140; N Avdan, *Visas and Walls: Border Security in the Age of Terrorism* (Philadelphia, University of Pennsylvania Press, 2019) ch 5; L Laube, 'The Relational Dimension of Externalizing Border Control: Selective Visa Policies in Migration and Border Diplomacy' (2019) 7 *Comparative Migration Studies* 1, 14–18.

[42] K Natter, 'Tunisia's Migration Politics Throughout the 2011 Revolution: Revisiting the Democratisation – Migrant Rights Nexus' (2022) 43 *Third World Quarterly* 1551, 1561.

[43] Mixed Migration Centre, 'Quarterly Mixed Migration Update: North Africa, Quarter 3' (2024) 10–12, www.mixedmigration.org/resource/quarterly-mixed-migration-update-na-q3-2024/, which also mentions visas being reinstated for Moroccans.

[44] There is extensive literature on carrier sanctions eg, Feller (n 22); S Scholten and P Minderhoud, 'Regulating Immigration Control: Carrier Sanctions in the Netherlands' (2008) 10 *European Journal of Migration and Law* 123; T Bloom and V Risse, 'Examining Hidden Coercion at State Borders: Why Carrier Sanctions Cannot Be Justified' (2014) 7 *Ethics & Global Politics* 65; T Rodenhäuser, 'Another Brick in the Wall: Carrier Sanctions and the Privatisation of Immigration Control' (2014) 26 *International Journal of Refugee Law* 223; T Baird and T Spijkerboer, 'Carrier Sanctions and the Conflicting Legal Obligations of Carriers: Addressing Human Rights Leakage' (2019) 11 *Amsterdam Law Forum* 4.

twentieth century.[45] They have long been used as a tool for containment: in the 1930s and 1940s, Britain used carrier sanctions and stationed immigration liaison officers abroad to keep Jewish refugees from reaching Palestine (then under British Mandate rule) by ship.[46] Today, carrier sanctions are the norm and are implemented by nearly all States (not only in the Global North) to enforce their visa policies.[47]

Carriers are legally obliged to verify that passengers are duly documented at the point of departure and refuse boarding if not. Otherwise, they will face financial and other sanctions and bear responsibility for removing the individuals denied entry. In refusing boarding, carriers purport to comply with international, EU or domestic law, which impose obligations on States to adopt carrier sanction legislation.[48] In Europe, for instance, all Schengen and EU Member States are required to have carrier sanctions legislation in place. Fines must be a minimum of 3,000 and a maximum of EUR 5,000 per passenger or a lump sum of EUR 500,000 for each infringement. States can also impose 'penalties of another kind, such as immobilisation, seizure, and confiscation of the means of transport, or temporary suspension or withdrawal of the operating licence'.[49]

Airlines are often supported by immigration liaison officers (ILOs) and airline liaison officers (ALOs) posted at major international airports and ports. They work to prevent irregular migration by assisting carriers with pre-departure and document checks of prospective travellers and help to facilitate information sharing and cooperation with local authorities, including on people smuggling. Key destination states, including Australia, Canada, the EU, the UK and the US, post ILOs in strategic locations worldwide.[50] ILOs may implement pre-clearance programmes to screen passengers prior to embarkation (which can involve discriminatory profiling, as section IV.B examines). Many States

[45] See Feller (n 22) 49–53; Rodenhäuser (n 44) 226; FitzGerald (n 3) 63–64, 166–68, 221–22.

[46] FitzGerald (n 3) 22, 25–31.

[47] See eg, Immigration (Emergency Provisions) Act 1947 (Myanmar) s 13(2), (3); Immigration Act 1979 (Thailand) ss 70, 71; globally, DEMIG, 'DEMIG POLICY Data', www.migrationinstitute.org/data/demig-data/demig-policy-1; on South America; Acosta (n 36) 96, 126.

[48] International Civil Aviation Organization, Convention on Civil Aviation (adopted 7 December 1944, entered into force 4 April 1947) 15 UNTS 295 (Chicago Convention) arts 13, 37(j), Annex 9; Palermo Protocols, art 11(1)–(4); The Schengen acquis – Convention implementing the Schengen Agreement of 14 June 1985 between the Governments of the States of the Benelux Economic Union, the Federal Republic of Germany and the French Republic on the gradual abolition of checks at their common borders [2000] OJ L 239/19 (CISA) art 26. See Rodenhäuser (n 44) 226–29.

[49] CISA, art 26; Council Directive 2001/51/EC supplementing the provisions of Article 26 of the Convention implementing the Schengen Agreement of 14 June 1985 [2001] OJ L 187/45 (Carriers Liability Directive) arts 3–5. See T Baird, 'Carrier Sanctions in Europe: A Comparison of Trends in 10 Countries' (2017) 19 *European Journal of Migration and Law* 307; Moreno-Lax, *Accessing Asylum* (n 22) ch 5.

[50] See eg Regulation (EU) 2019/1240 of the European Parliament and of the Council of 20 June 2019 on the creation of a European network of immigration liaison officers [2019] OJ L 198/88 (ILOR); Moreno-Lax, *Accessing Asylum* (n 22) 121, 133–42; FitzGerald (n 3) ch 4, 168–70, 221.

now also require airlines to transmit Advance Passenger Information before the flight departs, enabling States to pre-vet passengers against watchlists and databases and provide airlines with a Board/No-Board response.[51] Some countries in the Global South also deploy liaison officers, including Pakistan;[52] Sri Lanka, which co-chairs the Regional Immigration Liaison Officer Network alongside Australia;[53] and the Indian-administered Information Fusion Centre–Indian Ocean Region, which hosts ILOs from 14 partner States to enhance maritime safety and security.[54] Like visas, the routine sharing of information and techniques between ILOs across regions can create similar understandings of 'risk', influencing who is filtered and targeted across regions.[55]

ii. Privatisation and Outsourcing

Like various migration control functions, visa processing has been privatised and outsourced.[56] Many States today require visa applicants to submit their applications at visa application centres (VACs) operated by private companies rather than their embassies and consulates. Private companies can be authorised to provide information on visa requirements, application forms and supporting documents, collect data (including biometrics) and applications, transmit applications to consulates, manage appointments, and return travel documents and decisions to applicants.[57] VFS Global, BLS International and TLScontact are among the major transnational corporations that act as external service providers for governments.[58] VFS Global, the leading provider, has 3592 VACs in 158 countries across five continents, with 69 client governments, ranging from Brazil, India, Japan, Russia, South Africa, Turkey, the UAE and Vietnam.[59]

[51] ICAO, 'API Guidelines and PNR Reporting Standards', www2023.icao.int/security/fal/sitepages/api%20guidelines%20and%20pnr%20reporting%20standards.aspx. See recently, I Chan, 'New Hong Kong Immigration System Barring 'Undesirables' from Boarding Flights to City Comes into Effect' (*HKFP*, 4 September 2024) www.hongkongfp.com/2024/09/04/new-hong-kong-immigration-system-barring-undesirables-from-boarding-flights-to-city-comes-into-effect/.

[52] UNODC, 'UNODC Facilitates Orientation Workshop for Immigration Liaison Officers Seconded to New Link Offices in Italy, Spain, Turkey, the U.A.E and the UK' (28 July 2022) www.unodc.org/copak/en/Stories/SP1/unodc-facilitates-orientation-workshop-for-immigration-liaison-officers-seconded-to-new-link-offices-in-italy--spain--turkey--the-u-a-e-and-the-uk.html.

[53] RSO, 'The Bali Process', www.rso.baliprocess.net/rso-networks/rilon/; The Bali Process, 'Technical Experts Working Group – Irregular Movement by Air (2011)' (2011) www.baliprocess.net/event/technical-experts-working-group-irregular-movement-by-air-2011/.

[54] IFC-IOR, 'IFC-IOR', ifcior.indiannavy.gov.in/about_us.

[55] See N Ostrand, 'Overseas Immigration Liaison Officers: "Knowledge Brokers" and Transnational Spaces of Mid-Level Negotiations Shaping Extraterritorial Migration Control Practices' (2022) 10 *Migration Studies* 41; Low (n 38) 12; Lee (n 38) 543.

[56] See generally T Gammeltoft-Hansen and NN Sørensen, *The Migration Industry and the Commercialisation of International Migration* (Abingdon/New York, Routledge, 2013).

[57] See eg Visa Code, arts 40, 43.

[58] VFS Global, 'Welcome to VFS Global' (2025) www.vfsglobal.com/en/individuals/index.html; BLS International, 'About BLS International' (2024) www.blsinternational.com; TLS Contact, 'What We Do', (2025) www.tlscontact.com/en/.

[59] VFS Global (n 58).

The UK, Schengen States and EU Member States, for instance, require applicants of various nationalities to submit their applications at private VACs.[60]

Visa services may also be outsourced to IOM, which has operated VACs in more than 50 countries since 1994.[61] IOM has operated programmes for States such as Australia, Canada, Germany, South Korea and the UK and partnered with VFS Global to operate certain VACs and service diplomatic missions.[62] IOM describes its role as 'expanding, implementing and enhancing regular pathways globally, by facilitating tailored services' for the visa submission and processing cycle, including information dissemination, eligibility screening, document collection and verification, interview facilitation, biometrics and health assessments.[63] It is worth noting that ICMPD provides operational and technical support to enhance the visa systems of partner countries and EU candidates, help them align with the EU's common visa policy, and support visa liberalisation dialogues.[64] ICMPD also operates Migrant Resource Centres, which provide advice on visa applications and complementary pathways.[65] In addition, ICMPD co-developed the EU's Integrated Border Management (IBM) concept, whose first tier involves 'measures taken in third countries' such as providing advice and training to consular officials and carriers through liaison officers and document experts. To this end, ICMPD facilitates training sessions and capacity-building activities.[66] ICMPD does not, however, appear to be directly involved in visa processing.

[60] See Visa Code Handbook C(2020) 395 final Annex 28 – List of Member States' consular presence, representation arrangements and forms of cooperation for the collection of visa applications, collection by Honorary Consuls or outsourcing of the collection of visa applications.

[61] IOM, 'IOM Visa Application Centres' (Fact Sheet, 2023) www.iom.int/sites/g/files/tmzbdl486/files/documents/2023-07/visa-application-centres.pdf.

[62] See IOM, 'IOM Opens UK Visa Application Office in Guyana' (Press Release, 21 February 2014) www.iom.int/news/iom-opens-uk-visa-application-office-guyana.

[63] See eg IOM, 'IOM and Immigration and Visa Support Solutions' (Fact Sheet, 2011) www.iom.int/files/live/sites/iom/files/What-We-Do/docs/11-IBM-Fact-Sheet-Immigration-and-Visa-Support-Solutions-2011.pdf; IOM, 'Annual Report for 2015' (13 June 2016) C/107/4, para 83; IOM, 'Visa Application Processing Solutions' (Information Sheet) www.iom.int/sites/g/files/tmzbdl486/files/our_work/DMM/IBM/ibm-visaapplicationprocessingsolutions_booklet.pdf.

[64] MPF, 'Visa Capacity Building in Bosnia and Herzegovina (VCBB)' www.migrationpartnershipfacility.eu/mpf-projects/60-visa-capacity-building-in-bosnia-and-herzegovina-vcbb/preview; ICMPD, 'ENIGMMA-2: Sustaining Migration Management in Georgia', www.icmpd.org/our-work/projects/sustaining-migration-management-in-georgia-enigmma-2.

[65] ICMPD, 'ICMPD Opens More Migrant Resource Centres in Iraq, Pakistan' (7 June 2024) www.icmpd.org/news/icmpd-opens-more-migrant-resource-centres-in-iraq-pakistan.

[66] EU, *Guidelines for Integrated Border Management in European Commission External Cooperation* (Brussels, EU, 2010) 20–21, 57, 68–70, ch 8, www.icmpd.org/file/download/48280/file/Guidelines%2520for%2520Integrated%2520Border%2520Management%2520in%2520European%2520Commission%2520External%2520Cooperation%2520EN.pdf; ICMPD, 'ICMPD Facilitated FIA, Pakistan and Immigration Police, Bangladesh Delegations' Study Visit on Document Security to Denmark' (13 November 2024) www.budapestprocess.org/icmpd-facilitated-fia-pakistan-and-immigration-police-bangladesh-delegations-study-visit-on-document-security-to-denmark/; ICMPD, 'Border Management and Security Programme', www.icmpd.org/our-work/capacity-building/border-management-and-security-programme.

More and more would-be migrants are dealing only with private actors or IOM at the frontline, moving processing away from the State itself. While nationals from the Global South will ordinarily encounter almost no border controls, those from the Global South often face numerous shifting borders, perhaps beginning with a visit to a privatised VAC and involving various intermediaries.[67] The plurality of actors involved has transformed migration control governance: States are seeking not only to streamline visa processes and minimise costs but also to dilute responsibility.

iii. Virtual Borders and Automation

Through privatisation and outsourcing, visa controls 'may operate entirely passively, with no need for the state to establish its presence extraterritorially'.[68] Many States now also rely on digital technologies to manage migration and asylum, including accepting online visa applications, issuing e-visas and ETAs, and deploying artificial intelligence/machine learning in their decision-making.[69] States are relying on automated processes to issue electronic visas and make visa decisions.[70] In 2020, in response to a legal challenge, the UK Home Office suspended a secret 'visa streaming' algorithm, which graded applicants as red, amber or green based on nationality. It said it was redesigning the process to consider issues surrounding unconscious bias and the use of nationality.[71] In 2026, the EU's new travel authorisation system, ETIAS, will be operational, which uses automatic profiling to screen visa-exempt nationals based on security, illegal immigration and health risk profiles. Authorisations will be automatically approved if there are no 'hits' and manually processed otherwise, with the

[67] K Jones, H Sha and MRA Bhuiyan, 'Overcoming and Reproducing Inequalities: Mediated Migration in the "Global South"' in H Crawley and JK Teye (eds), *The Palgrave Handbook of South–South Migration and Inequality* (Cham, Palgrave Macmillan, 2024); F Infantino, *Outsourcing Border Control: Politics and Practice of Contracted Visa Policy in Morocco* (New York, Palgrave Macmillan, 2016) 6.

[68] T Gammeltoft-Hansen, *Access to Asylum: International Refugee Law and the Globalisation of Migration Control* (Cambridge, CUP, 2011) 135.

[69] EE Korkmaz (ed), *Digital Identity, Virtual Borders and Social Media: A Panacea for Migration Governance?* (Cheltenham, Edward Elgar Publishing, 2021).

[70] See eg RWM Wong and AHW Chun, 'eBrain – Using AI for Automatic Assessment at the Hong Kong Immigration Department' (2007) www.cs.cityu.edu.hk/~hwchun/research/PDF/eBrain_IAAI.pdf; Stats NZ, *Algorithm Assessment Report* (Wellington, Te Tari Taiwhenua Internal Affairs, 2018) 17; P Molnar and L Gill, 'Bots at the Gate: A Human Rights Analysis of Automated Decision Making in Canada's Immigration and Refugee System' (2018) Citizen Lab and International Human Rights Program Research Report No 114, 14–15, 23–25, 34–35, 38, www.citizenlab.ca/wp-content/uploads/2018/09/IHRP-Automated-Systems-Report-Web-V2.pdf; AS Akinlabi, 'Implementation of e-VISA application system and automated landing and exit card' (Nigeria Immigration Service, Press Release, 2 May 2025) www.immigration.gov.ng/implementation-of-the-e-visa-application-system-andautomated-landing-and-exit-card/.

[71] H Warrell, 'Home Office under Fire for using Secretive Visa Algorithm' (*Financial Times*, 9 June 2019); JCWI, 'We Won! Home Office to Stop using Racist Visa Algorithm' (4 August 2020) www.jcwi.org.uk/news/we-won-home-office-to-stop-using-racist-visa-algorithm.

outcome accessible to carriers.[72] In 2021, the EU's Visa Information System was also reformed so that all short-stay visa applications are automatically profiled against specific risk indicators.[73] Additionally, private companies contracted by States and airlines may themselves use automated technologies.[74] Automated decision-making elicits serious concerns about the quality of decisions, bias and discrimination, discussed below.

D. Common Features across Visa Regimes

These processes and elements reveal several common features that can be distilled across visa regimes. Visas are designed to forestall departure through extraterritorialisation and outsourcing, as well as being discretionary, selective and costly for those nationalities who do not benefit from waivers or ETAs. Visa regimes possess both temporal and spatial elements. Temporally, visas play a proactive and preventative function, seeking to control, pre-select and deter movement at the source and during transit. Spatially, visas allow States to exercise border control functions well beyond their frontiers.[75] They have been aptly categorised by Guild as 'the border abroad' and 'virtual border'.[76] Given that non-nationals have no general right of entry, visas are one of the most powerful mechanisms by which States exercise their immigration control prerogative and police movement from abroad.[77] This 'complex network of privatisation'[78] and outsourcing to IOM creates potential difficulties in establishing jurisdiction and attributing wrongful conduct to the State.

[72] Regulation (EU) 2018/1240 of the European Parliament and of the Council of 12 September 2018 establishing a European Travel Information and Authorisation System (ETIAS) and amending Regulations (EU) No 1077/2011, (EU) No 515/2014, (EU) 2016/399, (EU) 2016/1624 and (EU) 2017/2226 [2018] OJ L 236/1, arts 20, 33, 45; Regulation (EU) 2018/1241 of the European Parliament and of the Council of 12 September 2018 amending Regulation (EU) 2016/794 for the purpose of establishing a European Travel Information and Authorisation System (ETIAS) [2018] OJ L 236. See also N Vavoula, 'Artificial Intelligence (AI) at Schengen Borders: Automated Processing, Algorithmic Profiling and Facial Recognition in the Era of Techno-Solutionism' (2021) 23 *European Journal of Migration and Law* 457.

[73] Regulation (EU) 2021/1134, art 9j.

[74] See eg Sopra Steria contracted by UK Home Office, Warrell (n 71).

[75] V Mitsilegas, 'Extraterritorial Immigration Control, Preventive Justice and the Rule of Law in Turbulent Times: Lessons from the Anti-Smuggling Crusade' in S Carrera, JS Vara and T Strik (eds), *Constitutionalising the External Dimensions of EU Migration Policies in Times of Crisis: Legality, Rule of Law and Fundamental Rights Reconsidered* (Cheltenham, Edward Elgar Publishing, 2019) 291–92.

[76] Guild, 'Border Abroad' (n 23); E Guild, 'Citizens Without a Constitution, Borders Without a State: EU Free Movement of Persons' in A Baldaccini, E Guild and H Toner (eds), *Whose Freedom, Security and Justice? EU Immigration and Asylum Law and Policy* (Oxford, Hart Publishing, 2007) 51.

[77] D Bigo and E Guild, 'Policing at a Distance: Schengen Visa Policies' in D Bigo and E Guild (eds), *Controlling Frontiers: Free Movement Into and Within Europe* (Chesterfield, Ashgate, 2005) 234; Neumayer (n 12) 73–74, 76–78.

[78] T Bloom, 'The Business of Migration Control: Delegating Migration Control Functions to Private Actors' (2015) 6 *Global Policy* 151, 151.

III. JURISDICTION AND ATTRIBUTION

A. Visa Refusals and Denial of Embarkation as an Exercise of Jurisdiction

Whether a visa refusal brings the individual within the State's jurisdiction is a contentious issue and is highly dependent on the adjudicative body interpreting the matter. As discussed in chapter two, jurisdictional tests are interpreted much more generously by UN bodies and other regional bodies than by the Strasbourg Court. The denial of boarding by carriers is simpler, provided the conduct of carriers can also be attributed to the State.

i. Visa Refusals

In the 2020 case of *MN v Belgium*, the Strasbourg Court held that visa refusals do not involve the exercise of jurisdiction under Article 1 of the ECHR.[79] *MN* concerned a Syrian family who had fled Aleppo and applied for urgent humanitarian visas at the Belgian embassy in Beirut under Article 25 of the Visa Code. Belgium refused the visas, stating that the Code only covers short-stay visas, not asylum.[80]

The applicants claimed that refusing their visa applications exposed them to the risk of ill-treatment contrary to Article 3. The Grand Chamber declared the case inadmissible, holding that applying for a visa at the Belgian embassy did not bring the applicants within Belgium's jurisdiction and, therefore, no Convention protections were triggered. The Court stated that 'the mere fact that an applicant brings proceedings in a State Party with which he has no connecting tie cannot suffice to establish that State's jurisdiction over him' and 'to find otherwise would amount to enshrining a near-universal application of the Convention on the basis of the unilateral choices of any individual, irrespective of where in the world they find themselves'.[81] This would create an unlimited obligation under Article 3 to allow entry for those at risk of ill-treatment, negating the State's right to control entry.[82] Nor did the diplomatic agents exercise de facto control over the applicants, who were free to come and go.[83]

The Court prioritised the State's immigration control prerogative over the protection of refugees and appeared to accept the flawed policy arguments of the State interveners that acceding to the applicants' claims would disrupt the protection system by introducing disorder and instability.[84] As a result, the

[79] *MN v Belgium*, App no 3599/18 (ECtHR, 5 March 2020).
[80] Remarkably similar to the case before the CJEU, *X and X v Belgium*, Case C-638/16 PPU, EU:C:2017:173.
[81] *MN* (n 79) paras 79–81, 86–90, 123.
[82] ibid para 124.
[83] ibid para 118.
[84] ibid para 90.

Court sustained the 'systemic exclusion of refugees from the international legal order' – unable to access asylum and safe routes – while cynically referencing the endeavours made by States to facilitate access to asylum procedures through their embassies.[85]

Nonetheless, principled arguments existed to support a finding of jurisdiction, including the Court's own jurisprudence. The activities of diplomatic or consular agents are recognised in international law as lawful exercises of extra-territorial jurisdiction and visa processing one of their recognised functions.[86] Nevertheless, the weight of authority requires factual control. Prior to *MN*, the Court had only examined visa issuance on the merits where there was a pre-existing private or family link between the applicant and State, specifically where refugees had been denied family reunification.[87] In such cases, jurisdiction is implied. However, a pre-existing link is not necessary. As several intervenors submitted, is well-established in the case law that jurisdiction encompasses the decisions of diplomatic and consular agents.[88] As reflected in *Al-Skeini*, 'the acts of diplomatic and consular agents, who are present on foreign territory in accordance with provisions of international law, may amount to an exercise of jurisdiction when these agents *exert authority and control over others*'.[89] Chapter two demonstrated that the Strasbourg Court does not always demand physical control over the individual. In *Xhavara* (collision with a vessel on the high seas), *Kovačić v Slovenia* (legislation freezing foreign-currency account withdrawals abroad), and *Andreou v Turkey* (Turkish-Cypriot troops open firing on demonstrators in Greek-Cypriot territory), jurisdiction arose based on specific acts involving proximity.[90] In *Nada v Switzerland*, the Court held that Switzerland,

[85] ibid para 126; AN Reyhani, 'Expelled from Humanity: Reflections on M.N. and Others v Belgium' (*Verfassungsblog*, 6 May 2020) www.verfassungsblog.de/expelled-from-humanity/.

[86] See Vienna Convention on Consular Relations (adopted 24 April 1963, entered into force 19 March 1) 596 UNTS 261 (VCCR) arts 3, 5(d); *Banković v Belgium* (2007) 44 EHRR SE5, para 73; *MN* (n 79) para 83, 91, 93.

[87] See eg *X and Y v Switzerland* (1977) 9 DR 57; *Tuquabo-Tekle v Netherlands*, App no 60665/00 (ECtHR, 1 December 2005); *Haydarie v Netherlands*, App no 8876/04 (ECtHR, 20 October 2005); *Schembri v Malta*, App no 66297/13 (ECtHR, 19 September 2017). See also *East African Asians v UK* (1973) 3 EHRR 76 (Commission Decision) paras 185–187; *MN* (n 79) para 109.

[88] *MN* (n 79) paras 91, 93, 95. See the debate between G Noll, 'Seeking Asylum at Embassies: A Right to Entry under International Law?' (2005) 17 *International Journal of Refugee Law* 542 and K Ogg, 'Protection Closer to Home? A Legal Case for Claiming Asylum at Embassies and Consulates' (2014) 33 *Refugee Survey Quarterly* 81 on extraterritorial application.

[89] *Al-Skeini v UK* (2011) 53 EHRR 18, para 134 (emphasis added). See also *X v Federal Republic of Germany*, App no 1611/62 (Commission Decision, 25 September 1965) 168; *X v UK* (1977) 12 DR 73, para 1; *WM v Denmark* (1992) 73 DR 193, para 1; *R (Sandiford) v The Secretary of State for Foreign and Commonwealth Affairs* [2014] UKSC 44, [2014] 1 WLR 2697, para 19; *R (Islam) v Secretary of State for the Home Department* [2019] EWHC 2169 (Admin), para 46.

[90] *Xhavara v Italy and Albania*, App no 39473/98 (ECtHR, 11 January 2001); *Kovačić v Slovenia*, Apps nos 44574/98, 45133/98 and 48316/99 (ECtHR, 9 October 2003) 51–52; *Pad v Turkey*, App no 60167/00 (ECtHR, 28 June 2007) para 54; *Andreou v Turkey*, App no 45653/99 (ECtHR, 27 October 2009) para 25. See also *Georgia v Russia (II)*, App no 38263/08 (ECtHR, 21 January 2021) paras 131–32; Moreno-Lax, *Accessing Asylum* (n 22) 278–81.

by banning the applicant from entering or transiting through Switzerland in order to leave the Italian enclave of Campione, exercised jurisdiction.[91]

Visa refusals have a proximate, foreseeable impact on the right to leave of nationals requiring a visa. As the applicants emphasised at the *MN* hearing, if there was no requirement for a visa and no power over their fate, they could simply board a plane.[92] It is this assumption of authority or control over their exercise of rights that matters, not physical contact or individual choices.[93] While applicants entering and leaving a consulate do so voluntarily, this is not analogous to an individual voluntarily returning to their State of origin.[94] In refusing a visa, the authorities assume sufficient control over the specific applicant, specifically their *exercise* of the right to leave, creating a functional and/or causal relationship between that individual and the State.[95] Several factors illustrate this: the State has control over the applicant's fate and whether they can leave and seek entry lawfully; the refusal brings that applicant directly within the State's authority and control through its decision and immigration laws, emanating from State territory but producing effects abroad, similar to the travel ban in *Nada*; and it is reasonable for the State to secure the individual's right by granting the visa and to avoid foreseeable violations. In contrast to Strasbourg, the Inter-American Court has held that protection from *refoulement* applies to the conduct of diplomatic agents 'whenever the nexus of personal jurisdiction can be established with the particular person'.[96] Similarly, the Committee on the Rights of Persons with Disabilities held that Australia's refusal to issue a work visa to the applicant for failing to satisfy the health requirement brought the applicant within the State's jurisdiction, recognising the power of the State to control the behaviour of non-nationals outside its territory through its visa process and ensuring people with disabilities can utilise immigration proceedings to exercise their liberty of movement.[97] Visa refusals can, therefore, amount to effective control or trigger jurisdiction based on a direct causal or functional relationship, even if this is not yet the case before Strasbourg. Directness and foreseeability thus delimit jurisdiction and responsibility for any ensuing violation of the right to leave. Finding jurisdiction would also not impose an unlimited obligation of entry in relation to *non-refoulement*; strict conditions for granting visas and a minimum threshold for triggering Article 3's positive obligations remain.

[91] *Nada v Switzerland* (2013) 56 EHRR 18, paras 121–22. See also *X and Y* (n 87) 73.

[92] Citing *X and Y* (n 87); *Nada* (n 91).

[93] See for support *R (B) v Secretary of State for the Foreign and Commonwealth Office* [2004] EWCA Civ 1344, [2005] 2 WLR 618, paras 63–66. cf *Duarte Agostinho v Portugal*, App no 39371/20 (ECtHR, 9 April 2024) paras 205–06. See also Ogg (n 88) 99–102.

[94] cf *Khan v UK*, App no 11987/11 (ECtHR, 28 January 2014).

[95] Gammeltoft-Hansen (n 68) 124–25, 145–46, 150–57.

[96] *Advisory Opinion on the Institution of Asylum and its Recognition as a Human Right in the Inter-American Protection System*, IACtHR, OC-25/18 (30 May 2018) paras 174–76, 188, 192.

[97] *Grainne Sherlock v Australia*, Communication No 20/2014 (19 March 2021) UN Doc CRPD/C/24/D/20/2014, para 7.4.

On first appearances, visa refusals resulting from online processes raise more complex questions. Some have argued that the claim for jurisdiction likely diminishes when visa processing is conducted at privatised VACs, applications are handled by a third State, or applications are submitted online.[98] While visa processing may increase remoteness in the causal chain, processing and handling by a privatised VAC or IOM does not raise separate jurisdictional issues so long as the relevant conduct is attributable to the State. Given that physical control is not *sine qua non*, effective control or jurisdiction based on a direct causal or functional relationship can be established over online (or postal) applications based on the abovementioned factors. In the 2024 case of *Wieder and Guarnieri v the UK*, the Strasbourg Court held that the interception, processing and interrogation of electronic communications falls within the State's jurisdiction if such surveillance activities occurred within its territory, even if the individual concerned was located abroad.[99] This case arguably has significant implications for other areas involving technological advancements. Virtual methods, whether online visa refusals or digital surveillance, interfere with rights akin to the more direct physical intervention. It would be inconceivable for adjudicative bodies to deny technological advancements rendering the 'exercise of manual, physical power over individuals unnecessary' and allow States to freely engage in practices affecting individuals extraterritorially by holding onto physical notions of control.[100] Indeed, the decision of the CRPD Committee concerned an electronic visa application. Jurisdiction is arguably established when the individual applies as this is the key moment when the State assumes sufficient power and control over their exercise of rights.

ii. Denial of Embarkation

The denial of boarding by carriers is less contentious, as refusing to let an individual embark can more readily be understood as the exercise of effective control. Some scholars argue that while arrest and detention at the border would amount to control over the person, routine border controls do not.[101] However, the acts of carriers in inspecting documentation and actively denying boarding undoubtedly amount to physical power over the interdicted person.[102] In *Women*

[98] Gammeltoft-Hansen (n 68) 135. See also C Costello, *The Human Rights of Migrants and Refugees in European Law* (Oxford, OUP, 2016) 244–45.

[99] M Milanovic, 'Wieder and Guarnieri v UK: A Justifiably Expansive Approach to the Extraterritorial Application of the Right to Privacy in Surveillance Cases' (*EJIL: Talk!*, 21 March 2024) www.ejiltalk.org/wieder-and-guarnieri-v-uk-a-justifiably-expansive-approach-to-the-extraterritorial-application-of-the-right-to-privacy-in-surveillance-cases/.

[100] M Milanovic, 'Human Rights Treaties and Foreign Surveillance: Privacy in the Digital Age' (2015) 56 *Harvard International Law Journal* 81, 120.

[101] Gammeltoft-Hansen (n 68) 193–95; Costello (n 98) 119.

[102] See V Moreno-Lax, 'Must EU Borders have Doors for Refugees? On the Compatibility of Schengen Visas and Carriers' Sanctions with EU Member States' Obligations to Provide International Protection to Refugees' (2008) 10 *European Journal of International Law* 315, 337–38; M den Heijer,

on Waves v Portugal, the Strasbourg Court found that Portugal had violated a Dutch organisation's right to freedom of expression by sending a warship to block entry into Portugal's territorial waters.[103] This had a direct impact on the organisation despite the absence of physical contact or violence.[104] Similarly, airlines and other transport operators exercise physical coercion over the individual's movement at the point of departure. Though individuals may have other means to leave, what is pertinent is that a direct causal or functional relationship exists between the denial of embarkation and obstruction of leaving.[105] Indeed, Strasbourg has recognised extraterritorial jurisdiction when State agents have subjected individuals to checkpoints.[106] Similarly, *Roma Rights* can be read as demonstrating effective control when individuals are prevented from leaving by plane, where the House of Lords found British authorities to have exercised governmental authority when intercepting Roma asylum seekers at Prague airport in breach of their non-discrimination obligations.[107]

Visa regimes raise complex jurisdictional issues. However, visa refusals and denials of boarding can amount to the exercise of jurisdiction. Despite the decision in *MN*, it is arguable that visa refusals can, in principle, meet Article 1 of the ECHR. *A fortiori*, the lower jurisdictional tests under other human rights treaties are also met. Even if the above arguments are not yet accepted under the ECHR, this is the general trend of extraterritorial jurisdiction. It recognises that States cannot obstruct access to territory and rights free of responsibility, especially when attempting to bypass their obligations towards asylum seekers.

B. Attribution to the Destination State

To establish a violation of the right to leave for visa refusals and denial of embarkation, the conduct of carriers, visa companies and IOM must be attributable to the destination State (or EU). ARSIWA and ARIO set out the rules on attribution.

Europe and Extraterritorial Asylum (Oxford, Hart Publishing, 2012) 302; Moreno-Lax, *Accessing Asylum* (n 22) 319. cf Rodenhäuser (n 44) 244–45.

[103] *Women on Waves v Portugal*, App no 31276/05 (ECtHR, 3 February 2009).

[104] Costello (n 98) 248.

[105] Rodenhäuser (n 44) 245–46; S Taylor, 'Offshore Barriers to Asylum Seeker Movement: The Exercise of Power without Responsibility?' in J McAdam (ed), *Forced Migration, Human Rights and Security* (Oxford, Hart Publishing, 2008) 115.

[106] *Jaloud v Netherlands* (2015) 60 EHRR 29, paras 149–52.

[107] *R v Immigration Officer at Prague Airport, ex p European Roma Rights Centre* [2004] UKHL 55, [2005] 2 AC 1, paras 45, 98, cf para 21. See E Guild and V Stoyanova, 'The Human Right to Leave Any Country: A Right to be Delivered' in P Czech, L Heschl, K Lukas and M Nowak, *European Yearbook on Human Rights 2018* (Plymouth, Intersentia, 2018) 378–79.

i. Denial of Embarkation by Carriers

The conduct of non-State actors can sometimes be attributed to the State, including when governments delegate their functions to parastatal or private entities.[108] The conduct of carriers is attributable to the State when they are empowered by the law of the State to exercise elements of governmental authority and are acting in that capacity when they commit a wrongful act (ARSIWA, Article 5).[109] The ARSIWA Commentary states that 'Private or State-owned airlines may have delegated to them certain powers in relation to immigration control', recognising immigration control as a governmental authority.[110] In checking travel documentation, refusing boarding in potential violation of the right to leave, and being obligated to assume responsibility for undocumented non-nationals, carriers are clearly exercising governmental authority – becoming surrogate consular and border officials.[111] As for an empowering law, States have carrier sanctions legislation in place.[112] In the EU, Member States are required by EU law to introduce carrier sanctions legislation.[113] Although the EU may be exercising normative control over the conduct of Member States, carriers should not be understood as agents of the EU acting under its control such that their conduct would be attributed to the EU.[114] Otherwise, all Member State acts applying an EU directive in an area of shared competence would be ipso facto dually attributable to the EU. The EU may instead bear indirect responsibility for direction and control of Member States (both in the area of visa policy and the area of carrier sanctions).

Against the backdrop of watchful ILOs, the conduct of carriers is also attributable to the State when they act on the specific instructions of the State's immigration officials to prevent inadequately documented passengers from boarding (ARSIWA, Article 8).[115] The 'advisory' role of ILOs is doubtful in practice. Though the final decision rests with the airline, studies show that ILO 'advice' is almost always followed.[116] This is understandable. Carriers

[108] ARSIWA Commentary, 42–43 paras 1–2.

[109] ARSIWA Commentary, 43 paras 2, 5.

[110] ARSIWA Commentary, 43 para 2.

[111] Moreno-Lax, *Accessing Asylum* (n 22) 7, 313–16. cf *DZ v Blue Air – Airline Management Solutions SRL*, Case C-584/18, EU:C:2020:324, paras 70–81.

[112] See eg Migration Act 1958 (Cth) s 229; Immigration and Asylum Act 1999 (UK) ss 32–33; Immigration and Refugee Protection Act, SC 2001, c 27 (Canada) (IRPA 2001) s 148; Immigration and Refugee Protection Regulations, SOR/2002-227 (Canada) (IRPR 2002) ss 279–280.

[113] CISA, art 26(1)(b), (2); Carriers Liability Directive, recital 1.

[114] ARIO, art 6. cf art 7, ARIO 56, para 11.

[115] ARSIWA, art 8l; Gammeltoft-Hansen (n 68) 186–88; Moreno-Lax, *Accessing Asylum* (n 22) 317–18.

[116] See Scholten and Minderhoud (n 44) 138; S Scholten, *The Privatisation of Immigration Control through Carrier Sanctions: The Role of Private Transport Companies in Dutch and British Immigration Control* (Leiden, Brill Nijhoff, 2015) 130–33, 275. This is not, however, to say local actors do not play an active part in informing decisions.

are not refusing boarding for their own interests but because they are legally obliged to do so.[117] Despite their initial opposition to sanctions legislation, carriers have a financial incentive to comply and be zealous in their efforts.[118] Through penalisation, ILOs and checks on passengers by immigration officers upon disembarkation, States coerce the 'gatekeeper' into mandatory action.[119] Therefore, the conduct of carriers is attributable to the State as an exercise of governmental authority or when they act on the instructions of ILOs, even when such conduct exceeds authority or contravenes instructions.[120]

ii. Visa Processing

The delegation of visa processing and handling by States to private firms and IOM raises issues similar to and distinct from those involving carriers. Given the State's right to control entry, the handling and processing of applications for entry visas by private companies is attributable to the State as an exercise of governmental authority (ARSIWA, Article 5).[121] Companies must have been empowered by law to exercise this authority pursuant to some legal provision of the State.[122] Private visa companies may be empowered through legislation[123] or by government contract.[124] The Commentary contemplates that 'private security firms may be contracted to act as prison guards' to exercise 'public powers'.[125]

However, private companies and States clearly specify that intermediaries do not have any influence over the decision.[126] IOM also communicates to applicants that the decision rests solely with the State.[127] Accordingly, the issue of attribution does not necessarily arise as granting or refusing a visa is an official action of the State, for which it bears responsibility (ARSIWA, Article 4). Therefore,

[117] Rodenhäuser (n 44) 233.

[118] Feller (n 22) 63–64.

[119] Scholten and Minderhoud (n 44) 128–44. See also Bloom and Risse (n 44); Moreno-Lax, *Accessing Asylum* (n 22) 317–18; FitzGerald (n 3) 64, 68–69.

[120] ARSIWA, art 7; ARSIWA Commentary, 48 para 8.

[121] See VCCR, art 5(d); *Hirsi Jamaa v Italy* (2012) 55 EHRR 21, 76–78 (Separate Opinion Albuquerque J).

[122] J Crawford, *State Responsibility: The General Part* (Cambridge, CUP, 2013) 132; H Tonkin, *State Control Over Private Military and Security Companies in Armed Conflict* (Cambridge, CUP, 2011) 111–12.

[123] See Visa Code, arts 43(2), 45.

[124] See eg VFS Global, 'VFS Global Wins Contract to Provide Germany Visa Services in 14 Countries in Asia Pacific' (*CISION PR Newswire*, 29 October 2018) www.prnewswire.co.uk/news-releases/vfs-global-wins-contract-to-provide-germany-visa-services-in-14-countries-in-asia-pacific-698860921.html; M Gibbs, 'VFS: Who is the Company Subcontracted by the Home Office to Process Visa Applications?' (*The Independent*, 18 August 2019) www.independent.co.uk/news/uk/home-news/vfs-global-home-office-outsourcing-visa-applications-a9061476.html.

[125] ARSIWA Commentary, 43 para 2; Crawford (n 122); Tonkin (n 122) 111–12. cf Gammeltoft-Hansen (n 68) 182, 185, 187.

[126] See eg Visa Code, art 43(4); Infantino (n 67) 42, 46; VFS Global (n 58).

[127] IOM, 'IOM and Immigration' (n 63) 1.

while States may outsource parts of the process, the chain of responsibility is unbroken. These arguments apply equally to online applications. In practice, however, private actors filter out applicants. In her ethnographic study of EU visa policy in Morocco, Infantino found that private contractors play a pivotal role in exercising the discretion inherent in their everyday tasks. Private VAC workers influence the outcome by judging the eligibility of applicants for specific visas and by making mistakes, such as when uploading data to consulates, pre-vetting documentation or providing inaccurate information. This may result in the wrongful exclusion of migrants, a trend identified by others.[128] Therefore, it remains important to attribute the conduct of private companies to the State to account for the whole process, including errors, through Article 5. States also have an obligation to protect applicants under their jurisdiction from violations by non-state actors. However, neither ARSIWA nor ARIO contain a rule that explicitly permits attribution to the State of the conduct of IOs. Accordingly, section V.B will assess IOM's responsibility for aiding and assisting in potential violations (alongside the EU's indirect responsibility).

It follows that when scrutinising the conduct of carriers and private visa companies in the following sections for compliance with the right to leave, this is on the basis that their conduct is attributable to the destination State they act on behalf of.

IV. VISA REFUSALS AND DENIAL OF EMBARKATION: VIOLATIONS OF THE RIGHT TO LEAVE

This section considers whether visa refusals and the denial of embarkation by carriers amount to violations of the right to leave. Applying the key requirements under the right to leave and the general framework established in Part I of this book, it is argued that both visa refusals and denials of embarkation interfere with the right but likely pursue legitimate aims. Nevertheless, they fail the legality requirement. There is a lack of foreseeability and regular review regarding which States end up, and remain, on blacklists. Visa refusals and interceptions by carriers are highly discretionary measures, risk arbitrariness, and individuals may be unable to challenge the outcomes. Regarding proportionality, the effectiveness of visas and carrier sanctions is also questionable and more protective options are available to States. They bear down heavily on asylum seekers and refugees, who are disproportionately harmed by visa regimes and excluded from accessing regular pathways. Lastly, visa refusals and denials of embarkation are inconsistent with other fundamental rights owed to migrants, notably obligations of *non-refoulement*, non-discrimination and the right to life.

[128] Infantino (n 67) 11, 16, 28, 42–59. See Bloom (n 78) 152–53; Moreno-Lax, *Accessing Asylum* (n 22) 113; Gibbs (n 124).

A. Visa Refusals

i. Interference

Prima facie visa requirements and refusals interfere with the right to leave, which is a contentious proposition in light of the widespread acceptance of visa regimes. Visa policies make leaving dependent on having permission to enter the destination State, either through visa-free access or possessing a visa. The jurisprudence on the right illustrated numerous types of interferences. However, in *Consorts Demir v France*, the Strasbourg Court refused to consider denying an entry visa as engaging the right to leave, holding that Article 2 Protocol 4 does not confer any right to obtain an entry visa.[129] Nevertheless, the Court did not adequately explain why visa refusals cannot fall within the scope of the right and be understood as *interfering* with leaving at the point of departure, as opposed to generating a positive *right* to be granted a visa.[130] As Strasbourg has held in other cases, 'any measure' which denies an individual the use of a document which would have permitted them to leave the country amounts to an interference with the right to leave.[131] When the CRPD Committee found that Australia's refusal to issue a visa breached the applicant's freedom of movement on an equal basis with others, it implicitly acknowledged an interference with her right to leave.[132] Recall that the right encapsulates departure from any country, departure to a place of the individual's choice, and that obligations under the right apply extraterritorially.

By requiring certain nationalities to possess a visa to enter a country, their ability to leave for their chosen destination is suppressed, requiring them to apply for a visa, travel irregularly or not at all. An unsuccessful applicant cannot leave the State they are in and legally travel to the State which has declined their visa, although they may be able to travel elsewhere (addressed below). Den Heijer argues that a visa refusal's practical and legal effect only occurs when the visa requirement is enforced through pre-clearance controls, such as by carriers.[133] However, it is just as much an interference with the right to leave to force a person to leave a country 'legally', rendering travel without permission unlawful. In a case concerning the freedom to leave one's residence, Strasbourg held that the obligation to ask the authorities for permission to leave each time does not correspond to freedom of movement.[134] Transit visas pose a greater interference, being doubly extraterritorial. They prevent people from being

[129] *Consorts Demir v France*, App no 3041/02 (ECtHR, 4 April 2006) para 23.

[130] See den Heijer, *Europe* (n 102) 157; E Guild, *The Right to Leave a Country* (Issue Paper, Council of Europe Commissioner for Human Rights 2013) 64–65; Guild and Stoyanova (n 107) 375.

[131] *SE v Serbia*, App no 61365/16 (ECtHR, 11 July 2023) para 75; *LB v Lithuania*, App no 38121/20 (ECtHR, 14 June 2022) para 79.

[132] *Sherlock* (n 97).

[133] den Heijer, *Europe* (n 102) 161.

[134] *Ivanov v Ukraine*, App no 40450/04 (ECtHR, 15 October 2009) para 85.

able to travel through places such as Australia, North America, Europe, Turkey or the UAE for onward travel to their ultimate destination. Notably, in a case against Russia, interrupting the applicants' journey by pulling them off a train to Azerbaijan and forcing them to wait for 12 days for an (exit) transit visa, interfered with and violated their right to leave.[135] As will be discussed, transit visas can pose significant obstacles for asylum seekers. The plurality of actors making leaving difficult for nationals of those States deemed an asylum risk is significant when considering the notion of a global travel ban for refugee-producing States.

While destination States may argue that the right to leave is only opposable to departure States when non-nationals are concerned, nothing limits the right in this manner. As den Heijer has argued, destination States may also interfere with the right when they impose immigration measures that prevent non-nationals from leaving another country.[136] As Part I concluded, the fact that visas operate as a pre-entry control should not affect their dual characterisation as an exit control. Otherwise, destination States would be free to inhibit leaving as they pleased.[137] As early as 1989, in the context of carrier sanctions, NGOs urged the UN Sub-Commission to declare that States must refrain from preventing, even indirectly, non-nationals from leaving their country of origin.[138] Classifying visas as an interference correctly recognises that departure States and States exercising extraterritorial control have obligations under the right to leave, which ensures its effectiveness and upholds its object and purpose, including protecting departure independently of entry. States cannot hide behind a collectivised reading of the right, ignoring the binary nature of obligations (contracting State–individual under jurisdiction).[139] Every State bound by the right must guarantee it to those within their jurisdiction and respect its independent nature, including States imposing visas.[140] States can, thus, be in violation of the right regardless of whether entry will be granted.

As demonstrated in chapter two, an interference does not presuppose a complete inability to leave for everywhere, and the availability of alternatives should not affect the right's threshold. Individuals have the right to leave in any direction, and the inability to travel to one State amounts to an interference despite the fact the individual could travel elsewhere.[141] As Strasbourg held in

[135] *Shioshvili v Russia*, App no 19356/07 (ECtHR, 20 December 2016) paras 58–62.

[136] Den Heijer, *Europe* (n 102) 157.

[137] ibid 160.

[138] Report of the Secretary General, 'The Right of Everyone to Leave any Country, including his Own, and to Return to his Country' (1989) UN Doc E/CN.4/Sub.2/1989/44/Add.1, 11–12.

[139] Moreno-Lax, 'EU Borders' (n 102) 353–55; GS Goodwin-Gill and J McAdam, *The Refugee in International Law*, 4th edn (Oxford, OUP, 2021) 430.

[140] ibid; Guild and Stoyanova (n 107) 394.

[141] cf *Mogos v Romania*, App no 20420/02 (ECtHR, 13 October 2005) para 111, where the Court held that the applicants' inability to leave the transit centre and country was due to their refusal to re-enter Romania and regularise their status and not attributable to the State.

SE v Serbia, the applicant, a recognised Syrian refugee, would have been able to 'travel to other countries of his choice to which he could have been admitted had he been able to comply with one of the essential prerequisites for that', namely a valid travel document.[142] Rather, the availability of alternatives may be relevant to proportionality. Therefore, the dual effect of visas in hindering individuals at the start of the journey, alongside their effect on entry, is an interference.

ii. In Accordance with Law

Any interference with the right to leave must be in accordance with or provided by law. It is not contentious that visa policies have a basis in law. The question is whether the listing and visa refusal processes satisfy the quality of law test, requiring them to be clear, foreseeable and accompanied by adequate procedural safeguards.

a. Listing Process

There is often a lack of transparency around how States end up on visa blacklists, the evidence used, and the possibilities for removal. The whitelisting and blacklisting of countries is inherently a foreign policy decision shaped by diplomatic relations, strategic alliances and perceived risks. This means the quality of law assessment under the right to leave will be fairly lax, despite issues with foreseeability and arbitrariness.

The EU's visa regime is particularly accessible compared to other regimes and thus, provides a useful analytical framework. EU law specifies that listing is taken:

> on the basis of a case-by-case assessment of a variety of criteria relating, inter alia, to illegal immigration, public policy and security, economic benefit, in particular in terms of tourism and foreign trade, and the Union's external relations with the relevant third countries, including, in particular, considerations of human rights and fundamental freedoms, as well as the implications of regional coherence and reciprocity.[143]

This demonstrates the wide discretion afforded to the EU in listing a State; the criteria are vague, non-exhaustive, and not sufficiently precise to allow States (or nationals) to foresee whether they will be blacklisted. The EU's listing history demonstrates that there has been movement between lists, highlighting the existence of periodic reviews.[144] Several benchmarks and factors

[142] *SE* (n 131) para 78.
[143] Reg (EU) 2018/1806, art 1.
[144] Reg (EU) 2018/1806, recital 3, art 8(4); M den Heijer, 'Visas and Non-discrimination' (2018) 20 *European Journal of Migration and Law* 470, 480–85; E Guild and M Grundler, 'The EU Visa Policy: To Deter and to Facilitate' in E Tsourdi and P De Bruycker (eds), *Research Handbook on EU Migration and Asylum Law* (Cheltenham, Edward Elgar Publishing, 2022) 390–406.

are typically considered for movement onto the whitelist: document security; migratory risks including irregular migration, readmission, asylum, and border and migration management; public order and security; and external relations and fundamental rights.[145] In considering list amendments, waivers have been granted for geopolitical reasons with visa liberalisation being a key bargaining chip in international relations.[146] For instance, the EU has granted visa waivers to Albania, Bosnia and Herzegovina, Kosovo, Montenegro, North Macedonia, Serbia, Georgia, Moldova and Ukraine following visa liberalisation dialogues, representing the first step towards EU membership.[147] This was controversial for the Western Balkan States, which had been blacklisted amidst the Yugoslav Wars and the ensuing refugee crisis.[148] As discussed under proportionality, the EU conditions liberalisation and threatens restrictive measures on a State's performance in asylum and border control.[149] The risk of or absence of irregular migration is also afforded priority. Ecuador and Bolivia were moved to the blacklist in 2006 because of concerns over illegal immigration and public policy concerns.[150] Visa requirements were recently reimposed on Vanuatu over concerns that its investor citizenship scheme posed increased internal security and public order risks.[151] Conversely, Colombia and Peru were whitelisted based on factors including significant economic growth, low levels of irregular migration, reduced security threats, cooperation on return, and a strong EU relationship.[152]

[145] See eg Commission, 'Joint Staff Working Paper First Progress Report of the Implementation by the Republic of Moldova of the Action Plan on Visa Liberalisation' SEC (2011) 1075 final, 1; Regulation (EU) 2025/11 of the European Parliament and of the Council of 19 December 2024 amending Regulation (EU) 2018/1806 as regards Vanuatu [2025] OJ 2025/11.

[146] Czaika, de Haas and Villares-Varela (n 13) 4, 7–11; den Heijer, 'Visas' (n 144) 483–85.

[147] Commission, 'Communication from the Commission to the European Parliament and the Council on the monitoring of the EU's visa free regimes' (30 May 2023) COM/2023/297 final; M Petrovic, 'Freedom of Movement in the European Union: Visa Liberalisation in the Western Balkan Countries' (2010) LSE Migration Studies Unit Working Papers No 2010/04, www.lse.ac.uk/government/Assets/Documents/pdf/research-groups/msu/WP-2010-04.pdf.

[148] See generally F Trauner and E Manigrassi, 'When Visa-free Travel Becomes Difficult to Achieve and Easy to Lose: The EU Visa Free Dialogues after the EU's Experience with the Western Balkans' (2014) 16 *European Journal of Migration and Law* 125.

[149] ibid; T Strik, 'The Global Approach to Migration and Mobility' (2017) 5 *Groningen Journal of International Law* 310, 317–18.

[150] Council Regulation (EC) No 453/2003 of 6 March 2003 amending Regulation (EC) No 539/2001 [2003] OJ L 69/10, recital 1; Council Regulation (EC) No 1932/2006 of 21 December 2006 amending Regulation (EC) No 539/2001 [2006] OJ L 405/23, recital 2; Commission, 'Proposal for a Council Regulation amending Regulation (EC) No 539/2001' COM (2002) 679 final, 2–3; Commission, 'Proposal for a Council Regulation amending Regulation (EC) No 539/2001' COM (2006) 84 final, 2–3.

[151] Reg (EU) 2025/11. See Reg (EU) 2018/1806, art 8 on the visa suspension mechanism.

[152] Regulation (EU) No 509/2014 of the European Parliament and of the Council of 15 May 2014 amending Council Regulation (EC) No 539/2001 [2014] OJ L 149/67, recitals 5, 6; Commission, 'Report from the Commission to the European Parliament and the Council on the Fulfilment by Colombia of the relevant criteria in view of the negotiation of a visa waiver agreement between the European Union and Colombia' COM (2014) 665 final; Commission, 'Report from the Commission to the European Parliament and the Council On the Fulfilment by Peru of the relevant criteria in

Nonetheless, there remains a lack of transparent, published reasoning for why most States are blacklisted, impacting their nationals' right to leave. As Moreno-Lax and den Heijer argue, the inclusion of the bulk of blacklisted States has never been properly justified or reviewed.[153] The absence of a requirement to justify precisely why a State is blacklisted makes it impossible to ascertain the criteria at play.[154] Arguably, this leads to a failure of the EU visa policy to adequately safeguard nationals against arbitrariness. The same issues squarely arise for the ATV list. Apart from its stated aim of combatting illegal migration and the EU's annual review of Member States' decisions to impose additional ATVs, the specific criteria for listing a State and the timing of EU-wide reviews remain imprecise and opaque.[155]

Quality of law issues appear to be a problem across visa regimes, which is unsurprising given the political nature of listing. For example, while Australia has a universal visa requirement, it differentiates between States by allowing nationals with an 'eligible passport' to apply online for certain visas. The instrument specifying these countries does not explain their inclusion or the exclusion of others.[156] The US position is slightly clearer on which States qualify for visa-free travel: the State must have and maintain a low visa refusal rate (below 3 per cent) and issue machine-readable passports. However, the State is assessed against inherently vague criteria, including security interests, law enforcement and the enforcement of immigration laws.[157] The Trump administration's 2017 travel ban preventing the entry of nationals from primarily African, Asian and Middle Eastern States and the 2025 travel ban further illustrate how visa regimes can fall within broad and unconstrained executive powers under domestic law, resulting in unpredictability and arbitrariness.[158]

In some Global South States, the criteria for white or blacklisting are either not easily accessible or lack clear codification. Where such criteria do exist, they are often vague or grant authorities broad discretionary powers. For instance, Mexican and Turkish law authorises the government to unilaterally

view of the negotiation of a visa waiver agreement between the European Union and Peru' COM (2014) 663 final.

[153] Moreno-Lax, *Accessing Asylum* (n 22) 89–94; den Heijer, 'Visas' (n 144) 487.

[154] Guild, 'Border Abroad' (n 23) 92–104.

[155] Visa Code, recital 5, art 3(3). See R Cholewinski, 'Borders and Discrimination in the European Union' (Immigration Law Practitioners' Association and Migration Policy Group, 2002) 20–37, https://www.migpolgroup.com/_old/wp-content/uploads/2016/10/152.bordersandDiscrimination_exec_summary_01.02.pdf.

[156] Migration (Specification of eVisitor eligible passport) Instrument (LIN 23/064) 2023; Migration (IMMI 18/084: Specification of ETA-Eligible Passports) Instrument 2018.

[157] See INA 8 USC s 1187. See also Mau and others, *Liberal States* (n 12) 60–62, 70–73; B Ryan, 'Extraterritorial Immigration Control: What Role for Legal Guarantees?' in B Ryan and V Mitsilegas (eds), *Extraterritorial Immigration Control: Legal Challenges* (Leiden, Martinus Nijhoff, 2010) 8–10.

[158] See NAFSA, 'Travel Ban: NAFSA Resources' (20 January 2021) www.nafsa.org/professional-resources/browse-by-interest/executive-order-travel-ban-nafsa-resources; S Bojang Jnr and E Conroy, 'Trump's Travel Ban: Over Half the Countries on the List are in Africa' (*The Africa Report*, 18 March 2025) www.theafricareport.com/379171/trumps-travel-ban-the-22-african-countries-on-the-list/.

decide to waive the visa requirement for nationals of certain countries.[159] Brazilian law specifies that visa exemptions are granted at its discretion to States that ensure reciprocity of treatment and other nationalities subject to the national interest.[160] New or updated lists may be published online, in the official gazette, or amended without explanation.[161] South Africa's official website states that the visa exemption list is 'subject to change without notice', while the law gives the Minister broad power to exempt any category of persons.[162] Before 2024, when Kenya transitioned to an ETA system for all visitors regardless of nationality, its immigration law sorted States into three lists: visa-free, visa on application, and referred visa.[163] The only explicit reference to criteria pertained to referred visas – required for nationals of countries such as Afghanistan, Kosovo, Senegal and Tajikistan – relating to applicants 'against whom there is some local objections or doubt in the country where the application is made'. However, even under an ETA system, applicants from certain nationalities will still face greater scrutiny. It bears mentioning that despite the right to leave being an *individual* right, any review and removal from the blacklist requires State-level action.

b. Visa Issuance

The quality of law test will be applied more stringently with respect to visa refusals for individuals. While visa rules may be relatively straightforward and publicly available, the problem lies in the highly discretionary and opaque nature of visa decisions and the lack of procedural safeguards.

Even when an applicant ostensibly satisfies the stated requirements, the visa may nevertheless be refused. The broad and imprecise nature of visa criteria affords the authorities wide powers of interpretation to base their decisions, often with limited accountability.[164] There are various grounds on which a visa may be refused. These include an inability to demonstrate a genuine intention to

[159] Law on Foreigners and International Protection, Law No 6458 of 2013 (Turkey) art 18; Migratory Act (Ley de Migración) 2011 (Mexico) art 37(III)(a).

[160] Decree No 9199 of November 20, 2017 (Brazil) subsection 3. See Brazil reinstating visas for Australia, Canada and the US, 'Government to Resume Visa Requirement for Americans Entering Brazil' (*Folha de S. Paulo*, 9 April 2025) www1.folha.uol.com.br/internacional/en/world/2025/04/government-to-resume-visa-requirement-for-americans-entering-brazil.shtml.

[161] See Immigration Regulations of 1968 (Malawi); Immigration (Amendment) Regulations 2024 (Malawi) reg 3, sch 2; Royal Thai Consulate-General, 'Visa Exemption and Visa on Arrival to Thailand' (18 July 2024) thaiconsulatela.thaiembassy.org/en/publicservice/visa-exemption-and-visa-on-arrival-to-thailand.

[162] Immigration Act 13 of 2002 (South Africa) s 10A(4); Department of Home Affairs, 'Countries Exempt from South African Visas', www.dha.gov.za/index.php/immigration-services/exempt-countries.

[163] The Kenya Citizenship and Immigration Regulations 2012, sch 5. For the new law, see the Kenya Citizenship and Immigration (Amendment) Regulations 2023.

[164] F Infantino, *Schengen Visa Implementation and Transnational Policymaking: Bordering Europe* (New York, Palgrave Macmillan, 2019) 55–64.

return – often evidenced by the absence of return travel arrangements; insufficient or unconvincing justification for the purpose and duration of the intended stay; insufficient proof of financial means to support the stay; the use of false documentation; prior criminal convictions or criminal activity; or posing a threat to security, public health, public policy or international relations.[165] As chapter two discussed, these latter terms are vague and open to interpretation. States also do not generally define what constitutes a threat to public policy or security.[166] Decision-makers, thus, enjoy near unfettered discretion in assessing whether an individual poses a security, migratory or other risk, combined with subjective judgements of veracity and intention.[167]

In Australia, visa applicants can be subject to a sweeping character test. A visa can be refused because the person has a substantial criminal record, poses a potential danger to the community, or their *general conduct* indicates they are not of good character.[168] This test has received much criticism for affording the Minister extremely broad discretionary powers and lacking safeguards.[169] As a result, there is a risk of arbitrariness, and applicants may be unable to reasonably foresee the outcome of their application or how considerations will be applied or weighted. Although Australia may be on the far end of the spectrum, these features are likely inherent to many, if not all, visa systems. As Jansen posits, visa issuance is 'widely experienced as dependent more on the whims of individual functionaries than on transparent criteria. Its discretionary nature – a favour, not a right'.[170] Though such criteria may not be any

[165] See eg INA 8 USC ss 1182, 1184(b), 1201(g) (2018); IRPA 2001 (Canada) ss 34–39; IRPR 2002 (Canada) ss 14–20, 179; Immigration Act 2002 (South Africa) ss 10–11, 29–30; Visa Code, arts 21(1), (3), (6)–(7), 32(1); Law of the Republic of Indonesia Number 6 of 2011 on Immigration, art 42; Law No 13.445 of May 24, 2017 (Brazil), arts 10, 11 and 45.

[166] See Visa Code, art 32(1)(a)(vi); Immigration and Foreigners Act, 2025 (India) s 3(1). See also H Staples, 'Adjudicating the External Schengen Border' in K Groenendijk, E Guild and P Minderhoud (eds), *In Search of Europe's Borders* (The Hague, Kluwer Law International, 2003) 235, 245; Bigo and Guild (n 77) 244–45.

[167] See *Koushkaki v Bundesrepublik Deutschland*, Case C-84/12, EU:C:2013:862, paras 55–63 on the wide discretion afforded to authorities; Infantino, *Schengen Visa* (n 164) 177–215.

[168] Migration Act 1958 (Cth) s 501; Migration Regulations 1994 (Cth) sch 4; Minister for Immigration, Citizenship and Multicultural Affairs (Cth), 'Direction No. 110 – Visa refusal and cancellation under section 501 and revocation of a mandatory cancellation of a visa under section 501CA' (7 June 2024).

[169] See Australian Human Rights Commission, 'Background Paper: Human Rights Issues Raised by Visa Refusal or Cancellation under Section 501 of the Migration Act' (2013) https://humanrights.gov.au/our-work/asylum-seekers-and-refugees/publications/background-paper-human-rights-issues-raised-visa; Law Council of Australia, Submission No 29 to Senate Legal and Constitutional Affairs Committee, Parliament of Australia, *Migration Amendment (Strengthening the Character Test) Bill 2019* (14 August 2019); Visa Cancellations Working Group, Submission No 19 to Senate Legal and Constitutional Affairs Legislation Committee, *Migration Amendment (Strengthening the Character Test) Bill 2021* (17 December 2021).

[170] S Jansen, 'After the Red Passport: Towards an Anthropology of the Everyday Geopolitics of Entrapment in the EU's "Immediate Outside"' (2009) 15 *Journal of the Royal Anthropological Institute* 815, 818. See also F Zampagni, 'Unpacking the Schengen Visa Regime. A Study on Bureaucrats and Discretion in an Italian Consulate' (2016) 31 *Journal of Borderlands Studies* 251.

more vague than other areas of administrative discretion, visa regimes seek to establish powers and discretion, not rules and standards.[171]

There is also a risk of poor-quality decision-making, including errors by private visa contractors. Staples, in their 2003 study of the jurisprudence of national courts on the Schengen visa rules, found that the system resulted in arbitrary decisions and lacked legal certainty.[172] However, the Visa Code introduced in 2009 may have helped to address these issues by harmonising procedures and the criteria. The UK Independent Chief Inspector of Borders and Immigration, tasked with monitoring the efficiency and effectiveness of the Home Office's functions, has expressed concern on different occasions about the quality of decision-making and inconsistency, such as visas being incorrectly refused after staff 'disregarded or misinterpreted' evidence or where applicants failed to provide information not requested.[173] Many States may also experience inefficiency, corruption and resource limitations, leading to poorly managed visa systems and inconsistent decisions.

The increased reliance on automated systems and algorithmic risk assessments in visa processing exacerbates arbitrariness, opaqueness, and the lack of procedural fairness and oversight.[174] Automated systems often operate as 'black boxes', where the processes and reasoning behind rejections are unclear and not easily understood by applicants and even officials. This, combined with uncertainty over whether there was human oversight and *who* or *what* made the decision, creates obstacles for individuals in challenging adverse outcomes and on what grounds, including for discrimination or errors. Before the visa streaming tool's suspension, the UK Independent Chief Inspector of Borders and Immigration warned that it could become 'a de facto decision-making tool' because of the danger of confirmation bias.[175] Visa regimes are discretionary and opaque by design, which automation perpetuates.

As the right to leave jurisprudence illustrated, wide discretion is less problematic if adequate procedural safeguards exist. The ability to challenge a visa refusal is critical to realising the right to leave, for a first refusal may pave the way

[171] Costello (n 98) 89.

[172] Staples (n 166) particularly 223–35, 245–46.

[173] See eg ICIBI, 'Inspection Report of the UK Border Agency Visa Sections in Africa' (June 2012) 5–7, sect 4, www.gov.uk/government/publications/inspection-report-of-the-uk-border-agency-visa-sections-in-africa-june-2012; ICIBI, 'Inspection Report of the Amman Visa Section' (October 2015) 4–5, sect 4, www.gov.uk/government/publications/inspection-report-of-the-amman-visa-section-october-2015.

[174] See Molnar and Gill (n 70) particularly pts 5.1, 5.3, 6.1–6.2; A Rinaldi and SA Teo, 'The Use of Artificial Intelligence Technologies in Border and Migration Control and the Subtle Erosion of Human Rights' (2025) 74 *International & Comparative Law Quarterly* 61; GY Tian, T McFarland and S Guo, 'Automated Decision Making and Deportation: Legal Concerns and Regulation' (2025) *Griffith Law Review* 1.

[175] ICIBI, 'An Inspection of Entry Clearance Processing Operations in Croydon and Istanbul' (July 2017) 5–6, sect 7. https://www.gov.uk/government/publications/inspection-report-on-entry-clearance-processing-operations-in-croydon-and-istanbul-july-2017.

for future refusals.[176] In the case of short-stay or temporary visas, appeal rights may be absent, limited or difficult to exercise. Levels of transparency and appeal rights differ vastly across countries and regions. For example, when a Schengen visa is refused, individuals possess a right of judicial appeal under national law against the Member State refusing the visa and must be provided with information regarding the appeal procedure.[177] Though informed of their rights, they will have to start proceedings from a third State and cannot present their case in person unless granted permission to enter or appear via video.[178] In some Asian and African countries, rejected applicants can appeal from abroad.[179] Re-applying with additional documentation addressing the rejection reason may often be less costly and faster than a potentially lengthy appeal process.[180] However, re-applying or appealing is particularly difficult in countries where authorities deny visas without explanation.[181]

In other States, appeal rights are more precarious and available only in limited circumstances. The UK does not grant appeal rights for visitor or student visa refusals unless the applicant raises a human rights or protection claim, leaving them to re-apply, seek judicial review, or request administrative review in the case of students.[182] Canada has no formal appeal process, while in the case of New Zealand, overseas temporary visa applicants generally do not have a right to reconsideration.[183] Similarly, in Australia, non-citizens can only submit an application for review if they have review rights and applicants overseas are generally not entitled to these rights.[184] Visa applicants without ties to the US

[176] See eg Migration Act 1958 (Cth) ss 501E, 501F; US Department of State, 'Visa Denials – INA Section 214(b) – Visa Qualifications and Immigrant Intent' www.travel.state.gov/content/travel/en/us-visas/visa-information-resources/visa-denials.html. cf Visa Code, art 21(9) but see art 32(5) on refusals being recorded.

[177] Visa Code, arts 32(3), 47(1)(h), annex VI; *El Hassani v Minister Spraw Zagranicznych*, Case C-403/16, EU:C:2017:960, paras 37–42; Guild and Grundler (n 144) 402–04 discussing that as an implication of the Court finding that a visa can only be refused based on a listed ground, it must follow that 'there is an obligation to issue a visa if the criteria for its issue are satisfied.'

[178] See Staples (n 166) 228–33.

[179] See Immigration Act 13 of 2002 (South Africa) s 8(3)–(7); AskGov Singapore, 'How Do I Appeal Against My Visa Rejection?' (27 January 2025) www.ask.gov.sg/ica/questions/clos83fvx01mb5k0ww9yau2xd.

[180] See on re-applying in Brazil at points 30 and 31: Ministério das Relações Exteriores, 'Visa FAQ', www.gov.br/mre/pt-br/embaixada-helsinque/consular-services/visa-faq.

[181] See Ministry of Foreign Affairs Singapore, 'Frequently Asked Questions on Visa', www.mfa.gov.sg/Overseas-Mission/Chennai/Visa-Information/Frequently-Asked-Questions-on-Visa; Ministry of Foreign Affairs of Japan, 'Frequently Asked Questions', www.mofa.go.jp/j_info/visit/visa/faq.html. A Google search reveals numerous posts on forums like TripAdvisor, where people report being denied visas to countries across various regions, including Asia, the Middle East, and South America, without explanation.

[182] Nationality, Immigration and Asylum Act 2002 (UK) s 82(1).

[183] Government of Canada, 'How Do I Get Help If My Visa Application Is Refused?' (7 November 2012) www.ircc.canada.ca/english/helpcentre/answer.asp?qnum=422&top=16; New Zealand Immigration, 'Appealing Against a Decision to Refuse a Visa', www.immigration.govt.nz/about-us/news-centre/appealing-against-a-decision-to-refuse-a-visa/.

[184] Migration Act 1958 (Cth) ss 338, 500.

(ie, a US spouse or close family) are virtually powerless, hindered by the doctrine of 'consular nonreviewability'.[185] In many parts of the Global South, there is no publicly available information on the availability of appeal rights or appeal process. It is also important to note that even when a visa is granted, individuals may still be refused entry at the border, as a visa (or waiver) constitutes only a prima facie case for admission.

While limiting appeals may be justifiable from a cost and efficiency perspective, this does not negate the significant quality of law issues impacting visa processes. Visa applicants are non-voluntary customers, often having no choice but to use private companies.[186] Outsourcing to third parties and relocation away from the border makes it difficult, perhaps impossible, for them to assert their legal rights. The individual may only ever encounter a private company or IOM, making frontline workers useful scapegoats.[187] Delegation thus removes such activities from democratic and legal control mechanisms.[188] Outsourcing and automation multiply the chances of arbitrary visa processes and prevent individuals from vindicating their right to leave. The State and safeguards are conveniently hidden.

iii. Proportionality

Although visa listing and refusal processes likely fail to meet the legality test to varying degrees across jurisdictions, there remains scope for States to improve compliance through systemic reforms. Accordingly, adjudicative bodies' analysis of whether visa requirements or refusals violate the right to leave would largely hinge on proportionality. This entails examining whether such measures pursue a legitimate aim, are rationally connected to that aim, are strictly necessary to achieve it, and strike a fair balance between the individual's right to leave and the objectives pursued.

a. Legitimate Aim

The longstanding and widespread use of visas by States has rendered them one of the least contested migration controls, often treated as inherently legitimate and insulated from challenge. In the *Roma Rights* case, Lord Bingham asserted that 'it could not plausibly be argued that a visa regime would have been contrary to the practice of the nations'.[189] The UNHCR also recognises

[185] See *Trump v Hawaii* 138 S Ct 2392, 2418–20 (2018); DS Dobkin, 'Challenging the Doctrine of Consular Non-reviewability in Immigration Cases' (2010) 24 *Georgetown Immigration Law Journal* 113; G Baca, 'Visa Denied: Why Courts should Review a Consular Officer's Denial of a U.S.-Citizen Family Member's Visa' (2015) 64 *American University Law Review* 591.

[186] Infantino, *Schengen Visa* (n 164) 37.

[187] See ibid 5, 62–80.

[188] Bloom and Risse (n 44) 76.

[189] *Roma Rights* (n 107) para 28. See also Goodwin-Gill and McAdam (n 139) 417.

visa requirements (and carrier sanctions) as generally permissible measures by States to manage entry to their territory, including requirements that may prove onerous for people from refugee-producing countries.[190] Accordingly, visas *could* be understood to fall within the scope of lawfully permissible measures restricting the right to leave.

However, this work does not contend that visas are unlawful *in toto* or against the practice of nations. Rather, it demonstrates that visas cannot always be understood as a lawful restriction on the right to leave, given the common issues that can arise across visa regimes and visa types. While immigration control may be a legitimate expression of State sovereignty and due regard must be given to State practice, this does not insulate visas from challenge. It should also be interrogated whether the State's right to control *entry* automatically entitles it to control *exit*. As is conventional practice within human rights law adjudication, courts can declare certain aspects of a practice incompatible with a right to ensure its effectiveness. This is particularly important given that the right to leave is underexplored vis-à-vis destination States.

Visa policies may pursue several legitimate aims justifying restrictions on the right to leave, specifically national security, public order, public safety, health and the prevention of crime.[191] As the general criteria for visa issuance demonstrate, visas seek to facilitate welcome cross-border movement while simultaneously controlling and curbing movement that poses security, health and other migratory risks.[192] The EU's visa policy captures these aims clearly: it is directed at 'facilitating legitimate travel and tackling illegal immigration', 'strengthening freedom, security and justice' in the EU, and assessing whether applicants are a threat to public policy, security or public health.[193] As delved into below, visa regimes also seek to limit the arrival of asylum seekers and refugees, for example when States reimpose visa requirements following an increase in asylum applications.[194]

There are indeed risks associated with migration and mobility, including the spread of disease and viruses (as shown by the Covid-19 pandemic), human trafficking and smuggling, and threats to security and public safety associated with terrorism and crime.[195] It is not contentious that visa policies fall within the scope of public order – ensuring the functioning of society based on fundamental

[190] UNHCR, 'Annex to UNHCR Note on the "Externalization" of International Protection: Policies and Practices related to the Externalization of International Protection' (28 May 2021) para 16.

[191] See Feller (n 22) 50; FitzGerald (n 3) 53.

[192] Neumayer (n 12) 74.

[193] Visa Code, recital 3, arts 21, 32(1); Reg (EU) 2018/1806, art 1. See also IRPA 2001 (Canada) s 3(1).

[194] See Reg (EU) 2018/1806, art 8(2)(a)(b); Trauner and Manigrassi (n 148) 126, 132–44.

[195] See on security and crime, Neumayer (n 12) 76; M Mittelstadt and others, 'Through the Prism of National Security: Major Immigration Policy and Program Changes in the Decade since 9/11' (Fact Sheet, MPI, 2011) www.migrationpolicy.org/research/post-9-11-immigration-policy-program-changes.

principles. Visas aim to facilitate order and control migration through selectivity – preventing irregular migration while simultaneously promoting tourism, trade and other beneficial activities. However, even far-reaching legitimate aims are constrained by a State's international obligations. Measures that restrict departure in order to prevent individuals from seeking asylum are unlikely to be legitimate. Therefore, targeting asylum seekers and refugee-producing countries should not be understood as a legitimate public order aim. The legitimacy of discriminatory visa policies is also questionable, addressed under the consistency limb of the right to leave. States may also invoke national security, which is only properly implicated in cases of a serious threat to the nation itself, not merely local or isolated threats. This sets a high bar for imposing visa requirements and refusals based on national security, though it is possible in certain individual cases.

Two deeper problems are at play. First, States *construct* the notion of 'illegal immigration', turning those who would otherwise cross the border lawfully into 'illegal' and 'irregular' migrants through their visa policies and immigration laws.[196] Without a documentary requirement, such movement would be lawful. As the Committee on Migrant Workers has articulated, 'Migration irregularity is not the result of a decision of the migrant, but of restrictive policies of the State that prevent the exercise of the right to freedom of movement'.[197] Second, some States may claim to pursue legitimate goals, but their true aim is to avoid their international obligations toward asylum seekers. Migration is highly politicised, and its risks are routinely exaggerated. The rhetoric of politicians and the media often leverages migrants as a threat to the security, economy, health, identity and fabric of society. Positive labels such as 'tourist', 'expat' or 'businessperson' are disproportionately afforded to individuals of certain nationalities or racial backgrounds, while 'illegal migrant' is seldom associated with a backpacker or student who has overstayed their visa.[198] As FitzGerald aptly expresses:

> Even though the chances of an asylum seeker committing a terrorist act are infinitesimally small, the narrative that these controls are necessary to protect security provides a plausible alternative to the narrative that the controls deliberately or in effect prevent asylum seekers from seeking safety.[199]

[196] Costello (n 98) ch 3. See also E Guild, 'Who is an Irregular Migrant?' in B Bogusz and others (eds), *Irregular Migration and Human Rights: Theoretical, European and International Perspectives* (Leiden: Martinus Nijhoff, 2004).

[197] CMW, 'General Comment No. 5 (2021) on Migrants' Rights to Liberty and Freedom from Arbitrary Detention and Their Connection with Other Human Rights' (21 July 2022) UN Doc CMW/C/GC/5, para 36.

[198] See A Tsoukala, 'Looking at Migrants as Enemies' in D Bigo and E Guild (eds), *Controlling Frontiers: Free Movement Into and Within Europe* (Cardiff, Ashgate, 2005); Bigo and Guild (n 77) 237; Avdan (n 41) 186–88, 190–91; C Dauvergne, 'Sovereignty, Migration and the Rule of Law in Global Times' (2004) 67 *Modern Law Review* 588, 599.

[199] FitzGerald (n 3) 261.

Adjudicative bodies should scrutinise the motives underlying visa requirements rather than accepting their legitimacy at face value. States should not be permitted to make vague security or public order assertions, feeding into vilifying rhetoric that masks the real aim and discriminatory treatment involved. However, adjudicative bodies, particularly the Strasbourg Court, are likely to afford the State a high degree of deference.[200] Given the State's right to control entry, many visa policies will likely be deemed to serve a legitimate aim with little interrogation. The remainder of the proportionality test is therefore critical in ensuring minimum impairment of the right to leave.

b. Rational Connection, Necessity and Balancing

This section identifies key concerns regarding the proportionality of visa restrictions to achieving their intended objectives. It highlights clear issues with the suitability of visa policies, the existence of more protective alternatives, the assessment of applicants against predetermined group stereotypes, and the disproportionate impact of visa regimes on asylum seekers and refugees.

The first step in the proportionality analysis – suitability – requires a rational connection between the measure adopted and the objective pursued. There are serious doubts about whether visa requirements are capable of effectively preventing irregular migration and people smuggling and trafficking. Visas narrow the availability of lawful travel options and, for many nationalities, can be difficult to obtain, increasing irregular movement, the risk of trafficking and the need for smugglers.[201] Studies have shown that while visa refusals appear to increase irregular migration, visa requirements are a relatively strong deterrent. However, this deterrent effect is effectively counterbalanced by the considerable deflection of migrants into irregularity.[202] Other studies have shown that the re-introduction of visa restrictions by Mexico and South American countries for Ecuadorians, Haitians and Venezuelans led to a significant increase in irregular migration and the use of smugglers.[203] So-called 'illegal' migration remains the 'product of the laws that seek to combat it'.[204] Nevertheless,

[200] See also *Trump* (n 185) 2418–20.

[201] See Bloom and Risse (n 44) 74; N Avdan, 'Human Trafficking and Migration Control Policy: Vicious or Virtuous Cycle?' (2012) 32 *Journal of Public Policy* 171; Guild and Stoyanova (n 107) 390.

[202] M Czaika and M Hobolth, 'Deflection into Irregularity? The (Un)intended Effects of Restrictive Asylum and Visa Policies' (2014) IMI Working Paper Series 84, www.migrationinstitute.org/publications/wp-84-14; M Czaika and M Hobolth, 'Do Restrictive Asylum and Visa Policies Increase Irregular Migration into Europe?' (2016) 17 *European Union Politics* 345.

[203] See Cintra (n 34); HRW, *"This Hell Was My Only Option": Abuses Against Migrants and Asylum Seekers Pushed to Cross the Darién Gap* (New York, HRW, 2023); O Hammoud-Gallego, 'The Short-Term Effects of Visa Restrictions on Migrants' Legal Status and Well-Being: A Difference-in-Differences Approach on Venezuelan Displacement' (2024) 182 *World Development* 1; Mixed Migration Centre, 'Smuggling and Migration in South America: Insights from Migrants' (2025) www.mixedmigration.org/resource/smuggling-and-migration-in-south-america/.

[204] Costello (n 98) 67.

visas may be logically capable of addressing concerns related to security, crime, safety and health; however, their actual effectiveness in doing so remains open to question.[205] Second, visas are not strictly necessary to achieve these aims as reasonable, less restrictive alternatives exist. Migration control could occur at the border rather than in the State of origin or departure. Scholars have proposed a more liberal migration policy or one combined with limited detention and the return of migrants declared inadmissible, ensuring public scrutiny and judicial control in destination States rather than leaving people outside in countries of transit or of persecution.[206] There are problems and implications with such an approach. Control at the border is less effective for remote control purposes and is associated with greater pressure at border crossings, high costs of detention and deportation, greater administrative and financial costs, and obstacles to returning the individual.[207]

Nonetheless, processing at the destination State's border represents a more protective alternative for migrants. Resource implications can be partially addressed, including requiring rejected migrants to pay for their return journey when possible.[208] Moreover, as demonstrated below, most people will be allowed entry and the costs associated with processing asylum seekers who arrive spontaneously can be reduced by introducing humanitarian corridors. Adopting a human rights-centred approach, rather than a State-centred one, allows more protective alternatives to be accepted as reasonable, rendering visa regimes not strictly necessary. However, when it comes to restricting the right to leave during public health crises, some departure controls – such as temporarily restricting the entry of non-essential travellers – may be necessary. However, as the WHO and UNHCR warned during the pandemic, blanket travel bans and border closures are likely to be ineffective and counterproductive, risking further spread of a virus as migrants take more hidden routes or end up in 'orbit' in search of a State willing to admit them.[209]

If the State's overriding objective is to prevent so-called 'unwanted' migrants altogether, equally effective but less restrictive alternatives are unlikely to exist. This requires a proportionality assessment in the strict sense, striking a fair

[205] Avdan, *Visas* (n 41) 191–92, 196–97, questions their effectiveness in curbing terrorism and criminal activity.

[206] Baird and Spijkerboer (n 44) 17, 19.

[207] See eg Christian (n 18) 216, 228–29; UNHCR, 'Protection Policy Paper: The Return of Persons Found Not to be in Need of International Protection to their Countries of Origin: UNHCR's Role' (November 2010); den Heijer, *Europe* (n 102) 163.

[208] Guild and Stoyanova (n 107) 390–91.

[209] UNHCR, 'Key Legal Considerations on Access to Territory for Persons in Need of International Protection in the Context of the COVID-19 Response' (16 March 2020) paras 5–8; WHO, 'Updated WHO Recommendations for International Traffic in Relation to COVID-19 Outbreak' (29 February 2020) www.who.int/news-room/articles-detail/updated-who-recommendations-for-international-traffic-in-relation-to-covid-19-outbreak. See also N Banulescu-Bogdan, M Benton and S Fratzke, 'Coronavirus is Spreading across Borders, but it is not a Migration Problem' (Commentary, MPI, 2020) www.migrationpolicy.org/news/coronavirus-not-a-migration-problem.

balance between the individual's right to leave and the objectives pursued. Where an individual is subject to widespread visa requirements or frequent refusals, this is likely to destroy the essence of the right – unless they pose a clear security or health risk. This cannot, however, be the only scenario where visas are disproportionate.[210] Statistical evidence from the EU highlights their disproportionate nature (as well as the reasonableness of alternatives). Visas significantly impact mobility, despite the number of people entering the EU irregularly or refused admission at the border paling compared to the vast numbers entering lawfully, accompanied by generally low refusal rates, which indicate that travellers are not customarily deemed to pose risks.[211]

As established in the jurisprudence from chapter two, restrictions will not be considered necessary if they are automatic and fail to account for individual circumstances. While visas may not be a wholly blanket and indiscriminate measure, individuals from blacklisted States are guilty until proven innocent. Paradoxically, passports identify unique individuals but, combined with visas, dismantle that 'uniqueness by classifying them into a collectivity restricted by default in terms of cross-border mobility'.[212] This places the burden on applicants to prove they are the exception and do not constitute a risk, notwithstanding their membership of a State which, by definition, is deemed suspicious.[213] This may prove impossible and is especially challenging when algorithms classify individuals as 'risky' based on pre-determined threat levels rather than individual behaviour or factors within their control.[214] To strike a fair balance, significant weight must be given to individual circumstances, avoiding a broad-brush approach based on preconceived characteristics.

c. Disproportionate Impact on Asylum Seekers and Refugees

Although the right to leave benefits nationals and non-nationals alike, a stricter test is warranted when assessing violations of the *right to leave to seek asylum*, explored in chapter four. Visa policies disproportionately harm asylum seekers and (would-be) refugees. This is evident in the widespread blacklisting of refugee-producing States, the instrumentalisation of incentives and sanctions to pressure States to readmit asylum seekers and curb irregular migration, and

[210] cf M Zieck, 'Refugees and the Right to Freedom of Movement: From Flight to Return' (2018) 39 *Michigan Journal of International Law* 21, 41–45.

[211] E Guild and S Carrera, 'EU Borders and Their Controls: Preventing Unwanted Movement of People in Europe?' (2013) CEPS Essay No 6, particularly 6, 12–14, www.ceps.eu/ceps-publications/eu-borders-and-their-controls-preventing-unwanted-movement-people-europe/; Guild and Grundler (n 144) 396.

[212] Jansen (n 170) 817.

[213] See J Carling, 'Migration in the Age of Involuntary Immobility: Theoretical Reflections and Cape Verdean Experiences' (2002) 28 *Journal of Ethnic and Migration Studies* 5, 32–33; Bigo and Guild (n 77) 89.

[214] See N Vavoula, *Immigration and Privacy in the Law of the European Union: The Case of Information Systems* (Leiden, Brill Nijhoff, 2022).

the fact most asylum seekers and refugees cannot meet standard visa criteria or overcome arduous procedures.

Visas have been used for decades to deter refugees and asylum seekers – and have been criticised for just as long for obstructing the right to seek asylum.[215] For example, in the 1980s, the UK introduced visas for countries such as Afghanistan, Iraq, Iran and Sri Lanka in response to a rise in asylum applications (alongside carrier sanctions), and Germany introduced visas for Afghans, Bangladeshis, Indians and Sri Lankans.[216] Similarly, Canada overtly used visas as a tool to deter asylum seekers, reinstating them for the Czech Republic and Hungary whenever asylum applications from Roma individuals increased, which continued until Canada moved to treat EU Member States as safe countries of origin.[217] In response to the millions of Venezuelans fleeing the country in 2017 and 2018, States such as Chile, Ecuador and Peru introduced entry requirements for Venezuelans, who could previously enter with relative ease.[218] In May 2023, Egypt introduced new visa requirements for all Sudanese nationals, forcing many people fleeing the conflict, which had broken out a month prior, to cross the border irregularly.[219] Blacklists generally overlap with the leading source countries for refugees, which is further illustrated by the Passport Index, highlighting the power – or lack thereof – of certain passports.[220] Transit visas also target (some but not all) refugee-producing countries, such as the list of countries whose nationals require an ATV by some or all EU Member States, including Afghanistan, the DRC, Ethiopia, Eritrea, Somalia, Sudan, Syria and Yemen.[221]

States may also explicitly link their visa policies to reducing asylum, which inhibits the regular movement of asylum seekers and refugees. Visa facilitation is often made conditional on a State's cooperation on readmission and strengthening

[215] See eg Council of Europe, 'Parliamentary Assembly Recommendation 1163 (1991) on the Arrival of Asylum-Seekers at European Airports' (23 September 1999) paras 7–10; UNHCR, 'UNHCR Position: Visa Requirements and Carrier Sanctions' (September 1995); Christian (n 18) 223–24.

[216] B Ryan, 'Extraterritorial Immigration Control: What Role for Legal Guarantees?' in B Ryan and V Mitsilegas (eds) *Extraterritorial Immigration Control: Legal Challenges* (Leiden, Martinus Nijhoff, 2010) 9; Moreno-Lax, *Accessing Asylum* (n 22) 114; FitzGerald (n 3) 164–66.

[217] A Macklin, 'A Safe Country to Emulate? Canada and the European Refugee' in H Lambert, J McAdam and M Fullerton (eds), *The Global Reach of European Refugee Law* (Cambridge, CUP, 2013); FitzGerald (n 3) 60–61.

[218] D Acosta, C Blouin and LF Freier, *La emigración venezolana: respuestas latinoamericanas* (Salamanca, Fundación Carolina, 2019) 30; Mixed Migration Centre (n 203) 3, 8–9.

[219] Amnesty International, '"Handcuffed Like Dangerous Criminals": Arbitrary Detention and Forced Returns of Sudanese Refugees in Egypt' (2024) 8–9, www.amnesty.org/en/documents/mde12/8101/2024/en/.

[220] Henley & Partners, 'Passport Index', www.henleypassportindex.com/passport; UNHCR, 'Communication from the European Commission on A Common Policy on Illegal Immigration (COM(2001) 672 final) 4; UNHCR, 'Refugee Data Finder' (2024) www.unhcr.org/refugee-statistics/data-summaries.

[221] Visa Code, annex IV; List of third countries whose nationals are required to be in possession of an airport transit visa when passing through the international transit area of airports situated on the territory of one/some Member States.

its border controls. Conversely, failure to comply can lead to the use or threatened use of punitive measures such as making visas more difficult and expensive to obtain or trade sanctions.[222] For instance, as part of the 2016 EU–Turkey deal, the EU committed to lifting visas for Turkish citizens in exchange for the readmission of all irregular migrants crossing into Greece and preventing irregular migration.[223] However, Turkey has yet to be granted visa-free access due to outstanding benchmarks, including full implementation of the readmission agreement and harmonisation of its visa list.[224] This exemplifies 'Fortress Europe': the 'creation of a borderless Europe was always a doubly constitutive process: removing fences within, it built higher fences around'.[225] This can also be understood as 'visa cascading', where affluent destination States pressure transit States to emulate their restrictive visa regimes and impose visa requirements on refugee-producing States or those posing a risk of significant irregular migration, limiting their access to transit countries. Australia has influenced Malaysia and Indonesia to adopt visa requirements for Afghans, Iraqis, Iranians and Syrians.[226] Similarly, pressure or requests from the US have led Mexico, Costa Rica, Panama and Honduras to introduce new visa requirements and transit visas for nationalities arriving at the US southern border in greater numbers, as well as the harmonisation of visa lists between Canada and the US.[227] Since 2022, countries across the Americas have taken over 300 new visa policy actions to restrict irregular migration.[228] Mirroring the externalisation practices of the Global North (and at odds with their general reputation as being more open to migrants than the former), in the 2000s, Argentina pressured Brazil to stop issuing visas to Senegalese nationals given their rising asylum applications and, in the 2010s, Brazil pressured Peru and Ecuador to lift visa waivers for Haitians to prevent their arrival.[229]

[222] See Visa Code art 25a; Australia, Migration Amendment (Removal and Other Measures) Act 2024 (Cth) ss 199A, 199F–199G, allowing the government to designate a country as a 'removal concern country' where it is not cooperating in the removal of its nationals, and barring visa applications from nationals of that country, subject to certain exceptions.

[223] European Council, 'EU-Turkey Statement' (18 March 2016); Czaika, de Haas and Villares-Varela (n 13) 7–10; Avdan, Visas (n 41) 168–78. See also Strik (n 149); H Grabbe, 'Stabilising the East While Keeping Out the Easterners: Internal and External Security Logics in Conflict' in S Lavenex and EM Uçarer (eds), *Migration and the Externalities of European Integration* (Lanham, Lexington Books, 2002); Laube (n 41) 12–16.

[224] Commission, 'Staff Working Document Turkey 2018 Report' SWD (2018) 153 final, 48–49.

[225] Jansen (n 170) 819–20.

[226] See 'Jakarta Declaration on Addressing Irregular Movement of Persons' (20 August 2013) 2; F Mussi and F Tan, 'Comparing Cooperation on Migration Control: Italy–Libya and Australia–Indonesia' in F de Londras and S Mullaly (eds), *Irish Yearbook of International Law 2015* (Oxford, Hart Publishing, 2017) 97–98; AL Hirsch, 'Externalisation and Access to Asylum: An Investigation into Australia's Migration Control Cooperation with Indonesia' (DPhil thesis, Monash University 2022) 48, 71–72.

[227] FitzGerald (n 3) ch 4; Women's Refugee Commission, 'Visa Regimes: A Threat to Migrants' Access to Safety and Asylum' (2022) www.womensrefugeecommission.org/research-resources/visa-regimes-a-threat-to-migrants-access-to-safety-and-asylum/.

[228] Los Angeles Declaration (n 37).

[229] Vammen (n 34); Cintra (n 34). See also Acosta (n 36) 125; N Cintra and P Nabuco Martuscelli, 'Wall of Visas: How Race Impacts the Externalization of (Forced) Migration Control in South-South Migration Corridors' (2025) *Ethnic and Racial Studies* 1.

Therefore, many asylum seekers and refugees must obtain a visa to access the global mobility regime; however, most cannot meet strict criteria or evidence requirements. Even when States do not explicitly target asylum seekers, claiming asylum is, by definition, not accommodated within visa regimes, except in rare cases such as humanitarian visas or protected entry programmes. As the UNHCR has critiqued, visa policies do not differentiate between asylum seekers and refugees and the broader class of nationals requiring a visa, ignoring the protection they are entitled to.[230] For short-stay visas, individuals must typically possess a valid passport, specify their dates and purpose, provide details of their accommodation and means of subsistence, and prove their intention to leave afterwards.[231]

First, an asylum seeker, refugee or stateless person may not possess a valid passport or travel document.[232] Requiring asylum seekers and refugees to obtain a passport or visa ignores the very issues giving rise to their protection needs.[233] Often, the authorities responsible for issuing travel documents constitute the source of persecution or threat, or individuals may be unable or unwilling to avail themselves of the authorities' protection.[234] In collapsed States, there will be no competent issuing agency. Even with a passport, individuals may be unable to travel to an embassy or unable to wait around for a visa when facing imminent threats to their safety.[235] This reality underscores the relevance of Article 31 of the Refugee Convention, which prohibits penalising refugees and asylum seekers for irregular entry, recognising the general inability to meet entry requirements. Second, unless asylum seekers lie about their intentions, they cannot prove the temporary nature of their stay.[236] If there are doubts about an individual's reliability, the authenticity of their documents, or they are perceived as posing a risk of irregular migration, a visa will typically be refused. Providing evidence of an address in the country of destination, family ties or funds for the stay – or even paying for the visa itself – may be prohibitive.[237] Unequal visa regimes reportedly cost the world's poorest over €100 million yearly, with rejected visa costs flowing from poor to rich countries.[238] Asylum seekers requiring an ATV

[230] Moreno-Lax, 'EU Borders' (n 102) 317–18; Moreno-Lax, *Accessing Asylum* (n 22) 100–06; UNHCR, 'Communication from European Commission' (n 220) 5.

[231] MB Salter, 'The Global Visa Regime and the Political Technologies of the International Self: Borders, Bodies, Biopolitics' (2006) 31 *Alternatives* 167, 176–77. See for the EU: Moreno-Lax, *Accessing Asylum* (n 22) 96–99, 103–06.

[232] A Brouwer and J Kumin, 'Interception and Asylum: When Migration Control and Human Rights Collide' (2003) 21 *Refuge* 6, 8–9.

[233] UNHCR, 'UNHCR Position on Conventions Recently Concluded in Europe (Dublin and Schengen Conventions)' (16 August 1991). See also Moreno-Lax, 'EU Borders' (n 102) 326–27, particularly fn 85.

[234] UNHCR, 'UNHCR Position' (n 215); Feller (n 22) 56, 61.

[235] See UNHCR, 'Dublin' (n 233).

[236] JC Hathaway, *The Rights of Refugees under International Law* (Cambridge, CUP, 2005) 291–93.

[237] UNHCR, 'Dublin' (n 233).

[238] M Foresti, O Mantegazza and K Maghoma, 'Africans Pay the Price of Visa Denials to Europe' (*Africa at LSE*, 24 June 2024) blogs.lse.ac.uk/africaatlse/2024/06/24/africans-pay-the-price-of-visa-denials-to-europe/.

have usually already been classified as a migratory risk. Their right to leave is more disproportionately impacted, as they will not be granted a visa to *even transit* through a State if they risk claiming asylum.[239]

Obtaining a visa may also be physically impossible. States do not have consulates or VACs in every country, yet applications may still need to be made in person, requiring migrants to make long, difficult or irregular journeys to the nearest VAC. For instance, it appears that no EU Member State has a presence in Eswatini, The Gambia, Liberia or Somalia and all visa sections in Afghanistan, South Sudan and Syria are temporarily closed or not issuing visas.[240] Tellingly, the number of Schengen visas issued to Syrians before the conflict was over 30,000, dropping to almost zero in 2013.[241] After conflict broke out in Sudan in 2023, many countries closed their embassies, as did private visa centres.[242] Physical impossibility or a policy of non-issuance to certain nationalities is plainly disproportionate and in violation of the right to leave.

Neither in law nor in practice are visas accessible to most asylum seekers and refugees. Visas requirements are 'the most explicit blocking mechanism for asylum flows', denying most refugees legal migration opportunities.[243] As Costello and Vasanthakumar have noted, this does not mean that refugees do not come; rather, irregular arrivals often occur when containment strategies backfire, as exemplified by Europe's 2015 'refugee crisis'.[244] If States are serious about ending irregular migration, they should facilitate the arrival of asylum seekers by providing safe and regular routes – less restrictive alternatives which have been advocated for years.[245] Alongside increasing resettlement options, States and the EU should introduce and expand complementary pathways such as community sponsorship programmes, family reunification, labour mobility schemes, and educational opportunities, as well as protected entry and humanitarian corridors permitting individuals to apply for humanitarian visas at embassies or other outposts so they can travel lawfully to seek asylum.[246]

[239] See eg Immigration Rules (UK) app pt v 7.5; Visa Code, arts 14(2), 21(6).

[240] Visa Code Handbook, Annex 28.

[241] EU Agency for Fundamental Rights (FRA), *Legal Entry Channels to the EU for Persons in Need of International Protection: A Toolbox* (Vienna, FRA, 2015) 2; Moreno-Lax, *Accessing Asylum* (n 22) 107.

[242] eg VFS Global Sudan, visa.vfsglobal.com/sdn/en/gbr/.

[243] J Morrison and B Crosland, 'Trafficking and Smuggling of Refugees: The End Game in European Asylum Policy' (2001) UNHCR New Issues in Refugee Research Working Paper No 39, 1, 28, www.unhcr.org/research/working/3af66c9b4/trafficking-smuggling-refugees-end-game-european-asylum-policy-john-morrison.html.

[244] C Costello and A Vasanthakumar, 'Refugee Containment and the Costs of Creating False Dilemmas. A Response to Aleinikoff and Owen' (The Ethics of Migration Policy Dilemmas, Migration Policy Centre, 2022) 4–5, www.migrationpolicycentre.eu/wp-content/uploads/2023/10/2nd_dilemma_2nd_responsedf.

[245] CMW, 'General Comment No. 2 on the Rights of Migrant Workers in an Irregular Situation and Members of Their Families' (28 August 2013) UN Doc CMW/C/GC/2, para 17.

[246] See UNGA, 'Report of the United Nations High Commissioner for Refugees: Part II Global Compact on Refugees' (2 August 2018) UN Doc A/73/12, paras 90–96; UNGA, 'Global Compact for

Experts have suggested that adopting the latter would boost protection capabilities, dissuade some disorderly movement, and have strong savings potential compared to territorial asylum procedures.[247] Currently, many authorities are unlikely to grant visas for asylum purposes, and existing programmes remain ad hoc and discretionary (such as the EU failing to institutionalise humanitarian visas under the Visa Code). Or, as chapter six reveals, increased legal pathways may perversely result in pushbacks and the denial of territorial asylum. Denial of the right to seek asylum is thus a key feature of visa policies, and there are no apparent lawful alternatives when this is the intention. Therefore, the interests of asylum seekers and refugees should much more readily outweigh the interests of States in obstructing their search for refuge.[248]

Finally, it is vital to consider proportionality in the context of widespread blacklisting of refugee-producing States and visa cascading. Where many States blacklist refugee-producing States or refuse visas to the majority of applicants, this effectively amounts to a global travel ban and deprives individuals of an effective and practical right to leave. Blacklisting condemns individuals to unsafe conditions and irregularised travel, with whole regions inaccessible. Cumulative containment by States as currently exists for countries with the lowest passport power, such as Afghanistan and Syria, can be perceived as a collective violation of the right, leading to shared responsibility amongst States. Where knowledge exists of a substantial risk of harm by keeping visa requirements in place, States arguably have a duty to withdraw or temporarily suspend requirements (and carrier sanctions) until that risk dissipates.[249]

There is a strong case that visa policies fail the proportionality test. Visas remain largely inaccessible to asylum seekers and refugees, effectively denying their right to leave to seek asylum, sometimes with deadly consequences.

Safe, Orderly and Regular Migration' (11 January 2019) UN Doc A/RES/73/195, para 21; F Crépeau, 'Towards a Mobile and Diverse World: "Facilitating Mobility" as a Central Objective of the Global Compact on Migration' (2018) 30 *International Journal of Refugee Law* 650; Koslowski (n 3) 170; T Wood, 'The Role of "Complementary Pathways" in Refugee Protection' (Report, Kaldor Centre for International Refugee Law, 2020) https://www.unsw.edu.au/content/dam/pdfs/unsw-adobe-websites/kaldor-centre/2023-05-data/2023-07-complementary-pathways-refugee-protection.pdf.

[247] G Noll, J Fagerlund and F Liebaut, *Study on the Feasibility of Processing Asylum Claims outside the EU Against the Background of the Common European Asylum System and the Goal of a Common Asylum Procedure* (Copenhagen, Danish Centre for Human Rights and European Commission, 2003) particularly sects 5, 7. See also C Higgins, *Safe Journeys and Sound Policy: Expanding Protected Entry for Refugees* (Policy Brief 8, Kaldor Centre for International Refugee Law, 2019).

[248] Moreno-Lax, 'EU Borders' (n 102) 356–57; den Heijer, *Europe* (n 102) 166; Guild and Stoyanova (n 107) 391–93.

[249] UNHCR, 'Communication from European Commission' (n 220) 5; ECRE, 'Defending Refugees' Access to Protection in Europe (2007) 35, www.ecre.org/wp-content/uploads/2016/07/ECRE-Defending-Refugees-Access-to-Protection-in-Europe_December-2007.pdf; Moreno-Lax, *Accessing Asylum* (n 22) 312–13.

iv. Consistency with Other Rights

Lastly, restrictions on the right to leave must be consistent with other human rights. *Prima facie* visa policies may be inconsistent with the obligations of *non-refoulement* and non-discrimination, both of which have emerged as central concerns in this chapter. Other rights may also be implicated, depending on the context.

a. *Non-refoulement*

Establishing that visa requirements or visa refusals entail a risk of *refoulement* by the destination State falls to be considered under the Refugee Convention and international human rights law, with the latter being much more straightforward when individuals are exposed to a real risk of harm.

The generally accepted view under Article 33 of the Refugee Convention is that in imposing visa requirements and refusing visas to individuals with a well-founded fear of persecution but still inside their country of origin, the State does not breach its *non-refoulement* obligations.[250] On present understandings, Article 33 can only be breached by the destination State where an individual has crossed an international border, and there is a risk of indirect *refoulement* from a transit State. According to Gammeltoft-Hansen, merely refusing a visa does not necessarily provide a sufficient causal link to any future *refoulement*; it is enforcement of the visa requirement by another actor, such as an airline or the departure State, which may lead to *refoulement*.[251] However, a sufficient causal link between the refusal and risk of *refoulement* can exist. It is the initial visa requirement, followed by the visa refusal, which suppresses lawful departure in the first place and may compel an individual to continue to stay in or return to a situation of persecution. This does not only arise when the carrier or another State denies embarkation for the destination. Both denying a visa and enforcing visa requirements may violate Article 33 (and *non-refoulement* obligations under human rights law), where the individual's inability to leave puts them at risk of return to serious harm.[252] However, it is difficult to establish that the refusal of a visa to a person in transit constitutes a return to the State's frontier, as required by the Convention since the individual remains within the same (transit) State.[253] Nevertheless, a risk of indirect *refoulement* may exist.

Nevertheless, as argued in chapter four, a good faith interpretation of *non-refoulement* obligations, including under the Convention, requires States to organise their migration controls so individuals can seek asylum. Looking to

[250] See eg Hathaway, *Rights of Refugees* (n 236) 307–08, 310–12; Noll (n 88) 553; Moreno-Lax, *Accessing Asylum* (n 22) 264–65; Goodwin-Gill and McAdam (n 139) 417.
[251] Gammeltoft-Hansen (n 68) 134.
[252] Noll (n 88) 564–72; Ogg (n 88); Moreno-Lax, *Accessing Asylum* (n 22) 265.
[253] Noll (n 88) 556.

the object and purpose of the Refugee Convention supports an interpretation of *non-refoulement* that extends protection to would-be refugees who remain in their State of origin or a transit State as a direct consequence of departure and pre-entry controls. Visa policies are generally not implemented in good faith in this context; they are designed to contain asylum seekers where they are, as the preceding sections show, and to prevent *non-refoulement* and other obligations from being triggered at all.[254] Although visas are in widespread use and presumably, States believe they are complying with *non-refoulement* obligations (or have not considered this question), concluding that visa refusals cannot amount to *refoulement* arguably runs counter to the Refugee Convention's object and purpose. Accordingly, such an interpretation ought not lightly to be inferred from State practice.[255] Few States may uphold their obligations, and externalising States are actively seeking to bypass their obligations under the Convention.[256] Even if such arguments are not accepted (given the clear textual limitations of the Refugee Convention), and other jurisdictions support the determinations of the UK courts on this matter, visas can still be challenged under human rights law.

Under human rights law, establishing that a visa requirement or refusal leads to *refoulement* does not require the individual to be outside their State of origin. A refusal may amount to *refoulement* where it exposes the person to a real risk of irreparable harm in a particular territory and effectively compels them to return to, or remain in, that territory.[257] Exposure to such risk is sufficient – the threatened treatment need not be immediate or certain.[258] Despite the Strasbourg Court finding in *MN v Belgium* that visa refusals do not trigger *non-refoulement* obligations under the ECHR for want of jurisdiction, this book advances the position that refusing a visa to an individual seeking to exercise their right to leave, and who is in danger of ill-treatment, can nonetheless engage the State's positive obligations. States cannot turn a blind eye to an evident need for protection and are obliged to 'find out about the treatment to which the applicants would be exposed after their return'.[259] As Judge Albuquerque powerfully articulated in *Hirsi*, drawing on historical examples of protective visas granted during World War II, where a person is at risk of treatment contrary to Article 3 and seeks asylum at the embassy of a Contracting Party, that State has a positive obligation to protect the individual, including granting a visa to enable entry into its territory.[260] The high likelihood a visa refusal will lead to denial of boarding, as shown below, obliges States to take preventative measures, including issuing humanitarian visas or suspending visa

[254] Goodwin-Gill and McAdam (n 139) 416, 421–22, 434.
[255] Taylor (n 105) 109. See art 31(3)(b).
[256] ibid.
[257] Moreno-Lax, *Accessing Asylum* (n 22) 309–11, 313–20.
[258] Noll (n 88); Ogg (n 88) 106; ibid 309.
[259] *Hirsi Jamaa* (n 121) para 133; den Heijer, *Europe* (n 102) 140.
[260] *Hirsi Jamaa* (n 121) 70 (Separate Opinion Albuquerque J).

requirements temporarily.[261] While this may seem far-reaching, the applicant still needs to establish a real risk of harm and concerns over the 'burden' of refugees should be addressed through global responsibility sharing.

b. Discrimination

Visa policies may also violate the right to leave for unlawfully discriminating against individuals on racial, religious and gender-based grounds. The pressing question is whether visa policies constitute racial discrimination, directly or indirectly, given the blacklisting and differential treatment of specific nationalities, which has been the subject of growing attention.[262]

Discrimination involves any distinction, exclusion, restriction, or preference based on one or more prohibited grounds, such as race, national origin, sex, religion or other status, which has the purpose or effect of nullifying or impairing the enjoyment or exercise of rights.[263] Discrimination can be direct or indirect. In *Roma Rights*, immigration officials were targeting travellers of Roma ethnicity, which was 'inherently and systemically discriminatory' and amounted to direct race discrimination based on ethnic origin.[264] Conversely, indirect discrimination is where a general policy or measure, though facially neutral, has disproportionately prejudicial effects on a particular group even where it is not specifically aimed at that group and there is no discriminatory intent.[265] Indirect discrimination is only unlawful if it lacks an objective and reasonable justification.

Race-based immigration restrictions have a long history across the Americas and the British Empire, shaping many of today's migration regimes.[266] However, States cannot lawfully discriminate between non-citizens on racial grounds.[267] If it can be shown that States impose visa requirements or restrictions directly

[261] UNHCR, 'Communication from the European Commission' (n 220) 5; Moreno-Lax, *Accessing Asylum* (n 22) 311–13.

[262] See den Heijer, 'Visas' (n 144); M Grundler, '"Treatment Accorded to Aliens Generally": Article 7(1) of the 1951 Refugee Convention as a Basis for Visa-Free Access to States Parties' Territory? An Examination of the Prohibition of Nationality Discrimination in the Refugee Convention' (2021) 33 *International Journal of Refugee Law* 469; Costello and Foster (n 2); UNGA, 'Report of the Special Rapporteur on the Human Rights of Migrants, Gehad Madi on the Phenomenon of Migrants Going Missing or Subjected to Enforced Disappearance – Human Rights Analysis' (28 April 2025) UN Doc A/HRC/59/49, para 36.

[263] HRC, 'General Comment No 18: Non-discrimination' (10 November 1989) UN Doc HRI/GEN/1/Rev.1 at 26, paras 6–7. See ECHR, art 14; ICCPR, arts 2(1), 26; ICERD, art 1.

[264] *Roma Rights* (n 107) paras 38, 73–75, 97.

[265] *Biao v Denmark*, App no 38590/10 (ECtHR, 24 May 2016) para 103; *Memedova v North Macedonia*, Apps nos 42429/16 and 2 others (ECtHR, 24 October 2023) para 89.

[266] See D Ghezelbash, 'Legal Transfers of Restrictive Immigration Law: A Historical Perspective' (2017) 66 *International and Comparative Law Quarterly* 235; E Lester, *Making Migration Law: The Foreigner, Sovereignty, and the Case of Australia* (Cambridge, CUP, 2018); FitzGerald and Cook-Martín (n 37).

[267] *Roma Rights* (n 107) para 101; *Biao* (n 265) paras 89–94. See also Guild, *Right to Leave* (n 130) 37–50, 54–55, 65.

based on race, ethnicity or religion, such measures will be difficult to justify under international law. For example, the Trump administration's 2017 so-called 'Muslim Ban' explicitly targeting seven Muslim-majority countries (Iran, Libya, Somalia, Sudan, Syria, Yemen) – all of which are predominantly Black and Brown nations – illustrates how visa policies may constitute unlawful direct discrimination.[268] Similarly, the response to Ukrainians fleeing Russia's invasion of Ukraine in February 2022 prompted many to point out the stark difference in treatment of Ukrainians compared with other refugees. Although Ukrainians already benefited from visa-free travel to the EU, the EU nonetheless activated its Temporary Protection Directive for the first time, granting Ukrainians the rights to temporary residency, work and social benefits, and free movement across Member States to choose their place of refuge.[269] Other States waived regular visa requirements and opened bespoke family reunion and sponsorship pathways facilitating easier access to their territory.[270] In contrast, foreigners from African, Asian and MENA countries, and Ukrainian ethnic minorities were faced with unequal, racialised treatment and violence.[271]

While this unequal treatment is stark, 'The global refugee regime treats different refugees differently, as a matter of course'.[272] During the Syrian civil war and increased arrivals to Europe, States responded by drastically reducing the number of visas granted to Syrian nationals and pursuing religious and country of origin bans, described as 'plainly discriminatory against refugees fleeing Muslim-majority countries'.[273] As Costello and Foster have usefully articulated, where everyone of a certain nationality or certain groups

[268] See H Panduranga, F Patel and MW Price, 'Extreme Vetting & the Muslim Ban' (Report, Brennan Center for Justice, 2017) www.brennancenter.org/our-work/research-reports/extreme-vetting-and-muslim-ban.

[269] Council of the European Union, 'Council Implementing Decision (EU) 2022/382 of 4 March 2022 establishing the existence of a mass influx of displaced persons from Ukraine within the meaning of Article 5 of Directive 2001/55/EC, and having the effect of introducing temporary protection' (4 March 2022) ST/6846/2022/INIT.

[270] eg Government of Canada, 'Immigration Measures and Support for Ukrainians and Their Families' (last updated April 2025) https://www.canada.ca/en/immigration-refugees-citizenship/services/immigrate-canada/ukraine-measures.html; UK Government, 'UK Visa Support for Ukrainian Nationals' (last updated February 2025) www.gov.uk/guidance/support-for-family-members-of-british-nationals-in-ukraine-and-ukrainian-nationals-in-ukraine-and-the-uk.

[271] See eg African Union, 'Statement of the African Union on the Reported Ill Treatment of Africans Trying to Leave Ukraine', www.au.int/en/pressreleases/20220228/statement-ill-treatment-africans-trying-leave-ukraine; HRW, 'Ukraine: Unequal Treatment for Foreigners Attempting to Flee' (*HRW*, 2022) www.hrw.org/news/2022/03/04/ukraine-unequal-treatment-foreigners-attempting-flee; HRW, 'Moldova: Romani Refugees from Ukraine Face Segregation' (*HRW*, 2022) www.hrw.org/news/2022/05/25/moldova-romani-refugees-ukraine-face-segregation.

[272] Costello and Foster (n 2) 244.

[273] See H Grant, 'UK Closing Doors to Syrian Migrants, Lawyers Say' (*The Guardian*, 11 March 2015) www.theguardian.com/uk-news/2015/mar/11/syrian-refugees-uk-visa-asylum-seekers-visa; ET Achiume, 'Race, Refugees, and International Law' in C Costello, M Foster and J McAdam (eds), *The Oxford Handbook of International Refugee Law* (Oxford, OUP, 2021) 50–51. cf Cintra and Nabuco Martuscelli (n 229) on Brazil's response to African compared with Syrian refugees.

of nationalities are targeted, a contextual and historical assessment should be undertaken, mindful of racialised colonial legacies.[274] Nevertheless, as the decision of the US Supreme Court in *Trump v Hawaii* demonstrates in upholding Trump's ban, the State's sovereign prerogative is often allowed to mask overt discriminatory intent.[275] Strasbourg has similarly been critiqued for legitimising deeply racialised borders and a narrow understanding of racial discrimination that ignores how specific measures are neither racially neutral nor intended to be.[276]

When and under what circumstances differences in treatment on the grounds of nationality amount to racial discrimination is even more contentious, including whether relevant prohibitions on discrimination encompass 'nationality'. Visa regimes are premised on differentiating between nationalities, with a person's nationality representing the determining factor as to whether they have access to visa-free travel.[277] Affording special treatment to some nationalities over others is generally understood as a legitimate exercise of the State's migration control prerogative and not unlawful discrimination.

Nationality is not an explicit ground of discrimination under most international treaties – including the ICCPR, ICERD and ECHR – only national origin.[278] This issue was addressed in the proceedings before the ICJ and CERD Committee concerning the expulsion and travel bans imposed on Qatari nationals by the UAE and Saudi Arabia. Under ICERD, 'racial' discrimination is understood broadly to encompass 'race, colour, descent, or national or ethnic origin' and Article 1(2) of ICERD explicitly excludes distinctions between citizens and non-citizens from the definition. The CERD Committee held that 'the absence of nationality in the definition of racial discrimination prohibited by the Convention does not affect the jurisdiction of the Committee'.[279] The Committee relied on an earlier general recommendation, which provides that Article 1(2) should not be construed as undermining the basic prohibition of discrimination and 'differential treatment based on citizenship or immigration status will constitute discrimination' if the criteria are not applied pursuant to a legitimate aim and are disproportionate to achieving that aim.[280] It concluded

[274] Costello and Foster (n 2) 250.

[275] See *Trump* (n 185); den Heijer, 'Visas' (n 144) 470–71.

[276] JT Theilen, 'Framing Migration in Human Rights: How the Reasoning of the European Court of Human Rights Legitimises Border Regimes' (2025) 27 *European Journal of Migration and Law* 66.

[277] *Roma Rights* (n 107) para 101; *Biao* (n 265) paras 89–94. See also Guild, *Right to Leave* (n 130) 37–50, 54–55, 65.

[278] cf ICRMW, art 1.

[279] *Decision on the Admissibility of the Inter-state Communication Qatar v Saudi Arabia* (27 August 2019) UN Doc CERD/C/99/6, paras 11–19; *Decision on the Admissibility of the Inter-state Communication Qatar v UAE* (27 August 2019) UN Doc CERD/C/99/4, paras 53–63.

[280] CERD, 'General Recommendation 30 on Discrimination Against Non-Citizens' (23 February-12 March 2004) UN Doc CERD/C/64/Misc.11/rev.3, paras 1, 2, 4, 7. See E Guild, 'The UN Global Compact for Safe, Orderly and Regular Migration: What Place for Human Rights?' (2019) 30 *International Journal of Refugee Law* 661, 662–63.

that only when those requirements are fulfilled and when a difference in treatment does not discriminate against any particular nationality, as required under Article 1(3) of the Convention, that such a difference will not constitute racial discrimination.[281] The ICJ declined to follow the CERD Committee and held that it had no jurisdiction to hear Qatar's application on the basis that 'national origin' in Article 1(1) of ICERD does not encompass 'present nationality'.[282] In a much-critiqued decision, the Court determined that race (which includes national origin) and nationality were mutually exclusive.[283] Contra to the ICJ's approach, the prohibitions on discrimination generally list suspect grounds in an illustrative, non-exhaustive manner. Accordingly, virtually all treaty bodies and many regional adjudicative bodies have confirmed nationality as a prohibited ground.[284]

Although this remains a significant area of contestation, this work proceeds on the basis that nationality falls within racial discrimination. The Strasbourg Court has recognised that most immigration policies differentiate based on nationality and, indirectly, race, ethnic origin and possibly colour. According to the Court, although States cannot implement 'purely racist' policies, preference for persons from States they have the closest ties with does not constitute racial discrimination.[285] Only 'very weighty reasons' could justify a difference in treatment based exclusively on the grounds of nationality.[286] The Human Rights Committee has held that differentiation on a suspect ground must be based on 'reasonable and objective criteria' but, in practice, has shown that such differentiation is difficult to justify.[287]

There is a weight of evidence demonstrating that visa regimes entail direct discrimination or, at the very least, indirect discrimination. Given the various legitimate aims States invoke in imposing visa requirements, adjudicative bodies may assume the objectivity and reasonableness of distinctions drawn between nationalities (and demonstrating before Strasbourg that visa policies have no justification

[281] Article 1(3) ICERD specifies that nothing in the Convention affects the laws of State parties 'concerning nationality, citizenship or naturalisation, provided that such provisions do not discriminate against any particular nationality'.

[282] *Application of the International Convention on the Elimination of All Forms of Racial Discrimination (Qatar v UAE)* (Preliminary Objections) [2021] ICJ Rep 71, paras 74–105.

[283] See Costello and Foster (n 2).

[284] V Chetail, 'Are Refugee Rights Human Rights? An Unorthodox Questioning of the Relations between Refugee Law and Human Rights Law' in R Rubio-Marín (ed), *Human Rights and Immigration* (Oxford, OUP, 2014) 151–56, particularly fns 403, 405. See also *Advisory Opinion on Juridical Condition and Rights of Undocumented Migrants*, IACtHR, OC-18/03 (17 September 2003).

[285] *Abdulaziz, Cabales and Balkandali v UK* (1985) 7 EHRR 471, para 84. See also GS Goodwin-Gill, *International Law and the Movement of Persons Between States* (Oxford, Clarendon Press, 1978) 83–87, 91–96.

[286] *Gaygusuz v Austria* (1997) 23 EHRR 364, para 42. See also *Biao* (n 265) para 93; *Andrejeva v Latvia*, App no 55707/00 (ECtHR, 18 February 2009) para 87; *British Gurkha Welfare Society v UK*, App no 44818/11 (ECtHR, 15 September 2016) para 81.

[287] *Gueye v France*, Communication No 196/1985 (3 April 1989) UN Doc CCPR/C/35/D/196/1985, paras 9.4–9.5. See Costello and Foster (n 2) 248, 251. See also HRC, 'General Comment No 18' (n 263) para 13.

unrelated to nationality will be especially challenging). Proportionality will, therefore, be crucial. As demonstrated, visa regimes have a disproportionately prejudicial effect on blacklisted nationalities on account of their *perceived* threat and migratory risk, with refugee-producing and low-income States specifically targeted. Scholars have argued that requiring visas from refugees from blacklisted countries, but not whitelisted countries, can constitute discrimination against refugees based on nationality under the Refugee Convention.[288]

Blacklists typically cover almost all States whose populations are least developed and primarily black or Muslim. While there may be objective grounds for blacklisting a specific State, there is a clear risk of listing due to prejudicial, speculative attitudes based on race, religion and class.[289] The blanket blacklisting of specific nationalities or groups of nationalities (ie, certain races or religions) is clearly disproportionate. According to den Heijer, the EU's lack of justification and review, particularly for all African countries, opens up its visa policy to accusations of racial and religious discrimination.[290] Similarly, Cholewinski has concluded that the EU's visa policy risks direct discrimination on the grounds of nationality and indirect discrimination based on race, ethnic origin or religion, given it fails to meet proportionality criteria in differentiating between countries.[291] Visa policies and individual assessments risk being based on predetermined stereotypes of certain nationalities, such as assumptions of 'overstayers' or 'asylum seekers' and exaggerated economic and national security concerns, which individuals often have limited ability to challenge.[292] This is evident for Africans, who are twice as likely to be refused a UK visitor visa, and for Schengen visas, rejection rates are as high as 40–50 per cent for Ghanese, Nigerians and Senegalese.[293] This is further exemplified by the US' 'extreme vetting' policy, which targets specific nationalities based on sweeping generalisations about religion and nationality rather than any individualised risk assessment.[294] Moreover, though superficially appearing

[288] Grundler (n 262); Costello and Foster (n 2) 257–69.

[289] See *Biao* (n 265) para 126; A Fresnoza-Flot, 'Three Ways in Which EU Mobility Policies and Their Implementation Treat Asians Unequally' (*Migration Research to Policy*, 2024) www.migrationresearchtopolicy.eu/2024/11/12/three-ways-eu-mobility-policies-and-their-implementation-treat-asians-unequally/.

[290] Den Heijer, 'Visas' (n 144) 474, 480–87. See also Moreno-Lax, *Accessing Asylum* (n 22) 90–94; SF Nicolosi, 'Going Unnoticed? Diagnosing the Right to Asylum in the Charter of Fundamental Rights of the European Union' (2017) 23 *European Law Journal* 94.

[291] Cholewinski (n 155) 2, 8, 20–35, 54–58.

[292] See *Roma Rights* (n 107) para 82; R Cholewinski, 'No Right of Entry' in CA Groenendijk, E Guild and PE Minderhoud (eds), *In Search of Europe's Borders* (The Hague, Kluwer Law International, 2003) 26–35; UNGA, 'Report of the Special Rapporteur on Contemporary Forms of Racism, Racial Discrimination, Xenophobia and Related Intolerance' (25 April 2018) UN Doc A/HRC/38/52, paras 55, 65.

[293] All-Party Parliamentary Group, 'Visa Problems for African Visitors to the UK' (Joint Report, 2019) 8–9, www.royalafricansociety.org/wp-content/uploads/2020/01/APPG-Report-on-Visa-problems-for-African-visitors-to-the-UK_v1.58web.pdf; Foresti, Mantegazza and Maghoma (n 238).

[294] The White House, 'Protecting the United States from Foreign Terrorists and Other National Security and Public Safety Threats' (21 January 2025) www.whitehouse.gov/presidential-actions/2025/01/protecting-the-united-states-from-foreign-terrorists-and-othernational-security-and-public-safety-threats/.

neutral, many algorithms embody pre-existing biases, suffer from feedback loops, and discriminate by design when persons holding 'suspect' nationalities are treated differently.[295] Policies which appear on their face to be neutral may also disproportionately impact women and certain ethnic groups and minorities based on class because of their weakened or lower socio-economic position globally.[296]

Impairing the rights of some non-citizens, such as their enjoyment of the right to leave, but not others, based on race, nationality or other stereotypes, is inimical to the prohibition on racial discrimination.[297] In conclusion, visa policies can plausibly amount to unlawful discrimination against certain nationalities and asylum seekers and refugees, in violation of the right to leave. However, as Achiume has argued, nationality remains 'largely bulletproof as a mechanism for racialised exclusion and differentiation', and adjudicative bodies may continue legitimising such discrimination between nationalities.[298]

B. Denial of Embarkation by Carriers

The denial of embarkation by carriers can also constitute a violation of the right to leave. As much of the relevant analysis has already been undertaken, this section will only briefly address the requirements under the right to leave. Carrier sanction frameworks share analogous features and, therefore, the conclusions drawn here apply broadly.

There is little doubt that preventing someone from boarding a plane, bus or ferry interferes with the right to leave. Carriers are not only preventing individuals from effectuating an illegal entry but also from leaving the country they are in (safely and regularly).[299] The Human Rights Committee has acknowledged that carrier sanctions interfere with the right, having expressed concern about their effect and 'other pre-frontier arrangements' on the right to leave. It requested that State party reports include information on carrier sanctions and other measures adversely affecting the right.[300]

[295] Molnar and Gill (n 70) sect 5.1; D Ozkul, 'Automating Immigration and Asylum: The Uses of New Technologies in Migration and Asylum Governance in Europe' (Refugee Studies Centre, 2023) www.rsc.ox.ac.uk/publications/automating-immigration-and-asylum-the-uses-of-new-technologies-in-migration-and-asylum-governance-in-europe.

[296] UNGA, 'Report of the Special Rapporteur' (n 292) paras 29–30; Spijkerboer (n 12) 457–58, 269.

[297] UNGA, 'Report of the Special Rapporteur' (n 292) paras 19, 67(b); Spijkerboer (n 12) 467; Guild, 'Global Compact' (n 280) 663.

[298] ET Achiume, 'Race, Borders, and Jurisdiction' (2022) 82 *ZaöRV* 465, 479–80.

[299] Den Heijer, *Europe* (n 102) 161.

[300] HRC, 'General Comment No 27: Article 12 (Freedom of Movement)' (2 November 1999) UN Doc CCPR/C/21/Rev.1/Add.9, para 10; HRC, 'Concluding Observations of the Human Rights Committee: Austria' (19 November 1998) UN Doc CCPR/C/79/Add.103, para 11. Austria responded by referencing national provisions waiving sanctions when asylum is granted and its *non-refoulement* obligations: HRC, 'Fourth Periodic Report: Austria' (20 November 2006) UN Doc CCPR/C/AUT/4, para 180.

Carrier sanctions are enshrined in national and EU laws, thus having a basis in law. Like visas, the issue lies in the lack of foreseeability for individuals about when they will be denied boarding, the wide discretion carriers have, and the lack of procedural safeguards to protect against arbitrary decisions by private actors. While individuals may reasonably foresee that they will be denied boarding if they lack the requisite documentation, it is unclear under what circumstances a carrier, perhaps advised by an ILO, will deny departure due to profiling or alleged risk factors – as racial profiling cases clearly illustrate.[301] Pre-screening activities that profile passengers based on risk factors using automation raise serious legality issues, including the opaqueness of algorithms and whether laws on data collection and information sharing are sufficiently clear and precise.[302] Critically, individuals must be able to challenge a denial by the carrier, the results of automated processes, and no-fly listings.[303] However, privatisation obscures the role of the State and the individual is likely only to be able to engage indirectly through the private actor (unless an ILO is present). As Bigo argues, 'What happens with an asylum seeker who is stopped by these agents and who risks being handed over to the authorities that he is trying to flee? … What appeals can he make?'[304]

International conventions require States to impose carrier sanctions – but only as a *limited* means to combat smuggling and trafficking.[305] Their long-standing use means they suffer from the same assumed lawfulness as visas. Costello points out that the lack of reference to carrier sanctions in the Global Compacts is 'a striking omission, given their central role in rendering refugees' flight and mobility dangerous' and the fact the compacts were intended to avert refugee crises and prevent unsafe migration by facilitating ordinary mobility.[306] Through omission, carrier sanctions are normalised in the global refugee regime.

[301] *Roma Rights* (n 107); *Williams Lecraft v Spain*, Communication No 1493/2006 (27 July 2009) UN Doc CCPR/C/96/D/1493/2006, para 7.2; *Memedova* (n 265).

[302] EM Kuşkonmaz, 'GCM Indicators: Objective 11: Manage Borders in an Integrated, Secure and Coordinated Manner' (*RLI Blog on Refugee Law and Forced Migration*, 8 July 2019) rli.blogs.sas.ac.uk/2019/07/08/gcm-indicators-objective-11-manage-borders-in-an-integrated-secure-and-coordinated-manner/.

[303] See also *Opinion 1/15 (EU-Canada PNR Agreement) of the Court*, 26 July 2017, EU:C:2017:592, paras 168–74.

[304] D Bigo, 'Criminalisation of "Migrants": The Side Effect of the Will to Control Frontiers and the Sovereignty Illusion' in B Bogusz, C Ryszard, A Cygan and E Szyszczak (eds) *Irregular Migration and Human Rights: Theoretical, European and International Perspectives* (Leiden, Martinus Nijhoff, 2004) 89.

[305] Chicago Convention, Annex 9; Palermo Protocols, art 11(1)–(4); CISA, art 26. See Feller (n 22); Rodenhäuser (n 44) 226–27.

[306] C Costello, 'Refugees and (Other) Migrants: Will the Global Compacts Ensure Safe Flight and Onward Mobility for Refugees?' (2018) 30 *International Journal of Refugee Law* 643, 644, 647–48. See also Crépeau (n 246).

As the enforcement arm of visa policies, they pursue the same legitimate aims. They were also introduced to avoid the 'administrative, financial and indeed social burden' of having to process 'failed' asylum seekers and enforce their removal.[307] However, using carrier sanctions to obstruct the flight of asylum seekers and would-be refugees should not be considered legitimate. The UNHCR has consistently voiced its concern that carrier sanctions may prevent asylum seekers from leaving the place where they fear persecution or other violence.[308] Avoiding economic and social costs also cannot be understood as falling within the public order aim. The Strasbourg Court has made clear, with reference to the Convention's drafting history, that economic reasons can never justify restricting the right to leave.[309]

Again, proportionality will be central to determining whether carrier sanctions violate the right to leave. The combination of visas and carrier sanctions has an undeniably disproportionate impact on asylum seekers, would-be refugees, and stateless and undocumented individuals.[310] International law and EU law make clear that carrier sanctions should be implemented consistently with international human rights and refugee standards, including *non-refoulement*.[311] Some legislation allows fines to be waived if individuals are subsequently admitted to asylum procedures or granted protection.[312] Nonetheless, studies demonstrate the ineffectiveness of these safeguards. The threat of sanctions typically results in carriers erring on the side of caution and refusing boarding to everyone regardless of potential protection needs.[313]

Visas and carrier sanctions represent the *precise structural conditions* which generate irregularised travel and the demand for people smugglers and falsified documents, resulting in migrants ending up in detention or trapped in transit, and the loss of life. Carrier sanctions deny the possibility of movement to *all* asylum seekers and migrants without documentation to save *some* from

[307] *Roma Rights* (n 107) para 2; den Heijer, *Europe* (n 102) 163–64.

[308] See Feller (n 22); UNHCR, 'Communication from European Commission' (n 220) 17–18.

[309] *Garib v Netherlands*, App no 43494/09 (ECtHR, 6 November 2017) para 109; den Heijer, *Europe* (n 102) 164.

[310] UNGA, 'Report of the Special Rapporteur on the Human Rights of Migrants' (3 August 2010) UN Doc A/65/222, paras 15, 39; Feller (n 22) 50; Hathaway, *Rights of Refugees* (n 236) 291; Costello, 'Refugees' (n 306) 647.

[311] Trafficking Protocol, arts 11(3), 14; Smuggling Protocol, arts 11(3), 19; CISA, art 26(1), (2); Carriers Liability Directive, recital 3, art 4(2).

[312] Carriers Liability Directive, recital 3, art 4(2). cf Migration Act 1958 (Cth) s 228B(2). See UNHCR, 'Communication from European Commission' (n 220) iii; ECRE (n 249) 28–29; Scholten (n 116) 82–84.

[313] Den Heijer, *Europe* (n 102) 184–87; Scholten (n 116) 249–58, 276–77. See also UNHCR, 'Dublin' (n 233); ECRE (n 249) 29–30.

traffickers – demonstrating their unsuitability to achieve certain objectives.[314] Baird and Spijkerboer aptly argue that:

> Carrier sanctions are an integral part of a system of migration control which results in migrants being unable to access the protection to which they are entitled under international law, and in migrants dying on their way to Europe, North America, Australia …[315]

Without carrier sanctions, the 'undocumented' could board planes and ferries. States are dressing up restrictive techniques as tackling smuggling and trafficking, despite awareness of their perverse effects and unsuitability, including forcing migrants into 'illegality'.[316] This destroys the essence of the right. Moreover, it cannot be proportionate that to 'exercise a *legal* entitlement to escape in search of international protection refugees need *generally* to breach the law'.[317] This is even more salient in light of *ND and NT v Spain*, where the Strasbourg Court concluded that the pushbacks did not amount to collective expulsion, partly because the applicants had failed to use existing legal pathways such as applying for a visa.[318] This blatantly disregards externalisation strategies and the general unavailability of legal pathways for Africans – with such pathways *nonetheless* falling outside the ECHR's protection given *MN v Belgium*.[319]

There are also significant concerns regarding compliance with the 'consistency with other rights' test. First, carrier sanctions may result in *refoulement*.[320] Although relevant savings clauses underscore that carrier sanctions must operate in accordance with *non-refoulement* obligations, some scholars argue that, apart from exceptional cases, refusing boarding does not foreseeably result in harm.[321] However, the risk of *refoulement* is inherent and well-known and is compounded by a lack of available data, making the true extent of the problem difficult to monitor. As the UNHCR and experts have highlighted, airline staff are neither authorised to grant protection nor professional immigration officers with sufficient expertise or training to identify protection needs and protect against *refoulement*, and are focused instead on profit and avoiding

[314] Bloom and Risse (n 44) 74–75.

[315] Baird and Spijkerboer (n 44) 6–7. See also Feller (n 22) 50; Hathaway, *Rights of Refugees* (n 236) 291; Taylor (n 105) 100.

[316] Rodenhäuser (n 44) 228; Czaika and Hobolth, 'Deflection into Irregularity?' (n 202).

[317] Moreno-Lax, 'EU Borders' (n 102) 356.

[318] *ND and NT v Spain*, Apps nos 8675/15 and 8697/15 (ECtHR, 13 February 2020) paras 209–12, 231.

[319] See S Carrera, 'The Strasbourg Court Judgement *N.D. and N.T. v Spain*: A *Carte Blanche* to Push Backs at EU External Borders?' (2020) EUI Working Paper RSCAS 2020/21, 10–17, cadmus.eui.eu/handle/1814/66629.

[320] UNHCR, 'Interception of Asylum-Seekers and Refugees: The International Framework and Recommendations for a Comprehensive Approach' (9 June 2000) UN Doc EC/50/SC/CRP.17; Rodenhäuser (n 44) 236–37; Goodwin-Gill and McAdam (n 139) 427.

[321] Bloom and Risse (n 44) 66–67; Baird and Spijkerboer (n 44) 9.

sanctions.[322] And ILOs and ALOs actively seek to curtail undocumented movement, including of asylum seekers, from ever reaching their destination.[323] Refusal of boarding can thus lead to migrants being stuck in their country of persecution or in transit at risk of *refoulement* and denied the right to seek asylum.

Regarding non-discrimination obligations, carriers (perhaps operating alongside a liaison officer) are likely to engage in discriminatory profiling based on ethnic origin, gender and asylum risk.[324] This likelihood is evidenced, for example, by the treatment of Roma individuals prevented from leaving countries in Europe and unaccompanied Saudi women at airports suspected of travelling to seek asylum in Australia.[325] Partner states may also turn away asylum seekers at airports to stop their onward journey to destination States.[326] This also infringes the right to seek asylum. Profiling on account of asylum risk or immigration status can amount to discrimination based on 'other status'.[327] Furthermore, although carrier sanctions impact men and women, given that women are more likely to be trafficked or experience other forms of violence during irregular journeys, a *prima facie* case of gender discrimination exists.[328] The CEDAW Committee has recognised that 'increased border control, refusal of entry, pushbacks, expulsion or detention limit the movement of women and girls fleeing from crises and conflict zones', heightening their vulnerability.[329] Expanding legal pathways would be far more effective in countering exploitation.[330]

[322] UNHCR, 'Dublin' (n 233); UNHCR, 'Interception' (n 320) para 17; Feller (n 22) 56–57, 63–64; Christian (n 18) 229; V Guiraudon, 'Before the EU Border: Remote Control of the "Huddled Masses"' in K Groenendijk, E Guild and P Minderhoud (eds), *In Search of Europe's Borders* (The Hague, Kluwer Law International, 2003) 202–04; Goodwin-Gill and McAdam (n 139) 424.

[323] See *Asch v Austria*, App no 12398/86 (ECtHR, 26 April 1991); *Roma Rights* (n 107); Commission Staff Working Document, 'Evaluation of the Council Regulation' (EC) 377/2004 on the Creation of an Immigration Liaison Officers Network' SWD (2018) 197 final, 4–5, 8; R Jefferies, 'Bringing Externalization Home: The International Civil Aviation Organization and "Entry Screening" in Australia' (2021) *Globalizations* 1; R Jefferies, D Ghezelbash and A Hirsch, 'Assessing Refugee Protection Claims at Australian Airports: The Gap Between Law, Policy, and Practice' (2021) 44 *Melbourne University Law Review* 1.

[324] See generally CERD, 'General Recommendation No 36 (2020) on Preventing and Combating Racial Profiling by Law Enforcement Officials' (17 December 2020) UN Doc CERD/C/GC/36.

[325] *Memedova* (n 265). See Guild , *Right to Leave* (n 130) 56; S McNeill, S O'Neill and M Fallon, 'Australian Border Force Accused of Targeting Women Suspected of Fleeing Saudi Arabia' (*ABC News*, 4 February 2019) www.abc.net.au/news/2019-02-04/border-force-accused-of-targeting-saudi-women-traveling-alone/10768036; R Boudjikanian, 'Hungarian Roma Regularly Prevented From Boarding Canada-bound Flights' (*CBC News*, 5 October 2015) www.cbc.ca/news/canada/montreal/hungarian-roma-refugee-claim-cbsa-air-transat-budapest-gabor-lukaçs-1.3257661.

[326] See on Australia, 'Cabinet Submission JH00/0275 – Indonesia – Cooperation to Combat People Smuggling and Illegal Immigration – Processing and Holding Centre – Decision JH00/0275/CAB, item, 22 August 2000, para 10.

[327] See *Hode and Abdi v the United Kingdom* (2013) 56 EHRR 27, paras 46–48.

[328] C Briddick, 'Some Other(ed) "Refugees"?: Women Seeking Asylum under Refugee and Human Rights Law' in SS Juss (ed), *Research Handbook on International Refugee Law* (Cheltenham, Edward Elgar Publishing, 2019) 283–84, 288–89.

[329] CEDAW, 'General Recommendation No. 38 (2020) on Trafficking in Women and Girls in the Context of Global Migration' (20 November 2020) UN Doc CEDAW/C/GC/38, paras 5, 24.

[330] See ibid paras 56–58.

Carrier sanctions may also be incompatible with right to life obligations. There is a clear link between carrier sanctions and increased migrant deaths, which push individuals into dangerous routes and narrow the options for safe travel.[331] In comparison, nationals with privileged access to the global mobility infrastructure enjoy the full protection of international law, with greater protection of their rights to life, family life, health, housing and work.[332] Even though millions of Ukrainians fled the country following Russia's full-scale invasion in 2022, the recorded fatalities were extremely low in contrast to the thousands of Black and Brown migrants from the Global South who have died in search of safety.[333] This underscores that providing safe routes and waiving or removing visa requirements and carrier sanctions is vital to preventing migrant deaths. Given the clear risks to other human rights and concerns around legality and proportionality, carrier sanctions appear to violate the right to leave. They prevent individuals from departing for their destination and force them onto longer, more expensive and unsafe routes.

V. SHARED RESPONSIBILITY OF STATES AND INTERNATIONAL ORGANISATIONS

This section explores the shared responsibility of States and IOs for their role in violating the right to leave under the law on international responsibility. As shown, visa refusals and denials of embarkation can breach the right to leave, including due to inadequate procedural safeguards, insufficient weight being afforded to the individual circumstances of people from blacklisted States, the inaccessibility and unavailability of visas for many asylum seekers and refugees, which prevents them from fleeing lawfully, and discriminatory practices and profiling.

A. Direct Responsibility and the Failure to Protect: Destination States and Territorial States

Violations of the right to leave during the implementation of visa regimes lead to the direct responsibility of destination States, given attribution and jurisdictional tests appear to be met. As chapter four outlined, States have a duty not to obstruct the right to leave, which demands the overhaul of many current visa

[331] T Spijkerboer, 'Moving Migrants, States, and Rights: Human Rights and Border Deaths' (2013) 7 *The Law & Ethics of Human Rights* 213; Border Deaths, 'Human Costs of Border Control', www.borderdeaths.org.

[332] T Spijkerboer, 'Wasted Lives. Borders and the Right to Life of People Crossing Them' (2017) 86 *Nordic Journal of International Law* 1; Spijkerboer, 'Global Mobility' (n 12) 467.

[333] Migration Data Portal, 'Crisis Movement' (20 February 2024) www.migrationdataportal.org/ukraine/crisis-movements.

regimes. At a minimum, States and the EU must improve on the quality of law shortcomings and ensure strict safeguards, including oversight mechanisms and avenues for appeal. Blacklists should be regularly reviewed, with unnecessary listings removed and greater transparency over the criteria used to draw up lists. Visas and other pathways should also be available to all migrants in practice, and assessments should be based on individualised and real risk, not group stereotypes or discriminatory or biased algorithms. Critically, States must ensure individuals are not denied legal routes to safety or subject to cumulative containment. States should adopt more protective alternatives by processing migrants at the border (as already exists for many nationals from the Global North) and increasing resettlement and complementary pathways. Though dependent on political will, such alternatives carry cost-saving potential and can reduce irregular movement, arguably promoting more circular and sustainable migration.

States will also bear responsibility for failing to protect migrants under their jurisdiction from violations of their right to leave by other actors. The precise scope of this protective duty will depend on the specific facts, taking into account reasonableness, proximity and the extent of knowledge.[334] Given the control that States wield over visa issuance and carriers, an obligation to protect undoubtedly arises. By assuming control over entry, 'the state places itself in proximate relationships with harm that might arise in relation to these activities even if this harm is not directly attributable to state agents. Control thus implies closer proximity and more demanding positive obligations'.[335] The State must show that it acted with due diligence, taking all reasonable steps to protect migrants from threats it knew or ought to have known of, and it must show that it responded adequately following a violation. As the above analysis demonstrated, there are foreseeable risks of harm under visa regimes, and this has been voiced by the UNHCR consistently and recognised in the savings clauses of international conventions and certain carrier sanctions legislation. It follows that destination States should bear responsibility where migrants suffer violations flowing from the infrastructure they created and retain control over. To fulfil their positive obligations, States and the EU ought to structure their relationships with carriers to prevent and address violations of the right to leave, right to life and obligations of *non-refoulement* and non-discrimination.[336] States should suspend visa requirements and carrier sanctions during crises without discrimination. Carriers should also be exempted from fines when individuals enter the asylum process and steps should be taken to ensure pre-clearance operations are not conducted in a discriminatory manner,

[334] V Stoyanova, 'Causation between State Omission and Harm within the Framework of Positive Obligations under the European Convention on Human Rights' (2018) 18 *Human Rights Law Review* 309, 320–24, 329.
[335] ibid 345.
[336] ibid 314–15, 322.

by providing carriers and ILOs with proper training on non-discrimination and refugee protection.[337]

The territorial State will also breach its positive obligation to secure the right to leave and protect migrants from violations by the destination State when carriers deny boarding. There is no impediment to several States exercising jurisdiction and sharing responsibility for separate breaches where their actions jointly affect the rights of individuals.[338] Alternatively, the territorial State could be seen as aiding and assisting the destination State under Article 16 of the ARSIWA in allowing its territory to be used to enforce visa regimes through carriers and ILOs.[339] Article 16 provides,

> A State which aids or assists another State in the commission of an internationally wrongful act by the latter is internationally responsible for doing so if: (a) that State does so with knowledge of the circumstances of the internationally wrongful act; and (b) the act would be internationally wrongful if committed by that State.

The ARSIWA commentary specifies that the support given must actually facilitate the wrongful act and significantly contribute to its commission.[340] However, *but for* the territorial State's actual or tacit consent, violations of the right could not occur in this context. Consequently, this is not aid and assistance; instead it gives rise to shared responsibility.[341] No circumstances precluding wrongfulness seem applicable that would otherwise excuse a breach by the destination or territorial State.

B. The EU and IOM

The responsibility of the EU and IOM under ARIO must also be assessed. Regarding the EU's visa policy, the leading case of *Bosphorus v Ireland* before the Strasbourg Court, cited in the ARIO commentary, is relevant here.[342] The Court held that where a Member State does no more than implement the

[337] See UNHCR, 'Communication from European Commission' (n 220) ii–iii, 17–18; *Roma Rights* (n 107) paras 89–91.

[338] See eg *Certain Phosphate Lands in Nauru* (*Nauru v Australia*) (Preliminary Objections) [1992] ICJ Rep 240, para 48; *Al-Skeini* (n 89) para 137; ARSIWA Commentary, 64 paras 3–5, 125 para 8.

[339] See ARSIWA Commentary, 66–67 para 8.

[340] ARSIWA Commentary, 66 paras 3, 5.

[341] See ARSIWA, art 47; ARSIWA, Commentary 124 paras 1, 3, 125 paras 6, 8; VP Tzevelekos, 'Reconstructing the Effective Control Criterion in Extraterritorial Human Rights Breaches: Direct Attribution of Wrongfulness, Due Diligence, and Concurrent Responsibility' (2014) 36 *Michigan Journal of International Law* 129, 164–69; S Besson, 'Concurrent Responsibilities under the European Convention on Human Rights: The Concurrence of Human Rights Jurisdictions, Duties, and Responsibilities' in A van Aaken and I Motoc (eds), *The European Convention on Human Rights and General International Law* (Oxford, OUP, 2018).

[342] ARIO, arts 17 and 61; ARIO Commentary, 68–69, 98–100, 103 para 5.

obligations flowing from its membership of the EU, there will be no violation of the ECHR provided the organisation offers equivalent Convention protection.[343] However, for the presumption to apply and the conduct to be attributable to the IO, the State must have no 'margin of manoeuvre' in implementing binding acts of the organisation.[344] A State will be fully responsible under the Convention where it exercises discretion afforded by EU law.[345] Notwithstanding, this does not rule out attribution of that same conduct to an IO.[346]

EU Member States remain responsible under the ECHR for violations of the right to leave, as they retain significant discretion when implementing the Visa Code, both in deciding whether to issue a visa or choosing to outsource visa processing. Accordingly, given the EU is not a party to the Convention, only Member States will bear responsibility before Strasbourg for violating the right when refusing a visa. By creating visa lists and establishing EU-wide visa policy, the EU may exercise normative control over Member States, possibly leading to dual attribution, but this remains a particularly complex and unsettled area of law.[347] As section III.B determined, the conduct of carriers cannot be dually attributed to the EU. Nonetheless, the EU may be responsible under customary international law and the EUCFR. For example, the EU may bear responsibility under EU law alongside the Member State, where the latter's ILO implements the EU visa regime at borders abroad and issues instructions to carriers. Migrants could bring an action for damages against the EU to the CJEU for sufficiently serious breaches of their right to leave (and others), though there are significant hurdles to overcome.[348]

[343] *Bosphorus v Ireland* (2006) 42 EHRR 1, paras 153–56.

[344] *Bosphorus* (n 343), paras 156–57; *Michaud v France*, App no 12323/11 (ECtHR, 6 December 2012) para 113; *Avotiņš v Latvia*, App no 17502/07 (ECtHR, 23 May 2016) para 105.

[345] See *Bosphorus* (n 343) paras 157–58; *Michaud* (n 344) para 103; *MSS v Belgium and Greece* (2011) 53 EHRR 2, paras 338–40.

[346] On dual and multiple attribution, see ARIO Commentary, 53 para 6, 54 para 4, 57 para 4 and on overcoming automatic attribution to the seconding State or IO based on effective or factual control, ARIO art 7; ARIO Commentary 56–60; A Nollkaemper and others, 'Guiding Principles on Shared Responsibility in International Law' (2020) 31 *European Journal of International Law* 15. See eg *Yassin Abdullah Kadi v Council of the European Union & Commission of the European Communities*, Case T-315/01, EU:T:2005:332, [2005] ECR II-3649 before the EU courts; *Al-Jedda v The United Kingdom*, App no 27021/08 (ECtHR, 7 July 2011) paras 76–86; *Nada* (n 91) paras 120–22. cf the much-critiqued decision, *Behrami and Behrami v France; Saramati v France, Germany and Norway* (2007) 45 EHRR SE 85.

[347] See on normative control, A Tzanakopoulos, *Disobeying the Security Council: Countermeasures Against Wrongful Sanctions* (Oxford, OUP, 2011) 33–45 (since publication, ARIO has been re-numbered: references to Articles 5 and 6 in the book refer to current Articles 6 and 7); C Contartese, 'Competence-Based Approach, Normative Control, and the International Responsibility of the EU and its Member States' (2019) 16 *International Organizations Law Review* 339.

[348] Consolidated Version of Treaty on the Functioning of the European Union [2008] OJ C115/47 (TFEU) arts 268, 340(2); EUCFR, art 41(3). See generally, M Fink, 'EU Liability for Contributions to Member States' Breaches of EU Law' (2019) 56 *Common Market Law Review* 1227; P Craig and G De Búrca, *EU Law: Text, Cases, and Materials*, 7th edn (Oxford, OUP, 2020) ch 17.

i. Indirect Responsibility for Direction, Control and Assistance

Given the difficulties surrounding attribution, the EU may incur derived responsibility for directing and controlling Member States in violation of the right to leave under Article 15 of ARIO.[349] However, this is a challenging argument, given the *Bosphorus* presumption. In setting black and whitelists, imposing visa and carrier sanctions requirements, and establishing the ILO network, the EU exercises direction and control through decisions binding Member States.[350] However, given that States have broad discretion in interpreting visa criteria and ultimate authority over visa issuance, this would not constitute direction and control by the EU over visa refusals violating the right to leave. It is arguable, however, that EU law mandating Member States to impose carrier sanctions meets the high threshold for direction and control, given States have much less room for manoeuvre in this area. This, too, remains contentious as States retain some discretion during implementation (ie, the type or amount of penalties, how they are enforced, and the mandates and programmes of ILOs). Article 15 requires the act to have been wrongful had it been committed by the EU and knowledge of the circumstances surrounding the breach – and these requirements are met. The EU cannot argue it was unaware that denials of embarkation may breach the right to leave. Given the overlapping competences, this situation arguably entails shared responsibility between the EU and the State. Following the organisation's directions does not constitute a defence.[351]

IOM's involvement in visa processing may trigger its responsibility for aid and assistance under Article 14 of ARIO. It must be shown that IOM aided or assisted the destination State in violating the right to leave, had knowledge of the circumstances of the violation, facilitated it, and that the act would have been wrongful if committed by IOM itself.[352] Operating VACs and performing various services, including application handling, taking biometrics and document verification, is likely to amount to aid and assistance. Such support must have significantly contributed to the breach of the right to leave.[353] Although the final decision rests with the State, IOM makes it significantly easier for States to perform their adjudicative role by undertaking several critical tasks on their behalf, clearly facilitating the violation. Although there is an ongoing debate over whether knowledge or intent is required, like the EU, it is difficult for IOM to argue it does not have knowledge that its assistance may lead to visa refusals and denials of leaving by carriers.[354] Lastly, opposability is satisfied,

[349] ARIO Commentary, 66–68 and 65–67 on the analogous ARSIWA rules applying in this context.
[350] The EU may also be instigating wrongful acts through visa cascading.
[351] See ARSIWA Commentary, 69 para 9; ARIO Commentary, 48 para 10.
[352] ARIO Commentary, 66.
[353] ARSIWA Commentary, 66 para 4.
[354] There is ongoing debate over the requisite mental element, with some arguing for a knowledge standard and others arguing for intention to facilitate the wrongful conduct: cf HP Aust, *Complicity and the Law of State Responsibility* (Cambridge, CUP, 2011) 230–49; V Lanovoy, *Complicity and its Limits in the Law of International Responsibility* (Oxford, Hart Publishing, 2016) 218–40.

as IOM is bound by the right to leave. It follows that IOM can bear responsibility for aid and assistance. IOM's limited involvement means it is unlikely to be directly responsible for any violations of the right (Article 6 ARIO). Nonetheless, by continuing to provide visa services to States that violate the right to leave, IOM risks breaching its due diligence obligations and failing to uphold its duty to protect migrants. It is worth noting that ICMPD's involvement in EU policy development, advice on visa pathways, and support for capacity building and training for consular officials in third countries appears too far removed from the actual processing of visas or denial of embarkation to constitute unlawful aid and assistance. However, in certain situations – depending on the nature and proximity of its support – it might reach the threshold for complicity.

VI. DISCRIMINATORY VISA REGIMES AND NORMALISED CARRIER SANCTIONS: A CONCLUDING CRITIQUE

This chapter showed that visa refusals and denials of embarkation can violate the right to leave, interfering with departure by suppressing lawful travel by plane, ferry and bus and disproportionately impacting migrants and asylum seekers from certain nationalities and racial backgrounds. Although ultimately contingent on the adjudicative body, destination States can be understood as exercising jurisdiction when they deny visas – an important conclusion given the routine insulation of visas from scrutiny under international law. States also exercise jurisdiction over individuals denied boarding by carriers, and issues of attribution can be overcome.

While not contending that visa regimes are inherently unlawful, this chapter has demonstrated that such practices frequently exceed the bounds of lawful restrictions on the right to leave. Visa regimes may pursue several legitimate aims, but often fail the legality and proportionality tests. By design, visa regimes are highly discretionary, obscure access to procedural safeguards, and render individuals relatively powerless against the State's migration control prerogative. Rather than achieving their aims, visa regimes foster irregular migration and drive reliance on smugglers, denying the right to seek asylum, violating the right to life, and exposing people to *refoulement*.

Carrier sanctions are *the* primary driver of dangerous journeys. Workable, more protective alternatives exist, as demonstrated in response to Ukraine, but political will is often missing. Visa blacklists, refusals and border profiling reflect deeply racialised practices that can be rooted in harmful stereotypes and inflated concerns over security and other risks, risking discrimination based on race, nationality and migration status. These practices give rise to the shared responsibility of States, the EU and IOM for their respective role in obstructing the right to leave and failing to discharge their positive obligations.

It should be seriously questioned whether a global (im)mobility infrastructure that normalises discrimination and exclusion and contributes to the precarious, deadly flight of migrants is compatible with international law. States and the EU must address the unlawful and structural problems in global visa and mobility systems, ensuring non-discriminatory, equitable access to travel, economic and study opportunities and that all migrants can seek asylum through safe and regular routes, irrespective of passport power. Ultimately, visa regimes must be reformed in order to uphold fundamental norms and prevent the ongoing harm inflicted on those forced into irregularity.

6

Pushbacks and Pullbacks at Sea and on Land

I. INTRODUCTION

STATES ARE INCREASINGLY implementing pushback and pullback practices at international borders around the world to prevent irregular migration and deny migrants access to their territory or asylum. By externalising their border controls and outsourcing enforcement to partner countries, States seek to circumvent their international obligations, with grave impacts on the human rights of migrants. These impacts are well-documented, particularly violations of the prohibitions on collective expulsion and *refoulement*.[1] Whether pushbacks and pullbacks at sea and on land violate the right to leave for (would-be) migrants has received comparatively little attention, which this chapter seeks to address.

This chapter argues that in most circumstances, pushbacks and pullbacks violate the right to leave, save when they can be considered a genuine rescue with disembarkation to a place of safety. Among other failings, they are highly disproportionate, indiscriminate measures that thwart the search for safety and lead to serious violations, disparately impacting people of colour and other protected groups. It delves into several complex questions, including the applicability of the right to leave when States act extraterritorially and through third parties, and the extent to which States of origin and transit can legitimately restrict this right in order to stem irregular migration towards major externalising regions such as Australia, Europe and the US.

It begins by tracing the shift from unilateral practices to forms of cooperative deterrence to 'border control by proxy', where destination States provide funding, equipment, training and technical support to partner States to prevent departure on their behalf. This foregrounds the role of the EU (including Frontex), IOM, the ICMPD and NATO in operationalising externalisation practices – often under the guise of capacity-building, humanitarian assistance

[1] See E McDonnell, 'Challenging Externalisation Through the Lens of the Human Right to Leave' (2024) 71 *Netherlands International Law Review* 119.

and regional security cooperation – as well as private actors. It then briefly outlines the relevant duties under the law of the sea and the legal basis for interdicting migrant vessels, which are pertinent to scrutinising the legality of pushbacks and pullbacks at sea. The chapter then demonstrates how the complexities surrounding jurisdiction and attribution, exacerbated by the myriad actors involved and attempts to sever the legal links between migrants and destination States, can nonetheless be overcome. After scrutinising whether pushbacks and pullbacks meet the requirements of the right to leave, the final section establishes the shared responsibility of States and IOs for violating the right to leave and failing to protect the rights of migrants at borders. Above all, such practices represent another form of exclusion and discrimination against migrants, routinely infringing upon their right to seek asylum, right to life and protection from ill-treatment. This chapter calls for an immediate end to pushback and pullback practices, and accountability when such violations occur, to ensure dignity and justice for people on the move.

II. SHIFTING AND EVOLVING PRACTICES

Destination States have employed various interception practices to contain and suppress migration out of States of origin and transit. These strategies have evolved and shifted over time, partly in response to successful legal challenges, and can be grouped into three broad categories: unilateral practices, cooperative deterrence, and remote control. States can, and do, implement such practices simultaneously.

It is worth noting that there is no legal definition of 'interception', a term used interchangeably with 'interdiction'. Its meaning is derived from State practice and has been defined by the UNHCR Executive Committee as follows:

> [i]nterception is one of the measures employed by States to:
>
> (i) prevent embarkation of persons on an international journey;
> (ii) prevent further onward international travel by persons who have commenced their journey; or
> (iii) assert control of vessels where there are reasonable grounds to believe the vessel is transporting persons contrary to international or national maritime law;
>
> where, in relation to the above, the person or persons do not have the required documentation or valid permission to enter;[2]

This definition encompasses measures on land, at sea or by air.

[2] EXCOM, 'No. 97 (LIV) – Conclusion on Protection Safeguards in Interception Measures' (2003) UN Doc A/AC.96/987, preamble. cf UNHCR, 'Interception of Asylum-seekers and Refugees: The International Framework and Recommendations for a Comprehensive Approach' (9 June 2000) UN Doc EC/50/SC/CRP.17, para 10, which encompasses 'passive' measures such as visas.

A. Unilateral Pushback Practices

Unilateral interceptions on the high seas form part of the traditional set of '*non-entrée*' measures.[3] Pushbacks are a well-known example of this. Although lacking an internationally agreed upon definition, 'pushbacks' have been defined at the UN-level as the various measures taken by States, sometimes together with third countries or non-State actors, which result in migrants being summarily forced back to the country, territory or out to sea (territorial or international waters) from where they attempted to cross or crossed an international border, without any individualised assessment of protection needs.[4] It is their summary nature that distinguishes them from lawful removals.

Pushbacks have a long history. In 1939, the St Louis ocean liner carrying around 1,000 Jewish refugees holding Cuban visas was prevented from landing on Cuban, Canadian and US shores. The ship was forced to return to Europe, where Belgium, Britain, France and the Netherlands agreed to admit the passengers; however, a quarter of those former passengers were later murdered by the Nazis.[5] The term 'pushback' appears to have originated during the Indochinese refugee crisis from the 1970s to the 1990s, where over three million asylum seekers from Vietnam, Cambodia and Laos left by boat, prompting Malaysia and Thailand to push thousands back out to sea.[6] It was not until the Comprehensive Plan of Action (CPA) adopted in 1989 by ASEAN States, Hong Kong, Western States and the UNHCR that pushbacks halted following international resettlement and repatriation commitments.[7] However, the CPA also enlisted Vietnam and Laos to prevent irregular departures, and instead promoted the Orderly Departure Program. While the CPA led to hundreds of thousands of refugees being resettled, it also led to large numbers forcibly returned home.[8]

Pushbacks have since become increasingly widespread. Since the 1980s, the US Coast Guard has pushed back Haitians, Cubans and other nationalities

[3] T Gammeltoft-Hansen and JC Hathaway, '*Non-Refoulement* in a World of Cooperative Deterrence' (2015) 53 *Columbia Journal of Transnational Law* 235, 244–48.

[4] UNGA, 'Report on Means to Address the Human Rights Impact of Pushbacks of Migrants on Land and at Sea' (2021) UN Doc A/HRC/47/30, paras 34–35.

[5] DS FitzGerald, *Refuge Beyond Reach: How Rich Democracies Repel Asylum Seekers* (Oxford, OUP, 2019) 24–33.

[6] See AC Helton, 'Asylum and Refugee Protection in Thailand' (1989) 1 *International Journal of Refugee Law* 20, 20–32.

[7] WC Robinson, 'The Comprehensive Plan of Action for Indochinese Refugees, 1989–1997: Sharing the Burden and Passing the Buck' (2004) 17 *Journal of Refugee Studies* 319. See on the right to leave A Wolman, 'The Role of Departure States in Combating Irregular Emigration in International Law: An Historical Perspective' (2019) 31 *International Journal of Refugee Law* 30, 44–47.

[8] SE Davies, '1989 Comprehensive Plan of Action (CPA) and Refugee Policy in Southeast Asia: Twenty Years Forward What Has Changed?' in A Abass and F Ippolito (eds), *Regional Approaches to the Protection of Asylum Seekers* (Abingdon/New York, Routledge, 2016).

attempting to reach US shores.[9] Many Haitian and Cuban asylum seekers intercepted on the high seas have also been taken to facilities at the US naval base on Guantánamo Bay.[10] Between the 1990s and 2000s, IOM was involved in these practices, undertaking interviews and data collection for asylum claims during 'shipboard' detention and then at Guantánamo.[11] Since 2018, the Trinidadian authorities have intensified immigration enforcement, intercepting and pushing back boats of Venezuelans and thwarting migration into and out of the country.[12] Pushbacks of Rohingya and Bangladeshi asylum seekers in the Bay of Bengal and Andaman Sea by Thailand, Malaysia and Indonesia have been an ongoing issue, most notably during the 2015 Andaman Sea crisis when thousands were left stranded at sea and refused disembarkation, marking a return to earlier policies.[13] As scholars have argued, such practices do not exclusively reflect 'the regional dominance of Australia or the complacency of Indonesia and Malaysia as docile transit or 'corridor' states' but their own mechanisms of externalisation.[14]

In 2001, Australia introduced a policy to intercept and turn back boats at sea. Under the infamous *Operation Sovereign Borders* (2013–), it conducts military-led 'turnbacks', returning boats to the country of departure, often the edge of Indonesian waters but sometimes making unauthorised incursions, and has placed migrants on self-navigating lifeboats with just enough fuel to wash up on Indonesian shores.[15] Like the US, Australia's pushback operations operate alongside its notorious offshore processing regime, where migrants intercepted at sea

[9] *Sale v Haitian Centres Council* 509 US 155 (1993); *The Haitian Centre for Human Rights v US*, IACHR, Case 10.675 Report No 51/96 (13 March 1997) OEA/Ser.L/V/II.95 Doc 7 Rev at 550. See FitzGerald (n 5) ch 5.

[10] IRAP, 'Offshoring Human Rights: Detention of Refugees at Guantánamo Bay' (Report, 2024) www.refugeerights.org/wp-content/uploads/2024/09/Offshoring-Human-Rights-Guantanamo-Bay-English-Report-September-2024.pdf.

[11] A Sherwood, I Lemay and C Costello, 'IOM's Immigration Detention Practices and Policies: Human Rights, Positive Obligations and Humanitarian Duties' in M Bradley, C Costello and A Sherwood (eds), *IOM Unbound?: Obligations and Accountability of the International Organization for Migration in an Era of Expansion* (Cambridge, CUP, 2023) 374–76.

[12] UN, 'Trinidad and Tobago: Court Ruling on Deportations will Gravely Impact Refugees and Migrants, UN Experts Say' (Press Release, 26 July 2023) www.ohchr.org/en/press-releases/2023/07/trinidad-and-tobago-court-ruling-deportations-will-gravely-impact-refugees#; SS Mohan, 'The Interrupting Island: Trinidad and Tobago and the Shifting Migration Trajectories of Venezuelans' in J Crush, A Chikanda and S Ramachandran (eds), *New Directions in South-South Migration* (Singapore, Springer Singapore, 2025).

[13] See BN Ghráinne, 'Left to Die at Sea: State Responsibility for the May 2015 Thai, Indonesian and Malaysian Pushback Operations' in F de Londras and S Mullally (eds), *The Irish Yearbook of International Law*, vol 10, 2015 (London, Hart Publishing, 2017); M Gleeson, 'Unprecedented but Unfulfilled: Refugee Protection and Regional Responses to the Andaman Sea "Crisis"' (2017) 38 *Antropologi Indonesia* 6, 8–10; K Jayangakula, 'Refugee Protection in Thailand' in S Lee and HE Lee (eds), *Asian Yearbook of International Law*, vol 28 (London, Brill, 2022).

[14] D Cantor and others, 'Externalisation, Access to Territorial Asylum, and International Law' (2022) 34 *International Journal of Refugee Law* 120.

[15] V Moreno-Lax, *The Interdiction of Asylum Seekers at Sea: Law and (Mal)practice in Europe and Australia* (Policy Brief 4, Kaldor Centre for International Refugee Law, 2017) 2–3, 10; Australian Government, 'Operation Sovereign Borders', osb.homeaffairs.gov.au/zero-chance.

are taken to facilities in third countries, notably Nauru and Papua New Guinea. In Europe, Greece systematically pushes migrants back to Turkey and engages in 'drift-backs', transferring migrants onto inflatable life rafts and abandoning them at sea and river borders, reminiscent of Australia's use of lifeboats.[16] The Greek and Turkish coastguards have reportedly encircled small migrant boats in a manner that creates dangerous bow waves, threatening to capsize the vessel and endanger the lives of those on board.[17]

Systematic and often violent pushbacks on land are well-documented along many migration routes. Thousands have been recorded at the EU's borders, including by Bulgaria, Croatia, Hungary, Germany, Greece, Latvia, Lithuania and Poland.[18] Similar practices occur elsewhere: from India to Bangladesh;[19] Thailand to Myanmar;[20] and Libya and Algeria into the Niger desert.[21] Iran and Turkey have pushed back Afghans as they attempted to cross the border, while de facto border closures by Jordan and Lebanon led to the systematic *refoulement* of Syrians.[22] In the Americas, pushbacks have occurred across multiple borders – from the US to Mexico under policies like 'Remain in Mexico'

[16] See *GRJ v Greece*, App no 15067/21 (ECtHR, 7 January 2025) (declared inadmissible *ratione personae*); *AE v Greece*, App no 15783/21 (ECtHR, 7 January 2025); N Keady-Tabbal and I Mann, 'Tents at Sea: How Greek Officials Use Rescue Equipment for Illegal Deportations' (*Just Security*, 22 May 2020) www.justsecurity.org/70309/tents-at-sea-how-greek-officials-use-rescue-equipment-for-illegal-deportations; Council of Europe, 'Memorandum on Migration and Border Control, Following the Commissioner's Visit to Greece From 3 to 7 February 2024' (17 April 2025) CommHR(2025)16, rm.coe.int/memorandum-on-greece-on-migration-and-border-control-following-visit-t/1680b5a661.

[17] HRW, 'Greece: Attacks on Boats Risk Migrant Lives' (22 October 2015) www.hrw.org/news/2015/10/22/greece-attacks-boats-risk-migrant-lives; Times of Malta, 'Migrant Boat Seen Being Attacked by Turkish Coastguard' (18 March 2016) www.timesofmalta.com/article/migrants-seen-being-attacked-by-turkish-coastguard.606081.

[18] See Border Violence Monitoring Network, *The Black Book of Pushbacks*, vols 1 and 2 (Brussels, 2020) borderviolence.eu/publications; 11.11.11 and others, 'Pushed, Beaten, Left to Die' (European Pushback Report, 2025) 11.be/sites/default/files/2025-02/20250217-Pushbacks-Report-2024-Pushed-Beaten-Left-to-die.pdf; N Mellersh, 'German Interior Ministry Enforces Tougher Border Policy, Turns Back Asylum Seekers' (*Info Migrants*, 16 May 2025) www.infomigrants.net/en/post/64607/german-interior-ministry-enforces-tougher-border-policy-turns-back-asylum-seekers.

[19] HRW, *'Trigger Happy': Excessive Use of Force by Indian Troops at the Bangladesh Border* (New York, HRW, 2010).

[20] K Olam and H Regan, 'Thailand Pushes Back Thousands Fleeing Myanmar as Death Toll Surpasses 500' (*CNN*, 30 March 2021) www.edition.cnn.com/2021/03/30/asia/thailand-myanmar-refugees-intl-hnk/index.html.

[21] See G Zandonini, 'Hundreds of Migrants Stuck in Niger Amid Coronavirus Pandemic' (*Al Jazeera*, 9 April 2020) www.aljazeera.com/news/2020/04/hundreds-migrants-stuck-niger-coronavirus-pandemic-200409131745319.html; UN, 'COVID-19 and People on the Move' (Policy Brief, June 2020) 19–20, unsdg.un.org/resources/policy-brief-covid-19-and-people-move; E Volkamnn, 'Libya Expels 600 Nigeriens in "Dangerous and Traumatising" Desert Journey' (*The Guardian*, 10 January 2025) www.theguardian.com/global-development/2025/jan/10/libya-expels-600-nigeriens-migrant-workers-eu.

[22] Amnesty International, 'Iran/Turkey: Fleeing Afghans Unlawfully Returned After Coming Under Fire at Borders' (Press Release, 31 August 2022) www.amnesty.org/en/latest/news/2022/08/iran-turkey-fleeing-afghans-unlawfully-returned-after-coming-under-fire-at-borders/; OG El-Taliawi, *The Politics of Refugee Policy in the Global South* (Kingston, McGill-Queen's University Press, 2024) chs 6 and 8.

and so-called asylum bans, and also from Mexico to Guatemala, and from Guatemala to Honduras.[23]

These practices operate alongside the global proliferation of walls and fences. Today, such barriers can be found in nearly every region, including the US–Mexico border, Morocco–Algeria, Saudi Arabia–Yemen, Turkmenistan–Uzbekistan, Pakistan–Afghanistan, South Africa–Zimbabwe, UK–France and Bulgaria–Turkey.[24] As highlighted in Part I, historically, walls were erected to keep enemies out, with the Berlin Wall an exceptional example designed to prevent citizens from exiting. Nowadays, most walls and fences are built to stop migrants from entering and to halt spontaneous movement across borders. New border walls are often high-tech and heavily policed, equipped with advanced surveillance technologies, including cameras, sensors and military-grade drones, to detect, track and deter migration across border landscapes and other cross-border activities.[25] These fortified boundaries have become key intelligence gathering sites, with data frequently shared with third States as part of cooperative deterrence strategies.

B. Cooperative Deterrence, Bilateral Agreements and Joint Operations

There has been a notable shift toward cooperative forms of deterrence, including interceptions, patrols, and joint operations carried out pursuant to bilateral and

[23] Amnesty International, 'USA: Government Must Stop Illegal Pushbacks of Asylum Seekers to Mexico' (Press Release, 11 April 2019) www.amnesty.org/en/latest/news/2019/04/usa-government-must-stop-illegal-pushbacks-of-asylum-seekers-to-mexico/; 'Mexican Police Push Back Hundreds of US-bound Migrants' (*BBC*, 24 January 2020) www.bbc.co.uk/news/av/world-latin-america-51235005/mexican-police-push-back-hundreds-of-us-bound-migrants; Amnesty International, 'Americas: Pushback Practices and Their Impact on the Human Rights of Migrants and Refugees' (2021) www.amnesty.org/es/wp-content/uploads/2021/05/AMR0136582021ENGLISH.pdf; R Schmidtke, 'Refugees International Eyewitness: Pushbacks of Venezuelans on the Guatemalan Border' (*Refugees International*, 31 October 2022) www.refugeesinternational.org/perspectives-and-commentaries/refugees-international-eyewitness-pushbacks-of-venezuelans-on-the-guatemalan-border/; HRW, 'US: Biden "Asylum Ban" Endangers Lives at the Border' (News Release, 11 May 2023) www.hrw.org/news/2023/05/11/us-biden-asylum-ban-endangers-lives-border.

[24] AR Benedicto and M Akkerman, 'A Walled World: Towards a Global Apartheid' (*TNI*, 18 November 2020) www.tni.org/en/publication/a-walled-world; E Vallet (ed), *Borders, Fences and Walls: State of Insecurity?* (Abingdon/New York, Routledge, 2016); M Paz, 'The Law of Walls' (2017) 28 *European Journal of International Law* 601; S Saddiki, *World of Walls: The Structure, Roles and Effectiveness of Separation Barriers* (Cambridge, Open Book Publishers, 2017); F Gülzau and S Mau, 'Visas and Border Infrastructures: What Makes Them Tighter or Looser?' E Recchi and M Safi (eds), *Handbook of Human Mobility and Migration* (Cheltenham, Edward Elgar Publishing, 2024) 203–11.

[25] R Jones and C Johnson, 'Border Militarisation and the Re-articulation of Sovereignty' (2016) 41 *Transactions of the Institute of British Geographers* 187; T Miller, 'More Than A Wall: Corporate Profiteering and the Militarization of US Borders' (Report, Transnational Institute, 2019) 19–22, www.tni.org/files/publication-downloads/more-than-a-wall-report.pdf; J Rigby and J Crisp, 'Fortress Europe: How 1,800km of Walls and Fences are Keeping Desperate Migrants Out' (*The Telegraph*, 20 December 2021) www.telegraph.co.uk/global-health/fortress-europe-borders-wall-fence-controls-eu-countries-migrants-crisis/; S Storey, 'The UK's AI Borders: Anduril's Autonomous Surveillance Towers' (*Migrants' Rights Network*, 27 April 2025) migrantsrights.org.uk/projects/hostile-office/the-digital-hostile-environment/ai-borders-anduril-autonomous-surveillance-towers/.

multilateral agreements.[26] However, cooperation with third States is not a new development. Since at least the 1980s, bilateral agreements have allowed destination States to patrol and intercept vessels bearing the coastal State's flag on the high seas and operate in the coastal State's territorial waters. Notable examples include agreements between Italy and Albania and Italy and Libya.[27] Such agreements have also authorised joint operations between destination States and third States. For instance, Italy's pushback campaign in the 2000s involved patrolling the Libyan coast and the high seas on vessels supplied by Italy, with mixed crews or exclusively Italian crews. This practice culminated in the *Hirsi Jamaa v Italy* case.[28]

More recently, Cyprus has pushed back boats of Syrian refugees to Syria and Lebanon, the latter under a bilateral readmission agreement.[29] Other instances of cooperative deterrence include Spain and Morocco's longstanding collaboration to apprehend and prevent migrants from crossing into the Spanish enclaves. Spain often hands over migrants to Morocco or notifies the Moroccan authorities when movement is detected at the border, prompting Morocco to 'pull back' the migrants.[30] Similarly, the US and Mexico have long worked together to apprehend migrants bound for the US.[31] The US has also entered into 'shiprider' agreements – which allow officials from one country to operate aboard the other's vessels – with countries such as Canada, the Dominican Republic and others in the Indo-Pacific region.[32] In South Asia,

[26] See eg M den Heijer, *Europe and Extraterritorial Asylum* (Oxford, Hart Publishing, 2012) ch 5; Gammeltoft-Hansen and Hathaway (n 3) 248–57; M Giuffré and V Moreno-Lax, 'The Rise of Consensual Containment: From "Contactless Control" to "Contactless Responsibility" for Forced Migration Flows' in SS Juss (ed), *Research Handbook on International Refugee Law* (Cheltenham, Edward Elgar Publishing, 2019) 82–92; NF Tan, 'International Models of Deterrence and the Future of Access to Asylum' in SS Juss (ed), *Research Handbook on International Refugee Law* (Cheltenham, Edward Elgar Publishing, 2019) 172–77.

[27] AT Gallagher and F David, *The International Law of Migrant Smuggling* (Cambridge, CUP, 2014) 95–110. See further den Heijer (n 26) 224–25; E Vari, 'Italy-Libya Memorandum of Understanding: Italy's International Obligations' (2020) 43 *Hastings International and Comparative Law Review* 105, 107–22.

[28] *Hirsi Jamaa v Italy* (2012) 55 EHRR 21.

[29] HRW, *'I Can't Go Home, Stay Here, or Leave': Pushbacks and Pullbacks of Syrian Refugees from Cyprus and Lebanon* (New York, HRW, 2024); UNHCR, 'UNHCR Concerned About Reports of Pushbacks of Syrians' (Press Release, 18 March 2025) www.unhcr.org/europe/news/press-releases/unhcr-concerned-about-reports-pushbacks-syrians.

[30] See *ND and NT v Spain*, App nos 8675/15 and 8697/15 (ECtHR, 13 February 2020); Council of Europe, 'Report of the Fact-finding Mission by Ambassador Tomáš Boček, Special Representative of the Secretary General on Migration and Refugees, to Spain, 18-24 March 2018' (3 September 2018) SG/Inf(2018)25, sect 3; R Brito, 'Migrant Arrivals Plunge in Spain after Deals with Morocco' (*Associated Press*, 26 April 2019) www.apnews.com/6e4c62e3255444c78196aef3f463fca0; 'Morocco foils 78,685 migrant attempts to reach Europe in 2024' (*Reuters*, 6 February 2025) www.reuters.com/world/africa/morocco-foils-78685-migrant-attempts-reach-europe-2024-2025-02-06/.

[31] See US Embassy & Consulates in Mexico, 'The Merida Initiative', mx.usembassy.gov/the-merida-initiative/.

[32] See eg Agreement Between the Government of the United States of America and the Government of the Dominican Republic Concerning Cooperation in Maritime Law Enforcement (20 May 2003) TIAS 03-520. See also N Klein, *Maritime Security and the Law of the Sea* (Oxford, OUP, 2011) 134–37; FitzGerald (n 5) 91–92.

Indonesia, Malaysia, the Philippines, Singapore and Thailand have concluded trilateral and multilateral agreements allowing joint naval and air patrols, surveillance and intelligence to address irregular migration and transnational crimes.[33] Under *Operation Sovereign Borders*, Australia conducts 'takebacks', where those intercepted are handed over to the State of departure, usually Sri Lanka or Vietnam. Indonesia and Australia also conduct joint maritime patrols and joint operations.[34]

In Europe, cooperation with third States is often under the auspices of Frontex, which is responsible for managing the EU's external borders. The Agency supports Member States and third countries through joint operations, rapid border interventions, and operational and technical assistance for search and rescue (SAR) missions and return processes.[35] Frontex has concluded working arrangements with non-EU States to address irregular migration.[36] For example, *Operation Hera* (2006–2007) was a joint operation coordinated by Frontex which patrolled the coasts of Senegal, Mauritania, Cape Verde and the Canary Islands and intercepted thousands of migrants, with coastal State 'shipriders' present on Frontex vessels.[37] Frontex officials can also be deployed to non-EU States for joint operations at their borders, and actively works with countries particularly in North Africa and the Levant to enhance their border security, through training workshops, visits, joint exercises and deployments.[38]

[33] See CC Low, 'Externalization of Border Control in ASEAN Countries' in AKMA Ullah (ed), *Handbook of Migration, International Relations and Security in Asia* (Singapore, Springer Singapore, 2024).

[34] ABF, 'Indonesia and Australia Conclude Joint Maritime Operation' (30 September 2022) www.abf.gov.au/newsroom-subsite/Pages/Indonesia-and-Australia-conclude-joint-maritime-operation-30-09-2022.aspx; AL Hirsch, 'Externalisation and Access to Asylum: An Investigation into Australia's Migration Control Cooperation with Indonesia' (DPhil thesis, Monash University 2022) 144, 168–69.

[35] Regulation (EU) 2019/1896 of the European Parliament and of the Council of 13 November 2019 on the European Border and Coast Guard and repealing Regulations (EU) No 1052/2013 and (EU) 2016/1624 [2019] OJ L 295/1 (Frontex Regulation) preamble 3, arts 3, 10, 36–37, 71–77. See also Regulation (EU) No 656/2014 of the European Parliament and of the Council of 15 May 2014 establishing rules for the surveillance of the external sea borders in the context of operational cooperation coordinated by the European Agency for the Management of Operational Cooperation at the External Borders of the Member States of the European Union [2014] OJ L 189/93 (Sea Borders Regulation) arts 5–9; Frontex, 'Operations', www.frontex.europa.eu/what-we-do/operations/operations/; M Fink, *Frontex and Human Rights: Responsibility in 'Multi-Actor Situations' under the ECHR and EU Public Liability Law* (Oxford, OUP, 2018) ch 2.

[36] Frontex Regulation, art 73; Frontex, 'Working Arrangements', www.frontex.europa.eu/what-we-do/beyond-eu-borders/working-arrangements/. See V Moreno-Lax, *Accessing Asylum in Europe: Extraterritorial Border Controls and Refugee Rights under EU Law* (Oxford, OUP, 2017) 173–78.

[37] Frontex, 'Longest Frontex Coordinated Operation – HERA, the Canary Islands' (Press Release, 19 December 2006) www.frontex.europa.eu/media-centre/news/news-release/longest-frontex-coordinated-operation-hera-the-canary-islands-WpQlsc; Frontex, 'HERA 2008 and NAUTILUS 2008 Statistics' (Press Release, 17 February 2009) www.frontex.europa.eu/media-centre/news/news-release/hera-2008-and-nautilus-2008-statistics-oP7kLN; den Heijer (n 26) 224–25.

[38] M Streppel, 'Analysis: Violence at a Distance: Frontex's Increasing Role Outside the EU' (*Statewatch*, 11 February 2025) www.statewatch.org/outsourcing-borders-monitoring-eu-externalisation-policy/bulletin-5/analysis-violence-at-a-distance-frontex-s-increasing-role-outside-the-eu/.

Frontex operates an extensive aerial surveillance system, which has led to its involvement in pullbacks by the Libyan and Tunisian coastguards and pushbacks by Greece.[39] Frontex planes and ships have been present when pushbacks have taken place, and are even alleged to have created waves and blocked refugee boats while waiting for the Greek Coast Guard.[40] NATO is also involved in maritime security in the region. It conducts operations in the Aegean and Mediterranean seas, sharing real-time surveillance data with the Greek and Turkish coastguards and Frontex via liaison officers, which has reportedly led to the interception and return of migrants, including to Libya.[41] While unilateral and cooperative deterrence practices remain key parts of the arsenal, destination States increasingly operate *through* third States.

C. Remote Forms of Controls: Pullbacks and Enlistment of Partner States

Destination States and the EU have shifted toward more remote forms of control, which have become a central pillar of externalisation. States in the Global North increasingly rely on countries of origin and transit to prevent migrants from leaving their territories, by enticing and pressuring these States to strengthen their border and exit controls and prevent new arrivals to their territory. This is often through 'pullbacks', where third States prevent migrants from leaving by intercepting and returning them to their place of departure as well as pre-emptive interceptions. Giuffré and Moreno-Lax refer to this phenomenon as 'contactless control'.[42] In return, third States are provided with funding, training, equipment and technical support and are incentivised (or cuts threatened) with foreign aid, trade concessions, access to labour markets, and lax visa requirements. Externalisation thus depends heavily on conditionality, to ensure third States

[39] See EBCG, 'Consolidated Annual Activity Report 2018' (12 June 2019) Reg No 5865, 45; Alarm Phone and others, 'Remote Control: The EU-Libya Collaboration in Mass Interceptions of Migrants in the Central Mediterranean' (Report, June 2020) www.eu-libya.info/img/RemoteControl_Report_0620.pdf; ECRE, 'Med: 118 Rescued, 211 into Quarantine while Italy Faces Legal Action for Pull-backs' (26 June 2020) www.ecre.org/med-118-rescued-211-into-quarantine-while-italy-faces-legal-action-for-pull-backs/; J Sunderland and L Pezzani, 'Airborne Complicity: Frontex Aerial Surveillance Enables Abuse' (*HRW, Border Forensics* 2022) www.hrw.org/video-photos/interactive/2022/12/08/airborne-complicity-frontex-aerial-surveillance-enables-abuse.

[40] See eg G Christides and others, 'EU Border Agency Frontex Complicit in Greek Refugee Pushback Campaign' (*Spiegel*, 23 October 2020) www.spiegel.de/international/europe/eu-border-agency-frontex-complicit-in-greek-refugee-pushback-campaign-a-4b6cba29-35a3-4d8c-a49f-a12daad450d7.

[41] NATO, 'Assistance for the Refugee and Migrant Crisis in the Aegean Sea' (20 June 2019) www.nato.int/cps/en/natohq/topics_128746.htm; B Cowles, 'Turkish Naval Ship Aids Pushback of Refugees to Libya' (*Morning Star*, 29 January 2020) morningstaronline.co.uk/article/turkey-aids-pushback-refugees-libya; NATO, 'Operation Sea Guardian' (26 May 2023) www.nato.int/cps/en/natohq/topics_136233.htm.

[42] Giuffré and Moreno-Lax (n 26) 97.

align their policies with the migration control objectives of the Global North.[43] Regional cooperation may aim to build capacity and expand legal migration pathways, but it is frequently employed as a tool of containment and acts as a fig leaf, at times, by appearing to offer positive solutions while simultaneously reinforcing restrictiveness and externalisation.

i. The Americas

Successive US administrations have long sought to prevent Central American migrants from reaching the US border by bolstering the migration control and enforcement capacity of Mexico and Central American States.[44] Mexico has become the key 'buffer zone' for the US, intensifying security operations and apprehending migrants travelling from the Northern Triangle into the US.[45] For many years, US foreign aid has been closely tied to migration enforcement and, at times, made contingent on recipient countries' efforts to stem irregular migration.[46] In October 2007, the Mérida Initiative was launched, with the US providing financial and technical assistance to Mexico and neighbouring States. This initiative aimed to create a modern US–Mexico border, curb irregular migration, and improve immigration enforcement and border security.[47] Between 2011 and 2017, over $100 million USD was allocated for training and equipment to secure Mexico's southern border.[48] Simultaneously, the US provided technical and financial assistance to strengthen Mexico's asylum system and refugee processing capacity.[49]

Under the threat of tariffs by the Trump administration in 2019 over increased irregular migration, Mexico significantly ramped up apprehensions of Central Americans, deploying more than 25,000 guards to its borders, and accepted the return of non-Mexican migrants under the Remain in Mexico policy.[50] The US also suspended foreign aid to El Salvador, Guatemala and

[43] See E Tsourdi and F Zardo, 'Migration Governance Through Funding: Theoretical, Normative, and Empirical Perspectives' (2025) 23 *Journal of Immigrant & Refugee Studies* 1.

[44] FitzGerald (n 5) 91–92, chs 6–7.

[45] A Isacson, M Meyer and H Smith, 'Mexico's Southern Border: Security, Central American Migration, and US Policy' (Report, WOLA, 2017) 7–11, www.wola.org/wp-content/uploads/2017/06/WOLA_Mexicos-Southern-Border-2017-1.pdf; FitzGerald (n 5) 123–46.

[46] See A Martín Gil, 'Managing Migration Through Foreign Aid in Mexico and Central America: The Role of U.S. Conditionality on Mexico's Migration Policies' (2025) 23 *Journal of Immigrant & Refugee Studies* 147.

[47] US Embassy & Consulates in Mexico (n 31).

[48] US Congressional Research Service, *Mexico: Evolution of the Mérida Initiative, 2007–2021* (Clare Ribando Seelke, IF10578, 2021).

[49] M Meyer and A Isacson, 'The "Wall" Before the Wall: Mexico's Crackdown on Migration at its Southern Border' (Report, WOLA, 2019) 43–44, www.wola.org/analysis/mexico-southern-border-report/.

[50] Meyer and Isacson (n 49) 7–20; S Pierce and J Bolter, 'Dismantling and Reconstructing the US Immigration System: A Catalog of Changes under the Trump Presidency' (Report, MPI, 2020) 28–29 www.migrationpolicy.org/research/us-immigration-system-changes-trump-presidency. See also FitzGerald (n 5) 139–41; M Chishti and C Putzel-Kavanaugh, 'The Limits of the Go-It-Alone

Honduras until they signed Asylum Cooperation Agreements ('safe third country' agreements), enabling the removal of asylum seekers to these countries to seek asylum there instead.[51] Under these agreements, US officials were deployed to train local counterparts on border management and asylum processing.[52] While the Biden administration focused more on addressing the root causes of migration and expanding legal pathways to prevent the need for irregular migration across the continent, it maintained restrictive Trump-era measures and remained reliant on regional partners to enforce their borders.[53] In 2022, Mexico agreed to accept the return of 30,000 migrants per month from Cuba, Haiti, Venezuela and Nicaragua attempting to enter the US irregularly, in exchange for the US admitting the same number of these nationals under a humanitarian parole program.[54] A return to the Trump administration, categorising immigration as 'an invasion', has already seen mass expulsions of migrants from Asian, Middle Eastern and African countries to facilities in countries across the region – some under the auspices of IOM's AVR program.[55] In response, the IACHR has expressed its concern over the increase in border externalisation and militarisation in the region.[56]

Scholars have examined the spill-over effect of North America's migration control efforts in Central America, which is reproducing forms of externalisation and reframing irregular migration and mobility as a security issue linked to organised crime.[57] This is manifesting in increased border policing, checkpoints,

Approach: U.S. Migration Management Increasingly Requires Other Countries' Cooperation' (*MPI*, 27 March 2024) www.migrationpolicy.org/article/us-immigration-management-cooperation.

[51] Martín Gil (n 46) 153.

[52] US Department of Homeland Security, 'DHS Agreements with Guatemala, Honduras and El Salvador' (Fact Sheet, November 2019) www.dhs.gov/sites/default/files/publications/19_1028_opa_factsheet-northern-central-america-agreements_v2.pdf.

[53] See the White House, 'U.S.-Mexico Joint Declaration' (1 March 2021) bidenwhitehouse.archives.gov/briefing-room/statements-releases/2021/03/01/u-s-mexico-joint-declaration/; The White House, 'The Biden Administration Blueprint for a Fair, Orderly and Humane Immigration System' (Fact Sheet, 27 July 2021) bidenwhitehouse.archives.gov/briefing-room/statements-releases/2021/07/27/fact-sheet-the-biden-administration-blueprint-for-a-fair-orderly-and-humane-immigration-system/; Chishti and Putzel-Kavanaugh (n 50).

[54] Homeland Security, 'DHS Announces New Migration Enforcement Process for Venezuelans' (12 October 2022) www.dhs.gov/archive/news/2022/10/12/dhs-announces-new-migration-enforcement-process-venezuelans; Homeland Security, 'DHS Continues to Prepare for End of Title 42; Announces New Border Enforcement Measures and Additional Safe and Orderly Processes' (5 January 2023) www.dhs.gov/archive/news/2023/01/05/dhs-continues-prepare-end-title-42-announces-new-border-enforcement-measures-and.

[55] Human Rights First and Refugees International, '"This is an Order from Trump:" Abuse, Expulsions, and Refoulement of People Seeking Asylum' (Report, 8 May 2025) www.refugeesinternational.org/reports-briefs/this-is-an-order-from-trump-abuse-expulsions-and-refoulement-of-people-seeking-asylum/; IOM, 'IOM Spokesperson: Statement On Assisted Voluntary Return (AVR) of Migrants in the United States' (12 May 2025) www.iom.int/news/iom-spokesperson-statement-assisted-voluntary-return-avr-migrants-united-states.

[56] IACHR, 'IACHR Urges States to Guarantee the Rights of Returned, Deported, or Expelled People' (Press Release, 15 May 2025) www.oas.org/en/IACHR/jsForm/?File=/en/iachr/media_center/PReleases/2025/102.asp.

[57] See S Kron and I Ness, 'Central America: Regional Migration and Border Policies' in I Ness and GD Woolf (eds), *The Encyclopedia of Global Human Migration* (London, Wiley, 2013);

detention and pushbacks. Moreover, since the mid-1990s, IOM has convened Regional Consultative Processes on Migration (RCPs) in the Americas, 'teaching' and institutionalising Global North standards of migration control.[58] For instance, Panamanian authorities have criticised Colombia for failing to effectively cooperate to combat smuggling and irregular migration through the Darién Gap, undermining the US-backed operation's objectives.[59]

ii. Asia-Pacific

Across the waters, Australia seeks to prevent, deter and contain irregular migration through regional cooperation with neighbouring States, using political pressure, development aid and funding to secure their involvement in Australia's externalisation regime.[60] Australia has spent billions of dollars funding immigration detention, offshore processing, capacity building and increased border controls with countries such as Indonesia, Malaysia, Sri Lanka and Vietnam.[61] According to Hirsch, this includes 'the increased use of biometric data, the use of anti-migrant-smuggling campaigns, increased intelligence and monitoring of ports, the harmonisation of restriction border policies across the region, and the development of a joint Assisted Voluntary Return (AVR) programme with IOM'.[62] It also stations liaison officers at key transport hubs, and a multi-agency

C Menjívar, 'Immigration Law Beyond Borders: Externalizing and Internalizing Border Controls in an Era of Securitization' (2014) 10 *Annual Review of Law and Social Science* 353; D Acosta and L Brumat, 'Argentina's Restrictive Turn on Migration: Trump's First Imitator in the Americas?' (*MPC*, 13 February 2017) migrationpolicycentre.eu/argentinas-restrictive-turn-on-migration-trumps-first-imitator-in-the-americas/; L Brumat, 'Migration and the "Rise of the Right" in South America: Is There an Increasing Anti-immigration Sentiment in the Southern Cone?' (*MPC*, 1 February 2019) migrationpolicycentre.eu/migration-rise-right-south-america-increasing-anti-immigration-sentiment-southern-cone/; N Winters and C Mora Izaguirre, '*Es Cosa Suya:* Entanglements of Border Externalization and African Transit Migration in Northern Costa Rica' (2019) 7 *Comparative Migration Studies* 27; W Vogt, 'Dirty Work, Dangerous Others: The Politics of Outsourced Immigration Enforcement in Mexico' (2020) 3 *Migration and Society* 50.

[58] R Andrijasevic and W Walters, 'The International Organization for Migration and the International Government of Borders' (2010) 28 *Environment and Planning D* 977; Kron and Ness (n 57) 2.

[59] C Yates and J Pappier, 'How the Treacherous Darien Gap Became a Migration Crossroads of the Americas' (MPI, 20 September 2023) www.migrationpolicy.org/article/darien-gap-migration-crossroads; International Crisis Group, 'Bottleneck of the Americas: Crime and Migration in the Darién Gap' (Report No 102, 2023) www.crisisgroup.org/latin-america-caribbean/andes/colombia-central-america/102-bottleneck-americas-crime-and-migration.

[60] See eg AL Hirsch, 'The Borders Beyond the Border: Australia's Extraterritorial Migration Controls' (2017) 36 *Refugee Survey Quarterly* 48; NF Tan, 'State Responsibility and Migration Control: Australia's International Deterrence Model' in T Gammeltoft-Hansen and J Vedsted-Hansen (eds), *Human Rights and the Dark Side of Globalisation: Transnational Law Enforcement and Migration Control* (Abingdon/New York, Routledge, 2017); M Lee, 'The Externalization of Border Control in the Global South: The Cases of Malaysia and Indonesia' (2022) 26 *Theoretical Criminology* 537.

[61] A Nethery and C Gordyn, 'Australia-Indonesia Cooperation on Asylum-Seekers: A Case of "Incentivised Policy Transfer"' (2014) 68 *Australian Journal of International Affairs* 177, 190; Hirsch, 'Borders Beyond' (n 60) 71, 75; Hirsch, 'Externalisation' (n 34).

[62] Hirsch, 'Externalisation' (n 34) 45–46.

task force led by the Australian Federal Police (AFP) gathers and shares intelligence on people-smuggling operations with local authorities for interception purposes.[63]

Indonesia has become of great strategic importance to Australia as a key transit State. The Regional Cooperation Agreement (RCA), established in 2000 between Australia, Indonesia and IOM, sees Indonesian authorities intercepting migrants attempting to travel irregularly to Australia or New Zealand. Australia has encouraged Indonesia to use detention as a deterrent and provided substantial funding to IOM for the refurbishment, extension, maintenance and training of immigration detention centres in Indonesia.[64] It has donated patrol boats, surveillance aircraft, motorcycles and detection equipment and deployed the AFP to provide training and technical assistance to local officials to support raids and interceptions intent on travelling to Australia.[65]

Regional cooperation also risks frustrating protection, mobility and genuine burden-sharing. The Bali Process was established in 2002 as a non-binding forum bringing together 45 States and four IOs under the chair of Australia and Indonesia to enhance cooperation on irregular migration and people smuggling. However, as the major RCP in the region, scholars have described how the Process is geared primarily towards Australia's interests and instrumentalised by the IOM to advance migration management.[66]

iii. Europe and the EU's External Agenda

The EU's external migration policy rests heavily on non-EU States, with billions of euros earmarked for migration control and containment. For many years, cooperation with third States to prevent irregular migration, among other objectives, has been a priority of the Union and its Member States.[67]

[63] See H Davidson, 'Almost 300 Asylum Seekers Prevented from Sailing to Australia in Past Year' (*The Guardian*, 11 November 2018) www.theguardian.com/australia-news/2018/nov/12/hundreds-of-asylum-seekers-disrupted-while-trying-to-sail-to-australia-in-past-year.

[64] A Nethery, B Rafferty-Brown and S Taylor, 'Exporting Detention: Australia-Funded Immigration Detention in Indonesia' (2013) 26 *Journal of Refugee Studies* 88, 94–95; AL Hirsch and C Doig, 'Outsourcing Control: The International Organization for Migration in Indonesia' (2018) 22 *International Journal of Human Rights* 681, 688–99; Sherwood, Lemay and Costello (n 11) 380–84.

[65] Hirsch, 'Borders Beyond' (n 60) 71–76; F Mussi and NF Tan, 'Comparing Cooperation on Migration Control: Italy–Libya and Australia–Indonesia' in F de Londras and S Mullally (eds), *The Irish Yearbook of International Law*, vol 10, 2015 (London, Hart Publishing, 2017); A Dastyari and A Hirsch, 'The Ring of Steel: Extraterritorial Migration Controls in Indonesia and Libya and the Complicity of Australia and Italy' (2019) 19 *Human Rights Law Review* 435, 439–42.

[66] See L Jansson, 'Everyday Efforts of the International Organization for Migration to (Re)create Migration Management in and Through the Bali Process: An Institutional Work Lens' (2025) *Journal of Ethnic and Migration Studies* 1285.

[67] Commission, 'Tampere: Kick-start to the EU's Policy for Justice and Home Affairs' (Fact Sheet, 2002) www.ec.europa.eu/councils/bx20040617/tampere_09_2002_en.pdf; Council of the European Union, 'Note on Global Approach to Migration: Priority Actions Focusing on Africa and the Mediterranean' (2005) 15744/05 ASIM 66 RELEX 761, data.consilium.europa.eu/doc/document/ST-15744-2005-INIT/en/pdf; FitzGerald (n 5) ch 8, particularly 177–80, ch 9.

Implementation of the European Integrated Border Management (IBM), which is now a shared responsibility of Frontex and Member States, explicitly comprises cooperation with and measures in third countries.[68] To this end, the EU has concluded hundreds of agreements with States across Africa, MENA and Eastern Europe, employing 'all leverages and tools' to incentivise them to manage migration, prevent departures, and readmit migrants.[69] These partnerships rely heavily on conditionality, including tying development cooperation, aid and other benefits (see chapter five) to effectively curbing irregular migration and intercepting and returning migrants.[70] At the same time, Global South States have strategically leveraged migration control to secure economic aid and political concessions.[71]

In the wake of the 2015 'refugee crisis', the EU coordinated its largest humanitarian programme to support Syrian refugees in Turkey – and ensure they remained there. Under the 2016 EU–Turkey deal, Turkey agreed to stem departures to Europe, with the EU funding border infrastructure, surveillance, and detention and deportation centres.[72] This deal became a harmful model for subsequent agreements. States in North Africa, sub-Saharan Africa and elsewhere have become Europe's 'new frontier' for migration control.[73] The EU,

[68] See Council of the European Union, 2768th Council Meeting, C/06/341 (Press Release, 4 December 2006) www.ec.europa.eu/commission/presscorner/detail/en/pres_06_341; Commission, 'Guidelines for Integrated Border Management in European Commission External Cooperation' (Brussels, 2011) www.icmpd.org/file/download/48280/file/Guidelines%2520for%2520Integrated%2520Border%2520Management%2520in%2520European%2520Commission%2520External%2520Cooperation%2520EN.pdf.

[69] Commission, 'Establishing a new Partnership Framework with third countries under the European Agenda on Migration' (Communication) COM (2016) 385 final; Commission, 'EU Action Plan for the Western Mediterranean and Atlantic Routes' (6 June 2023) home-affairs.ec.europa.eu/eu-action-plan-western-mediterranean-and-atlantic-routes_en; Council of the European Union, *The External Dimension of Migration. From a Reactive to a Preventive Model* (Discussion Paper 12990/1/23 REV 1, 2023); Statewatch, 'EU Planning New Anti-Migration Deals with Egypt and Tunisia, Unrepentant in Support for Libya' (16 November 2023) www.statewatch.org/news/2023/november/eu-planning-new-anti-migration-deals-with-egypt-and-tunisia-unrepentant-in-support-for-libya/; Statewatch, 'Analysis: Violence at a distance: Frontex's increasing role outside the EU' (11 February 2025) https://www.statewatch.org/outsourcing-borders-monitoring-eu-externalisation-policy/bulletin-5/analysis-violence-at-a-distance-frontex-s-increasing-role-outside-the-eu/; EU, 'Emergency Trust Fund for Africa' www.trust-fund-for-africa.europa.eu/index_en.

[70] Commission, 'A European Agenda on Migration' (Communication) COM (2015) 240 final, 5, 7–8; Commission, 'Emergency Trust Fund for Africa' (n 69). See T Raty and R Shilhav, *The EU Trust Fund for Africa: Trapped between Aid Policy and Migration Politics* (Briefing Paper, Oxfam 2020) 3–4, 10, pt 2.

[71] See eg G Tsourapas, 'The Refugee Rentier State and Norm Manipulation in the Arab World' in T Fakhoury and D Chatty (eds), *Refugee Governance in the Arab World: The International Refugee Regime and Global Politics* (London, Bloomsbury, 2025) chs 2, 3 6,7; D Chatty, *Syria: The Making and Unmaking of a Refuge State* (Oxford, OUP, 2018).

[72] Funding continued: Weise and others, 'The EU is Helping Turkey Forcibly Deport Migrants to Syria and Afghanistan' (*Politico*, 11 October 2024) www.politico.eu/article/the-eu-is-helping-turkey-forcibly-deport-migrants-to-syria-and-afghanistan/.

[73] eg European Council, 'Valletta Summit on Migration, 11-12 November 2015 – Action Plan and Political Declaration' (12 November 2015) www.consilium.europa.eu/en/press/press-releases/2015/11/12/valletta-final-docs/; European Council, 'Malta Declaration by the Members of

Italy and Malta's infamous cooperation with Libya has been central. After the Strasbourg Court closed a 'legal black hole' in *Hirsi Jamaa*, Italy sought to achieve the same aims as pushbacks by outsourcing to Libya what it is prohibited from doing directly. The EU and European States, in particular Italy, are providing substantial support to the Libyan authorities to enable them to stem migration and intercept migrants attempting to flee Libya – who are often pulled back into inhumane detention centres – in the form of funding, training, surveillance and equipment, including patrol boats.[74] EU and UK funds, training and equipment have similarly been used by regimes such as Morocco, Mauritania, Senegal and Tunisia to abandon migrants in the desert, pull back boats at sea, and conduct mass deportations.[75] Conflicts across the Afro-Asian region led the EU to conclude a strategic partnership with Egypt in 2024, providing millions of Euros in support for preventing migration, building on previous assistance to the Egyptian Coast Guard to restrict irregular migration.[76] Millions in training, equipment and capacity building has also been provided to Lebanon by European States, which has led to the pullback of Syrian refugees headed for Cyprus and Italy.[77]

There has thus been a strategic shift to *refoulement* by proxy. Coastal States, in particular Italy and Malta, have also engaged in 'privatised pushbacks' and proxy pullbacks, co-opting passing merchant vessels and requiring them to pull

the European Council on the External Aspects of Migration: Addressing the Central Mediterranean Route' (Press Release, 3 February 2017) www.consilium.europa.eu/en/press/press-releases/2017/02/03/malta-declaration/.

[74] Libya–Italy MoU, preamble, arts 1, 2(2), (3). See S Uselli (trs), 'Italy-Libya agreement: the Memorandum text' (*ASGI*, 7 February 2017) www.asgi.it/antidiscriminazione/italy-libya-agreement-the-memorandum-text/; Vari (n 27) 107–22; A Pijnenburg, 'From Italian Pushbacks to Libyan Pullbacks: Is *Hirsi 2.0* in the Making in Strasbourg?' (2018) 20 *European Journal of Migration and Law* 396, 399–404; AP Santos, 'UK Strikes £1M Deal with Libya to Combat Irregular Arrivals into Europe' (*Info Migrants*, 11 March 2024) www.infomigrants.net/en/post/55736/uk-strikes-£1m-deal-with-libya-to-combat-irregular-arrivals-into-europe.

[75] N Gasteli and others, 'How EU Funds Enable North African Countries to Push Back Europe-bound Migrants Into the Desert' (*Le Monde*, 21 May 2024) www.lemonde.fr/en/le-monde-africa/article/2024/05/21/how-eu-funds-enable-north-african-countries-to-push-back-europe-bound-migrants-into-the-desert_6672115_124.html; L Carretero, 'Tunisia: Hundreds of Migrants Intercepted at Sea Are Nowhere to Be Found' (*Info Migrants*, 2 April 2025) www.infomigrants.net/en/post/63724/tunisia-hundreds-of-migrants-intercepted-at-sea-are-nowhere-to-be-found; B Bathke, 'Spain Sends Drones, Personnel to Senegal to Stop Boats Departing for Canary Islands' (*Info Migrants*, 31 October 2023) www.infomigrants.net/en/post/52920/spain-sends-drones-personnel-to-senegal-to-stop-boats-departing-for-canary-islands; UK Government, 'UK Partnership with Tunisia to Target Root Causes of Irregular Migration' (Press Release, 31 January 2025) www.gov.uk/government/news/uk-partnership-with-tunisia-to-target-root-causes-of-irregular-migration.

[76] S Samy, 'Egypt's New Asylum Law: Aided by EU Support, Fuelled by Repression' (*euobserver*, 13 January 2025) www.euobserver.com/eu-and-the-world/ar788ee6c9; Statewatch, 'European Support for Egypt: Billions of Euros for a Dictatorial "Partner" in Migration Control' (27 March 2025) www.statewatch.org/analyses/2025/european-support-for-egypt-billions-of-euros-for-a-dictatorial-partner-in-migration-control/.

[77] HRW, *I Can't Go Home* (n 29) pt viii.

and take back migrants to Libya.[78] This shift has been accompanied by the alarming disengagement of search and rescue (SAR) assets by European States, the criminalisation of NGO rescue vessels, and refusals to allow disembarkation.[79] The EU's *Operation Sophia* withdrew all naval assets in 2019, leaving only aircraft which passes surveillance data to repressive regimes.

The EU's externalisation strategy has also tied aid and other incentives to enforcing and enacting new restrictive laws, including pushing partner States to criminalise exit, irregular migration and smuggling.[80] Before the coup in Niger, a complaint was made to the ECOWAS Court of Justice challenging the legality of Law No 36/2015, introduced in response to EU pressure on Niger to prevent onward movement, as a violation of the right to leave and free movement.[81] The EU's 'management' of migration plainly undermines the African Union and other regional bodies' free movement agendas (and sits uncomfortably with the EU's own model).[82] According to scholars, EU externalisation has contributed to the erosion of protection in Africa, as many African States have established refugee camps that keep refugees in their region of origin and processing centres near the border to restrict access to the territory.[83] Other

[78] *SDG v Italy*, Communication to the HRC (18 December 2019) declared inadmissible due to a lack of exhaustion of domestic remedies; P Kingsley, 'Privatised Pushbacks: How Merchant Ships Guard Europe' (*The New York Times*, 20 March 2020) www.nytimes.com/2020/03/20/world/europe/mediterranean-libya-migrants-europe.html; P Kingsley, 'Latest Tactic to Push Migrants from Europe? A Private, Clandestine Fleet' (*The New York Times*, 27 April 2020) www.nytimes.com/2020/03/20/world/europe/mediterranean-libya-migrants-europe.html; Alarm Phone, 'Also in the Central Mediterranean Sea: Black Lives Matter!' (6 July 2020) www.alarmphone.org/en/2020/07/06/also-in-the-central-mediterranean-sea-black-lives-matter/.

[79] See Frontex, 'Frontex Launching New Operation in Central Med' (Press Release, 1 February 2018) www.frontex.europa.eu/media-centre/news/news-release/frontex-launching-new-operation-in-central-med-yKqSc7; Council Decision (CFSP) 2020/472 of 31 March 2020 on a European Union military operation in the Mediterranean (EUNAVFOR MED IRINI) [2020] OJ L 101/4; Commissioner for Human Rights, 'Third Party Intervention by the Council of Europe Commissioner for Human Rights under Article 36, paragraph 3, of the European Convention on Human Rights Application No 21660/18 *SS and Others v Italy* CommDH(2019)29' (15 November 2019) paras 13–15; EU Agency for Fundamental Rights, 'Search and Rescue Operations and Fundamental Rights' (June 2024) fra.europa.eu/en/publication/2024/june-2024-update-ngo-ships-sar-activities.

[80] eg Law No 02/03 (2003) Morocco; Law No 2004-6 (2004) Tunisia; Law 08-11 (2008), Law 09-01 (2009) and Law 24-06, Art 175 bis 1 (2024) Algeria; Law No 19 (2010) Libya; Law No 2015-36 (2015); V Badalič, 'Tunisia's Role in the EU External Migration Policy: Crimmigration Law, Illegal Practices, and Their Impact on Human Rights' (2019) 20 *Journal of International Migration and Integration* 85; D Perrin, 'Smuggling of Migrants: The Misused Spirit of the Palermo Protocol, in the Light of the Nigerien Experience' (*Border Criminologies*, 25 May 2020) https://blogs.law.ox.ac.uk/research-subject-groups/centre-criminology/centreborder-criminologies/blog/2020/05/smuggling.

[81] ASGI, 'Ecowas Court of Justice Called to Judge the Legality of Niger Law No. 36/2015' (2022) www.en.asgi.it/ecowas-court-of-justice-called-to-judge-the-legality-of-niger-law-no-36-2015/.

[82] See A Bisong, 'Win-win-win: Africa and Europe in 2019 Should Move Towards Solutions that Benefit Migrants Too' (*ECDPM*, 28 January 2019) www.ecdpm.org/talking-points/win-win-win-africa-europe-2019-move-towards-solutions-benefit-migrants-too/; L Kandilige and T Yeboah, 'West African Migration Regimes and the Externalization of EU Migration Management Policies' in G Heck and others (eds), *Making Routes: Mobility and Politics of Migration in the Global South* (Cairo, The American University in Cairo Press, 2024).

[83] See B Opi, 'Borders Recolonised – The Impacts of the EU Externalisation Policy in Africa' (2021) 3 *Journal of Decolonising Disciplines* 1, 11, 17–18; LS Gordon, 'Immigration Policy in

mechanisms to detain and contain migrants have also been developed, particularly across the Maghreb, including waiting zones in ports and airports and administrative detention.[84]

The EU routinely outsources project implementation of its migration and border control strategy to other entities, most notably IOM and ICMPD, which provide training, technical assistance, equipment and infrastructure to third States.[85] The ICMPD is a major recipient of EU funding to enhance border management capabilities in countries such as Lebanon, Tunisia, Turkey and across West Africa, supporting the IBM concept co-developed with the EU.[86] It has procured IT equipment for control rooms, surveillance systems and even K9 detection dogs for some beneficiary countries.[87] IOM has played various operational roles in Libya, including refurbishing detention centres, training the LBCG, and running a large AVR programme.[88] It has received funding to strengthen Egypt and Tunisia's migration management capacities, as well as to bolster border security in Burkina Faso, Mali, Mauritania and Niger. It has also trained Sudanese border guards and militias, some of whom are now key players in Sudan's ongoing civil war.[89] The EU's New Pact on Migration and Asylum, adopted in 2024, only entrenches Fortress Europe, enabling greater abuse through expanded detention and containment at EU borders, and further shifting responsibilities onto third States to prevent departures and process asylum claims.[90]

South Africa: Public Opinion, Xenophobia and the Search for Progress' in P Rugunanan and N Xulu-Gama (eds), *Migration in Southern Africa: IMISCOE Regional Reader* (Cham, Springer, 2022).

[84] D Perrin, 'Regulating Migration and Asylum in the Maghreb: What Inspirations for an Accelerated Legal Development?' in F Ippolito and S Trevisanut (eds), *Migration in the Mediterranean – Mechanisms of International Cooperation* (Cambridge, CUP, 2016) 197–204.

[85] See M Akkerman, 'Expanding the Fortress: The Policies, the Profiteers and the People Shaped by EU's Border Externalisation Programme' (Report, Transnational Institute and Stop Wapenhandel, 2018) www.tni.org/files/publication-downloads/expanding_the_fortress_-_1.6_may_11.pdf.

[86] ICMPD, 'Border Management and Security Programme' www.icmpd.org/our-work/capacity-building/border-management-and-security-programme; Akkerman (n 85) 82; M Esene, 'FMM West Africa: Support to Free Movement of Persons and Migration in West Africa' (*ICMPD*, 2021) www.icmpd.org/our-work/projects/support-to-free-movement-of-persons-and-migration-in-west-africa-fmm-west-africa; HRW, *I Can't Go Home* (n 29).

[87] MPF, 'Focus on Beneficiaries: K9 Division of the Georgian Border Police' (4 June 2020) www.migrationpartnershipfacility.eu/news/focus-on-beneficiaries-k9-division-of-the-georgian-border-police; ICMPD, 'Factsheet – Representation of ICMPD in Türkiye' (2024) www.icmpd.org/file/download/58885/file/ICMPD_T%25C3%25BCrkiyeGeneralInfoSheet_ENG_281122F.pdf.

[88] Sherwood, Lemay and Costello (n 11) 13.

[89] J Brachet, 'Policing the Desert: The IOM in Libya Beyond War and Peace' (2016) 48 *Antipode* 272, 276–77; Akkerman (n 85) 12–14, 45–46, 80–81; EU-IOM, 'EU-IOM Joint Initiative' (Flash Report No 24, January 2020) www.migrationjointinitiative.org/sites/default/files/files/articles/eu-iomjointinitiativeflashreport24en.pdf; PM Frowd, 'Borderwork Creep in West Africa's Sahel' (2022) 27 *Geopolitics* 1331; Sherwood, Lemay and Costello (n 11) 384.

[90] HRW, 'Civil Society Organisations Call on MEPs to Vote Down Harmful EU Migration Pact' (15 April 2024) www.hrw.org/news/2024/04/15/civil-society-organisations-call-meps-vote-down-harmful-eu-migration-pact; EU, 'Pact on Migration and Asylum' (21 May 2024) home-affairs.ec.europa.eu/policies/migration-and-asylum/pact-migration-and-asylum_en. See A Macklin, 'Exit

The remote control strategies of Global North States have dramatically reshaped the migration and human rights landscape across regions, spilling over into Global South States and leading to the criminalisation of migrants, as well as undermining regional free movement, hampering local economies and transforming rescues into interceptions.

III. THE LAW OF THE SEA

It is necessary to briefly summarise the key legal principles and obligations governing rescue and interdiction at sea, which are central to assessing the legality and legitimacy of pushbacks and pullbacks at sea under the right to leave any country. To ensure the full protection of migrants take often dangerous sea crossings in search of safety and dignity, it is essential that law of the sea duties are interpreted consistently and in compliance with international human rights and refugee standards, in accordance with the systemic integration principle.[91]

A. State Duties at Sea

One of the oldest maritime obligations is the duty to render assistance to any individual in distress at sea, regardless of nationality, status or circumstances.[92] States must require shipmasters flying their flag to rescue persons in distress, where there is a reasonable certainty of grave and imminent danger requiring immediate assistance.[93] States must also ensure rescued persons are delivered to a 'place of safety', which requires disembarkation to a place where their life is no longer threatened and basic needs are met, including protection from persecution and *refoulement*.[94] The obligation to save lives at sea and to guarantee

Rights, Seamless Borders and the New Carceral State' (2024) 73 *International & Comparative Law Quarterly* 891, pt IV on migrant detention as containment.

[91] See generally I Mann, *Humanity at Sea: Maritime Migration and the Foundations of International Law* (Cambridge, CUP, 2016); V Moreno-Lax and E Papastavridis, *'Boat Refugees' and Migrants at Sea: A Comprehensive Approach: Integrating Maritime Security with Human Rights* (Dordrecht, Brill Nijhoff, 2016).

[92] UNCLOS, arts 18(2), 58(2), 98(1), (2). See also International Convention for the Safety of Life at Sea (adopted 1 November 1974, entry into force 25 May 1980) 1184 UNTS 278 (SOLAS) ch V, reg 33(1.1); International Convention on Maritime Search and Rescue (adopted 27 April 1979, entry into force 22 June 1985) 405 UNTS 97 (SAR) annex, ch 2 para 2.1.10.

[93] UNCLOS, art 98(1). See also SOLAS, ch V, reg 33; SAR, para 1.3.13.

[94] SOLAS, ch V, reg 33(1.1), (6); SAR, paras 1.3.2 and 3.1.9; IMO Resolution MSC.167(78), Guidelines on the Treatment of Persons Rescued at Sea (adopted 20 May 2004), para 6.12; UNHCR, 'General Legal Considerations: Search-and-Rescue Operations involving Refugees and Migrants at Sea' (November 2017) paras 1, 6, 16–17; UNHCR, 'Legal Considerations on the Roles and Responsibilities of States in Relation to Rescue at Sea, Non-Refoulement, and Access to Asylum' (2022).

protection for those rescued further imposes on States obligations to conduct effective investigations to prosecute and ensure accountability for the serious crimes and serious human rights violations that take place at sea, such as trafficking in persons and aggravated smuggling as well as other human right violations. Coastal States must maintain adequate and effective SAR services in their region and bear primary responsibility for the swift coordination of search and rescue efforts to save lives at sea and ensure survivors are disembarked to safety.[95]

B. Legal Foundation for Interdicting Migrant Vessels

The legal basis for interdicting migrant vessels is complex, contested and, crucially, circumscribed by international law.[96] Interdiction involves boarding and inspecting vessels suspected of prohibited conduct, and if confirmed, taking specific enforcement measures, such as the vessel's arrest.[97] The duty to rescue *does not equate* to a general right of interdiction, with SAR operations distinct from interdiction.[98] To this end, the UNHCR, IOM and other UN actors have emphasised the importance of preventing and addressing distress situations, while ensuring rescue and interception operations prioritise human rights, guarantee access to asylum, and do not expose refugees and other migrants to further risks or harm.[99]

Article 87 of UNCLOS sets out the fundamental principle of freedom of the high seas. Vessels on the high seas are subject to the exclusive jurisdiction of their flag State, and other States may only interdict and exercise enforcement jurisdiction over foreign vessels when they have lawful justification.[100] For instance, Article 110 of UNCLOS permits a warship to board a foreign vessel where there are reasonable grounds for suspecting the vessel is engaged in specified conduct, such as piracy or the slave trade, or that the vessel is without nationality ('right of visit'). Additionally, interdiction may be authorised by treaty or consent of the flag or coastal State whose SAR zone the vessel is in, as

[95] SOLAS, ch V, regs 7, 33(1.1); SAR, chs 2-3; UNCLOS, art 98(2); UNHCR, 'Legal Considerations on Roles' (n 94).

[96] See D Guilfoyle, *Shipping Interdiction and the Law of the Sea* (Cambridge, CUP, 2009); E Papastavridis, *The Interception of Vessels on the High Seas: Contemporary Challenges to the Legal Order of the Oceans* (London, Hart Publishing, 2013) ch 8.

[97] Guilfoyle (n 96) 4.

[98] EXCOM (n 2) preamble; V Moreno-Lax, 'Seeking Asylum in the Mediterranean: Against a Fragmentary Reading of EU Member States' Obligations Accruing at Sea' (2011) 23 *International Journal of Refugee Law* 174, 176–77.

[99] UNHCR and others, 'Distress at Sea: A call for a Humanitarian and Precautionary Approach' (Joint Statement, 2024) www.unhcr.org/sites/default/files/2024-12/joint-statement-on-distress-at-sea.pdf.

[100] UNCLOS, arts 92, 94. See Papastavridis (n 96).

the aforementioned bilateral agreements provide for.[101] The Smuggling Protocol allows interdiction of vessels suspected of migrant smuggling with express flag State consent.[102] States can also board and search a vessel suspected of smuggling without nationality and, if suspicion is confirmed, take appropriate measures in accordance with domestic and international law.[103] In contrast, the Trafficking Protocol only provides for State Parties to strengthen their border controls to prevent and detect trafficking.[104] UN Security Council authorisations, such as for the EU Naval Force (EUNAVFOR) operations off the coast of Libya, permit the inspection and seizure of vessels on the high seas suspected of smuggling or trafficking. However, any action must comply fully with human rights and refugee law standards and must not prevent seeking asylum.[105] As expanded upon below, enforcement-style measures cannot easily be derived from these clauses and States nonetheless remain bound to uphold their other international obligations, which is especially relevant to the legality and legitimacy of pushbacks and pullbacks.

The coastal State bears greater sovereignty when interception occurs in its territorial sea or contiguous zone. A State has full sovereignty over its territorial sea, subject to UNCLOS and other rules of international law, notably the right of innocent passage for ships.[106] Passage may be prejudicial where the ship loads or unloads people contrary to the coastal State's immigration laws.[107] Scholars disagree over whether passage to request international protection qualifies as innocent.[108] However, the right to seek asylum is a fundamental principle of international law, and the Refugee Convention prohibits penalisation for unauthorised entry, supporting the view that passage remains innocent. Regardless, coastal States may only take necessary measures to prevent non-innocent passage and must still comply with other rules of international law.[109] Similarly, a State may exercise 'control' in its contiguous zone as necessary to prevent or punish infringements of its immigration laws within the territorial sea.[110] Although there remains ambiguity over whether interdiction falls

[101] Guilfoyle (n 96) 5, ch 13; Papastavridis (n 96) 281–89.

[102] Smuggling Protocol, arts 8(2), (5); Papastavridis (n 96) 80–81.

[103] Smuggling Protocol, art 8(7).

[104] Trafficking Protocol, art 11(1).

[105] UN Security Council Resolution 2240 (9 October 2015) UN Doc S/RES/2240, paras 5–8, 10–13; UNSC Res 2491 (3 October 2019) UN Doc S/RES/2491, para 2. See Council Decision (CFSP) 2020/472; Guilfoyle (n 96) 222–225; E Papastavridis, 'EUNAVFOR MED Operation Sophia and the Question of Jurisdiction over Transnational Organized Crime at Sea' (2016) 30 *QIL Zoom-in* 19, 27–30, 75–77.

[106] UNCLOS, arts 2, 17.

[107] ibid arts 19(1), 2(g).

[108] cf GS Goodwin-Gill and J McAdam, *The Refugee in International Law*, 4th edn (Oxford, OUP, 2021) 340–42 with Moreno-Lax, 'Seeking Asylum' (n 98) 191–92; Moreno-Lax, *Interdiction* (n 15) 4. See also N Markard, 'The Right to Leave by Sea: Legal Limits on EU Migration Control by Third Countries' (2016) 27 *European Journal of International Law* 591, 599–606; Klein (n 32) 30–31.

[109] UNCLOS, arts 2(3), 25(1), 27(1); Goodwin-Gill and McAdam (n 108) 340.

[110] UNCLOS, art 33.

within this scope, any exercise of jurisdiction remains constrained by refugee and human rights law.[111]

Thus, when scrutinising pushbacks and pullbacks, law of the sea considerations must be duly accounted for, particularly the limits on interdiction and preservation of human rights protections.

IV. JURISDICTION AND ATTRIBUTION

The above survey of the most prominent practices at international borders around the world revealed different types of pushbacks and pullbacks, each raising distinct issues: physical interceptions; 'active' but indirect deterrence measures, involving officials or ships, such as bow wave manoeuvres; and walls and physical infrastructure that may block entry and drive migrants away. Simultaneously, several outsourcing modalities exist, comprising countries of origin and transit, private actors, the EU and other IOs. This leads to complex questions of jurisdiction, attribution and responsibility allocation.

A. Pushbacks and Pullbacks as an Exercise of Jurisdiction

While pushbacks at or near a State's border or in international waters clearly involve the intercepting/destination State exercising jurisdiction over migrants, pullbacks by a third country with the support of the destination State are far more controversial.

i. Pushbacks

As various adjudicative bodies have held, jurisdiction exists where the State exerts factual control over vessels or persons or through activities occurring on board ships flying the flag of that State.[112] This has been the case for pushbacks in the ground-breaking *Hirsi Jamaa* case;[113] during the interception, boarding, and towing to port of a vessel on the high seas;[114] rescues at sea;[115] return of an

[111] See ibid arts 58(1), 86, 87(1); Moreno-Lax, 'Seeking Asylum' (n 98) 190–91. See also Human Rights at Sea, 'Geneva Declaration on Human Rights at Sea' (2022).

[112] See on jurisdiction at sea E Papastavridis, 'The European Convention of Human Rights and Migration at Sea: Reading the "Jurisdictional Threshold" of the Convention Under the Law of the Sea Paradigm' (2020) 21 *German Law Journal* 417; UNHCR, 'Legal Considerations on Roles' (n 94).

[113] *Hirsi Jamaa* (n 28) paras 75, 77–78, 81. See also *Medvedyev v France* (2010) 51 EHRR 39, para 65; *Sonko v Spain*, Communication No 368/2008 (25 November 2011) UN Doc CAT/C/47/D/368/2008, para 10.3; *Sharifi v Italy and Greece*, App no 16643/09 (ECtHR, 21 October 2014); *Banakova v Lithuania*, App no 11167/12 (ECtHR, 31 May 2016) para 63.

[114] *Medvedyev* (n 113) paras 63–67.

[115] *JHA v Spain*, Communication No 323/2007 (10 November 2008) UN Doc CAT/C/41/D/323/2007, para 8.2.

individual refused entry to their country of origin by private ship;[116] and mere collision with a vessel.[117] Blockades and using warships to prevent entry have also amounted to jurisdiction and, by extension, active deterrence measures involving violence, the threat of, or otherwise producing a 'chilling effect' that stops or diverts migrants, such as patrols and encirclement, should meet the threshold for effective control.[118] Vessels and migrants are deprived of the only course of action available to them: navigation. The same applies to land pushbacks. Numerous international and regional cases have found migrants to be within the State's jurisdiction when subject to pushbacks.[119] Open firing on people, the use of force, and vehicle checkpoints have also involved the exercise of jurisdiction.[120] States participating in joint operations can be considered to have jurisdiction when they are both exercising such authority or control.[121]

For walls and fences, much will turn on the test adopted, and the adjudicative body concerned. When guarded and policed, physical barriers have the same diversion effect as direct pushbacks. However, so does a wall with no guards, which nonetheless directly impacts one's right to leave and ability to assert a right of entry.[122] Therefore, pushbacks and other measures that drive migrants away or back over the border can be understood as effective control or as triggering jurisdiction based on a functional or causal relationship.

ii. Pullbacks

With respect to pullbacks, destination States are actively trying to sever jurisdictional links and avoid *Hirsi*-like results. The State of origin or transit performing the pullback plainly exercises effective control, akin to pushbacks. The key question is whether migrants also fall within the destination State's jurisdiction by virtue of the funding, training, equipment and intelligence support provided

[116] *Mansouri v Italy*, App no 63386/16 (ECtHR, 29 April 2025) paras 47–51.

[117] *Xhavara v Italy and Albania*, App no 39473/98 (ECtHR, 11 January 2001) 5–6.

[118] *Women on Waves v Portugal*, App no 31276/05 (ECtHR, 3 February 2009); Moreno-Lax, *Interdiction* (n 15) 9–10; Papastavridis, 'European Convention' (n 112) 424–26, 429–30.

[119] *MA v Lithuania*, App no 59793/17 (ECtHR, 11 December 2018) paras 70, 4–6 (Separate Opinion Albuquerque J); *MK v Poland*, Apps nos 40503/17, 42902/17 and 43643/17 (ECtHR, 23 July 2020) paras 129–32. See also *DD v Spain*, Communication No 4/2016 (1 February 2019) UN Doc CRC/C/80/D/4/2016, para 14.3; *ND and NT* (n 30) paras 104–11; *ARE v Greece*, App no 15783/21 (ECtHR, 7 January 2025).

[120] *Andreou v Turkey*, App no 45653/99 (ECtHR, 27 October 2009) para 25; *Al-Skeini v UK* (2011) 53 EHRR 18, para 136; *Jaloud v Netherlands* (2015) 60 EHRR 29, paras 149–52.

[121] EU Agency for Fundamental Rights (FRA), *Scope of the Principle of 'Non-Refoulement' in Contemporary Border Management: Evolving Areas of Law* (Luxembourg, FRA, 2016) 28; *AS, DI, OI and GD v Italy*, Communication No 3042/2017 (4 November 2020) UN Doc CCPR/C/130/D/3042/2017, paras 7.3–7.8; *AS, DI, OI and GD v Malta*, Communication No 3043/2017 (13 March 2020) UN Doc CCPR/C/128/D/3043/2017, paras 6.3–6.7; *Nabhari v Australia*, Communication No 3663/2019 (25 October 2024) UN Doc CCPR/C/142/D/3663/2019, paras 7.5–7.15.

[122] See Paz, 'Law of Walls' (n 24); M Paz, 'The Legal Reconstruction of Walls: *N.D. & N.T. v. Spain*, 2017, 2020' (2020) 22 *NYU Journal of Legislation & Public Policy* 693, 697, 709–13.

to the third State. Three possible routes exist for establishing jurisdiction in pullback cases: effective control, functional/cause and effect, and complicity.

In June 2025, the Strasbourg Court issued its long-awaited decision in *SS v Italy*, declaring it inadmissible.[123] The case concerned a violent pullback by the Libyan Coast Guard (LBGC) in 2017, after it interfered with the rescue of nearly 150 people by the NGO Sea-Watch, resulting in 20 deaths and the return of 47 people to inhumane conditions. The 17 survivors alleged violations of their rights to life, protection from torture and ill-treatment, *refoulement* and collective expulsion. In a deeply disappointing decision, the Court ruled Italy did not exercise jurisdiction over the migrants when acting through its proxy, the LBCG; its extensive support to Libya was deemed insufficient to establish effective control or authority over the individuals.[124]

Yet, there was overwhelming evidence before the Court supporting Italy's effective control over the pulled-back migrants. Italy donated the vessel conducting the pullback, and eight of the thirteen crew members were trained under *Operation Sophia*, to which Italy was a key contributor. The Rome MRCC sent the distress signal to the LBCG and Sea-Watch, directed them toward the dinghy, and an Italian helicopter was present overhead.[125] Italy continuously coordinated and controlled the interception and rescue, directing the LBCG to 'take charge', and creating the conditions enabling the violations to materialise.[126] Without Italian and EU support, the previously non-existent LBCG would not have been capable of conducting pullbacks: their backing facilitated Libya's declaration of a SAR region and the establishment of a joint rescue coordination centre.[127] Instead, the Court concluded that coordinating a rescue does not create a jurisdictional link.[128] As the applicants and experts have argued, the decisive influence exercised by destination States over third countries (consider also Australia over Indonesia, the US over Mexico, and the EU over Turkey) is

[123] *SS v Italy*, App 21660/18 (ECtHR, 20 May 2025). See also *CO and AJ v Italy*, App no 40396/18 (ECtHR, 30 March (not yet communicated)).

[124] *SS* (n 123) paras 91–108; I Mann, 'S.S. and Others v. Italy: Killing by Omission, Confirmed by Design' (*EJIL:Talk!*, 19 June 2025) www.ejiltalk.org/s-s-and-others-v-italy-killing-by-omission-confirmed-by-design/; V Moreno-Lax, 'SS and Others v Italy – or doubling down on Banković' (*EJIL:Talk!*, 19 June 2025) www.ejiltalk.org/ss-and-others-v-italy-or-doubling-down-on-bankovic/.

[125] See Forensic Oceanography, 'Mare Clausum: Italy and the EU's Undeclared Operation to Stem Migration Across the Mediterranean' (Report, May 2018) content.forensic-architecture.org/wp-content/uploads/2019/05/2018-05-07-FO-Mare-Clausum-full-EN.pdf.

[126] V Moreno-Lax, 'The Architecture of Functional Jurisdiction: Unpacking Contactless Control – On Public Powers, *SS and Others v Italy*, and the "Operational Model"' (2020) 21 *German Law Journal* 385, 406; Moreno-Lax, 'SS and Others' (n 124). See also L Riemer, 'From Push-backs to Pull-backs: The EU's New Deterrence Strategy Faces Legal Challenge' (*FluchtforschungsBlog*, 16 June 2018) www.blog.fluchtforschung.net/from-push-backs-to-pull-backs-the-eus-new-deterrence-strategy-faces-legal-challenge/; Pijnenburg, 'Italian Pushbacks' (n 74) 411.

[127] Commissioner for Human Rights (n 79) paras 20, 35; G Ciliberto, 'Libya's Pull-Backs of Boat Migrants: Can Italy Be Held Accountable for Violations of International Law?' (2018) 4 *Italian Law Journal* 489, 527–28; Forensic Oceanography (n 125) 19–56.

[128] *SS* (n 123) paras 103–06.

comparable to *Ilaşcu* and *Catan*, despite their unique factual circumstances.[129] Without such influence, third States would neither be willing nor capable of obstructing departure, as in the past, but the Court rejected this.[130]

The Court nonetheless reaffirmed that States remain bound by their obligations on rescue, refugee protection and State responsibility and highlighted the serious concerns of numerous bodies about the outsourcing of migration control.[131] It also warned against creating 'an area outside the law' at sea, yet ultimately disregarded these rules and instead confirmed that European States can violate migrants' rights free from responsibility.[132] Despite this ruling, principled legal arguments support a finding that destination States exert significant influence and control over pullbacks, constituting effective control.

Second, jurisdiction can be established based on the direct and foreseeable impact of a State's actions and policies on migrants, applying a functional or causal approach. This remains true where the State did not coordinate the specific pullback and where physical contact is lacking. Externalisation practices create the *precise* conditions that lead to pullbacks and ensuing violations. As the UNHCR argued in *SS*, when the coordination or involvement of an MRCC is likely to determine the course of events, human rights obligations are engaged.[133] Similarly, a complaint was made to the Human Rights Committee concerning Italy's role in privatised pushbacks, contending that by orchestrating the interdiction jointly with the LBCG, Italy decisively contributed to and violated the individual's right to leave Libya.[134] Furthermore, as NGO interveners in *SS* argued, during rescue operations on the high seas, State agents exercise authority over rescuees in a manner that has proximate and foreseeable effects on their rights, thereby constituting effective control under maritime law.[135] Control over responses to distress signals and knowledge of distress at sea should thus be decisive in establishing jurisdiction.[136] Destination States' extensive border surveillance systems demonstrate not only knowledge but also functional control over migrant movements, highlighting their capacity to prevent violations.[137]

Recent jurisprudence supports this approach: the Human Rights Committee found that Italy exercised jurisdiction and violated the right to life of over 200 migrants whose vessel sank in the Mediterranean, even though the incident

[129] *SS* (n 123) paras 56, 65, 72; Pijnenburg, 'Italian Pushbacks' (n 74) 413–15; Giuffré and Moreno-Lax (n 26) 105–07; Moreno-Lax, 'Architecture' (n 126) 408–11.

[130] *SS* (n 123) para 97.

[131] ibid paras 110–12.

[132] ibid para 111.

[133] ibid para 70. See also para 105 on 'direct impact'.

[134] *SDG* (n 78) paras 17, 56–58, 62–68, 100.

[135] *SS* (n 123) para 71. cf Moreno-Lax, 'Architecture' (n 126) on a functional public powers model.

[136] Papastavridis, 'European Convention' (n 112) 435.

[137] UNGA, 'Report of the Special Rapporteur of the Human Rights Council on Extrajudicial, Summary or Arbitrary Executions on Unlawful Death of Refugees and Migrants' (15 August 2017) UN Doc A/72/335, para 64. See *SDG* (n 78) para 10.

occurred within Malta's SAR region and under its concurrent jurisdiction.[138] The Committee found that a 'special relationship of dependency' was established based on the initial distress call to the Italian MRCC, the proximity of an Italian naval vessel, and Italy's ongoing involvement. The migrants were therefore 'directly affected' in a 'reasonably foreseeable' manner by Italy's delayed rescue.[139]

Critically, containment and return 'are not accidental, unforeseen, or unintended'; they are a 'planned and expected' consequence of externalisation.[140] The Committee Against Torture and Human Rights Committee have found on multiple occasions that Australia exercised jurisdiction over migrants detained offshore, based on the cumulative effect of establishing, building and funding the centres and significant levels of control and influence over the management and operation of the centres.[141] Likewise, there is a functional and direct causal relationship between pulled-back migrants and the destination State's material support to third States performing pullbacks.[142] This even extends to truly 'contactless' cases, where the State provides resources and deliberately turns a blind eye to ensuing violations. Such States retain the capacity to uphold their obligations, but instead, foster curtailment of the right to leave.[143]

Lastly, the aid and assistance provided by Italy and other States can be viewed through a complicity lens. Building on Jackson's analysis, who argues that the *Soering* rule should be re-imagined to prohibit all forms of extraterritorial complicity, not solely complicity in torture.[144] Recognising jurisdiction in cases of aid and assistance would rightly prevent destination States from facilitating human rights violations through externalisation without accountability. Regrettably, in *SS*, Strasbourg refrained from addressing any arguments raised regarding Article 16 of ARSIWA and broader State responsibility.[145]

While Strasbourg maintains its restrictive, harmful stance on jurisdiction, other adjudicative bodies should find jurisdiction in similar pullback cases, especially given their firm rejection of pushbacks. This would prevent serious

[138] *AS v Italy* (n 121); *AS v Malta* (n 121).

[139] *AS v Italy* (n 121) paras 7.8, 8.4–8.5.

[140] Moreno-Lax, 'Architecture' (n 126) 387, 410.

[141] CAT, 'Concluding Observations on the Combined Fourth and Fifth Periodic Reports of Australia' (23 December 2014) UN Doc CAT/C/AUS/CO/4-5, para 17; HRC, 'Concluding Observations on the Sixth Periodic Report of Australia' (1 December 2017) UN Doc CCPR/C/AUS/CO/6, para 35; *MI v Australia*, Communication No 2749/2016 (31 October 2024) UN Doc CCPR/C/142/D/2749/2016; *Nabhari* (n 121); NF Tan, 'The Manus Island Regional Processing Centre: A Legal Taxonomy' (2018) 20 *European Journal of Migration and Law* 427, 444–47.

[142] See A Pijnenburg, 'Containment Instead of *Refoulement*: Shifting State Responsibility in the Age of Cooperative Migration Control?' (2020) 20 *Human Rights Law Review* 306, 325.

[143] See on positive obligations den Heijer (n 26) 48; Pijnenburg, 'Italian Pushbacks' (n 74) 410.

[144] M Jackson, 'Freeing *Soering*: The ECHR, State Complicity in Torture and Jurisdiction' (2016) 27 *European Journal of International Law* 817; Pijnenburg, 'Containment' (n 142) 327. See also *Hirsi Jamaa* (n 28) 78 (Separate Opinion Albuquerque J).

[145] *SS* (n 123) paras 30, 70–71.

responsibility gaps as States increasingly perform pushbacks by proxy, and ensure destination States cannot strategically evade their obligations despite obvious control. The right to leave should therefore be opposable not only to departure but also destination States, allowing both to share jurisdiction during pullbacks.

B. Attribution to States and International Organisations

Given the many actors that may be involved in pushbacks and pullbacks, it is necessary to determine to which State and/or IO such conduct is attributable.

i. Pushbacks

Pushbacks performed directly by the destination State raise no attribution issues as they are carried out by State organs (ie, border forces or naval units), satisfying Article 4 of ARSIWA.[146] When States conduct joint operations and patrols (such as in South Asia, by Indonesia and Australia, or previously Italy and Albania), this should trigger attribution to each State, depending on the level of command or authority each State's officials have.[147] When rescue operations are conducted by private vessels, there is generally no link between the rescued people and the flag State.[148] However, where private vessels are entrusted to exercise governmental authority or act on instructions from a destination State's MRCC to 'rescue' migrants and cooperate with a partner State, such conduct is attributable to the destination State under Articles 5 or 8 of ARSIWA.[149] In situations involving instructions, the destination State's coordination is decisive in directing the vessel's actions and determining the fate of the migrants, ie, Italy and Malta instructing merchant vessels to return migrants to Libya.[150] The control link would be even stronger where private vessels are officially contracted for such purposes.[151] Dual attribution is also likely with the third State involved, ie, Libya, in jointly directing the vessel and forcing migrants to disembark under Articles 4 and 8 of ARSIWA.[152]

[146] *MK* (n 119) para 130; Gammeltoft-Hansen and Hathaway (n 3) 268.

[147] See ARSIWA Commentary, 44 para 3, 64; *Certain Phosphate Lands in Nauru (Nauru v Australia)* (Preliminary Objections) [1992] ICJ Rep 240.

[148] Papastavridis, 'European Convention' (n 112) 432.

[149] See *Mansouri* (n 116) paras 57–62, where events were attributable to Italy who had vested public-authority powers in the captain of a private ship to confine an individual on board and return them to their country of origin.

[150] *SDG* (n 78) para 100; UNHCR, 'Submission by the Office of the United Nations High Commissioner for Refugees in the case of *S.S. and Others v Italy* (Appl No 21660/18) before the European Court of Human Rights' (14 November 2019)' para 4.5; Papastavridis, 'European Convention' (n 112) 432.

[151] Alarm Phone (n 78); ARSIWA Commentary, 43 para 2, 47 para 1.

[152] See *SDG* (n 78) paras 6, 14.

In the Mediterranean and Aegean Seas, EU Member States may engage in pushbacks during Frontex and NATO operations, raising complex attribution issues. In Frontex operations, attribution depends on whether the conduct is attributable only to the host State, participating States, and/or the EU.[153] Scholars have highlighted longstanding concerns about the unclear division of responsibilities between the Agency and Member States and lack of transparency and accurate information on arrangements.[154] During joint operations, the host State retains operational command, with teams of Frontex standing corps, including Frontex staff and national guards deployed and seconded by Member States to Frontex.[155] Technical equipment and assets come from Members and Frontex. Although the host State instructs teams and formally has full operational command, participating States maintain some authority and command over their assets and personnel.[156] States contributing large assets can also issue instructions and retain command over their vessels, aeroplanes, and personnel, and can also sometimes authorise measures against vessels.[157] As such, the actual chain of command is far less established and the 'multi-layered authority structure' allows all actors to influence operations.[158]

The conduct of deployed personnel is *prima facie* attributable to their contributing entity under Article 4 ARSIWA and Article 6 ARIO.[159] However, where officials are placed under the host State's exclusive command and exercise governmental authority (ie, perform interdictions) on its behalf, Article 6 ARSIWA transfers attribution from the participating State to the host.[160] No clear rule governs the attribution of IO organs (Frontex staff) to the host State. It has been assumed that Article 6 of ARSIWA applies by analogy to these secondments.[161] Though Frontex presents itself as a mere coordinator, it plays a decisive role in operations. It funds operations, manages and deploys resources, coordinates tactical and operational planning, and provides intelligence, considerably limiting host State control.[162] Frontex officers have reportedly also

[153] For comprehensive studies on Frontex responsibility see R Mungianu, *Frontex and Non-Refoulement: The International Responsibility of the EU* (Cambridge, CUP, 2016); Fink (n 35).
[154] See den Heijer (n 26) 268–69; JJ Rijpma, 'External Migration and Asylum Management: Accountability for Executive Action Outside EU-territory' (2017) 2 *European Papers* 571, 588; Moreno-Lax, *Accessing Asylum* (n 36) 160.
[155] Frontex Regulation, preamble 17, 20–22, arts 54–57, 70, 78, 82(6); Fink (n 35) 45–58.
[156] Frontex Regulation, art 82(4), (8).
[157] Sea Borders Regulation, arts 2(5), 6(4)–(6), 7(4)–(6), (9), (11); Frontex Regulation, arts 43(5), 45; M Fernandez 'The EU External Borders Policy and Frontex-Coordinated Operations at Sea: Who is in Charge? Reflections on Responsibility for Wrongful Acts' in V Moreno-Lax and E Papastavridis (eds), *'Boat Refugees' and Migrants at Sea: A Comprehensive Approach: Integrating Maritime Security with Human Rights* (Dordrecht, Brill Nijhoff, 2016) 393–94; Fink (n 35) 69–70, 124–26, 140.
[158] Fernandez (n 157); Fink (n 35) 66–67, 124–25.
[159] Fink (n 35) 111–13, 122.
[160] See den Heijer (n 26) 267–68; Mungianu (n 153) 61–73; Rijpma (n 154) 588.
[161] ARSIWA Commentary, 45 para 9; Fink (n 35) 122–23.
[162] Sea Borders Regulation, preamble 18, art 2(6), (7); Frontex Regulation, arts 21, 38, 43(2), (3), 44; I Majcher, 'Human Rights Violations during EU Border Surveillance and Return Operations: Frontex' Shared Responsibility or Complicity?' (2015) 7 *Silesian Journal of Legal Studies* 45, 60–64;

engaged in independent patrols in Greece, which would lead to attribution to the EU (Article 6 ARIO).[163] Frontex's operational role suggests that Frontex teams could, at times, be under its effective control per Article 7 ARIO.[164]

Consequently, Frontex teams cannot always be said to be *exclusively* under the host State's command, rendering Article 6 of ARSIWA inapplicable. The ARIO Commentary envisions multiple attribution, while the Frontex Regulation recognises the shared responsibility of the Agency and national authorities.[165] Thus, pushbacks during joint operations could be attributable to the host State, participating States (except where only minor equipment is provided), and Frontex/the EU (Articles 4 ARSIWA, 6 and 7 ARIO).[166] Later in the chapter, rebuttal of the *Bosphorus* presumption and issues of responsibility for complicity and failure to protect are explored.

NATO missions follow a different structure. In the Aegean, NATO patrols involve a multinational maritime force comprising assets permanently placed at NATO's disposal by allied States, supplemented by allied ships, and operating alongside Greek and Turkish units. Under the command of a lead State's Rear Admiral and NATO's central authority, it can be presumed NATO exercises effective control over the force, making any pushback attributable to it under Article 7 of ARIO, even if individual States act against instructions.[167] However, if Greece, Turkey or another State retain sufficient command over their assets, dual attribution with NATO is possible. NATO's *Operation Sea Guardian* in the Mediterranean follows much the same structure, although allied States can operate independently, which may allow for dual attribution depending on the circumstances.[168]

It briefly bears mentioning that under shiprider agreements, the conduct of shipriders from third States cannot be attributed solely to the destination State: each State retains enforcement powers and jurisdiction, meaning Article 6 of ARSIWA does not apply.[169] Such operations are best classified as concerted

Fernandez (n 157) 398–402; Moreno-Lax, *Accessing Asylum* (n 36) 180; M Gkliati, 'The Next Phase of The European Border and Coast Guard: Responsibility for Returns and Push-backs in Hungary and Greece' (2022) 7 *European Papers* 171, 189–90.

[163] Gammeltoft-Hansen and Hathaway (n 3) 268–69.

[164] See Fink (n 35) 136–41; Gkliati (n 162) 185–86.

[165] ARIO Commentary, ch II 54 para 4. See also *Jaloud* (n 120) para 146; Frontex Regulation, preamble 12, art 7(1); Gammeltoft-Hansen and Hathaway (n 3) 275–76; Majcher (n 162) 54–55, 64.

[166] Fernandez (n 157) 398–403.

[167] NATO, 'Assistance' (n 41) including fact sheet; ARIO, art 8; Cowles (n 41). See also N David, *The International Responsibility of NATO and its Personnel during Military Operations* (Boston, Brill Nijhoff, 2017) 155–65; T Dannenbaum, 'Dual Attribution in the Context of Military Operations' in AS Barros, C Ryngaert and J Wouters (eds), *International Organizations and Member State Responsibility* (Leiden, Brill Nijhoff, 2017).

[168] NATO, 'Operation Sea Guardian', www.mc.nato.int/missions/operation-sea-guardian.

[169] Den Heijer (n 26) 269–70; M Giuffré, 'State Responsibility Beyond Borders: What Legal Basis for Italy's Push-backs to Libya?' (2012) 24 *International Journal of Refugee Law* 692, 724–25; Markard (n 108) 611, 614. See for Canada-US, Integrated Cross-Border Maritime Law Enforcement Operations Act, SC 2012, c 19 (Canada) s 12.

acts, leading to joint responsibility.[170] Where shipriders are used during Frontex operations, Frontex may share responsibility, directly or indirectly, with both the host and third State.

ii. Pullbacks

Pullbacks are performed by the third State on behalf of the destination State or EU, raising distinct challenges. Pullbacks are directly attributable to that third State under Article 4 of ARSIWA (or Article 8 if private vessels are co-opted, as with Libya).[171] Even if institutions are fragmented, such as those partially controlled by militias like the LBCG, Article 4 will generally be satisfied if they are held out as formally operating under the State's Ministry of Defence and acting as a State organ.[172]

The key issue is whether pullbacks can be attributed to the destination State (or EU) for potential violations of the right to leave. Conduct, such as directing and instructing third parties, providing support, funding and equipment, and placing border guards in the territory of another State, will generally be directly attributable to the sending/destination State per Article 4. However, according to the ARSIWA Commentary, Article 6 does not cover inter-State cooperation and Article 8 only concerns non-State actors, leaving no clear attribution route to the destination State for the pullback itself under ARSIWA.[173] Coastguards or officials from third States are not fully integrated with the destination State's machinery, especially when operating in their own territory.[174] Some guidance may be offered by the Strasbourg Court's extraordinary rendition case law, in which the unlawful conduct has been attributed to the respondent State 'for acts performed by foreign officials on its territory with the acquiescence or connivance of its authorities', but generally the Court tends to address complicity through positive obligations.[175] As such, section VI will explore the responsibility of destination States for failing to uphold their positive obligations and for complicity and direction and control over pullbacks.

[170] ARSIWA, art 47; *Hirsi Jamaa* (n 28) 78 (Separate Opinion Albuquerque J); GS Goodwin-Gill, 'The Right to Seek Asylum: Interception at Sea and the Principle of *Non-Refoulement*' (2011) 23 *International Journal of Refugee Law* 443, 453. cf den Heijer (n 26) 269.

[171] Gammeltoft-Hansen and Hathaway (n 3) 268; Giuffré (n 169) 723; Giuffré and Moreno-Lax (n 26) 107.

[172] Libya–Italy MoU, art 1(c); Forensic Oceanography (n 125) 19, 31, 37–39.

[173] ARSIWA Commentary, 44 paras 2, 4. cf UNHCR, 'Submission' (n 150) para 4.5; Gammeltoft-Hansen and Hathaway (n 3) 268; GLAN, 'Submission to the Independent Fact-Finding Mission on Libya on the EU and Member States' Responsibilities for Libyan Abuses Against Migrants' (2021) para 10.

[174] ARSIWA Commentary, 44 fn 130 mentions *Xhavara* (n 117) on Italian patrols not being attributable to Albania; Pijnenburg, 'Italian Pushbacks' (n 74) 412; V Stoyanova, 'The Right to Leave Any Country and the Interplay between Jurisdiction and Proportionality in Human Rights Law' (2020) 32 *International Journal of Refugee Law* 403, 419–20.

[175] *El-Masri v Former Yugoslav Republic of Macedonia* (2013) 57 EHRR 25, para 206; Pijnenburg, 'Italian Pushbacks' (n 74) 412–13.

For EU (not Frontex) partnerships with third States, attribution of pullbacks under Article 7 of ARIO depends on whether the EU exercises effective control. While the EU provides extensive support and conditions aid and visa liberalisation on third States stemming irregular migration and conducting 'rescues', it is implausible that the third State loses command over its organs. During Frontex operations in third States, that State acts as host and instructs the Frontex team per the Operational Plan.[176] The Frontex team deployed comprises Member States' officials who are placed under the third State's control and command, which suggests that their conduct is attributable to the third State, applying Article 6 ARSIWA.[177] However, as noted above, ambiguity remains about whether the conduct of Frontex officials can be attributed to the host State. Frontex Liaison Officers deployed to non-EU states likely possess some control and may issue directions to the third State.[178] Given that the EU, Frontex and participating Member States play a critical role in joint operations with third States, adopting a multiple attribution framework that attributes the pullback to each party under ARSIWA or ARIO would be most appropriate. Alternatively, the derived responsibility of the EU and Member States can be assessed.

In summary, pushbacks are attributable to the destination State, including privatised ones, and may also be dually attributable to a third State. Depending on the precise circumstances – and reiterating the lack of transparency – pushbacks during Frontex operations are attributable to the host State, major contributing States and the EU, provided multiple attribution is accepted. For NATO missions, dual attribution arises only where control is shared with the intercepting State. Pullbacks arguably cannot be attributed to the destination State and attribution to the EU or Frontex would require multiple attribution. Where attribution fails, recourse to derived responsibility is necessary.

V. PUSHBACKS AND PULLBACKS AS VIOLATIONS OF THE RIGHT TO LEAVE

The analysis now examines whether pushbacks and pullbacks at sea and on land violate the right to leave. Pushbacks and pullbacks are addressed together, as they raise many analogous issues, with key differences noted. It is concluded that, except where classified as genuine rescues, pushbacks and pullbacks violate the right to leave of (would-be) migrants. They are highly disproportionate, blanket and indiscriminate measures that undermine the essence of the right and obstruct the search for asylum, preventing the duty to admit from arising. While States may claim legitimate aims, these are often vague, conceal true motives,

[176] Frontex Regulation, art 43(1).
[177] ibid arts 54(6), 73(3), 76(1); Rijpma (n 154) 593–94; Fink (n 35) 43–45.
[178] Frontex Regulation, art 77.

and can be counterproductive. Pushbacks and pullbacks also fail to meet the 'in accordance with law' requirement and are accompanied by serious, well-documented human rights violations.

A. Interference

First, it must be determined whether pushbacks and pullbacks interfere with the right to leave. As chapter two established, any measure curtailing departure can constitute an interference, including attacks on migrant boats as in *Victims of the Tugboat '13 de Marzo' v Cuba*.[179] Pullbacks are a blatant interference with leaving, as affirmed by UN experts.[180] Recall that the Committee on Migrant Workers has also stated that Libya's pullback of migrants at sea violates the right of migrant workers and their families to leave.[181] Notably, in *SS v Italy* the right to leave was not pleaded, given the jurisdictional hurdles.[182]

In contrast, the right to leave has been invoked in a pending Human Rights Committee complaint against Italy, Malta and Libya, which argues that a pullback by the LBCG, with Italian and Maltese cooperation, violates the right to leave Libya and leads to the denial of other fundamental rights.[183] Similarly, another complaint against Italy contended that a privatised pushback to Libya on the high seas, orchestrated by Italy, constituted an undue interference with the right to leave, incompatible with a *bona fide* interpretation and implementation of the right.[184]

Pullbacks, by design and effect, obstruct departure for destination States. Arrangements like the EU–Turkey deal, US–Mexico agreement, and the Australian–Indonesian model all require third States to act as gatekeepers and to deny exit and contain migrants in their country of origin or transit.[185] Whether occurring just before departure, like pre-emptive 'rescues', further out at sea or when migrants attempt to cross a land border, pullbacks deny exit. Although under UNCLOS departure is technically complete once the vessel leaves the territorial sea, pullbacks beyond this nonetheless frustrate the right to leave and deprive it of meaningful effect.[186] States should not be able to wait until the boat

[179] IACHR, Case 11.436, Report No. 47/96 (16 October 1996) OEA/Ser.L/V/II.95 Doc 7 Rev at 127.

[180] UNGA, 'Report of the Special Rapporteur on Torture and Other Cruel, Inhuman or Degrading Treatment or Punishment' (23 November 2018) A/HRC/37/50, para 55.

[181] CMW, 'Concluding Observations on the Initial Report of Libya' (8 May 2019) UN Doc CMW/C/LBY/CO/1 paras 32–33.

[182] See McDonnell (n 1).

[183] ASGI and CIHRS, 'Complaint to the UN Human Rights Committee Over the Role of Italy, Malta, and Libya in Violating the Right to Leave Libya, Resulting in Denial of the Rights of Asylum Seekers' (Press Release, 24 July 2020) www.statewatch.org/media/1267/un-asgi-cihrs-complaint-libya-pull-backs-pr-24-7-20.pdf.

[184] *SDG* (n 78) paras 94–100.

[185] Giuffré and Moreno-Lax (n 26) 95, 107.

[186] UNCLOS, art 2. This maps national airspace, Chicago Convention, arts 1–2.

crosses the territorial sea and inhibit leaving *carte blanche*.[187] A good faith interpretation recognises interference even beyond the territorial sea.

Engaging the right is a low threshold: individuals need not prove no alternatives exist, and they possess the right to exit in any direction.[188] Nevertheless, even when other corridors theoretically remain open, containment arrangements severely limit lawful and safe departure, with alternatives often being dangerous and effectively unavailable. Migrants in transit have several 'choices': return home; leave for neighbouring States where they may also face ill-treatment or hardship (ie, a migrant in Libya who has escaped from detention might be able to leave to Egypt but not Italy); wait for evacuation, an asylum hearing or resettlement in a potentially harmful or intolerable situation (ie, under the Remain in Mexico policy or in limbo in Indonesia); or leave and try to secure admission to a destination State.[189]

As chapter two argued, alternatives should not preclude engagement of the right.[190] Instead, complete denial of leaving shows their disproportionate nature. Nor does the fact that pullbacks simultaneously operate to prevent 'unlawful' entry bar their classification as an interference. Rights protect individual interests, not State prerogatives.[191] Critically, as chapter three concluded, given the right to leave's independent nature, States cannot justify pullbacks by pointing to destination States' possible refusal to admit. Third States are enlisted precisely to prevent migrants asserting their right of entry.

Whether pushbacks interfere with leaving is more contentious, as they often occur well after departure and may primarily target entry. However, as Part I's analysis shows, the proper focus is whether the measure also controls exit and deprives the right to leave of meaningful effect by obstructing the migrant's search for refuge and a State to admit them – an interpretation supported by a former Council of Europe Commissioner on Human Rights.[192] As argued, *Xhavara* was wrongly decided, overlooking how Italy's actions simultaneously prevented exit and entry. It should not be decisive that the measure took place on the high seas, after formal departure occurs.[193] Some pushbacks occur at borders where exit and entry cannot easily be separated, such as the short stretch between Turkey and Greece, where many Greek Islands lie so close to the Turkish mainland that their territorial waters adjoin, making departure relatively contingent on immediate entry into another State. Regardless, as Part I demonstrated, destination States remain duty-bound to respect the right and

[187] VCLT, arts 26, 31(1); den Heijer (n 26) 161–62; Markard (n 108) 596–97.

[188] Markard (n 108) 596.

[189] Stoyanova, 'Right to Leave' (n 174) 412. See for children, V Digidiki and J Bhabha, 'Against the Best Interests of the Child: The Global Injustice of Migrant Externalization' in L Weber and C Tazreiter (eds), *Handbook of Migration and Global Justice* (Cheltenham, Edward Elgar Publishing, 2021).

[190] cf Stoyanova, 'Right to Leave' (n 174) 407–10.

[191] ibid 413–14.

[192] E Guild, *The Right to Leave a Country* (Issue Paper, Council of Europe Commissioner for Human Rights, 2013) 7–8, 53.

[193] cf Stoyanova, 'Right to Leave' (n 174) 415.

not obstruct departure from third States. Accordingly, moving beyond a strictly territorialised reading of the right to leave, pushbacks in such instances can be deemed interferences.

Joint operations in a third State's territorial waters involving pushbacks by destination States cannot be said to focus only on entry; they seek to control exit to avoid having to control the entry of irregular migrants altogether.[194] Returns to the edge of territorial waters, handovers to a partner country, and pushbacks on land deprive the right to leave of substance and obstruct the right to seek asylum.[195] This is stark when migrants are repeatedly pushed back or face dangerous manoeuvre tactics that force them to turn back for fear of drowning. Similarly, walls also interfere with the right, preventing migrants from crossing into another State and triggering protective obligations.[196] Migrants are back where they began – the place from which they fled.

Of course, not every return or refusal of entry interferes with the right to leave. A distinction must be drawn between a migrant being denied entry at the border following proper consideration of their individual circumstances and a summary pushback without due process.[197] In 1997, the Human Rights Committee affirmed that France's refusal to let asylum seekers disembark at its ports to claim asylum engaged the right to leave.[198] As Stoyanova observes, the more meaningful consideration the State gives to individual circumstances, the easier it is to conclude that the operation concerns unauthorised entry, and depending on subsequent measures, *non-refoulement* (or collective expulsion) would be the applicable obligation.[199] However, as the sections below explain further, this is not the case for pushbacks, which can result in *refoulement* and render the right to leave ineffective.

In conclusion, pullbacks interfere with the right to leave. While more complex, pushbacks should also be understood as an interference. Accordingly, the right to leave constrains how States conduct interceptions, and unless pushbacks and pullbacks meet strict requirements, they will amount to violations.

B. In Accordance with Law

The second requirement under the right to leave is whether pushbacks and pullbacks are 'in accordance with law'. This entails a legal basis and compliance with the quality of law test outlined in chapter two. It is widely accepted that

[194] R Weinzierl and U Lisson, *Border Management and Human Rights: A Study of EU Law and the Law of the Sea* (Berlin, German Institute for Human Rights, 2007) 3, 70; Markard (n 108) 616; Fink (n 35) 44.

[195] Den Heijer (n 26) 160–61, 258–59.

[196] Paz, 'Law of Walls' (n 24) 604, 613–14.

[197] See den Heijer (n 26) 161–62.

[198] HRC, 'Concluding Observations of the Human Rights Committee: France' (4 August 1997) UN Doc CCPR/C/79/Add.80, para 20.

[199] Stoyanova, 'Right to Leave' (n 174) 415–16.

most pushback and pullback operations rest on unstable legal foundations, are highly arbitrary, and lack the foreseeability and safeguards required by international law.[200]

The first key question is whether these practices are prescribed by law (domestic, EU or international). As previously noted, pushbacks differ from lawful refusals of entry or removals under domestic law. Domestic legal frameworks often include saving clauses, requiring compliance with international human rights and refugee law, indicating that pushbacks are unlikely to actually meet domestic or EU laws.[201] Furthermore, as set out in chapter two, non-binding or publicly inaccessible sources, such as internal policies or administrative orders, typically fail to meet the legality standard. This includes, for example, the expedited removal of asylum seekers at the US border, authorised by presidential orders and proclamations issued by successive administrations.[202] By contrast, certain national and EU laws do purport to provide authority: Australian law, for instance, permits vessels to be boarded and 'taken' to another destination, while EU law empowers Frontex to intercept vessels suspected of smuggling or circumvention of border controls and hand over those on board to a third State.[203] Frontex and EUNAVFOR operations are further grounded in EU Council decisions.[204] The US has often relied on agreements with third countries to legitimise interdiction operations at sea and cooperation at land borders.[205]

Contemporary practices in Europe increasingly involve the legalisation of pushbacks and the possibility of derogating from asylum law in response to so-called 'migratory crises' or 'instrumentalisation'. This was exemplified by the influx of migrants at the EU–Belarus border from 2021. Migrants were reified as 'weapons' in a 'hybrid attack' orchestrated by Belarus, which relaxed its visa regime for several refugee-producing countries, facilitated their arrival to Minsk, and stopped preventing irregular migration to the EU.[206]

[200] See eg den Heijer (n 26) 256, 259; E Papastavridis, '"Fortress Europe" and FRONTEX: Within or Without International Law?' (2010) 79 *Nordic Journal of International Law* 75, 99–100; Stoyanova, 'Right to Leave' (n 174) 427.

[201] See eg Regulation (EU) 2016/399 of the European Parliament and of the Council of 9 March 2016 on a Union Code on the rules governing the movement of persons across borders (Schengen Borders Code) [2016] OJ L 77/1, arts 3–4, 6(5)(c), 14; *ND and NT* (n 30) on Spanish domestic laws.

[202] See Amnesty International and others, 'Explainer on U.S. Deportations and Expulsions During the COVID-19 Pandemic' (21 May 2020) www.amnestyusa.org/wp-content/uploads/2020/05/Explainer-on-Deportations-and-Expulsions-During-the-COVID-19-Pandemic-1.pdf; HRW, 'US: Biden' (n 23).

[203] Maritime Powers Act 2013 (Cth) s 21, pt 3 divs 2, 7–9 (MPA); Sea Borders Regulation, arts 6–8. See also P Mathew, 'Legal Issues Concerning Interception' (2003) 17 *Georgetown Immigration Law Journal* 221 on Australia's reliance on powers in the contiguous zone to justify turnbacks.

[204] See TEU, arts 42(4), 43(2); Council Decision (CFSP) 2020/472.

[205] KH Tennis, *Outsourcing Control: The Politics of International Migration Cooperation* (Montreal, McGill-Queen's University Press, 2020) chs 2–3.

[206] See V Moreno-Lax, 'The "Crisification" of Migration Law: Insights from the EU External Border' in SB Elias, K Cope and J Goldenziel (eds), *The Oxford Handbook of Comparative Immigration Law* (Oxford, OUP, 2023); A Ancite-Jepifánova, 'Beyond the "Hybrid Attack"

In response, Latvia, Lithuania and Poland amended their domestic laws to authorise pushbacks.[207] Thousands of migrants were repeatedly pushed back by both Latvian and Belarusian forces, stranding them between borders without access to protection. In 2024, as part of the new Pact, the EU adopted a crisis and force majeure regulation, further entrenching 'exceptional' measures, as well as new accelerated border procedures with fewer safeguards.[208] Finland and the UK have also enacted laws authorising pushbacks, citing Russia's instrumentalisation of migration and Channel crossings, respectively.[209] However, such authority under domestic or regional law does not guarantee compliance with international law, which imposes significant constraints on these practices.

While SAR operations have a legal basis under the law of the sea, interdiction and enforcement actions are more controversial. UNCLOS and the Smuggling Protocol do not clearly authorise actions beyond stop-and-search.[210] Article 8(7) of the Smuggling Protocol refers to 'appropriate measures' against stateless vessels if evidence is found confirming suspicions, but this is vague and open to abuse.[211] Scholars generally agree that enforcement-style actions – interdictions, returns to port, arrest or detention – exceed the right of visit.[212] Therefore, even when authorised by domestic or EU law, pushbacks and pullbacks go beyond what is permissible under international law. Even where flag and coastal States authorise actions in their waters, enforcement measures cannot override international obligations, particularly when enforcement exceeds what is necessary to protect the coastal State's immigration interests.[213]

Paradigm: EU-Belarus Border Crisis and the Erosion of Asylum-Seeker Rights in Latvia, Lithuania and Poland' (2024) 15 *Avant* 1.

[207] Ancite-Jepifánova (n 206) 1. In May 2025, Lithuania instituted proceedings at the ICJ against Belarus, alleging breaches of the Smuggling Protocol by facilitating large-scale smuggling of irregular migrants into Lithuania: *Alleged Smuggling of Migrants (Lithuania v Belarus)* 19 May 2025.

[208] Regulation (EU) 2024/1359 of the European Parliament and of the Council of 14 May 2024 addressing situations of crisis and force majeure in the field of migration and asylum and amending Regulation (EU) 2021/1147 [2024] OJ L 2024/1359; ECRE, 'ECRE Comments Paper: Regulation on Addressing Situations of Crisis and Force Majeure in the Field of Migration and Asylum' (2024) www.ecre.org/comments-paper-regulation-on-addressing-situations-of-crisis-and-force-majeure-in-the-field-of-migration-and-asylum/.

[209] Nationality and Borders Act 2022 (UK) sch 7 (NABA); Finland, which some scholars have defended: J Pirjola, 'Hostile Instrumentalized Migration and the Right to Seek Asylum: Reflecting the European Legal Framework' (2025) 27 *European Journal of Migration and Law* 1.

[210] Guilfoyle (n 96) ch 8; Papastavridis, *Interception* (n 96) 264–67; T Coventry, 'Appropriate Measures at Sea: Extraterritorial Enforcement Jurisdiction over Stateless Migrant Smuggling Vessels' (2019) *Maritime Safety and Security Law Journal* 5, 9–10, 15–21.

[211] See for analogy *Medvedyev* (n 113) para 95.

[212] Goodwin-Gill and McAdam (n 108) 335–37; Moreno-Lax, 'Seeking Asylum' (n 98) 186–88 and fns; Papastavridis, *Interception* (n 96) 264–67. See also Klein (n 32) ch 3, cf 143 citing Becker.

[213] Smuggling Protocol, art 8(2); Goodwin-Gill and McAdam (n 108) 337–39. cf Papastavridis, 'Fortress' (n 200) 93.

A significant issue in both limbs of the legality test is the opaque and informal nature of many migration control agreements. While some agreements – such as EUNAVFOR mandates or some US deals – are public and formalised, many are informal, publicly inaccessible and non-binding.[214] This includes EU mobility partnerships, dialogues, memoranda of understanding (MoUs) and statements, and Australia's exchange of letters with Indonesia and IOM, all of which lack legal precision and public scrutiny.[215] Frontex's Operational Plans, likewise, are not public, and the details surrounding operations are largely unknown.[216] While Frontex is mandated to uphold human rights and has appointed fundamental rights monitors, these measures have proved insufficient to ensure effective oversight or prevent the Agency's involvement in past violations.[217] Partnerships under which third States agree to perform pullbacks are often embedded in aid, trade and visa deals. While such arrangements may proclaim compliance with international obligations, they lack sufficient transparency and oversight, thus undermining essential safeguards.

Where a legal basis does exist, it often fails to meet the quality of law test. Many authorising laws and agreements lack legal certainty and procedural safeguards, failing to protect migrants from arbitrary interference with their right to leave. They fail to specify the grounds, conditions, or procedures for interception or obstruction of departure with sufficient precision.[218] The consequence for migrants remains unclear. Agreements and laws either broadly authorise interception or frame their aim as preventing irregular migration.[219] For instance, the 2017 Italy–Libya MoU only mentions 'stemming illegal migration', without legal clarity on pullbacks.[220] As the Strasbourg Court held in *Medvedyev*, vague or ad hoc authorisations cannot satisfy the requirement that measures be 'prescribed by law,' especially where physical security is at stake.[221] Consequently, legal bases that do not explicitly grant States the power to prevent migrants from leaving should be understood as not permitting such actions.[222] Current frameworks leave migrants unable to foresee how or when

[214] See den Heijer (n 26) 259–61.

[215] C Molinari, 'The EU and its Perilous Journey Through the Migration Crisis: Informalisation of the EU Return Policy and Rule of Law Concerns' (2019) 44 *European Law Review* 824; Giuffré and Moreno-Lax (n 26) 95; V Stoyanova, 'The Right to Life under the EU Charter and Cooperation with Third States to Combat Human Smuggling' (2020) 21 *German Law Journal* 436, 443–44.

[216] Fink (n 35) 339–41.

[217] Frontex Regulation, arts 109–10. T Strik, 'Frontex's Expanding Mandate: Has Democratic Control Caught Up?' (2024) 30 *European Law Journal* 217.

[218] Den Heijer (n 26) 260–61.

[219] See eg Sea Borders Regulation arts 6–8; NABA (UK) schedule 7.

[220] Art 1(a). See E Guild and V Stoyanova, 'The Human Right to Leave Any Country: A Right to Be Delivered' in W Benedek and others (eds), *European Yearbook on Human Rights 2018* (Plymouth, Intersentia, 2018) 387; Giuffré (n 169) 702–05 on the absence of express provisions authorising pushbacks to Libya under earlier agreements.

[221] *Medvedyev* (n 113) paras 82–102. See also *Khlaifia v Italy*, App no 16483/12 (ECtHR, 1 September 2015) para 102.

[222] Den Heijer (n 26) 259–61.

their right to leave will be infringed, where they will be taken, whether they will be detained, or if their protection claims will be assessed. As a result, State authorities have almost unfettered discretion, resulting in arbitrariness.

The legal basis must also guarantee procedural safeguards, including independent review, access to asylum procedures, and effective remedies. In many cases, pushbacks and pullbacks occur outside clear procedural frameworks, with safeguards absent, ineffective or merely theoretical.[223] For example, under Australian law, boat turnbacks remain valid irrespective of Australia's international obligations, and the rules of natural justice do not apply.[224] In the US, restrictions on access to asylum enable summary expulsions outside regular removal processes, denying individuals basic due process, including the right to a hearing and opportunity to claim asylum. While the US Supreme Court upheld expedited removal without habeas corpus review in 2020, courts have repeatedly struck down asylum bans in recent years.[225]

In contrast, EU law requires full compliance with fundamental rights and international standards.[226] Before any return or before handing intercepted migrants over to a third State, Frontex must assess their personal circumstances, inform them of the proposed destination, and allow them to express that disembarkation there would amount to *refoulement*.[227] Yet, it is unclear how these obligations are complied with, given that onboard screenings are inherently inadequate and routinely fail to ensure effective protection from *refoulement* and collective expulsion, as argued in chapter three.[228] In Australia and the US, onboard screening is often cursory, while some migrants receive no screening at all, and demonstrating a fear of return or potential protection needs can lead to offshore processing on Nauru or Guantánamo.[229] Despite paying lip service to the letter of the law, many screenings will amount to summary returns with no effective assessment of individual protection needs.

These failures are enabled by the hidden nature of pushbacks and pullbacks, conducted 'out of sight and out of mind'. Australia has a policy of secrecy for

[223] ibid 164, 259–60.

[224] MPA 2013, ss 22A, 22B, 75A, 75B. However, the High Court clarified that under the relevant legislation, the maritime officer must be satisfied the destination is safe for the individual, *CPCF v Minister for Immigration and Border Protection* (2015) 255 CLR 514, paras 11–13, 104–119, 294.

[225] *Department of Homeland Security v Thuraissigiam* 140 S Ct 1959 (2020). eg *Huisha-Huisha v Mayorkas*, No 21-100 (2022); *Arizona v Mayorkas*, 598 US__(2022); *East Bay Sanctuary Covenant v Biden*, No 23-16032 (2024); *Las Americas Immigrant Advocacy Center v US Department of Homeland Security*, No 24-1702 (2025).

[226] See Frontex Regulation, arts 1, 36(2), 71–73, 80.

[227] Sea Borders Regulation, art 4.

[228] Moreno-Lax, *Interdiction* (n 15) 11–12. See also *Hirsi Jamaa* (n 28) para 185; den Heijer (n 26) 311–12.

[229] See eg Commonwealth, *Estimates*, Senate, 23 February 2015, 136–39; for US practice see *Haitian Centre* (n 9) paras 57, 120; D Ghezelbash, *Refuge Lost: Asylum Law in an Interdependent World* (Cambridge, CUP, 2018) chs 4, 5, particularly 100–03, 129–30; A Dastyari and D Ghezelbash, 'Asylum at Sea: The Legality of Shipboard Refugee Status Determination Procedures' (2020) 32 *International Journal of Refugee Law* 1, 16–24.

'on-water' matters, while Greek border practices, such as bow wave encirclement or abandonment on inflatable life rafts, often occur at night or far out at sea.[230] Given that many migrants go missing, lose their lives or are returned to third countries, migrants will find challenging their interception and accessing legal redress, in most cases, effectively impossible.[231] This is especially the case when courts, such as the Strasbourg Court, impose insurmountable evidentiary standards.[232] In 2024 alone, the LBCG pulled back nearly 21,000 migrants, many of whose fate remains unknown.[233]

Ultimately, migrants are denied effective remedies and are unable to vindicate their right to leave and other fundamental rights. IOs often remain shielded from accountability in the context of externalisation.[234] In the EU, the CJEU dismissed a challenge to the EU–Turkey statement on the grounds that it was not an EU act.[235] EUNAVFOR operations similarly fall outside the Court's jurisdiction, although the CJEU has gradually begun to expand its jurisdiction over certain aspects of the Common Foreign and Security Policy (CFSP).[236] Access to redress for actions by Frontex remains largely inaccessible to migrants due to legal, procedural and structural obstacles.[237] Several cases have been brought before the CJEU regarding Frontex's operations in the Aegean Sea and involvement in pushbacks, but all have been dismissed to date.[238] Following investigations uncovering Frontex's complicity in and cover-up of pushbacks by Greece, the Agency's new Executive Director vowed to end illegal pushbacks and

[230] Ghezelbash (n 229) 138.

[231] See *SDG* (n 78) para 104. But see Rome Court decisions ordering Italy to issue visas to pushed and pulled back migrants, SarítaLibre, 'Adam è a Roma! Il Tribunale ritiene l'Italia responsabile per aver trasmesso ai libici la posizione della sua barca' (24 March 2025) saritalibre.it/tribunale-libici-italia/.

[232] See *GRJ* (n 16).

[233] M MacGregor, 'Libya's Coast Guard has Intercepted and Returned Nearly 21,000 Migrants in 2024' (*Info Migrants*, 12 May 2024) www.infomigrants.net/en/post/61570/libyas-coast-guard-has-intercepted-and-returned-nearly-21000-migrants-in-2024.

[234] See T Spijkerboer, 'Bifurcation of People, Bifurcation of Law: Externalisation of Migration Policy before the EU Court of Justice' (2018) 31 *Journal of Refugee Studies* 216.

[235] *NF, NG and NM v Council*, Cases T-192/16, T-193/16 and T-257/16, EU:T:2017:128, EU:T:2017:129, EU:T:2017:130. See also *JR v Greece*, App no 22696/16 (ECtHR, 25 January 2018), finding that detention on a Greek hotspot pending their deportation under the EU-Turkey statement was lawful. See also, on the Libyan Supreme Court using formalities to uphold the Libya-Italy MoU, M Achour and T Spijkerboer, 'The Libyan Litigation about the 2017 Memorandum of Understanding between Italy and Libya' (*EU Immigration and Asylum Law and Policy*, 2 June 2020) www.eumigrationlawblog.eu/the-libyan-litigation-about-the-2017-memorandum-of-understanding-between-italy-and-libya/.

[236] TEU, art 24(1); TFEU, art 275; Rijpma (n 154) 594. But see *KS and KD v Council of the European Union*, Case C-29/22 P, EU:C:2024:725; L Schubert, 'Doing Too Much and Too Little: The CJEU's Approach to Judicial Review of Fundamental Rights Breaches in the CFSP After KD and KS' (*EJIL:Talk!*, 30 October 2024) www.ejiltalk.org/doing-too-much-and-too-little-the-cjeus-approach-to-judicial-review-of-fundamental-rights-breaches-in-the-cfsp-after-kd-and-ks/.

[237] See Majcher (n 162) 70–74; Fink (n 35) 4–5, 9, ch 4, 348–49.

[238] *SS and ST v Frontex*, Case T-282/21, EU:T:2022:235; *WS v Frontex*, Case T-600/21, EU:T:2023:492; *Hamoudi v Frontex*, Case T-136/22, EU:T:2023:821 (an appeal has now been filed under C-136/24). See McDonnell (n 1) 130; G Cornelisse, 'EU Boots on the Ground and Effective Judicial Protection Against Frontex' Operational Powers in Return: Lessons from Case T-600/21' (2024) 26 *European Journal of Migration and Law* 356.

Frontex has since launched investigations into several such incidents involving Greece.[239]

In conclusion, pushbacks and pullbacks typically fall far short of the legality requirements. They are designed to deflect migrants and operate in legal grey zones devoid of transparency and adequate safeguards. Although greater compliance is theoretically possible, most contemporary pushbacks and pullbacks fail at this stage, violating the right to leave.

C. Proportionality

This section examines whether pushbacks and pullbacks are proportionate to achieving the objectives they purport to serve. As will be demonstrated, compliance with the right to leave and other fundamental obligations necessitates ending such practices altogether.

i. Legitimate Aim

States may invoke a range of aims that plausibly fall within the permissible limitations on the right to leave, such as public order, public safety, protection of health and prevention of crime. However, the seemingly legitimate justifications of saving lives, supporting partner countries in border management, and preventing trafficking fail to withstand closer scrutiny.

a. Saving Lives and Protecting Migrants

States routinely frame restrictive migration measures as necessary to save lives by deterring and preventing migrants from embarking on perilous journeys.[240] Such justifications easily fall within the public safety and health exceptions, including to fulfil the duty to rescue persons in distress at sea and protect the right to life of individuals within the State's jurisdiction.[241] States, therefore, have a duty to protect the lives of those seeking to leave through irregular, dangerous means.

[239] OLAF, 'Final Report on Frontex' (2011) CASE No OC/2021/0451/A1, fragdenstaat.de/dokumente/233972-olaf-final-report-on-frontex/; R Maltezou and Y Souliotis, 'EU Border Agency Reviewing 12 Cases of Potential Rights Violations by Greece' (*Reuters*, 8 April 2025) www.reuters.com/world/europe/eu-border-agency-reviewing-12-cases-potential-rights-violations-by-greece-2025-04-08/; FRONTEX, 'Statement of Frontex Executive Management Following Publication of OLAF Report' (14 October 2022) www.frontex.europa.eu/media-centre/news/news-release/statement-of-frontex-executive-management-following-publication-of-olaf-report-amARYy; O Bizot, 'New Frontex Chief Vows to End Illegal Pushbacks of Migrants at Border' (*Euro News*, 19 January 2023) www.euronews.com/my-europe/2023/01/19/new-frontex-chief-vows-to-end-illegal-pushbacks-of-migrants-at-border.

[240] eg COM (2016) 385 final, 1–2.

[241] HRC, 'General Comment No 36 (2018) on Article 6 of the International Covenant on Civil and Political Rights, on the Right to Life' (30 October 2018) UN Doc CCPR/C/GC/36, paras 4, 6–7, 22, 63.

However, the good faith of these justifications is questionable. Under the guise of humanitarianism, States engage in pushbacks and pullbacks, fully aware of the ill-treatment, detention and dangers migrants will be exposed to in the place of return.[242] Rescue has been repurposed as interdiction, with destination States and Frontex manipulating the key legal concepts of 'distress' and 'place of safety'.[243] Even as they provide humanitarian aid to improve the reception conditions and asylum capacity of third countries, strengthen their search and rescue operations, promote and fund economic development, and facilitate legal pathways for third-country nationals, this occurs within the overarching aim of preventing irregular migration.[244] Under a thin humanitarian veil, States claim to save lives while simultaneously endangering them. As the UN Special Rapporteur on Extrajudicial, Summary or Arbitrary Executions warned, it cannot be acceptable 'to discourage exit out of countries where lives are endangered on the grounds that doing so saves lives from the dangers of border crossing: that is simply permitting a more secret death elsewhere'.[245] This is abundantly clear when States and the EU ignore distress calls, delay rescue leading to shipwrecks, or facilitate pullbacks to unsafe territories.[246]

Since most migrant boats are unseaworthy and 'in distress' by definition, the justifiability of coastal States obstructing departure reveals a potential conflict between the right to leave and duty of rescue, as discussed below.[247] Nonetheless, as courts and the UNHCR have affirmed, States cannot circumvent responsibility by framing pushbacks and pullbacks as rescues.[248] Disembarkation must occur in a genuine place of safety, which in the European context is generally only available in European States.[249] As argued in chapter two, restricting the right to leave becomes illegitimate when it frustrates the exercise of the

[242] See *SDG* (n 78) paras 10, 27, 65; D Davitti, 'Biopolitical Borders and the State of Exception in the European Migration "Crisis"' (2018) 29 *European Journal of International Law* 1173, 1183–84, 1187; Giuffré and Moreno-Lax (n 26) 97, 103; Macklin (n 90) 910–15.

[243] See V Moreno-Lax, 'Protection at Sea and the Denial of Asylum' in C Costello, M Foster and J McAdam (eds), *The Oxford Handbook of International Refugee Law* (Oxford, OUP, 2021).

[244] See Esene (n 86); A Amante and G Fonte, 'Italy Working with EU on Debt-relief Plan for Africa Tied to Development Projects' (*Reuters*, 20 June 2025) www.reuters.com/world/africa/italy-working-with-eu-debt-relief-plan-africa-tied-development-projects-2025-06-20/.

[245] UNGA, 'Special Rapporteur – Unlawful Death of Refugees and Migrants' (n 137) para 59.

[246] OHCHR, 'Note on Migrant Rescues in the Mediterranean' (Press Briefing, 8 May 2020) www.ohchr.org/EN/NewsEvents/Pages/DisplayNews.aspx?NewsID=25875&LangID=E; Alarm Phone and others (n 39); HRW, 'Greece: 6 Months On, No Justice for Pylos Shipwreck' (13 December 2023) www.hrw.org/news/2023/12/14/greece-6-months-no-justice-pylos-shipwreck; European Ombudsman, 'Decision on how the European Border and Coast Guard Agency (Frontex) complies with its fundamental rights obligations with regard to search and rescue in the context of its maritime surveillance activities, in particular the Adriana shipwreck' (26 February 2024) (OI/3/2023/MHZ).

[247] Moreno-Lax, 'Seeking Asylum' (n 98) 195–96.

[248] eg *Hirsi Jamaa* (n 28) para 79; UNHCR, 'Legal Considerations on Roles' (n 94) para 4.6.

[249] See A Farahat and N Markard, *Places of Safety in the Mediterranean: The EU's Policy of Outsourcing Responsibility* (Berlin, Heinrich-Böll-Stiftung, 2020).

right to seek asylum, as externalisation overtly aims to do. Unless States can demonstrate that their actions genuinely protect the lives of migrants, through bona fide rescues and disembarkation to a place of safety, such measures lack legitimacy.

During the Covid-19 pandemic, States across the Global South and North engaged in pushbacks and closed their borders, often without exceptions for asylum seekers, under the pretext of public health.[250] As the UNHCR stressed, 'denial of access to territory without safeguards to protect against *refoulement* cannot be justified on the grounds of any health risk'.[251] Similarly, Justice Gorsuch of the US Supreme Court observed that Title 42 was employed to severely restrict immigration, criticising the courts for allowing 'themselves to be used to perpetuate emergency public-health decrees for collateral purposes'.[252] Consequently, pushbacks and pullbacks that negate the right to seek asylum and risk *refoulement*, cannot be justified on public health grounds or to protect the right to life.

b. Human Trafficking and Smuggling

Pushbacks and pullbacks are also justified as measures to combat human trafficking and smuggling, objectives linked to the international public order explored in chapter two.[253] Both the Smuggling and Trafficking Protocols oblige States to strengthen border controls as necessary and, in the case of the Smuggling Protocol, to cooperate to the fullest extent possible to suppress migrant smuggling by sea.[254] As Hathaway aptly argues, the Protocols' emphasis on intensified border control provides destination States with a legal basis to implement deterrence measures and collaborate with third States, bolstering their capacity to stymie the flight of asylum seekers.[255] On the surface, the Palermo Protocols make it legitimate for States to control departure.

[250] See UN, 'Policy Brief: COVID-19 and People on the Move' (2020) 19–20, www.unsdg.un.org/resources/policy-brief-covid-19-and-people-move; D Ghezelbash and NF Tan, 'The End of the Right to Seek Asylum? COVID-19 and the Future of Refugee Protection' (2021) 32 *International Journal of Refugee Law* 668; AFP, 'Another Rohingya Boat Turned Back from Malaysia Waters' (*New Straits Times*, 11 June 2020); MV Espinoza, 'Migration Governance in South America: Change and Continuity in Times of "Crisis"' in H Crawley and JK Teye (eds), *The Palgrave Handbook of South–South Migration and Inequality* (Cham, Palgrave Macmillan, 2024) 643–44.

[251] UNHCR, 'Key Legal Considerations on Access to Territory for Persons in Need of International Protection in the Context of the COVID-19 Response' (16 March 2020) para 6.

[252] *Arizona v Mayorkas* 598 U. S. ____ (2023) 6.

[253] See eg Commission, 'Migration on the Central Mediterranean Route. Managing Flows, Saving Lives' (Communication) JOIN (2017) 4 final, 2, 5-9; The Bali Process, 'The Bali Process on People Smuggling, Trafficking in Persons and Related Transnational Crime' www.baliprocess.net.

[254] Trafficking Protocol, arts 5, 9–11; Smuggling Protocol, arts 7, 8(2), (5), 10–14.

[255] JC Hathaway, 'The Human Rights Quagmire of "Human Trafficking"' (2008) 49 *Virginia Journal of International Law* 1, 6, 12–13, 25–35, 41. See also C Harvey and RP Barnidge, 'Human Rights, Free Movement, and the Right to Leave in International Law' (2007) 19 *International Journal of Refugee Law* 1, 14; Wolman (n 7) 49–51.

In practice, the Smuggling Protocol has been interpreted too broadly, often criminalising many forms of mobility and humanitarian assistance, and being misused as a tool against migration more generally.[256] The Protocol defines migrant smuggling narrowly: as the procurement of illegal entry for financial or material benefit, which applies only to transnational offences involving organised criminal groups.[257] Accordingly, legitimate anti-smuggling efforts must target transnational, organised crime for gain. Crucially, the Protocols do not authorise free interference with the right to leave. They explicitly require that the rights of migrants be protected, and implementation of their provisions must not prejudice other obligations under international law, referencing commitments to free movement.[258] As such, the Protocols do not authorise pushback or pullback operations that violate the right to leave, the right to seek asylum, protection from *refoulement* and collective expulsion, or penalise asylum seekers in breach of Article 31 of the Refugee Convention. As Harvey and Barnidge argue, 'the right to leave one's own country is a fundamental human right, and this remains the case, notwithstanding a migrant's attempt to be smuggled'.[259] Thus, while States may invoke anti-smuggling objectives under the Palermo framework, any measures must be narrowly construed and remain fully consistent with the requirements under the right to leave.

c. Immigration Control and Preventing Irregular Migration

The broader aim of pushbacks and pullbacks is to prevent irregular migration and unlawful entry, enabling destination States to control immigration. Signatories to the Global Compact for Migration committed to manage national borders by facilitating safe, regular movement while preventing irregular migration.[260] This allows third States to claim that restricting departure to official ports with valid documentation serves legitimate public order goals. International human rights law also clearly accommodates the interests of States in controlling their borders.[261]

[256] See *R v Appulonappa* 2015 SCC 59, [2015] 3 SCR 754 (Canada); R Landry, 'The "Humanitarian Smuggling" of Refugees: Criminal Offence or Moral Obligation?' (2016) RSC Working Paper Series No 119, www.rsc.ox.ac.uk/publications/the-humanitarian-smuggling-of-refugees-criminal-offence-or-moral-obligation; AF Eltayeb, 'Why Is the EU-Khartoum Process So Wrong on So Many Levels' (*Sudan Tribune*, 6 November 2017) www.sudantribune.com/article62098/; S Kneebone and A Missbach, 'The Human Rights Implications of Australian and Indonesian Anti-Smuggling Laws' (2018) 4 *International Journal of Migration and Border Studies* 379; Perrin, 'Smuggling' (n 80).

[257] Smuggling Protocol, arts 3(a), 4.

[258] Trafficking Protocol, arts 2, 4–6, 11, 14; Smuggling Protocol, arts 2, 4–6, 9, 11, 16, 19. See Goodwin-Gill and McAdam (n 108) 418–20.

[259] Harvey and Barnidge (n 255) 14.

[260] UNGA, 'Global Compact for Safe, Orderly and Regular Migration' (11 January 2019) UN Doc A/RES/73/195, para 27.

[261] Stoyanova, 'Right to Life' (n 215) 450.

However, as this book demonstrates, the right to leave cannot be curtailed solely because entry into another State might be denied, undermining claims that controlling *entry* justifies restricting *exit*. It remains doubtful whether third States, including those designated as safe third countries, may lawfully restrict departure to prevent irregular migration to destination States. That public order encapsulates international concerns does not, in itself, justify such interference. As noted in chapter two, a UK proposal to this effect was rejected during ICCPR negotiations.[262] Markard similarly argues that under UNCLOS, enforcement actions in territorial waters and the contiguous zone is limited to preserving the coastal State's immigration laws, not those of others.[263] In *Stamose v Bulgaria*, the Strasbourg Court held that only compelling circumstances would justify restricting the right to leave to prevent breaches of another State's immigration laws.[264] Accordingly, pullbacks may only be legitimate where such compelling circumstances exist, such as where irregular migration is truly unmanageable (and not fostered by destination States) or part of responsibility sharing frameworks that guarantee effective protection for migrants.

Nevertheless, principled arguments exist to refute the legitimacy of pushbacks and pullbacks on these grounds. Fundamentally, such measures serve to externalise migration control and deflect obligations onto another State or evade them altogether, frustrating the right to seek asylum and preventing migrants from asserting any right of entry. As Chetail notes, the Global Compact glaringly omits any reference to the right to leave, revealing the political agenda espousing a preventive approach to migration.[265] While third States may have a shared interest in combatting smuggling and trafficking, these partnerships often reflect a desire to avoid sanctions or receive promised benefits. Legitimising pushbacks and pullbacks on this basis goes against a good faith reading of international obligations.

ii. Rational Connection, Necessity and Balancing

Accordingly, pushbacks and pullbacks may only be justified when narrowly and genuinely tailored to combatting smuggling or trafficking or protecting life and health, not as broad tools of migration deterrence. Proportionality requires that such measures must be suitable to achieving their stated objectives, the least intrusive means available, and strike a fair balance between the State's and individual interests, particularly for asylum seekers. Importantly, the burden lies on the State to demonstrate that its measures meet these criteria.

[262] Giuffré and Moreno-Lax (n 26) 98–99. See M Nowak, *UN Covenant on Civil and Political Rights: CCPR Commentary*, 2nd edn (Kehl am Rhein, NP Engel, 2005) 279.

[263] UNCLOS, arts 17, 19(2)(g), 33; Markard (n 108) 605, 613.

[264] *Stamose v Bulgaria*, App no 29713/05 (ECtHR, 27 November 2012), para 36.

[265] V Chetail, 'The Global Compact for Safe, Orderly and Regular Migration: A Kaleidoscope of International Law' (2020) 16 *International Journal of Law in Context* 253, 255–57.

Whether pushbacks and pullbacks are rationally connected to their purported goals is highly questionable. States and the EU have not substantiated claims that these practices effectively reduce deaths, dismantle organised smuggling networks, or prevent trafficking.[266] On the contrary, their overarching aim of immigration control often undermines these objectives and related international obligations. A key example is the decades-long UK–France cooperation, with the UK paying France to prevent irregular Channel crossings with little success.[267] As chapter five illustrated, visas and carrier sanctions exclude migrants from safe, regular channels, which pushes migrants into life-threatening journeys and towards smugglers – consequences recognised by various UN bodies.[268]

The criminalisation of smuggling and the intensification of border controls may also transform 'simple' smuggling into highly risky trafficking situations.[269] Even if preventing irregular migration were a legitimate aim and some arrivals were deterred through harsher policies, borders are notoriously porous, and externalisation merely diverts migration flows.[270] Partnering with authoritarian regimes with abysmal human rights records to bolster their ability to stop migrant boats only risks driving more migration.[271]

These measures are also not strictly necessary as reasonable, less restrictive alternatives exist. The Strasbourg Court has held that States must take operational steps to address trafficking and provide migrants with effective protection.[272] In *ND and NT*, the Court emphasised the relevance of States

[266] See P Tinti and T Reitano, *Migrant, Refugee, Smuggler, Savior* (Oxford, OUP, 2017); K Williams and A Mountz, 'Between Enforcement and Precarity: Externalization and Migrant Deaths at Sea' (2018) 56 *International Migration* 74; Stoyanova, 'Right to Life' (n 215) 454–55; Stoyanova, 'Right to Leave' (n 174) 429–31.

[267] L Blythe, 'UK-France Cooperation on Border Control: Efficacy, Deterrence and Human Rights' (2025) RSC Working Paper Series 142, https://www.rsc.ox.ac.uk/publications/uk-france-cooperation-on-border-control-efficacy-deterrence-and-human-rights.

[268] CMW and CRC, 'Joint General Comment No. 3 (2017) of the Committee on the Protection of the Rights of All Migrant Workers and Members of Their Families and No. 22 (2017) of the Committee on the Rights of the Child on the general principles regarding the human rights of children in the context of international migration (16 November 2017) UN Doc CMW/C/GC/3-CRC/C/GC/22, paras 41–43; Stoyanova, 'Right to Life' (n 215) 450–55.

[269] See eg Hathaway (n 255) 6, 12–13; T Spijkerboer, 'Wasted Lives. Borders and the Right to Life of People Crossing Them' (2017) 86 *Nordic Journal of International Law* 1, 8.

[270] See MS Cerrutti and PF Marcelino, 'Recent African Immigration to South America: The Cases of Argentina and Brazil in the Regional Context' in J Martínez Pizarro and L Reboiras Finardi (eds), *Development, Institutional and Policy Aspects of International Migration Between Africa, Europe and Latin America and the Caribbean* (Santiago, UN, 2012) on Argentina and Brazil as new destinations; I Steiner, 'Safe Third Country Agreement Expansion Causes Asylum Seekers to Explore New Routes' (*Wilson Center*, 14 September 2023) www.wilsoncenter.org/blog-post/safe-third-country-agreement-expansion-causes-asylum-seekers-explore-new-routes; IOM, *The Annual Global Overview of Migration Routes 2024* (Geneva, IOM, 2025) 26, 29, 39.

[271] N Squires, 'How Italy Stopped the Migrant Boats' (*The Telegraph*, 19 January 2025) www.telegraph.co.uk/world-news/2025/01/19/italy-migrant-boats-giorgia-meloni-africa-tunisia-libya/.

[272] *Rantsev v Cyprus and Russia* (2010) 51 EHRR 1, paras 283–93; *Chowdury v Greece*, App no 21884/15 (ECtHR, 30 March 2017) paras 86–89. See C Briddick, 'Some Other(Med) "Refugees"?:

providing genuine, effective access to legal entry channels. Although the case risks legitimising collective expulsions, it can counterintuitively be read as urging States to secure legal pathways.[273] It cannot be necessary for States to close or reduce the availability of regular pathways and then obstruct the only options migrants have left. As argued in chapter five, reasonable and more effective alternatives to reducing irregular and spontaneous arrivals include expanding humanitarian corridors, family reunification, and work and study opportunities. Such pathways cater to the State's right to control entry, while facilitating orderly arrivals and enhancing the protection of migrants against loss of life, trafficking and exploitation.[274] To save lives at sea, dedicated SAR operations should be a priority.[275] In the context of safeguarding public health and life, the use of pushbacks and blanket entry bans during the Covid-19 pandemic was neither strictly necessary nor proportionate to achieving legitimate public health objectives. Indiscriminate measures excluding asylum seekers without evidence of health risk or safeguards against *refoulement* are discriminatory and incompatible with international standards.[276] Viable alternatives, such as testing, limited quarantine and self-isolation, were available and effectively used for other travellers.[277]

Of course, where States are unwilling to receive certain migrants altogether, equally effective alternatives may not exist, necessitating a balancing of the right to leave against the State's interest in preventing irregular migration – an interest that should not be readily accepted as a legitimate aim. As noted in chapter two, the lawfulness of a person's presence in the territory is relevant, but indiscriminate or automatic measures cannot satisfy proportionality. Pushbacks and pullbacks systematically obstruct departure and the search for safety, disregarding individual circumstances. Indeed, this is the intention behind such practices and agreements with third countries, destroying the essence of the right to leave especially in light of their current implementation.[278]

Women Seeking Asylum under Refugee and Human Rights Law' in SS Juss (ed), *Research Handbook on International Refugee Law* (Cheltenham, Edward Elgar Publishing, 2019) 287–88.

[273] D Thym, 'A Restrictionist Revolution? A Counter-Intuitive Reading of the ECtHR's *N.D. & N.T.*-Judgment on "Hot Expulsions"' (*EU Migration Law Blog*, 17 February 2020) www.eumigrationlawblog.eu/a-restrictionist-revolution-a-counter-intuitive-reading-of-the-ecthrs-n-d-n-t-judgment-on-hot-expulsions/. See also *MN v Belgium*, App no 3599/18 (ECtHR, 5 March 2020) para 126.

[274] Stoyanova, 'Right to Life' (n 215) 454–56. See on eliminating abuse and legal channels: V Stoyanova, 'Dancing on the Borders of Article 4: Human Trafficking and the European Court of Human Rights in the *Rantsev* Case' (2012) 30 *Netherlands Quarterly of Human Rights* 163, 175–79.

[275] Guild (n 192) 434.

[276] UNHCR, 'Key Legal Considerations' (n 251) para 6. See also HRW, 'US: COVID-19 Policies Risk Asylum Seekers' Lives' (2 April 2020) www.hrw.org/news/2020/04/02/us-covid-19-policies-risk-asylum-seekers-lives.

[277] UNHCR, 'Key Legal Considerations' (n 251) paras 6–8.

[278] Markard (n 108) 602; Guild and Stoyanova (n 220) 386, 391–93; Giuffré and Moreno-Lax (n 26) 85, 99–100; *SDG* (n 78) para 86.

They also render the right to seek asylum illusory, depriving it of practical effect. As affirmed by the UNHCR, interceptions and rescues must not result in summary returns that deny access to protection or risk *refoulement*.[279] Individuals unable to flee their country of origin following a pullback or pushback are precluded from becoming a refugee under the Refugee Convention. Pullbacks prevent access to the rights and protections individuals would otherwise be entitled to under human rights and refugee law upon reaching the destination State. Even where migrants are nearing border infrastructure or make contact with the authorities, they may still face pushbacks. Such measures display a lack of good faith, undermining the State's duty to admit those with protection needs and penalising individuals for their mode of arrival.[280] Given the right to flee to seek asylum, the absence of viable travel alternatives, and the serious harms migrants are exposed to when contained in third States, the individual interests at stake significantly outweigh those asserted by States.

For those departing by sea, a tension arises between the migrant's agency and the duty of rescue. Individuals retain the right to decide to leave and determine for themselves where they will be safest, whatever the associated risks, and that choice should be respected if made freely.[281] However, States remain obliged to rescue those in distress. This can be reconciled by holding that interception does not breach the right to leave if it constitutes a genuine rescue, conducted in full compliance with refugee and human rights standards, including *non-refoulement* and disembarkation in a place of safety. The UNHCR has made clear that disembarkation arrangements must not frustrate rescued persons' right to leave, especially when they are fleeing serious harm.[282] As scholars argue, maritime obligations must be interpreted in harmony with human rights and refugee law, rejecting a fragmentary approach.[283] The mere fact that a boat has not requested rescue is irrelevant; an objective assessment of distress must be made. This does not, however, justify pullbacks disguised as 'pre-emptive rescues'. Ultimately, the disproportionality of pushbacks and pullbacks is reinforced by their undermining of other fundamental rights.

[279] EXCOM (n 2) (a); UNHCR, 'Legal Considerations on Roles' (n 94) para 3.7.

[280] Weinzierl and Lisson (n 194) 67; Goodwin-Gill and McAdam (n 108) 433–36.

[281] JC Hathaway, 'The False Panacea of Offshore Deterrence' (2006) 26 *Forced Migration Review* 56, 57; Markard (n 108) 608; University of Michigan, 'The Michigan Guidelines on Refugee Freedom of Movement' (2018) 39 *Michigan Journal of International Law* 5, para 6; Guild and Stoyanova (n 220) 437.

[282] UNHCR, 'Legal Considerations on Roles' (n 94) para 3.4.

[283] See Moreno-Lax, 'Seeking Asylum' (n 98); Giuffré (n 169) 708; E Papastavridis, 'The Interplay Between Maritime Interdiction Operations and Human Rights Law' (2014) 1 *Acta Criminologica: Southern African Journal of Criminology* 36.

D. Consistency with Other Rights

Lastly, restrictions on the right to leave must be consistent with other human rights. As the Strasbourg Court has reiterated in several cases, problems in managing large influxes of migrants cannot justify recourse to practices that breach the Convention.[284] As alluded to, pushbacks and pullbacks infringe a range of other human rights, thereby reinforcing their incompatibility with the right to leave. When restrictions violate rights of *jus cogens* status, such as the right to life, they must be construed as disproportionate and unlawful.[285]

Although the specific harms migrants experience vary by context, abuse is a systemic and well-documented feature of interceptions at sea and on land. These include violations such as *refoulement*, collective expulsion, torture, inhuman and degrading treatment, slavery, arbitrary detention, deprivation of life, and enforced disappearances.[286] GLAN's 2020 case, pending at the time of writing, argues that Greece's systemic pushbacks at the Evros land border constitute enforced disappearance, involving incommunicado detention, confiscation of belongings, and summary expulsion to Turkey. The applicant was stripped of his German residence permit and passport (proof of his legal and refugee status), preventing him from leaving Turkey and re-entering his own country for over 1,000 days, in breach of his freedom of movement.[287] The migrant experience is marked by border violence at every stage of the journey.[288] As the UN Special Rapporteur on Extrajudicial, Summary or Arbitrary Executions has described, the situation is a 'human rights and humanitarian crisis' and the 'tolerance for its fatalities' is 'grave and disturbing'.[289]

Partner States are arguably selected not only due to geographical proximity but also because of their weak oversight mechanisms and willingness to cooperate, which are often influenced by regional hegemonic pressure. Similarly, some States are banking on partner authorities' poor human rights records, especially violations of migrants' rights, to deter irregular crossings.[290] In key partner States such as Niger and Tunisia, the abuse of migrants is rife and asylum systems like Mexico's routinely fail to meet international standards;

[284] *Khlaifia* (n 221) para 241. See also *MSS v Belgium and Greece* (2011) 53 EHRR 2, para 223; *Hirsi Jamaa* (n 28) paras 113–38, 146–57, 183–86, 197–206, 122, 179; *ND and NT* (n 30) paras 195–99.

[285] Den Heijer (26) 166.

[286] See also McDonnell (n 1) sect 4.1.

[287] *FAA v Greece*, Registered with the HRC, 5 November 2021 (filed *FAJ v Greece*) www.glanlaw.org/_files/ugd/14ee1a_4e9dea36dd1043d48e6a50dbe5b78f04.pdf. See for developments, de:border migration justice collective, 'F.A.A. v Greece: Illegal expulsions and enforced disappearance at Evros' https://debordercollective.org/interventions/pushbacks-as-enforced-disappearances/faa-greece-hrcttee/.

[288] UNGA, 'Special Rapporteur – Unlawful Death of Refugees and Migrants' (n 137) sects 2–3; I Mann, 'Border Violence as Crime' (2021) 42 *University of Pennsylvania Journal of International Law* 675.

[289] UNGA, 'Special Rapporteur – Unlawful Death of Refugees and Migrants' (n 137) para 1.

[290] ibid para 91.

other States, such as Indonesia, may not be party to the Refugee Convention.[291] Migrants in Libya face crimes against humanity, while the cruel and inhumane treatment of people sent to Australia's offshore detention centres is well-documented.[292]

Wealthy countries are shifting their responsibilities onto third countries with less capacity to provide effective protection, which are under-resourced, often have poor human rights records, and already host the vast majority of the world's refugees.[293] Despite the designation of certain countries, such as Guatemala, Rwanda, Turkey and Malaysia, as 'safe third countries', there is broad consensus that these countries do not meet the necessary protection standards for migrants.[294] Nonetheless, other countries continue to follow suit.[295] Notably, while the Supreme Court of Canada ultimately upheld the Canada–US safe third country agreement in recent litigation, the Court acknowledged significant concerns regarding the risk of detention upon return, the conditions of such detention, and potential *refoulement* from the US.[296] More broadly, the practice by both Global North and South States of rapidly removing people to an expanding list of 'safe' countries of origin which are not in fact safe, often occurs without adequate safeguards and further risks breaching core protection standards.[297]

[291] See Dastyari and Hirsch (n 65) 8–10, 17–21; G Zandonini and F Bellina, 'Niger, Part 1: At the Centre of a Brewing Militant Storm' (*The New Humanitarian*, 28 March 2019) www.thenewhumanitarian.org/special-report/2019/03/28/niger-part-1-centre-brewing-militant-storm; Meyer and Isacson (n 49) 28–38.

[292] See among many UNGA, 'Report of the Special Rapporteur on the Human Rights of Migrants on his Mission to Australia and the Regional Processing Centres in Nauru' (24 April 2017) UN Doc A/HRC/35/25/Add.3; Letter from the Office of the Prosecutor of the ICC to Andrew Wilkie MP (12 February 2020) uploads.guim.co.uk/2020/02/14/200213-Andrew-Wilkie-Response-from-International-Criminal-Court-Australian-Government-treatment-of-asylum-seekers_(1).pdf; UN News, 'Libya: Crimes Against Humanity Committed Since 2016 – Rights Probe' (27 March 2023) www.news.un.org/en/story/2023/03/1135052.

[293] See recently HRW, *'Nobody Cared, Nobody Listened': The US Expulsion of Third-Country Nationals to Panama* (New York, HRW, 2025).

[294] See on Malaysia, *Plaintiff M70/2011 v Minister for Immigration and Citizenship* (2011) 244 CLR 144; Guatemala, HRW and Refugees International, *Deportation with a Layover: Failure of Protection under the US-Guatemala Asylum Cooperative Agreement* (New York, HRW, 2020); Rwanda, E McDonnell, 'UK Supreme Court Finds UK-Rwanda Asylum Scheme Unlawful' (*HRW*, 15 November 2023) www.hrw.org/news/2023/11/15/uk-supreme-court-finds-uk-rwanda-asylum-scheme-unlawful; Turkey, RSA, 'The Council of State Annuls the Designation of Turkey as a "Safe Third Country" for Asylum Seekers' (27 March 2025) www.rsaegean.org/en/council-of-state-annuls-the-designation-of-turkey-as-a-safe-third-country/.

[295] See Reuters, 'Immigrants Set for Libya Deportation Sat on Tarmac for Hours, Attorney Says' (*The Guardian*, 9 May 2025) www.theguardian.com/us-news/2025/may/09/libya-deportations-immigrants-trump.

[296] *Canada (Minister of Citizenship and Immigration) v Canadian Council of Refugees* 2021 FCA 72; *Canadian Council for Refugees v Canada (Citizenship and Immigration)* 2023 SCC 17.

[297] See *Krajský soud v Brně*, Case C-406/22, EU:C:2024:841; F Khan and N Rayn, 'Country Fiche South Africa' (*ASILE*, 2020) 10–12 www.asileproject.eu/wp-content/uploads/2021/03/Country-Fiche_South-Africa_Final_Pub.pdf; Commission, 'Commission Proposes to Frontload Elements of the Pact on Migration and Asylum As Well As a First EU List of Safe Countries of Origin' (Press Release, 15 April 2025) ec.europa.eu/commission/presscorner/detail/en/ip_25_1070;

Pushbacks and pullbacks involving such partner States pose a clear risk of *refoulement* under Article 33 of the Refugee Convention and human rights law. Pushbacks at international borders have been found to amount to *refoulement* and, in many instances, also collective expulsion.[298] The applicability of *non-refoulement* obligations during pullbacks raises complex questions that have not yet been adjudicated. As explored in chapters three and five, *non-refoulement* under human rights law is interpreted broadly: it applies regardless of whether the individual has crossed an international border. Accordingly, both push-backs and pullbacks will breach *non-refoulement* obligations when migrants are exposed to a real risk of serious harm, including by being forced to remain in or return to unsafe territory.[299]

Article 33 of the Convention requires individuals to be outside their country of origin and prohibits 'return to the frontiers' of that country. Similarly, Article 3 of CAT requires return to 'another State'. Since pullbacks typically occur within a transit State's territory, return will amount to *refoulement* under both instruments provided the risk threshold is met. Likewise, pushbacks to transit States can be understood as the re-transfer of jurisdiction back to the transit State.[300] The core issue lies in determining whether pullbacks by a third State within its territory qualify as a return to frontiers or another State. A black letter interpretation would suggest otherwise. Nonetheless, like restrictive visa regimes, pullbacks run contrary to a good faith reading of Article 33 of the Convention (and CAT), effectively preventing individuals asserting their right of entry stemming from such obligations and undermining access to protection.[301]

Pushbacks and pullbacks involve repeated loss of life, routinely violating the right to life, which applies at all times and without discrimination.[302] Scholars have established a direct link between increased border controls and rising migrant deaths on routes to Europe, Australia and the US.[303] The right to life

EuroMed Rights, 'Stop Considering Egypt, Tunisia and Morocco "Safe" Countries!' (16 April 2025) www.euromedrights.org/publication/stop-considering-egypt-tunisia-and-morocco-safe-countries/.

[298] See OHCHR, 'Greece: Rights Violations Against Asylum Seekers at Turkey-Greece Border Must Stop – UN Special Rapporteur' (Press Release, 23 March 2020) www.ohchr.org/EN/NewsEvents/Pages/DisplayNews.aspx?NewsID=25736&LangID=E; IACHR, 'IACHR Expresses Deep Concern about the Situation of Migrants and Refugees in the United States, Mexico, and Central America' (Press Release 180/19, 23 July 2019) www.oas.org/en/iachr/media_center/PReleases/2019/180.asp; McDonnell, 'Challenging Externalisation' (n 1).

[299] Moreno-Lax, *Accessing Asylum* (n 36) 309–11, 313–20; Pijnenburg, 'Containment' (n 142) 318–20; Goodwin-Gill and McAdam (n 108) 315–18.

[300] See *Al-Saadoon and Mufdhi v UK* (2010) 51 EHRR 9, paras 140, 143; Pijnenburg, 'Containment' (n 142) 320.

[301] See Goodwin-Gill and McAdam (n 108) 430–32, 434.

[302] UNGA, 'Special Rapporteur – Unlawful Death of Refugees and Migrants' (n 137) paras 14–15.

[303] Spijkerboer, 'Wasted Lives' (n 269); K Williams and A Mountz, 'Between Enforcement and Precarity: Externalization and Migrant Deaths at Sea' (2018) 56 *International Migration* 74; D Kerwin and DE Martínez, 'Forced Migration, Deterrence, and Solutions to the Non-Natural Disaster of Migrant Deaths Along the US-Mexico Border and Beyond' (2024) 12 *Journal on Migration and Human Security* 127.

of many irregular migrants is 'protected' through the prevention of departure, interceptions or SAR, which contrasts with the strong protections afforded to other travellers.[304] As the Rapporteur on Extrajudicial, Summary or Arbitrary Executions has remarked, 'it is impossible to protect the right to life while simultaneously attempting to deter entry by endangering life'.[305] Excessive use of force amounting to arbitrary deprivation of life is prevalent, such as the shooting of Ethiopian refugees trying to flee Yemen by Saudi Arabia, the firing of rubber bullets and tear gas by Spanish authorities near Ceuta, or against Rohingyas and Bangladeshis on the high seas.[306] Indian authorities have reportedly forced Rohingya refugees off an Indian navy vessel and into the Andaman Sea, giving them life jackets and making them swim to an island in Myanmar territory.[307] The reasonably foreseeable risk to life is abundantly clear when distress calls are ignored, coastguards aggressively manoeuvre, or migrants are abandoned at sea.

These risks further reveal how pushbacks and pullbacks disproportionately discriminate against specific groups, including based on nationality (ie, Syrians under the EU–Turkey deal), race, ethnicity or religion (ie, Rohingya Muslim refugees fleeing Myanmar or black Africans in Morocco), and immigration status (ie, irregular mode of arrival or undocumented).[308] All people, regardless of migration status or identity, must be protected from harm without discrimination during border control operations and, if in distress at sea, rescued in a timely manner.[309] Those dying at international borders are mostly Black and Brown migrants, highlighting the racism and neo-colonialism underpinning deadly externalisation and containment practices.[310] Pushbacks and pullbacks can also

[304] T Spijkerboer, 'Moving Migrants, States, and Rights: Human Rights and Border Deaths' (2013) 7 *TLEHR* 213; Spijkerboer, 'Wasted Lives' (n 269).

[305] UNGA, 'Special Rapporteur – Unlawful Death of Refugees and Migrants' (n 137) paras 25–35, 59. See also *Sonko* (n 113).

[306] UNGA, 'Special Rapporteur – Unlawful Death of Refugees and Migrants' (n 137); HRW, *'They Fired on Us Like Rain' Saudi Arabian Mass Killings of Ethiopian Migrants at the Yemen-Saudi Border* (New York, HRW, 2023).

[307] OHCHR, 'Alarmed by Reports of Rohingya Cast into the sea from Indian Navy Vessels, UN Expert Launches Inquiry of "Unconscionable, Unacceptable Acts"' (Press Release, 15 May 2025) www.ohchr.org/en/press-releases/2025/05/alarmed-reports-rohingya-cast-sea-indian-navy-vessels-un-expert-launches.

[308] OHCHR (n 307) para 36; Giuffré and Moreno-Lax (n 26) 99; E Tyszler, 'From Controlling Mobilities to Control Over Women's Bodies: Gendered Effects of EU Border Externalization in Morocco' (2019) 7 *Comparative Migration Studies* 25, 6–7. See *R v Immigration Officer at Prague Airport, ex p European Roma Rights Centre* [2004] UKHL 55, [2005] 2 AC 1; *Memedova v North Macedonia*, Apps nos 42429/16 and 2 others (ECtHR, 24 October 2023).

[309] Weinzierl and Lisson (n 194) 38, 69.

[310] See L Mayblin, *Asylum After Empire: Colonial Legacies in the Politics of Asylum Seeking* (London, Roman & Littlefield International, 2017); M Lemberg-Pedersen, 'Manufacturing Displacement. Externalization and Postcoloniality in European Migration Control' (2019) 5 *Global Affairs* 247; S Reardon-Smith, 'Linking Land and Sea: Intersections between Indigenous Peoples' Dispossession and Asylum Seekers' Containment by Australia' (2024) 7 *Migration and Society* 153; A Gündoğdu, 'From the Colony to the Border: The Lawful Lawlessness of Racial Violence' in

have a disproportionate impact on women, children and other groups who are at heightened risk of harm. Women fleeing crisis or conflict may face racialised and gendered vulnerabilisation at borders.[311] Black women are especially at risk, experiencing multiple layers of marginalisation due to the intersection of race, gender and immigration status. Women, girls and LGBTIQ+ individuals may be subjected to sexual and gender-based violence, whether by people smugglers, authorities policing the border, or through structural discrimination.[312]

Rather than identifying or protecting potential victims of human trafficking or violence, many are expelled, arbitrarily detained or denied access to protection. A complaint has been brought to the CEDAW Committee against Italy and Libya by Nigerian women who were trafficked and found it almost impossible to leave Libya, and even when they did attempt to flee, were pulled back to Libya, imprisoned and exposed to further exploitation and abuse.[313] Despite their special status in international law, children are exposed to severe discrimination and violence during border operations. Their best interests are routinely ignored; for instance, children are forcibly separated from their families, pushed back at borders or denied rescue, and left without adequate access to basic services.[314]

In summary, pushbacks and pullbacks gravely undermine the rights of migrants. They violate not only the right to leave but likely a spectrum of interrelated and fundamental rights.

VI. INTERNATIONAL RESPONSIBILITY FOR PUSHBACKS AND PULLBACKS

In light of this conclusion, it is necessary to examine which actors bear and share responsibility for their role in violating the right to leave during pushback and pullback operations. This section will first consider the primary responsibility of States and IOs, before turning to questions of derived responsibility. It will briefly be argued that no circumstances precluding wrongfulness apply.

A Shachar and S Benhabib (eds), *Lawless Zones, Rightless Subjects: Migration, Asylum, and Shifting Borders* (Cambridge, CUP, 2025).

[311] See CEDAW, 'General Recommendation No. 38 (2020) on Trafficking in Women and Girls in the Context of Global Migration' (20 November 2020) UN Doc CEDAW/C/GC/38, para 24; Tyszler (n 308); A Talbot, A Vogl and S Dehm, 'The Gender- and Sexuality-Based Harms of Refugee Externalization: A Role for Human Rights Due Diligence' (2024) 23 *International Journal of Refugee Law* 60.

[312] See Tyszler (n 308); R Buxton and S Ritholtz, *The Way Out: Justice in the Queer Search for Refuge* (California, University of California Press, forthcoming).

[313] ASGI, 'Legal Framework. Italian and Libyan Responsibilities for the Violation of Articles 2 and 6 of the CEDAW' (December 2021) www.asgi.it/wp-content/uploads/2021/12/Juridical-Framework_1.pdf. See also Sherwood, Lemay and Costello (n 11) 389.

[314] Digidiki and Bhabha (n 189); CMW and CRC (n 268) paras 40–41.

A. Direct Responsibility and Accountability Gaps

Pushbacks trigger the direct responsibility of the State carrying out the interception, as such conduct is attributable to that State (including when privatised). When destination and third States conduct joint operations and patrols that result in unlawful conduct, or jointly direct privatised pushbacks or pullbacks, if jurisdictional and attribution tests are met this will give rise to joint responsibility under Article 47 of ARSIWA.

During joint Frontex operations, Frontex, the host State, and participating States play a significant role in the operation. Pursuant to Articles 6 and 7 of ARIO (and following the analysis in section IV.B above), the EU bears responsibility for pushbacks that violate the right to leave during Frontex-led operations, adopting a multiple attribution framework. Where the EU, the host State and participating States contribute significant assets, share operational command, or operate akin to joint organs at national coordinator centres, as seems to be the case, joint responsibility as co-perpetrators under Articles 47 and 48 of ARSIWA and ARIO appears to arise.[315] Notably, Hirsch has argued that the Bali Process may also amount to a joint organ formed by multiple States to conduct activities on behalf of the whole group.[316] A nuanced approach should assign responsibility proportionally to each actor's contribution to the overall harm. The EU is also responsible for unlawful actions committed *independently* by Frontex officers during solo patrols or when supporting EUNAVFOR or NATO operations at sea.[317]

Although the EU cannot be brought before the Strasbourg Court, the *Bosphorus* presumption can be rebutted to hold Frontex host and contributing States responsible for pushbacks, following the reasoning in *Al-Jedda v UK* and *Nada v Switzerland*.[318] Although EU law (ie, the Frontex Regulation, Schengen Borders Code) conditions conduct, States retain discretion in implementing border measures and deciding the precise actions they adopt in order to comply (or not) with fundamental rights. The operational role played by both host and participating States allows them to ensure that interceptions amount to genuine SAR and avoid conduct that amounts to *refoulement* or endangers life.[319] Frontex may separately be subject to an action for damages before the CJEU, but this requires overcoming the significant barriers outlined above. Similarly, NATO can bear responsibility for pushbacks performed by its multinational forces. If before Strasbourg, the *Bosphorus* presumption will only be rebuttable

[315] See Gammeltoft-Hansen and Hathaway (n 3) 272–76; Gkliati (n 162) 188–90.
[316] See also Hirsch, 'Borders Beyond' (n 60) 43–55.
[317] See Frontex, 'Liaison Officers Network', www.frontex.europa.eu/partners/liaison-officers-network/; ARIO, art 8; ARIO Commentary, 60–61.
[318] *Al-Jedda v UK* (2011) 53 EHRR 23, paras 76–86; *Nada v Switzerland* (2013) 56 EHRR 18, paras 120–23.
[319] See Fernandez (n 157) 400; Fink (n 35) 96–97, 168, 176–79.

where the national coastguard also exercised effective control and discretion in pushing and pulling migrants back, which will be fact-specific.

Pullbacks lead to the direct responsibility of the third State conducting them. They cannot also be attributed to the destination State under ARSIWA, requiring recourse to the rules of derived responsibility. A multiple attribution approach would support the primary responsibility of the EU for pullbacks it effectively controls, such as those by the LBCG or during Frontex operations hosted by third States (Article 7 ARIO). Given evidentiary and legal hurdles to proving effective control in light of the third State's preeminent role, derived responsibility remains a clearer path.

Third States allowing destination States to operate in their territory remain responsible for failing to uphold the right to leave and other positive obligations.[320] Given that destination States have jurisdiction, they are duty-bound to effectively protect the right to leave of migrants from infringements by third States, private actors and IOs. Entering into cooperative agreements does not absolve them of their positive obligations nor because the partner State is the 'direct' perpetrator.[321] When partnering with third States, destination States and the EU, must effectively assess the human rights risks of such cooperation. Where it is foreseeable that operations will result in harm, any assistance must be conditioned on effective safeguards and mitigation. Otherwise, there should be a presumption against engagement.[322] Due diligence policies must not – as they often do – become rubber stamps, while the commission of abuse continues with support.[323]

However, destination States and the EU are not merely failing to protect; they are often actively facilitating and requiring third States to hamper migrants' departure through pushbacks and pullbacks. Given their extensive involvement and the well-documented, easily verifiable risks, States and the EU possess actual or constructive knowledge that these arrangements will cause harm (as does NATO).[324] This should lead to the concurrent responsibility of the destination State, the EU and NATO for failure to protect and prevent violations with the third State conducting the pullback.[325] Moreover, the duty of rescue at sea does not depend on jurisdiction. Practices such as ignoring distress calls, replacing SAR with military operations, and criminalising rescue vessels undoubtedly

[320] And maybe the violation itself if the approach in *El-Masri* (n 175) is followed.

[321] See *Saadi v Italy* (2009) 49 EHRR 30, para 126; *Hirsi Jamaa* (n 28) para 129; Moreno-Lax, 'Seeking Asylum' (n 98) 201–02; C Ferstman, 'Human Rights Due Diligence Policies Applied to Extraterritorial Cooperation to Prevent "Irregular" Migration: European Union and United Kingdom Support to Libya' (2020) 21 *German Law Journal* 459, 466–70.

[322] UNHCR, 'Submission' (n 150) paras 5.8–6.1.

[323] Ferstman (n 321) 460, 468, 470–71, 486.

[324] *Hirsi Jamaa* (n 28) paras 121, 131, 137, 156; *MSS* (n 284) paras 258–59; UNHCR, 'Submission' (n 150) paras 5.8–5.9; Ciliberto (n 127) 527–28; Giuffré and Moreno-Lax (n 26) 102–03, 106–07. See Gkliati (n 162) 187 on the power of Frontex border guard teams to prevent violations.

[325] *Corfu Channel Case (UK v Albania)* (Merits) [1949] ICJ Rep 4, 17–18, 22–23; Goodwin-Gill (n 170) 453; Giuffré and Moreno-Lax (n 26) 107.

violate that duty.[326] In many cases, States, Frontex and NATO are systematically leaving people to die through a policy of non-assistance or even using their own vessels to create waves, allowing other States to conduct pull and pushbacks, and failing to rescue migrants or protect them from foreseeable violations.[327]

To uphold the right to leave, the duty of rescue and other fundamental obligations, destination States, third States and IOs must cease all forms of pushbacks and pullbacks and involvement therein, and end policies of non-assistance and criminalisation of rescue. They should provide victims with effective access to remedies, such as visas and protection. States should refrain from deploying officials and assets to Frontex and NATO operations or terminate participation when pushbacks and pullbacks are known to be occurring. Under its Regulation, Frontex is obligated to monitor, investigate and suspend or terminate operations when there are persisting or serious rights violations.[328] Frontex must comply with this duty, as it did in Hungary; however, it has failed to do so in Greece despite investigations into its own conduct and clear breaches by Greece.[329] Activities must be limited to genuine rescues, ensuring timely disembarkation to a place of safety and effective access to asylum procedures, accompanied by dedicated SAR operations that prioritise protection.[330] Robust monitoring and accountability mechanisms should be implemented to ensure international standards are upheld worldwide.[331] As Stoyanova underscores, the cumulative effect of migration policies must not leave migrants with no reasonable pathway to exercise their right to leave and seek asylum.[332]

B. Indirect Responsibility for Assistance, Direction and Control

Even where attribution or jurisdiction cannot be established, destination States and IOs may still bear responsibility for aiding and assisting or directing and

[326] See SOLAS, ch V, reg 33(1); SAR, 4.2.1, 4.3; Moreno-Lax, *Interdiction* (n 15) 6–7.

[327] See HRC, 'General Comment No 36' (n 241) paras 6–7, 22; Fink (n 35) 153–60.

[328] Frontex Regulation, arts 46, 109(2)(b).

[329] See 'EU Migration Chief Welcomes Frontex Suspension of Operations in Hungary' (*Euronews*, 28 January 2021) www.euronews.com/2021/01/28/eu-migration-chief-welcomes-frontex-suspension-of-operations-in-hungary; Maltezou and Souliotis (n 239).

[330] Moreno-Lax, *Interdiction* (n 15) 12–13; Statewatch, 'To SAR or Not to SAR, Part 1: Why Is Frontex Expected to Save Lives at Sea?' (*Statewatch*, 15 July 2021) www.statewatch.org/analyses/2021/to-sar-or-not-to-sar-part-1-why-is-frontex-expected-to-save-lives-at-sea/; UNHCR and others (n 99).

[331] 'Open Letter: The UN Human Rights Council Should Urgently Respond to the Global Pattern of Deaths, Torture and Other Grave Human Rights Violations at International Borders' (19 June 2023) www.reliefweb.int/report/world/open-letter-un-human-rights-councilshould-urgently-respond-global-pattern-deaths-torture-and-other-grave-human-rights-violationsinternational-borders; OHCHR, 'Intersessional Panel Discussion on the Human Rights of Migrants in Transit' (15 May 2024) www.ohchr.org/en/events/events/2024/intersessional-panel-discussion-human-rights-migrants-transit-15-may-2024.

[332] Stoyanova, 'Right to Life' (n 215) 439, 456–58.

controlling other actors to commit violations of the right to leave (Articles 16/17 ARSIWA, Articles 14/15 ARIO).

States such as Australia, the US and EU Member States are aiding and assisting third States like Indonesia, Libya, and Mexico to violate the right to leave within the meaning of Article 16 of ARSIWA.[333] This assistance typically includes funding, training, technical support, secondment of officials, surveillance data, and capacity-building.[334] This assistance must be given with a view to facilitating the commission of an internationally wrongful act. It is hard to think of a more paradigmatic case. Partner States are given aid and assistance for the explicit purpose of engaging in pullbacks and preventing departure, with the assistance materially supporting and enabling pullbacks.[335] Destination States are fully aware, if not intending, that such conduct will lead to such outcomes and of the prevailing situation in third States, satisfying the knowledge and contribution requirements of Article 16. The right to leave is opposable to third States, for instance, under the ICCPR or customary international law.

This complicity arguably extends to other foreseeable abuses, such as arbitrary detention or ill-treatment in third countries. As the Rapporteur on Extrajudicial, Arbitrary and Summary Executions has stated, where systematic abuses are known in third countries, destination States must cease support for migration control.[336] Though Article 16 remains untested in the context of externalisation, principled arguments exist for its application here.[337] As argued above, *Soering*-type cases can be extended to prohibit all forms of extraterritorial complicity and positive obligations tailored to hold States accountable for violations they facilitate.

Under Article 17 ARSIWA, destination States may also incur responsibility where they exercise direction and control over third States. Article 17 requires a relationship of domination, not one of 'oversight' or 'mere influence', while direction 'connotes actual direction of an operative kind'. Complete power is not required, meaning general instructions may suffice.[338] Although the threshold is high, and acknowledging the spectrum of direction and control exercised by destination States, ample evidence supports the conclusion that such relationships can meet this standard.

[333] See for support eg Markard (n 108) 615; JP Gauci, 'Back to Old Tricks? Italian Responsibility for Returning People to Libya' (*EJIL:Talk!*, 6 June 2017) www.ejiltalk.org/back-to-old-tricks-italian-responsibility-for-returning-people-to-libya/; Ciliberto (n 127) 522–25; Dastyari and Hirsch (n 65); Giuffré and Moreno-Lax (n 26) 101–03; Pijnenburg, 'Containment' (n 142) 327–31; Hirsch, 'Externalisation' (n 34) 144–48, 173–76, 219.

[334] Gammeltoft-Hansen and Hathaway (n 3) 279.

[335] Dastyari and Hirsch (n 65) 29–30; Giuffré and Moreno-Lax (n 26) 102–03.

[336] UNGA, 'Special Rapporteur – Unlawful Death of Refugees and Migrants' (n 137) paras 37, 40; European Court of Auditors, 'The EU Trust Fund for Africa: Despite New Approaches, Support Remained Unfocused' (Special Report, 2024) www.eca.europa.eu/ECAPublications/SR-2024-17/SR-2024-17_EN.pdf. See also GLAN (n 173) para 13.

[337] Gammeltoft-Hansen and Hathaway (n 3) 277–82.

[338] ARSIWA Commentary, 69 para 7; Giuffré and Moreno-Lax (n 26) 104.

The dynamics exemplify asymmetric power relations, where powerful States leverage considerable amounts of aid, condition reward, and apply diplomatic pressure to outsource their obligations. As Giuffré and Moreno-Lax argue, although States may not exert minute-by-minute control over their activities, the de facto binding nature of agreements and reciprocal commitments concluded with countries such as Turkey and Libya leaves them little discretion to avoid violating the right to leave while complying with the agreement.[339] Together, the EU and Italy reconstituted and trained the LBCG, which is only capable of acting because of the EU's significant support and instruction.[340] Though the LBCG is now partially self-reliant and has its own rescue coordination centre, this is the product of capacity-building. Moreover, many neighbouring States depend on aid from the EU and its Member States, limiting their ability to resist or refuse cooperation. In the Australian context, the situation is not one of mere encouragement or oversight. Australia is the more powerful player, able to exert significant pressure on States in the region. Australia engages in 'incentivised policy transfer', which is partly possible due to several States and former colonies relying on Australia for foreign aid.[341] Likewise, US pressure including threats, tariffs and aid cuts, has compelled Mexico and other Central American countries to intensify border control and increase interceptions.[342] In agreeing to accept third-country nationals expelled from the US to Costa Rica in February 2025, the Costa Rican President said: 'We are helping the economically powerful brother to the north, who if they impose a tax in our free zones, it'll screw us'.[343] Merely conditioning aid or other incentives on the criminalisation or obstruction of exit is unlikely, however, to establish a sufficient relationship of domination.

This is not to say third States are always wilful implementers or powerless pawns; they often bargain for mutually beneficial relationships and share common interests.[344] Nevertheless, *but for* the destination State, third States would likely not obstruct departure and in many cases, would be ill-equipped to do so. They often act on behalf of and in the interests of the destination State, frequently at the expense of their own citizens and interests, becoming the de

[339] Giuffré and Moreno-Lax (n 26) 103–04. See also Pijnenburg, 'Italian Pushbacks' (n 74) 424–26.

[340] Forensic Oceanography (n 125) 8–11, 19–56. See also Guild and Stoyanova (n 220) 360.

[341] Nethery and Gordyn (n 61). See also D Ghezelbash, 'Forces of Diffusion: What Drives the Transfer of Immigration Policy and Law Across Jurisdictions?' (2014) 1 *International Journal of Migration and Border Studies* 139; G Megalogenis, 'Neighbourhood Bully: Australia Views Asia Through the Wrong End of the Telescope' (*The Guardian*, 17 February 2019) www.theguardian.com/australia-news/2019/feb/18/neighbourhood-bully-australia-views-asia-through-the-wrong-end-of-the-telescope.

[342] See Martín Gil (n 46); Tsourdi and Zardo (n 43).

[343] HRW, *'The Strategy Is to Break Us': The US Expulsion of Third-Country Nationals to Costa Rica* (New York, HRW, 2025).

[344] eg S Kneebone, 'Australia as a Powerbroker on Refugee Protection in Southeast Asia' (2017) 33 *Refuge* 29; Winters and Izaguirre (n 57); Lee (n 60); A Missbach and M Phillips, 'Reconceptualizing Transit States in an Era of Outsourcing, Offshoring, and Obfuscation' (2020) 3 *Migration and Society* 19. See also *Namah v Pato* [2016] PGSC 13 (26 April 2016), where the PNG Supreme Court ruled detention on Manus Island unconstitutional.

facto buffer zones and new frontiers. Direction and control may also be evident where destination State officials, such as those in rescue coordination centres or posted in third countries, provide real-time locations and instruct third State officials to intercept or pull back migrants.[345] As above, knowledge and opposability are established. These patterns, though context-specific, often reveal domination and operational control.

Finally, even though Australia, European States, and the US have imposed conditionality and exerted significant diplomatic pressure, this is unlikely to constitute coercion under Article 18 of ARSIWA.[346] While elements of coercive diplomacy are present, most partner countries have voluntarily agreed to cooperate and have been incentivised to do so. Article 18 requires 'serious economic pressure' that effectively deprives the coerced State of any real possibility of complying with the obligation breached, a very high threshold only met in extreme cases (perhaps, Australia's relationship with Nauru, so heavily dependent on Australian support).[347]

i. International Organisations

Establishing the shared responsibility of the EU, ICMPD, IOM and NATO for violations of the right to leave is essential.

There is abundant evidence that the EU and Frontex are aiding and assisting in pullbacks and pushbacks, including by EU Member States (Article 14 ARIO).[348] EU policies are facilitating abuse in countries across North and West Africa, and other regions where its externalised border controls are implemented.[349] GLAN, in the context of Libya, has outlined the separate and joint international responsibilities of the EU and its Member States for enabling, contributing and maintaining unlawful conduct by Libyan actors, including serious breaches of peremptory norms.[350] The EU's funding, aid conditionality and provision of vast amounts of technical, logistical and material support have significantly contributed to the capacity of third States to perform pullbacks.[351] The provision of surveillance data, vessels and aircraft, the deployment of officials, and

[345] See Vari (n 27) 131–32.

[346] ARSIWA Commentaries, 69–70.

[347] Hirsch, 'Externalisation' (n 34) 150; JC Morris, *Asylum and Extraction in the Republic of Nauru* (New York, Cornell University Press, 2023).

[348] See Fernandez (n 157) 403–06.

[349] HRW, 'EU: Time to Review and Remedy Cooperation Policies Facilitating Abuse of Refugees and Migrants in Libya' (NGOs Joint Statement, 28 April 2020) www.hrw.org/news/2020/04/28/eu-time-review-and-remedy-cooperation-policies-facilitating-abuse-refugees-and.

[350] GLAN (n 173) paras 2, 9, 14, 19. See ARSIWA, art 41(2); ARIO, art 42(2).

[351] See D Davitti and A La Chimia, 'A Lesser Evil? The European Agenda on Migration and the Use of Aid Funding for Migration Control' in F de Londras and S Mullally (eds), *The Irish Yearbook of International Law*, vol 10, 2015 (London, Hart Publishing, 2017); T Spijkerboer and E Steyger, 'European External Migration Funds and Public Procurement Law' (2019) 4 *European Papers* 493, www.europeanpapers.eu/en/e-journal/european-external-migration-funds-and-public-procurement-law; European Court of Auditors (n 336).

other operational contributions by EUNAVFOR or Frontex to third States (ie, Libya, Tunisia and Turkey) and Member States (ie, Greece or Hungary) makes the EU complicit in pullbacks and pushbacks, alongside EU Member States contributing assets and otherwise participating by blocking onward movement and creating waves.[352] ARIO envisions shared responsibility for the same internationally wrongful act.[353]

Where interceptions cannot be attributed to NATO, sharing location data to the national coastguard that enables pushbacks can amount to complicity, as would support from NATO contributing States (Articles 14 ARIO and 16 ARSIWA). Where a pushback is only attributable to NATO, contributing States may nonetheless be complicit under Article 58 of ARIO. Frontex liaison officers also support NATO missions and NATO shares intelligence with Frontex, potentially aiding and assisting each other. However, for responsibility to arise, a sufficiently close nexus to the breach of the right to leave would need to be shown on the facts. IOM and ICMPD are also arguably complicit in interceptions, having partnered with the EU and Australia (only IOM). Their aid and assistance can, for example, be seen in the capacity-building, technical assistance and equipment provided to authorities in MENA, West Africa and Indonesia to manage and secure their borders.[354] In all of these situations, States and IOs are well-aware that violations are occurring, not least because they are active on the ground.[355] In particular, externalisation has been designed and executed at the EU level, while both the IOM and ICMPD play significant roles in co-developing, implementing and promoting restrictive standards of migration control. Lastly, opposability is met, with IOs bound by the right to leave.

Although not fully explored here, there is a strong case that Frontex and the EU may be directing and controlling violations of the right to leave by third States under Article 15 of ARIO, akin to powerful destination States. This may arise where EU forces or Frontex officers direct a specific pullback or operation, providing intelligence, coordination and capacity-building. Responsibility would then lie jointly with the EU and the third State.

C. Irregular Migration, Loss of Life and Consent to Interdict: Defences to Breaching the Right to Leave

No valid defences preclude wrongfulness for violations of the right to leave by States or IOs (consent, *force majeure*, distress and necessity, Articles 20

352 See Alarm Phone and others (n 39); Majcher (n 162) 67–69; Fink (n 35) 160–71; Gkliati (n 162).

353 ARIO, art 48. See also A Nollkaemper and others, 'Guiding Principles on Shared Responsibility in International Law' (2020) 31 *European Journal of International Law* 15, principle 7, paras 7–8.

354 Brachet (n 89) 276–77; Hirsch and Doig (n 64) 693–94, 697. See Australia's responsibility for other actions by IOM, Hirsch, 'Externalisation' (n 34) 199–207.

355 See on Frontex, Christides and others (n 40).

and 23-25 ARSIWA and ARIO). While coastal or flag States may consent to interdictions, measures must fall 'within the limits of that consent' and presumably States cannot lawfully consent to another actor infringing their nationals' rights.[356] As discussed, externalisation agreements rarely authorise outright prohibitions on leaving or other rights violations.

Force majeure, distress and necessity require that the actor has not substantially contributed to the situation.[357] Yet, the 'need' for pushbacks and pullbacks largely stems from destination States and EU policies that severely limit lawful travel and construct 'irregularity'. Even where States invoke migration crises, great loss of life or instrumentalisation as *force majeure*, the defence requires that it be 'materially impossible' to comply with human rights and that the conduct be involuntary – conditions not met here.[358] States and IOs demonstrably retain the capacity to uphold human rights even during crises, with alternatives to harmful practices readily available. This contrasts with Strasbourg's approach in *ND and NT v Spain*, which implies that where migrants take advantage of their large numbers and use force, and effective means of entry were otherwise available, this precludes the wrongfulness of an expulsion.

Necessity also requires that harmful measures be the *only* means of protecting an essential interest.[359] And even if irregular migration threatens the essential interests of the State, such measures must not 'seriously impair' another essential interest of the international community, which they evidently do in undermining the right to seek asylum and protection from *refoulement*.[360] Partner States can also decline to engage in pullbacks, even when under the direction or control of destination States, excluding them from invoking *force majeure*.[361] Relatedly, distress requires that there be no other reasonable way of saving life than to violate the right to leave. Though plausible, pushbacks and pullbacks, as opposed to SAR, often create 'greater peril' to life.[362] These justifications also fail in the context of a pandemic: it was not materially impossible to uphold rights, nor were pushbacks, border closures and other restrictive measures the only way to protect public health, as the proportionality analysis confirms.

[356] Papastavridis, 'Fortress' (n 200) 97–99.
[357] ARSIWA Commentary, 78 para 9, 80 para 9, 84 para 20.
[358] ibid 76–77 paras 2–4; Vari (n 27) 132–33.
[359] ARSIWA Commentary, 83–84 paras 15–17.
[360] Vari (n 27) 132–33. See also Papastavridis, 'Fortress' (n 200) 97; R Boed, 'State of Necessity as a Justification for Internationally Wrongful Conduct' (2014) 3 *Yale Human Rights and Development Law Journal* 1.
[361] ARSIWA Commentary, 69 para 9.
[362] ARSIWA Commentary, 78 para 1, 80 para 10.

VII. CONCLUDING REMARKS

This chapter has shown that pushbacks and pullbacks, at sea and on land, violate the right to leave of migrants unless they constitute genuine rescues with disembarkation in a true place of safety. Unlike removals following due process, these practices overwhelmingly fail to meet fundamental standards. Migrants are often returned to the very places they sought to leave without individualised assessments. Pushbacks and pullbacks are highly disproportionate, indiscriminate and inflict grave, well-documented violations. They not only destroy the essence of the right to leave but also obstruct access to asylum and prevent migrants from asserting their right to entry. Pushbacks and pullbacks are often dressed up as humanitarian efforts, and while regional cooperation can lead to improvements in reception capacity and migration management, partnerships must not legitimise violations of international law or discriminatory, exclusionary measures.

Destination States often believe they can deflect responsibility through outsourcing to third States, but this position is wholly unsustainable. Destination States remain responsible for directly violating the right to leave during pushbacks, failing to uphold positive obligations, and for aiding or directing third States to perform pullbacks. This entailed shared responsibility with third States, the EU, ICMPD, IOM and NATO, which is crucial to remedying accountability gaps.

To comply with the right to leave and other fundamental obligations, States and IOs must ensure safe migration pathways, halt all pushbacks and pullbacks, and restore effective SAR operations. Non-discrimination should underpin all migration policies, ensuring equal treatment and protection for women and children, and for all racial, ethnic and religious groups. Genuine humanitarian efforts must prioritise the rights and safety of migrants, including their right to leave and seek asylum. Regional cooperation should be grounded in human rights and supported by robust accountability mechanisms, not used to evade responsibility. Global North States can demonstrate genuine responsibility sharing and good faith by processing asylum claims at their borders, rather than outsourcing to 'safe' countries that lack capacity, resources and safeguards to ensure meaningful protection.

7

Conclusion

THIS WORK HAS uncovered how the human right to leave any country under international law is increasingly obstructed in a world of externalised migration control. Migrants are prevented both from entering a particular destination and from leaving another, in breach of the right to leave. As these abusive policies proliferate, many individuals from the Global South face systemic discrimination and exclusion from safe and regular migration routes, and are forced into ever more perilous journeys.

These final pages consolidate key findings and present targeted recommendations for States, IOs and other stakeholders, outlining a path forward away from externalisation and containment. By challenging the existing global (im)mobility regime, we can advance a rights-based, decolonial approach to migration and asylum that addresses asymmetrical power structures and upholds the dignity and human rights of all people without discrimination.

As this work has demonstrated, countries in the Global North have sought for decades to contain migrants within countries of origin and transit through restrictive measures, including visa systems, airlines preventing the departure of improperly documented migrants, border force agents stationed abroad, and offshore processing. With an ever-growing focus on preventing irregular migration, Global North States have increasingly outsourced migration control to partner States to forestall exit on their behalf, resulting in pullbacks, the criminalisation of exit, and detention. Beyond the State, private actors and IOs, notably the EU, ICMPD, IOM and NATO, play critical roles in designing, implementing and supporting externalisation policies.

Much of the discourse has centred on the externalisation strategies of Australia, the EU and the US – how they have 'exported' their restrictive and harmful policies to other wealthy nations while co-opting partner States to obstruct departure, including at the expense of the latter's own citizens.[1] However, as this book has sought to highlight, States in the Global South are not passive actors; they increasingly deploy their own externalisation policies, from Algeria to Brazil, South Africa to India, and beyond.

[1] See A Shachar and D Ghezelbash, 'How and Why "Ideas Travel" in Migration Law and Policy' in K Cope, S Burch Elias and J Goldenziel (eds), *The Oxford Handbook of Comparative Immigration Law* (Oxford, OUP, forthcoming) www.ssrn.com/abstract=4842136.

This work has provided a comprehensive exploration of the right to leave – a fundamental freedom for ensuring liberty, equality and international protection for people on the move with protection needs. Delving into the underexplored and underdeveloped right to leave, the book charts a general framework for assessing whether restrictions conform with the right to leave. Chapter two established how the right is and ought to be interpreted and operationalised. Through an in-depth examination of the sources of the right in international law and jurisprudence of global and regional adjudicative bodies, it clarified the right's core requirements, lawful limitations and scope. While the focus was mainly on the obligations owed by destination and departure States, the right to leave also imposes obligations on IOs. Chapter three challenged the dominant notion that States possess an almost unfettered right to exclude non-nationals as the epitome of State sovereignty. Instead, the work illuminated how ensuring protection from *refoulement* and collective expulsion imposes an obligation on States to grant migrants temporary admission to access asylum procedures. Other migrants may enjoy a right of entry for family reunification purposes or under free movement regimes. In doing so, it underscored the distinct yet interrelated relationship between exit and entry, arguing individuals should be able to exercise their right to leave irrespective of whether they possess any right of entry elsewhere. However, safe country concepts serve to legitimise the exclusion of asylum seekers.

The ability of asylum seekers to flee serious harm and seek refuge elsewhere hinges on being able to leave. As the opening chapters demonstrated, the right to leave is a precondition for exercising one's right to seek asylum, accessing refugee status, or securing protection from *refoulement* and expulsion – since making contact with a destination State should trigger a corresponding right of entry. Chapter four thus endorsed the notion of a '*right to leave to seek asylum*' and delved into the potential duties that accompany this right to ensure that it is fully respected and effectively realised for asylum seekers and refugees.

Building on the foundational framework in Part I, Part II examined the compatibility of key externalisation practices with the right to leave and the international legal responsibility of States and IOs for violations occurring in this context. Through detailed analyses in chapter five on visa regimes and carrier sanctions, and in chapter six on pushbacks and pullbacks, this work demonstrated how such measures can interfere with and violate the right to leave. Visa refusals and the denial of embarkation by carriers suppress lawful travel, disproportionately impacting migrants and asylum seekers from 'blacklisted' States and certain racial backgrounds. Pushbacks and pullbacks undermine the very essence of the right to leave and to seek asylum, resulting in grave violations. The only exception is when they constitute genuine rescues, with disembarkation in a place of safety. Through restrictive border control policies and practices, States construct the very problems they seek to avoid, pushing migrants into irregularity and vulnerability and increasing the demand for people smugglers.

The analysis illustrated that States and IOs exercising jurisdiction retain their obligations under international law, even when engaging in externalisation. Destination States, States of origin and transit, as well as the EU (including Frontex), the ICMPD, IOM and NATO, can all bear and share international responsibility for violations – whether as the direct perpetrator, for failing to uphold positive obligations, or through complicity and exerting direction and control over another actor.

Despite significant obstacles, the right to leave, jurisdictional thresholds, and the law of international responsibility limit the measures that can lawfully be imposed. Consequently, States and international actors engaged in externalisation cannot credibly claim adherence to the letter and spirit of international law while simultaneously undermining its core obligations. These actors remain responsible for violations resulting from externalisation, and attempts by destination States to shift responsibility onto third States is wholly untenable.

I. OPERATIONALISING THE RIGHT TO LEAVE IN MIGRATION POLICIES AND PRACTICES

There is a clear need for destination States, third States, IOs and private actors to operationalise and integrate the key aspects of the right to leave, along with the findings of this work, into their migration control policies and practices moving forward. If adopted, these recommendations would make the right to leave meaningful and effective for all – demonstrating that States and other actors are genuinely committed to tackling deadly, dangerous journeys.[2] These key aspects and recommendations are summarised here.

Foundational Principles

1. The right to leave is well-established in international law under treaty and customary law. It protects all individuals, regardless of migration status, and is subject to few legitimate exceptions.
2. Individuals have the right to leave any country for a country of their choice – with admission a distinct issue.

[2] See also: OHCHR, 'Recommended Principles and Guidelines on Human Rights at International Borders' (Geneva, UN, 2014) 7, 16, 38, www.ohchr.org/sites/default/files/Documents/Issues/Migration/OHCHR_Recommended_Principles_Guidelines.pdf; UNGA, 'Global Compact for Safe, Orderly and Regular Migration' (11 January 2019) UN Doc A/RES/73/195; FMR, 'Dangerous Journeys: Saving Lives and Responding to Missing Migrants and Refugees' (Issue 75, May 2025) www.fmreview.org/dangerous-journeys.

3. States must secure this right for nationals abroad and people within their territory or jurisdiction, including in cases of extraterritorial migration control.
4. No State may unlawfully obstruct departure from their territory and must issue travel documents to its nationals.
5. Legitimate aims must be narrowly construed and not prejudice other rights and obligations, including the right to seek asylum or non-discrimination obligations.
6. Restrictions must be provided by law, clearly defined, proportionate, and consistent with other human rights. Blanket, indefinite or automatic restrictions are incompatible with the right to leave.
7. The right to leave is independent of any right of entry elsewhere. States – and carriers acting as agents – cannot lawfully obstruct departure based on potential refusal of entry by a prospective destination or to stem irregular migration.

International Protection and Admission

1. The right to leave should be interpreted holistically, alongside the fundamental protections owed to asylum seekers and refugees, including the right to seek asylum, *non-refoulement* and collective expulsion.
2. States should grant temporary admission to migrants at their borders or under their control in order to ensure access to asylum procedures and procedural safeguards.
3. Safe country arrangements, if they continue at all, must not legitimise the shifting of asylum responsibilities or as a pretext for hampering migration, and must be subject to strict and robust criteria.
4. A stricter test should apply when assessing violations of the right to leave for asylum seekers and refugees, prioritising their protection needs.
5. States and IOs must not obstruct asylum seekers' departure or their search for a country to admit them. Migration laws and policies should be organised to enable individuals to leave and seek asylum, ensuring protection from *refoulement*, non-discrimination and other violations.
6. States of sojourn should issue travel documents to asylum seekers and refugees therein to ensure that they have access to regular travel opportunities.
7. States and IOs must take concrete steps to realise the right to leave to seek asylum, including facilitating departure and evacuation for stranded migrants and those in other precarious situations.

Externalisation and Migration Regimes

1. States should prioritise a systemic interpretation of their duties towards migrants, ensuring migration and border control measures comply with international human rights and refugee law and the law of the sea, and are performed in good faith.
2. To comply with these standards, States and IOs should abolish harmful externalisation and containment policies. States, the EU, ICMPD, IOM and NATO should reassess their activities and services that may contribute to violations of the right to leave or other rights.
3. States should adopt rights-based migration and asylum policies that prioritise the rights and safety of migrants, uphold international law, and promote responsibility sharing.[3] This includes ensuring access to fair and efficient asylum procedures within the State's own territory, rather than outsourcing to 'safe' countries with less capacity and resourcing.
4. Non-discrimination should underpin all migration policies, guaranteeing equal treatment and protection of women and children, people of all racial, ethnic and religious backgrounds, and other groups rendered vulnerable by these practices.
5. Bilateral and regional partnerships and agreements should prioritise genuine humanitarianism and enhance the protection of migrant rights, rather than advancing self-interest and containment strategies. Development aid, visa concessions and trade benefits should not be leveraged to undermine rights or shift responsibility away from destination States.
6. States should ensure accountability for violations against migrants by establishing independent oversight mechanisms, enhancing transparency, and providing effective remedies, including access to visas, asylum procedures, and other forms of justice.
7. States should ensure the availability of safe and regular routes on an equitable basis for migrants, including expanded refugee resettlement and complementary pathways for asylum seekers, alongside travel, education, work, labour and family reunification opportunities, without reinforcing exclusionary patterns, to reduce the need for irregular and unsafe migration.

Visa Regimes

1. States and IOs must address the discriminatory and structural issues in global visa and mobility systems.

[3] See UNGA, 'New York Declaration for Refugees and Migrants' (3 October 2016) UN Doc A/RES/71/1, para 68.

2. Visa regimes should be reformed to ensure that individuals from blacklisted States can obtain visas and to eliminate unnecessary blacklisting altogether. Visa decisions should be based on objective and precise criteria, and provide avenues to challenge refusals and denials of embarkation by carriers.
3. Carrier sanctions and ILO regimes should include strict safeguards such as robust accountability mechanisms, exemptions from penalties when individuals enter the asylum process, and adequate training on human rights and refugee standards.
4. Visa requirements and carrier sanctions should be suspended when a significant risk of harm exists for specific nationalities or groups.

Pushbacks and Pullbacks

1. States and IOs should immediately cease pushbacks and pullbacks at sea and on land, and all forms of involvement in operations where pushbacks or pullbacks are occurring or likely to occur.
2. Policies of non-assistance and the criminalisation of NGO rescue vessels performing lifesaving actions should be ended.
3. Operations should be limited to genuine rescues, with the protection of life and safety paramount. States and the EU must restore and resource effective SAR operations, ensuring timely disembarkation to real places of safety and access to asylum procedures.
4. Anti-smuggling laws and objectives should be narrowly construed in line with the Palermo Protocol to target transnational, organised groups profiting from human smuggling, rather than criminalising migrants or restricting movement itself.
5. States should create effective, independent monitoring mechanisms at and around borders to prevent abuses and ensure accountability and justice for victims.

II. THE WAY FORWARD: FROM CONTAINMENT TO GLOBAL MOBILITY

Implementing these recommendations would lead to significant and radical reform, with profound consequences for regimes that inhibit departure and prevent migrants from reaching their territories. It would help prevent abuses and remedy the situation of migrants stuck in their countries of origin and transit. It would also foster a much more liberal and equal global mobility regime than the one currently plagued by exclusion and discrimination. Free movement would again become the rule, and exclusion the exception.

We must remain attentive toward safe routes that, in practice, reinforce discriminatory patterns, are exploitative, or ultimately serve to restrict mobility, such as labour pathways to the West for Global South citizens being contingent on return, or those used as pretexts to end territorial asylum and penalise irregular arrivals.[4] Significantly, such reform would destabilise the interlocking system of externalisation, in which numerous States and actors have entrenched containment within global refugee and mobility regimes, *collectively containing* migrants worldwide.[5]

A. Border and Mobility Justice

A commitment to the right to leave is central to achieving border and mobility justice and to redressing enduring colonial and neocolonial inequalities.[6] As illustrated, the freedom to leave one's country has long been tied to broader struggles for personal liberty, resistance against oppressive regimes, and the search for asylum.

Although challenges persist, more protective and effective solutions are both possible and available. Yet meaningful reform ultimately hinges on the political will of policymakers to centre human rights, racial justice and equitable responsibility sharing, while firmly rejecting punitive alternatives. It also requires acknowledging that migration – an integral part of human history – will remain an ongoing reality, despite the best efforts of States and non-State actors to address its root causes or to prevent it.

Realistically, such a radical overhaul is not on the horizon. Incremental measures, like expanding safe pathways and ending pushbacks and pullbacks, are more likely to gain traction in liberal democracies and regional blocs with strong human rights traditions, whereas deeper structural reforms like dismantling carrier sanctions or ending discriminatory visa policies will face entrenched resistance. Ultimately, leading externalising States will likely forsake their formal commitment to the right to leave, or defend their practices as unobjectionable, rather than relinquish their preferred migration controls. Nevertheless, a better balance can be struck. While States retain the right to control entry, migration control should be executed consistently with their international obligations and in good faith. This does not mean States must provide entry to every migrant. Instead, it demonstrates that the right to leave and right to control entry need not clash. Any reform agenda must navigate these political realities to safeguard the right to leave in practice.

[4] R Marino and M Sallah, 'The Spain-Gambia Circular Migration MoU: Between Mobility Hopes and Criticism' (*migration-control.info*, 25 March 2025) www.migration-control.info/en/blog/the-spain-gambia-circular-migration-mou-between-mobility-hopes-and-criticism/; J Crisp, 'Managing Forced Migration: An Alternative to Dangerous Journeys?' (2025) 75 *Forced Migration Review* 115. cf LS Martini and T Megerisi, *Road to Nowhere: Why Europe's Border Externalisation is a Dead End* (London, European Council on Foreign Relations, 2023) 32–33.

[5] See DS FitzGerald, *Refuge Beyond Reach: How Rich Democracies Repel Asylum Seekers* (Oxford, OUP, 2019) 12, 14.

[6] See generally D Owen, 'Global Justice and the Governance of Transnational Migration' in L Weber and C Tazreiter (eds), *Handbook of Migration and Global Justice* (Cheltenham, Edward Elgar Publishing, 2021).

Closing accountability gaps and ending harmful externalisation practices requires a greater appreciation of the right to leave beyond States and IOs, empowering courts and civil society actors to advance the right through strategic litigation and legal mobilisation. Adjudicative bodies must take seriously the boundaries of the right to leave, especially domestic and regional bodies in the Global South, which play a vital role in litigating this right and declaring externalisation practices unlawful.[7] If partner States were held accountable for pullbacks, migrant detention or criminalising exit, destination States lacking the political will to reform would find it far harder to persuade Global South States to act on their behalf.[8] Practitioners and litigants can utilise the framework developed here to frame externalisation measures as violations of the right to leave, advance stronger normative standards, and compel reform.[9] This necessitates ongoing attentiveness to new modalities that may emerge once existing practices are struck down. By establishing a general framework, this work paves the way for further research, particularly on the externalisation practices of Global South States and whether other contemporary measures – within and beyond migration – undermine or uphold the right to leave.

I hope this book has illustrated the importance of placing the right to leave at the forefront of discussions on migration and asylum. As the starting point of any migrant journey, this right is indispensable in protecting the rights of asylum seekers, refugees and other migrants. Migrants are, first and foremost, individuals in need of protection. Therefore, even if migration control is legitimate, the State's prerogative to exclude should be understood as a secondary norm underpinned by human rights. The focus should always be on protecting people on the move and ensuring their 'right to have rights'.

If human rights continue to be placed second to State prerogatives and the right to leave systematically obstructed, migrants and citizens alike will have little hope of availing themselves of international protection and their rights will be routinely infringed. We will continue to see a global race to the bottom, as more States seek to shift and shirk their responsibilities, with deadly consequences. We must endeavour to make rights practical and effective, eliminate practices that force migrants into 'illegality' and harmful situations, and dismantle the global *(im)*mobility regime. It is therefore timely to re-imagine and restructure migration control in light of the right to leave.

[7] NF Tan and T Gammeltoft-Hansen, 'Topographical Approach to Accountability for Human Rights Violations in Migration Control' (2020) 21 *German Law Journal* 335.

[8] North Africa Post, 'Niger Condemns Algeria's Violations of Sub-Saharan Migrants' Rights' (1 May 2025) www.northafricapost.com/86651-niger-condemns-algerias-violations-of-sub-saharan-migrants-rights.html.

[9] See E McDonnell, 'Challenging Externalisation Through the Lens of the Human Right to Leave' (2024) 71 *Netherlands International Law Review* 119.

Bibliography

Abass, A and Ippolito, F (eds), *Regional Approaches to the Protection of Asylum Seekers: An International Legal Perspective* (Abingdon/New York, Routledge, 2016).

Achiume, ET, 'Migration as Decolonisation' (2019) 71 *Stanford Law Review* 1509.

Achiume, ET, 'Race, Refugees, and International Law' in C Costello, M Foster and J McAdam (eds), *The Oxford Handbook of International Refugee Law* (Oxford, OUP, 2021).

Achiume, ET, 'Race, Borders, and Jurisdiction' (2022) 82 *ZaöRV/Heidelberg Journal of International Law* 465.

Achiume, ET, 'Racial Borders' (2022) 110 *The Georgetown Law Journal LJ* 445.

Acosta, D, *The National Versus the Foreigner in South America: 200 Years of Migration and Citizenship Law* (Cambridge, CUP, 2018).

Acosta, D, Blouin, C and Freier, LF, *La emigración venezolana: respuestas latinoamericanas* (Salamanca, Fundación Carolina, 2019).

Adamson, FB and Tsourapas, G, 'The Migration State in the Global South: Nationalizing, Developmental, and Neoliberal Models of Migration Management' (2020) 54 *International Migration Review* 853.

Aiken, S and Neve, A, 'Refugee "Responsibility Sharing" – Challenging the Status Quo' (2023) 7 *PKI Global Justice Journal* 7.

Allain, J, 'The *Jus Cogens* Nature of *Non-refoulement*' (2001) 13 *International Journal of Refugee Law* 533.

Alvarez, J, 'Review of Dan Sarooshi, International Organizations and their Exercise of Sovereign Powers' (2007) 101 *American Journal of International Law* 674.

Ancite-Jepifánova, A, 'Beyond the "Hybrid Attack" Paradigm: EU-Belarus Border Crisis and the Erosion of Asylum-Seeker Rights in Latvia, Lithuania and Poland' (2024) 15 *Avant* 1.

Andrijasevic, R and Walters, W, 'The International Organization for Migration and the International Government of Borders' (2010) 28 *Environment and Planning D: Society and Space* 977.

Appleby, JK, 'The United States, Europe, and the Global Compacts: Honoring the Right to Remain and the Right to Migrate' (2025) 13 *Journal on Migration and Human Security* 151.

Arendt, H, *The Origins of Totalitarianism* (Harcourt, Brace and Company, 1951).

Aust, HP, *Complicity and the Law of State Responsibility* (Cambridge, CUP, 2011).

Avdan, N, 'Human Trafficking and Migration Control Policy: Vicious or Virtuous Cycle?' (2012) 32 *Journal of Public Policy* 171.

Avdan, N, *Visas and Walls: Border Security in the Age of Terrorism* (Philadelphia, University of Pennsylvania Press, 2019).

Baca, G, 'Visa Denied: Why Courts should Review a Consular Officer's Denial of a U.S.-Citizen Family Member's Visa' (2015) 64 *American University Law Review* 591.

Badalič, V, 'Tunisia's Role in the EU External Migration Policy: Crimmigration Law, Illegal Practices, and Their Impact on Human Rights' (2019) 20 *Journal of International Migration and Integration* 85.

Baird, T, 'Carrier Sanctions in Europe: A Comparison of Trends in 10 Countries' (2017) 19 *European Journal of Migration and Law* 307.

Baird, T and Spijkerboer, T, 'Carrier Sanctions and the Conflicting Legal Obligations of Carriers: Addressing Human Rights Leakage' (2019) 11 *Amsterdam Law Forum* 4.

Barnidge, RP, 'The Due Diligence Principle Under International Law' (2006) 8 *International Community Law Review* 81.

Bartels, L, 'The EU's Human Rights Obligations in Relation to Policies with Extraterritorial Effects' (2015) 25 *European Journal of International Law* 1071.

Battjes, H, *European Asylum Law and International Law* (Leiden, Martinus Nijhoff, 2006).

Bauböck, R, 'Free Movement and the Asymmetry Between Exit and Entry' (2006) 4 *Ethics & Economics* 1.

Bauböck, R, 'Free Movement Regimes: Is the EU Experience Exportable?' in E Recchi and M Safi (eds), *Handbook of Human Mobility and Migration* (Cheltenham, Edward Elgar Publishing, 2024).

Behrman, S, 'Refugee Law as a Means of Control' (2019) 32 *Journal of Refugee Studies* 42.

Bengel, K, 'Understanding the Nansen Passport: A System of Manipulation' (2022) 29 *Indiana Journal of Global Legal Studies* 217.

Benton, M and others, *COVID-19 and the State of Global Mobility in 2021* (Geneva/Washington DC, Migration Policy Institute and International Organization for Migration, 2022).

Berriane, M, de Haas, H and Natter, K, 'Introduction: Revisiting Moroccan Migrations' (2015) 20 *The Journal of North African Studies* 503.

Besson, S, 'The Extraterritoriality of the European Convention on Human Rights: Why Human Rights Depend on Jurisdiction and What Jurisdiction Amounts to' (2012) 25 *Leiden Journal of International Law* 857.

Besson, S, 'Concurrent Responsibilities under the European Convention on Human Rights: The Concurrence of Human Rights Jurisdictions, Duties, and Responsibilities' in A van Aaken and I Motoc (eds), *The European Convention on Human Rights and General International Law* (Oxford, OUP, 2018).

Bigo, D, 'Criminalisation of "Migrants": The Side Effect of the Will to Control Frontiers and the Sovereignty Illusion' in B Bogusz and others (eds), *Irregular Migration and Human Rights: Theoretical, European and International Perspectives* (Leiden, Martinus Nijhoff, 2004).

Bigo, D and Guild, E, 'Policing at a Distance: Schengen Visa Policies' in D Bigo and E Guild (eds), *Controlling Frontiers: Free Movement Into and Within Europe* (Chesterfield, Ashgate, 2005).

Bjorge, E, *The Evolutionary Interpretation of Treaties* (Oxford, OUP, 2014).

Bloom, T, 'The Business of Migration Control: Delegating Migration Control Functions to Private Actors' (2015) 6 *Global Policy* 151.

Bloom, T and Risse, V, 'Examining Hidden Coercion at State Borders: Why Carrier Sanctions Cannot Be Justified' (2014) 7 *Ethics & Global Politics* 65.

Boed, R, 'The State of the Right of Asylum in International Law' (1994) 5 *Duke Journal of Comparative & International Law* 1.

Boed, R, 'State of Necessity as a Justification for Internationally Wrongful Conduct' (2014) 3 *Yale Human Rights and Development Law Journal* 1.

Bordin, FL, *The Analogy between States and International Organizations* (Cambridge, CUP, 2019).

Bossuyt, MJ, *Guide to the "Travaux Préparatoires" of the International Covenant on Civil and Political Rights* (Dordrecht, Martinus Nijhoff, 1987).

Brachet, J, 'Policing the Desert: The IOM in Libya Beyond War and Peace' (2016) 48 *Antipode* 272.

Bradley, M, *The International Organization for Migration: Challenges, Commitments, Complexities* (Abingdon/New York, Routledge, 2020).

Bradley, M, Costello, C and Sherwood, A (eds), *IOM Unbound? Obligations and Accountability of the International Organization for Migration in an Era of Expansion* (Cambridge, CUP, 2023).

Brandl, U, 'The Human Right to Leave a Country: To Protect or Forget?' (Conflict and Compromise between Law and Politics in EU Migration and Asylum Policies conference, Brussels, February 2018).

Brennan, B and Anderson, B, 'Communities of Resistance: Migrant Organizing and Transnational Campaigning Past and Future' in B Anderson (ed), *Rethinking Migration Challenging Borders, Citizenship and Race* (Bristol, Bristol University Press, 2025).

Briddick, C, 'Some Other(ed) "Refugees"?: Women Seeking Asylum under Refugee and Human Rights Law' in SS Juss (ed), *Research Handbook on International Refugee Law* (Cheltenham, Edward Elgar Publishing, 2019).

Briddick, C and Costello, C, 'Introduction to the Symposium on Undoing Discriminatory Borders' (2021) 115 *American Journal of International Law Unbound* 328.
Brouwer, E, 'Extraterritorial Migration Control and Human Rights: Preserving the Responsibility of the EU and its Member States' in B Ryan and V Mitsilegas (eds), *Extraterritorial Immigration Control: Legal Challenges* (Leiden, Martinus Nijhoff, 2010).
Brouwer, A and Kumin, J, 'Interception and Asylum: When Migration Control and Human Rights Collide' (2003) 21 *Refuge* 6.
Buxton, R and Ritholtz, S, *The Way Out: Justice in the Queer Search for Refuge* (California, University of California Press, forthcoming).
Cantor, D and others, 'Externalisation, Access to Territorial Asylum, and International Law' (2022) 34 *International Journal of Refugee Law* 120.
Capone, F, 'The Alleged Tension between the Global Compact for Safe, Orderly and Regular Migration and State Sovereignty: "Much Ado about Nothing"?' (2020) 33 *Leiden Journal of International Law* 713.
Carens, JH, *The Ethics of Immigration* (Oxford, OUP, 2013).
Carling, J, 'Migration in the Age of Involuntary Immobility: Theoretical Reflections and Cape Verdean Experiences' (2002) 28 *Journal of Ethnic and Migration Studies* 5.
Cassarino, JP, 'Beyond the Criminalisation of Migration: A Non-Western Perspective' (2018) 4 *International Journal of Migration and Border Studies* 397.
Cassel, D, 'Extraterritorial Application of Inter-American Human Rights Instruments' in F Coomans and MT Kamminga (eds), *Extraterritorial Application of Human Rights Treaties* (Antwerp, Intersentia, 2004).
Cerna, CM, 'The Extraterritorial Scope of Human Rights Treaties: The American Convention on Human Rights' in F Coomans and MT Kamminga (eds), *Extraterritorial Application of Human Rights Treaties* (Plymouth, Intersentia, 2004).
Cerrutti, MS and Marcelino, PF, 'Recent African immigration to South America: The Cases of Argentina and Brazil in the Regional Context' in J Martínez Pizarro and L Reboiras Finardi (eds), *Development, institutional and policy aspects of international migration between Africa, Europe and Latin America and the Caribbean* (Santiago, UN, 2012).
Chatty, D, *Syria: The Making and Unmaking of a Refuge State* (Oxford, OUP, 2018).
Chetail, V, 'Freedom of Movement and Transnational Migrations: A Human Rights Perspective' in TA Aleinikoff and V Chetail (eds), *Migration and International Legal Norms* (The Hague, TMC Asser Press, 2003).
Chetail, V, 'Are Refugee Rights Human Rights? An Unorthodox Questioning of the Relations between Refugee Law and Human Rights Law' in R Rubio-Marín (ed), *Human Rights and Immigration* (Oxford, OUP, 2014).
Chetail, V, 'The Transnational Movement of Persons Under General International Law: Mapping the Customary Law Foundations of International Migration Law' in V Chetail and C Bauloz (eds), *Research Handbook on International Law and Migration* (Cheltenham, Edward Elgar Publishing, 2014).
Chetail, V, 'Sovereignty and Migration in the Doctrine of the Law of Nations: An Intellectual History of Hospitality from Vitoria to Vattel' (2016) 27 *European Journal of International Law* 901.
Chetail, V, *International Migration Law* (Oxford, OUP, 2019).
Chetail, V, 'The Global Compact for Safe, Orderly and Regular Migration: A Kaleidoscope of International Law' (2020) 16 *International Journal of Law in Context* 253.
Chetail, V, 'The International Organization for Migration and the Duty to Protect Migrants: Revisiting the Law of International Organizations' in J Klabbers (ed), *The Cambridge Companion to International Organizations Law* (Cambridge, CUP, 2022).
Chetail, V, 'Demystifying Sovereignty: Totem and Taboo of Migration Control in International Law' (2024) 118 *American Journal of International Law Unbound* 193.
Chime, IP and others, 'The AU Free Movement Protocol: Challenges in Its Implementation' (2023) 68 *Journal of African Law* 3.

Chimni, BS, 'The Geopolitics of Refugee Studies: A View from the South' (1998) 11 *Journal of Refugee Studies* 350.
Chimni, BS, 'Third World Approaches to International Law: A Manifesto' (2006) 8 *International Community Law Review* 3.
Cholewinski, R, 'No Right of Entry' in CA Groenendijk, E Guild and PE Minderhoud (eds), *In Search of Europe's Borders* (The Hague, Kluwer Law International, 2003).
Christian, BP, 'Visa Policy, Inspection and Exit Controls: Transatlantic Perspectives on Migration Management' (1999) 14 *Georgetown Immigration Law Journal* 215.
Ciliberto, G, 'Libya's Pull-Backs of Boat Migrants: Can Italy Be Held Accountable for Violations of International Law?' (2018) 4 *Italian Law Journal* 489.
Cintra, N, and Nabuco Martuscelli, P, 'Wall of Visas: How Race Impacts the Externalization of (Forced) Migration Control in South-South Migration Corridors' (2025) *Ethnic and Racial Studies* 1.
Collyer, M, 'Stranded Migrants and the Fragmented Journey' (2010) 23 *Journal of Refugee Studies* 273.
Contartese, C, 'Competence-Based Approach, Normative Control, and the International Responsibility of the EU and its Member States' (2019) 16 *International Organizations Law Review* 339.
Cornelisse, G, 'European Vessels, African Territorial Waters and "Illegal Emigrants": The Right to Leave and the Principle of (Il)Legality in a Global Regime of Mobility' (2008) *Challenge*.
Cornelisse, G, 'EU Boots on the Ground and Effective Judicial Protection Against Frontex' Operational Powers in Return: Lessons from Case T-600/21' (2024) 26 *European Journal of Migration and Law* 356.
Corten, O and Klein, P, 'The Limits of Complicity as a Ground for Responsibility: Lessons Learned from the *Corfu Channel* Case' in K Bannelier, T Christakis and S Heathcote (eds), *The ICJ and the Evolution of International Law: The Enduring Impact of the Corfu Channel Case* (Abingdon/New York, Routledge, 2012).
Costello, C, 'The Asylum Procedures Directive and the Proliferation of Safe Country Practices: Deterrence, Deflection and the Dismantling of International Protection?' (2005) 7 *European Journal of Migration and Law* 35.
Costello, C, *The Human Rights of Migrants and Refugees in European Law* (Oxford, OUP, 2016).
Costello, C, 'The Search for the Outer Edges of *Non-refoulement* in Europe: Exceptionality and Flagrant Breaches' in B Burson and DJ Cantor (eds), *Human Rights and the Refugee Definition: Comparative Legal Practice and Theory* (Leiden, Brill Nijhoff, 2016).
Costello, C, 'Refugees and (Other) Migrants: Will the Global Compacts Ensure Safe Flight and Onward Mobility for Refugees?' (2018) 30 *International Journal of Refugee Law* 643.
Costello, C and Foster, M, 'Non-refoulement as Custom and *Jus Cogens*? Putting the Prohibition to the Test' in M den Heijer and H van der Wilt (eds), *NYIL 2015: Jus Cogens: Quo Vadis?* (The Hague, TMC Asser Press, 2016).
Costello, C and Foster, M, '(Some) Refugees Welcome: When Is Differentiating Between Refugees Unlawful Discrimination?' (2022) 22 *International Journal of Discrimination and the Law* 244.
Costello, C and Mann, I, 'Border Justice: Migration and Accountability for Human Rights Violations' (2020) 21 *German Law Journal* 311.
Costello, C, Groenendijk, K and Storgaard, LH, *Realising the Right to Family Reunification of Refugees in Europe* (Issue Paper, Council of Europe Commissioner for Human Rights 2017).
Coventry, T, 'Appropriate Measures at Sea: Extraterritorial Enforcement Jurisdiction over Stateless Migrant Smuggling Vessels' (2019) *Maritime Safety and Security Law Journal* 5.
Craig, P and De Búrca, G, *EU Law: Text, Cases, and Materials*, 7th edn (Oxford, OUP, 2020).
Crawford, J, *State Responsibility: The General Part* (Cambridge, CUP, 2013).
Crawford, J and others, *The Law of International Responsibility* (Oxford, OUP, 2010).

Crawley, H and Teye, JK (eds), *The Palgrave Handbook of South–South Migration and Inequality* (New York, Palgrave Macmillan, 2024).
Crépeau, F, 'Towards a Mobile and Diverse World: "Facilitating Mobility" as a Central Objective of the Global Compact on Migration' (2018) 30 *International Journal of Refugee Law* 650.
Crisp, J, 'Managing Forced Migration: An Alternative to Dangerous Journeys?' (2025) 75 *Forced Migration Review* 115.
Crush, J, Chikanda, A and Ramachandran, S (eds), *New Directions in South-South Migration* (Singapore, Springer Singapore, 2025).
Czaika, M and Hobolth, M, 'Do Restrictive Asylum and Visa Policies Increase Irregular Migration into Europe?' (2016) 17 *European Union Politics* 345.
Czaika, M, de Haas, H and Villares-Varela, M, 'The Global Evolution of Travel Visa Regimes' (2018) 44 *Population and Development Review* 589.
Da Costa, K, *The Extraterritorial Application of Selected Human Rights Treaties* (Leiden, Martinus Nijhoff, 2013).
Damon-Feng, F, 'Refoulement as Pandemic Policy' (2022) 31 *Washington International Law Journal* 186.
Dannenbaum, T, 'Dual Attribution in the Context of Military Operations' in AS Barros, C Ryngaert and J Wouters (eds), *International Organizations and Member State Responsibility* (Leiden, Brill Nijhoff, 2017).
Dastyari, A and Ghezelbash, D, 'Asylum at Sea: The Legality of Shipboard Refugee Status Determination Procedures' (2020) 32 *International Journal of Refugee Law* 1.
Dastyari, A and Hirsch, A, 'The Ring of Steel: Extraterritorial Migration Controls in Indonesia and Libya and the Complicity of Australia and Italy' (2019) 19 *Human Rights Law Review* 435.
Dastyari, A, Nethery, A and Hirsch, A (eds), *Refugee Externalisation Policies: Responsibility, Legitimacy and Accountability* (Abingdon/New York, Routledge, 2022).
Daugirdas, K, 'How and Why International Law Binds International Organizations' (2016) 57 *Harvard International Law Journal* 325.
Dauvergne, C, 'Sovereignty, Migration and the Rule of Law in Global Times' (2004) 67 *Modern Law Review* 588.
Dauvergne, C, *The New Politics of Immigration and the End of Settler Societies* (Cambridge, CUP, 2016).
David, N, *The International Responsibility of NATO and Its Personnel during Military Operations* (Boston, Brill Nijhoff, 2017).
Davies, SE, '1989 Comprehensive Plan of Action (CPA) and Refugee Policy in Southeast Asia: Twenty Years Forward What Has Changed?' in A Abass and F Ippolito (eds), *Regional Approaches to the Protection of Asylum Seekers* (Abingdon/New York, Routledge, 2016).
Davitti, D, 'Biopolitical Borders and the State of Exception in the European Migration "Crisis"' (2018) 29 *European Journal of International Law* 1173.
Davitti, D and La Chimia, A, 'A Lesser Evil? The European Agenda on Migration and the Use of Aid Funding for Migration Control' in F de Londras and S Mullally (eds), *The Irish Yearbook of International Law*, vol 10, 2015 (London, Hart Publishing, 2017).
De Haas, H and Natter, K, 'Introduction: Revisiting Moroccan Migrations' (2015) 20 *The Journal of North African Studies* 503.
De Haas, H, Natter, K and Vezzoli, S, 'Growing Restrictiveness or Changing Selection? The Nature and Evolution of Migration Policies' (2018) 52 *International Migration Review* 324.
De Schutter, O, 'Human Rights and the Rise of International Organisations: The Logic of Sliding Scales in the Law of International Responsibility' in J Wouters and others (eds), *Accountability for Human Rights Violations by International Organisations* (Plymouth, Intersentia, 2010).
Dehm, S, 'Passport' in J Hohmann and D Joyce (eds), *International Law's Objects* (Oxford, OUP, 2018).
Dehm, S, 'Contesting the Right to Leave in International Law: The Berlin Wall, the Third World Brain Drain and the Politics of Emigration in the 1960s' in M Craven, S Pahuja, G Simpson (eds), *International Law and the Cold War* (Cambridge, CUP, 2019).
Dembour, MB, *When Humans Become Migrants: Study of the European Court of Human Rights with an Inter-American Counterpoint* (Oxford, OUP, 2015).

Den Heijer, M, *Europe and Extraterritorial Asylum* (Oxford, Hart Publishing, 2012).
Den Heijer, M, 'Shared Responsibility Before The European Court of Human Rights' (2013) 60 *Netherlands International Law Review* 411.
Den Heijer, M, 'Article 18 – Right to Asylum' in S Peers and others (eds), *The EU Charter of Fundamental Rights: A Commentary* (Oxford, Hart Publishing, 2014).
Den Heijer, M, 'Visas and Non-discrimination' (2018) 20 *European Journal of Migration and Law* 470.
Desmond, A, 'The Private Life of Family Matters: Curtailing Human Rights Protection for Migrants under Article 8 of the ECHR?' (2018) 29 *European Journal of International Law* 261.
Digidiki, V and Bhabha, J, 'Against the Best Interests of the Child: The Global Injustice of Migrant Externalization' in L Weber and C Tazreiter (eds), *Handbook of Migration and Global Justice* (Cheltenham, Edward Elgar Publishing, 2021).
Dobkin, DS, 'Challenging the Doctrine of Consular Nonreviewability in Immigration Cases' (2010) 24 *Georgetown Immigration Law Journal* 113.
Dowty, A, *Closed Borders: The Contemporary Assault on Freedom of Movement* (New Haven, Yale University Press, 1987).
Drewski, D and Gerhards, J, *Pan-African Solidarity and International Reputation: Uganda's Policy of Open Doors Toward Refugees* (Oxford, OUP, 2024).
Durieux, JF, 'Three Asylum Paradigms' (2013) 20 *International Journal on Minority and Group Rights* 147.
Düvell, F, 'Transit Migration: A Blurred and Politicised Concept' (2012) 18 *Population, Space and Place* 415.
Edwards, A, 'Human Rights, Refugees, and the Right "to Enjoy" Asylum' (2005) 17 *International Journal of Refugee Law* 293.
El-Enany, N, *Bordering Britain* (Manchester, Manchester University Press, 2020).
El-Taliawi, OG, *The Politics of Refugee Policy in the Global South*, vol 15 (Montreal, McGill-Queen's University Press, 2024).
Espinoza, MV, 'Migration Governance in South America: Change and Continuity in Times of "Crisis"' in H Crawley and JK Teye (eds), *The Palgrave Handbook of South–South Migration and Inequality* (Cham, Palgrave Macmillan, 2024).
European Union Agency for Fundamental Rights, *Legal Entry Channels to the EU for Persons in Need of International Protection: A Toolbox* (Vienna, FRA, 2015).
European Union Agency for Fundamental Rights, *Scope of the Principle of 'Non-Refoulement' in Contemporary Border Management: Evolving Areas of Law* (Luxembourg, EU, 2016).
Fakhoury, T and Chatty, D (eds), *Refugee Governance in the Arab World: The International Refugee Regime and Global Politics* (London, Bloomsbury, 2025).
Farahat, A and Markard, N, *Places of Safety in the Mediterranean: The EU's Policy of Outsourcing Responsibility* (Berlin, Heinrich-Böll-Stiftung, 2020).
Feller, E, 'Carrier Sanctions and International Law' (1989) 1 *International Journal of Refugee Law* 48.
Fernandez, M, 'The EU External Borders Policy and Frontex-Coordinated Operations at Sea: Who is in Charge? Reflections on Responsibility for Wrongful Acts' in V Moreno-Lax and E Papastavridis (eds), *'Boat Refugees' and Migrants at Sea: A Comprehensive Approach: Integrating Maritime Security with Human Rights* (Dordrecht, Brill Nijhoff, 2016).
Ferstman, C, *International Organizations and the Fight for Accountability* (Oxford, OUP, 2017).
Ferstman, C, 'Human Rights Due Diligence Policies Applied to Extraterritorial Cooperation to Prevent "Irregular" Migration: European Union and United Kingdom Support to Libya' (2020) 21 *German Law Journal* 459.
Fine, S and Ypi, L (eds), *Migration in Political Theory: The Ethics of Movement and Membership* (Oxford, OUP, 2016).
Fink, M, *Frontex and Human Rights: Responsibility in 'Multi-Actor Situations' under the ECHR and EU Public Liability Law* (Oxford, OUP, 2018).

Fink, M, 'EU Liability for Contributions to Member States' Breaches of EU Law' (2019) 56 *Common Market Law Review* 1227.

FitzGerald, DS, *Refuge Beyond Reach: How Rich Democracies Repel Asylum Seekers* (Oxford, OUP, 2019).

FitzGerald, DS and Cook-Martín, D, *Culling the Masses: The Democratic Origins of Racist Immigration Policy in the Americas* (Cambridge, HUP, 2014).

Flahaux, ML and de Haas, H, 'African Migration: Trends, Patterns, Drivers' (2016) 4 *Comparative Migration Studies* 1.

Forowicz, M, *The Reception of International Law in the European Court of Human Rights* (Oxford, OUP, 2010).

Foster, M, 'Protection Elsewhere: The Legal Implications of Requiring Refugees to Seek Protection in Another State' (2007) 28 *Michigan Journal of International Law* 223.

Foster, M, 'Responsibility Sharing or Shifting? "Safe" Third Countries and International Law' (2008) 25 *Refuge* 64.

Frelick, B, Kysel, IM and Podkul, J, 'The Impact of Externalization of Migration Controls on the Rights of Asylum Seekers and Other Migrants' (2016) 4 *Journal on Migration and Human Security* 190.

Frowd, PM, 'Borderwork Creep in West Africa's Sahel' (2022) 27 *Geopolitics* 1331.

Gallagher, AT and David, F, *The International Law of Migrant Smuggling* (Cambridge, CUP, 2014).

Gammeltoft-Hansen, T, *Access to Asylum: International Refugee Law and the Globalisation of Migration Control* (Cambridge, CUP, 2011).

Gammeltoft-Hansen, T, 'International Cooperation on Migration Control: Towards a Research Agenda for Refugee Law' (2018) 20 *European Journal of Migration and Law* 107.

Gammeltoft-Hansen, T and Hathaway, JC, '*Non-Refoulement* in a World of Cooperative Deterrence' (2015) 53 *Columbia Journal of Transnational Law* 235.

Gammeltoft-Hansen, T and Sørensen, NN, *The Migration Industry and the Commercialisation of International Migration* (Abingdon/New York, Routledge, 2013).

Garciandia, R, 'State Responsibility and Positive Obligations in the European Court of Human Rights: The Contribution of the ICJ in Advancing towards More Judicial Integration' (2020) 33 *Leiden Journal of International Law* 177.

Gardiner, R, *Treaty Interpretation*, 2nd edn (Oxford, OUP, 2015).

Ghezelbash, D, 'Forces of Diffusion: What Drives the Transfer of Immigration Policy and Law Across Jurisdictions?' (2014) 1 *International Journal of Migration and Border Studies* 139.

Ghezelbash, D, 'Legal Transfers of Restrictive Immigration Law: A Historical Perspective' (2017) 66 *International and Comparative Law Quarterly* 235.

Ghezelbash, D, *Refuge Lost: Asylum Law in an Interdependent World* (Cambridge, CUP, 2018).

Ghezelbash, D and Tan, NF, 'The End of the Right to Seek Asylum? COVID-19 and the Future of Refugee Protection' (2021) 32 *International Journal of Refugee Law* 668.

Ghráinne, BN, 'Left to Die at Sea: State Responsibility for the May 2015 Thai, Indonesian and Malaysian Pushback Operations' in F de Londras and S Mullally (eds), *The Irish Yearbook of International Law*, vol 10, 2015 (London, Hart Publishing, 2017).

Gil-Bazo, MT, 'The Charter of Fundamental Rights of the European Union and the Right to be Granted Asylum in the Union's Law' (2008) 27 *Refugee Survey Quarterly* 33.

Gil-Bazo, MT, 'Asylum as a General Principle of International Law' (2015) 27 *International Journal of Refugee Law* 3.

Giuffré, M, 'State Responsibility Beyond Borders: What Legal Basis for Italy's Push-backs to Libya?' (2012) 24 *International Journal of Refugee Law* 692.

Giuffré, M and Moreno-Lax, V, 'The Rise of Consensual Containment: From "Contactless Control" to "Contactless Responsibility" for Forced Migration Flows' in SS Juss (ed), *Research Handbook on International Refugee Law* (Cheltenham, Edward Elgar Publishing, 2019).

Gkliati, M, 'The Next Phase of The European Border and Coast Guard: Responsibility for Returns and Push-backs in Hungary and Greece' (2022) 7 *European Papers* 171.
Gleeson, M, 'Unprecedented but Unfulfilled: Refugee Protection and Regional Responses to the Andaman Sea "Crisis"' (2017) 38 *Antropologi Indonesia* 6.
Gleeson, M, 'Protection Deficit: The Failure of Australia's Offshore Processing Arrangements to Guarantee "Protection Elsewhere" in the Pacific' (2019) 31 *International Journal of Refugee Law* 415.
Goodwin-Gill, GS, *International Law and the Movement of Persons Between States* (Oxford, Clarendon Press, 1978).
Goodwin-Gill, GS, *The Refugee in International Law*, 2nd edn (Oxford, Clarendon Press, 1996).
Goodwin-Gill, GS, 'The Right to Leave, the Right to Return and the Question of the Right to Remain' in Gowlland-Debbas (ed), *The Problem of Refugees in the Light of Contemporary International Law Issues* (The Hague, Martinus Nijhoff, 1996).
Goodwin-Gill, GS, 'State Responsibility and the "Good Faith" Obligation in International Law' in Fitzmaurice, M and Sarooshi, D (eds), *Issues of State Responsibility before International Judicial Institutions: The Clifford Chance Lectures* (Oxford, Hart Publishing, 2004).
Goodwin-Gill, GS, 'R (ex parte European Roma Rights Centre et al) v Immigration Officer at Prague Airport and another (UNHCR intervening)' (2005) 17 *International Journal of Refugee Law* 427.
Goodwin-Gill, GS, 'The Extraterritorial Processing of Claims to Asylum or Protection: The Legal Responsibilities of States and International Organisations' (2007) 9 *UTS Law Review* 26.
Goodwin-Gill, GS, 'The Right to Seek Asylum: Interception at Sea and the Principle of *Non-Refoulement*' (2011) 23 *International Journal of Refugee Law* 443.
Goodwin-Gill, GS, '*Non-Refoulement*, Temporary Refuge, and the "New" Asylum Seekers' in DJ Cantor and JF Durieux (eds), *Refuge from Inhumanity? War Refugees and International Humanitarian Law* (Leiden, Brill Nijhoff, 2014).
Goodwin-Gill, GS and McAdam, J, *The Refugee in International Law*, 4th edn (Oxford, OUP, 2021).
Gordon, LS, 'Immigration Policy in South Africa: Public Opinion, Xenophobia and the Search for Progress' in P Rugunanan and N Xulu-Gama (eds), *Migration in Southern Africa: IMISCOE Regional Reader* (Cham, Springer, 2022).
Gowlland-Debbas, V, *The Problem of Refugees in the Light of Contemporary International Law Issues* (The Hague, Martinus Nijhoff, 1996).
Grabbe, H, 'Stabilising the East While Keeping Out the Easterners: Internal and External Security Logics in Conflict' in S Lavenex and EM Uçarer (eds), *Migration and the Externalities of European Integration* (Lanham, Lexington Books, 2002).
Grahl-Madsen, A, *The Status of Refugees in International Law: Asylum, Entry and Sojourn*, vol 2 (Leiden, AW Sijthoff, 1972).
Grahl-Madsen, A, *Territorial Asylum* (Stockholm, Almqvist & Wiksell International, 1980).
Grahl-Madsen, A, 'Asylum, Territorial' in P Macalister-Smith and G Alfredsson (eds), *The Land Beyond: Collected Essays on Refugee Law and Policy* (The Hague, Martinus Nijhoff, 2001).
Grahl-Madsen, A, 'The European Tradition of Asylum and the Development of Refugee Law' in P Macalister-Smith and G Alfredsson (eds), *The Land Beyond: Collected Essays on Refugee Law and Policy* (The Hague, Martinus Nijhoff, 2001).
Grundler, M, '"Treatment Accorded to Aliens Generally": Article 7(1) of the 1951 Refugee Convention as a Basis for Visa-Free Access to States Parties' Territory? An Examination of the Prohibition of Nationality Discrimination in the Refugee Convention' (2021) 33 *International Journal of Refugee Law* 469.
Guild, E, 'The Border Abroad: Visas and Border Controls' in K Groenendijk, E Guild and P Minderhoud (eds), *In Search of Europe's Borders* (Leiden, Kluwer Law International, 2003).
Guild, E, 'Who is an Irregular Migrant?' in B Bogusz and others (eds), *Irregular Migration and Human Rights: Theoretical, European and International Perspectives* (Leiden: Martinus Nijhoff, 2004).

Guild, E, 'Citizens Without a Constitution, Borders Without a State: EU Free Movement of Persons' in A Baldaccini, E Guild and H Toner (eds), *Whose Freedom, Security and Justice? EU Immigration and Asylum Law and Policy* (Oxford, Hart Publishing, 2007).

Guild, E, *The Right to Leave a Country* (Issue Paper, Council of Europe Commissioner for Human Rights, 2013).

Guild, E, 'The UN Global Compact for Safe, Orderly and Regular Migration: What Place for Human Rights?' (2019) 30 *International Journal of Refugee Law* 661.

Guild, E and Grundler, M, 'The EU Visa Policy: To Deter and to Facilitate' in E Tsourdi and P De Bruycker (eds), *Research Handbook on EU Migration and Asylum Law* (Cheltenham, Edward Elgar Publishing, 2022).

Guild, E and Stoyanova, V, 'The Human Right to Leave Any Country: A Right to Be Delivered' in W Benedek and others (eds), *European Yearbook on Human Rights 2018* (Plymouth, Intersentia, 2018).

Guilfoyle, D, *Shipping Interdiction and the Law of the Sea* (Cambridge, CUP, 2009).

Guiraudon, V, 'Before the EU Border: Remote Control of the "Huddled Masses"' in K Groenendijk, E Guild and P Minderhoud (eds), *In Search of Europe's Borders* (The Hague, Kluwer Law International, 2003).

Gülzau, F, and Mau, S, 'Visas and Border Infrastructures: What Makes Them Tighter or Looser?' in E Recchi and M Safi (eds), *Handbook of Human Mobility and Migration* (Cheltenham, Edward Elgar Publishing, 2024).

Gündoğdu, A, 'From the Colony to the Border: The Lawful Lawlessness of Racial Violence' in S Benhabib and A Shachar (eds), *Lawless Zones, Rightless Subjects: Migration, Asylum, and Shifting Borders* (Cambridge, CUP, 2025).

Haddad, E, *The Refugee in International Society: Between Sovereigns* (Cambridge, CUP, 2008).

Hailbronner, K, 'Comments on the Right to Leave, Return and Remain' in V Gowlland-Debbas (ed), *The Problem of Refugees in the Light of Contemporary International Law Issues* (The Hague, Martinus Nijhoff, 1996).

Hailbronner, K, 'Introduction into the EU Immigration and Asylum Law' in K Hailbronner (ed), *EU Immigration and Asylum Law: Commentary* (Munich, CH Beck, 2010).

Hakimi, M, 'State Bystander Responsibility' (2010) 21 *European Journal of International Law* 341.

Hammoud-Gallego, O, 'The Short-Term Effects of Visa Restrictions on Migrants' Legal Status and Well-Being: A Difference-in-Differences Approach on Venezuelan Displacement' (2024) 182 *World Development* 1.

Hancox, E, 'The Relationship Between the Charter and General Principles: Looking Back and Looking Forward' (2020) 22 *Cambridge Yearbook of European Legal Studies* 233.

Hannum, H, *The Right to Leave and Return in International Law and Practice* (Dordrecht, Martinus Nijhoff, 1987).

Hannum, H, 'The Strasbourg Declaration on the Right to Leave and Return' (1987) 81 *American Journal of International Law* 432.

Harvey, C and Barnidge, RP, 'Human Rights, Free Movement, and the Right to Leave in International Law' (2007) 19 *International Journal of Refugee Law* 1.

Hathaway, JC, 'The Emerging Politics of *Non-Entrée*' (1992) 91 *Refugees* 40.

Hathaway, JC, *The Rights of Refugees under International Law* (Cambridge, CUP, 2005).

Hathaway, JC, 'The False Panacea of Offshore Deterrence' (2006) 26 *Forced Migration Review* 56.

Hathaway, JC, 'The Human Rights Quagmire of "Human Trafficking"' (2008) 49 *Virginia Journal of International Law* 1.

Heck, G and others (eds), *Making Routes: Mobility and Politics of Migration in the Global South* (Cairo, The American University in Cairo Press, 2024).

Helfer, LR, 'Subregional Courts in Africa: Litigating the Hybrid Right to Free Movement of Persons' (2018) 16 *I-CON: International Journal of Constitutional Law* 235.

Helton, AC, 'Asylum and Refugee Protection in Thailand' (1989) 1 *International Journal of Refugee Law* 20.

Higgins, C, *Safe Journeys and Sound Policy: Expanding Protected Entry for Refugees* (Policy Brief 8, Kaldor Centre for International Refugee Law, 2019).

Higgins, R, 'The Right in International Law of an Individual to Enter, Stay in and Leave a Country' (1973) 49 *International Affairs* 341.

Hirsch, AL, 'The Borders Beyond the Border: Australia's Extraterritorial Migration Controls' (2017) 36 *Refugee Survey Quarterly* 48.

Hirsch, AL, 'Externalisation and Access to Asylum: An Investigation into Australia's Migration Control Cooperation with Indonesia' (DPhil thesis, Monash University 2022).

Hirsch, AL and Bell, N, 'The Right to Have Rights as a Right to Enter: Addressing a Lacuna in the International Refugee Protection Regime' (2017) 18 *Human Rights Review* 417.

Hirsch, AL and Doig, C, 'Outsourcing Control: The International Organization for Migration in Indonesia' (2018) 22 *International Journal of Human Rights* 681.

Hollifield, JF, 'The Emerging Migration State' (2004) 38 *International Migration Review* 885.

Horák, S, 'Visa Regimes and Regulatory Documents as an Obstacle for Tourism Development in Central Asia' in K Kantarci, M Uysal and VP Magnini (eds), *Tourism in Central Asia: Cultural Potential and Challenges* (New Jersey, Apple Academic Press, 2014).

Human Rights Watch, *"Trigger Happy": Excessive Use of Force by Indian Troops at the Bangladesh Border* (New York, HRW, 2010).

Human Rights Watch, *'They Fired on Us Like Rain' Saudi Arabian Mass Killings of Ethiopian Migrants at the Yemen-Saudi Border* (New York, HRW, 2023).

Human Rights Watch, *"This Hell Was My Only Option": Abuses Against Migrants and Asylum Seekers Pushed to Cross the Darién Gap* (New York, HRW, 2023).

Human Rights Watch, *"I Can't Go Home, Stay Here, or Leave": Pushbacks and Pullbacks of Syrian Refugees from Cyprus and Lebanon* (New York, HRW, 2024).

Human Rights Watch, *"Nobody Cared, Nobody Listened": The US Expulsion of Third-Country Nationals to Panama* (New York, HRW, 2025).

Human Rights Watch, *'The Strategy Is to Break Us': The US Expulsion of Third-Country Nationals to Costa Rica* (New York, HRW, 2025).

Human Rights Watch and Refugees International, *Deportation with a Layover: Failure of Protection under the US-Guatemala Asylum Cooperative Agreement* (2020).

Infantino, F, *Outsourcing Border Control: Politics and Practice of Contracted Visa Policy in Morocco* (New York, Palgrave Macmillan, 2016).

Infantino, F, *Schengen Visa Implementation and Transnational Policymaking: Bordering Europe* (New York, Palgrave Macmillan, 2019).

Jackson, M, *Complicity in International Law* (Oxford, OUP, 2015).

Jackson, M, 'Freeing *Soering*: The ECHR, State Complicity in Torture and Jurisdiction' (2016) 27 *European Journal of International Law* 817.

Jansen, S, 'After the Red Passport: Towards an Anthropology of the Everyday Geopolitics of Entrapment in the EU's "Immediate Outside"' (2009) 15 *Journal of the Royal Anthropological Institute* 815.

Jansson, L, 'Everyday Efforts of the International Organization for Migration to (Re)Create Migration Management in and Through the Bali Process: An Institutional Work Lens' (2025) *Journal of Ethnic and Migration Studies* 1285.

Jayangakula, K, 'Refugee Protection in Thailand' in S Lee and HE Lee (eds), *Asian Yearbook of International Law*, vol 28 (London, Brill, 2022).

Jefferies, R, 'Bringing Externalization Home: The International Civil Aviation Organization and "Entry Screening" in Australia' (2021) *Globalizations* 1.

Jefferies, R and McAdam, J, 'Locked in: Australia's COVID-19 Border Closures and the Right to Leave' (2023) 41 *Australian Year Book of International Law* 185.

Jefferies, R, Ghezelbash, D and Hirsch, A, 'Assessing Refugee Protection Claims at Australian Airports: The Gap Between Law, Policy, and Practice' (2021) 44 *Melbourne University Law Review* 1.

Jennings, R and Watts, A, *Oppenheim's International Law: Volume 1 Peace,* 9th edn (New York, Longman, 1992).

Johansen, SØ, *The Human Rights Accountability Mechanisms of International Organizations* (Cambridge, CUP, 2020).

Jones, K, Sha, H and Bhuiyan, MRA, 'Overcoming and Reproducing Inequalities: Mediated Migration in the "Global South"' in H Crawley and JK Teye (eds), *The Palgrave Handbook of South–South Migration and Inequality* (Cham, Palgrave Macmillan, 2024).

Jones, R and Johnson, C, 'Border Militarisation and the Re-articulation of Sovereignty' (2016) 41 *Transactions of the Institute of British Geographers* 187.

Juss, S, 'Free Movement and the World Order' (2004) 16 *International Journal of Refugee Law* 289.

Kai, L, 'Embracing the Chinese Exclusion Case: An International Law Approach to Racial Exclusions' (2018) 59 *William & Mary Law Review* 2617.

Kandilige, L and Yeboah, T, 'West African Migration Regimes and the Externalization of EU Migration Management Policies' in G Heck and others (eds), *Making Routes: Mobility and Politics of Migration in the Global South* (Cairo, The American University in Cairo Press, 2024).

Kanetake, M and Nollkaemper, A, 'The Application of Informal International Instruments Before Domestic Courts' (2014) 46 *George Washington International Law Review* 765.

Kanstroom, D, 'The "Right to Remain Here" as an Evolving Component of Global Refugee Protection: Current Initiatives and Critical Questions' (2017) 5 *Journal on Migration and Human Security* 614.

Keller, H and Walther, R, 'Evasion of the International Law of State Responsibility? The ECtHR's Jurisprudence on Positive and Preventive Obligations under Article 3' (2019) 24 *International Journal of Human Rights* 957.

Kent, G, 'The Human Rights Obligations of Intergovernmental Organizations' (2005) 42 *UN Chronicle* 32.

Kerwin, D and Martínez, DE, 'Forced Migration, Deterrence, and Solutions to the Non-Natural Disaster of Migrant Deaths Along the US-Mexico Border and Beyond' (2024) 12 *Journal on Migration and Human Security* 127.

Kinchin, N, 'The Implied Human Rights Obligations of UNHCR' (2016) 28 *International Journal of Refugee Law* 251.

Kiss, AC, 'Permissible Limitations on Rights' in L Henkin (ed), *The International Bill of Rights: The Covenant on Civil and Political Rights* (New York, Columbia University Press, 1981).

Klabbers, J, *Advanced Introduction to the Law of International Organizations* (Cheltenham, Edward Elgar Publishing, 2015).

Klabbers, J, 'Sources of International Organizations' Law: Reflections on Accountability' in d'Aspremont, J and Besson, S (eds), *Oxford Handbook of the Sources of International Law* (Oxford, OUP, 2017).

Klein, N, *Maritime Security and the Law of the Sea* (Oxford, OUP, 2011).

Kleist, JO, 'The Return of "Cold War" Refugee Policy' (2022) *International Politics & Society Journal.*

Kneebone, S, *Refugees, Asylum Seekers and the Rule of Law: Comparative Perspectives* (Cambridge, CUP, 2009).

Kneebone, S, 'Australia as a Powerbroker on Refugee Protection in Southeast Asia' (2017) 33 *Refuge* 29.

Kneebone, S and Missbach, A, 'The Human Rights Implications of Australian and Indonesian Anti-Smuggling Laws' (2018) 4 *International Journal of Migration and Border Studies* 379.

Koch, IE, 'Dichotomies, Trichotomies or Waves of Duties?' (2005) 5 *Human Rights Law Review* 81.

Kochenov, D, 'The Right to Leave Any Country Including Your Own in International Law' (2012) 28 *Connecticut Journal of International Law* 43.
Korkmaz, EE (ed), *Digital Identity, Virtual Borders and Social Media: A Panacea for Migration Governance?* (Cheltenham, Edward Elgar Publishing, 2021).
Koslowski, R, 'The International Travel Regime' in R Koslowski (ed), *Global Mobility Regimes* (New York, Palgrave Macmillan, 2011).
Kron, S and Ness, I, 'Central America: Regional Migration and Border Policies' in I Ness and GD Woolf (eds), *The Encyclopedia of Global Human Migration* (London, Wiley, 2013).
Lahav, G, 'Immigration and the State: The Devolution and Privatisation of Immigration Control in the EU' (1998) 24 *Journal of Ethnic and Migration Studies* 675.
Lambert, H, 'Temporary Refuge from War: Customary International Law and the Syrian Conflict' (2017) 66 *International & Comparative Law Quarterly* 723.
Lanovoy, V, *Complicity and its Limits in the Law of International Responsibility* (Oxford, Hart Publishing, 2016).
Laube, L, 'The Relational Dimension of Externalizing Border Control: Selective Visa Policies in Migration and Border Diplomacy' (2019) 7 *Comparative Migration Studies* 1.
Lauterpacht, E and Bethlehem, D, 'The Scope and Content of the Principle of *Non-Refoulement*: Opinion' in E Feller, V Türk and F Nicholson (eds), *Refugee Protection in International Law: UNHCR's Global Consultations on International Protection* (Cambridge, CUP, 2003).
Lauterpacht, H, *International Law and Human Rights* (London, Stevens and Sons, 1950).
Lawson, RA and Roychoudhury, S, 'Do Travel Visa Requirements Impede Tourist Travel?' (2016) 40 *Journal of Economics and Finance* 817.
Lee, M, 'The Externalization of Border Control in the Global South: The Cases of Malaysia and Indonesia' (2022) 26 *Theoretical Criminology* 537.
Lemberg-Pedersen, M, 'Manufacturing Displacement. Externalization and Postcoloniality in European Migration Control' (2019) 5 *Global Affairs* 247.
Lenard, PT, 'Exit and the Duty to Admit' (2015) 8 *Ethics & Global Politics* 25975.
Lester, E, *Making Migration Law: The Foreigner, Sovereignty, and the Case of Australia* (Cambridge, CUP, 2018)
Liu, G, *The Right to Leave and Return and Chinese Migration Law* (Leiden, Martinus Nijhoff, 2007).
Lockwood, BB, Finn, J and Jubinsky, G, 'Working Paper for the Committee of Experts on Limitation Provisions' (1985) 7 *Human Rights Quarterly* 35.
Long, K, 'In Search of Sanctuary: Border Closures, "Safe" Zones and Refugee Protection' (2013) 26 *Journal of Refugee Studies* 458.
Low, CC, 'Externalization of Border Control in ASEAN Countries' in AKMA Ullah (eds), *Handbook of Migration, International Relations and Security in Asia* (Singapore, Springer Singapore, 2024).
Macklin, A, 'A Safe Country to Emulate? Canada and the European Refugee' in H Lambert, J McAdam and M Fullerton (eds), *The Global Reach of European Refugee Law* (Cambridge, CUP, 2013).
Macklin, A, 'Exit Rights, Seamless Borders and the New Carceral State' (2024) 73 *ICLQ* 891.
Majcher, I, 'Human Rights Violations During EU Border Surveillance and Return Operations: Frontex' Shared Responsibility or Complicity?' (2015) 7 *Silesian Journal of Legal Studies* 45.
Mann, I, *Humanity at Sea: Maritime Migration and the Foundations of International Law* (Cambridge, CUP, 2016).
Mann, I, 'Border Violence as Crime' (2021) 42 *University of Pennsylvania Journal of International Law* 675.
Markard, N, 'The Right to Leave by Sea: Legal Limits on EU Migration Control by Third Countries' (2016) 27 *European Journal of International Law* 591.
Martín Gil, A, 'Managing Migration Through Foreign Aid in Mexico and Central America: The Role of U.S. Conditionality on Mexico's Migration Policies' (2025) 23 *Journal of Immigrant & Refugee Studies* 147.

Martini, LS, and Megerisi, T, *Road to Nowhere: Why Europe's Border Externalisation is a Dead End* (London, European Council on Foreign Relations, 2023).
Mathew, P, 'Legal Issues Concerning Interception' (2003) 17 *Georgetown Immigration Law Journal* 221.
Mau, S, 'Mobility Citizenship, Inequality, and the Liberal State: The Case of Visa Policies' (2010) 4 *International Political Sociology* 339.
Mau, S and others, *Liberal States and the Freedom of Movement: Selective Borders, Unequal Mobility* (Hampshire, Palgrave Macmillan, 2012).
Mau, S and others, 'The Global Mobility Divide: How Visa Policies Have Evolved over Time' (2015) 41 *Journal of Ethnic and Migration Studies* 1192.
Mayblin, L, *Asylum After Empire: Colonial Legacies in the Politics of Asylum Seeking* (London, Roman & Littlefield International, 2017).
McAdam, J, *Complementary Protection in International Refugee Law* (Oxford, OUP, 2007).
McAdam, J, 'An Intellectual History of Freedom of Movement in International Law: The Right to Leave as a Personal Liberty' (2011) 12 *Melbourne Journal of International Law* 27.
McDonnell, E, 'Challenging Externalisation Through the Lens of the Human Right to Leave' (2024) 71 *Netherlands International Law Review* 119.
Menjívar, C, 'Immigration Law Beyond Borders: Externalizing and Internalizing Border Controls in an Era of Securitization' (2014) 10 *Annual Review of Law and Social Science* 353.
Meron, T, 'Extraterritoriality of Human Rights Treaties' (1995) 89 *American Journal of International Law* 78.
Milanovic, M, *Extraterritorial Application of Human Rights Treaties: Law, Principles, and Policy* (Oxford, OUP, 2011).
Milanovic, M, 'Human Rights Treaties and Foreign Surveillance: Privacy in the Digital Age' (2015) 56 *Harvard International Law Journal* 81.
Missbach, A and Hoffstaedter, G, 'When Transit States Pursue Their Own Agenda' (2020) 3 *Migration and Society* 64.
Missbach, A and Phillips, M, 'Reconceptualizing Transit States in an Era of Outsourcing, Offshoring, and Obfuscation' (2020) 3 *Migration and Society* 19.
Mitsilegas, V, 'Extraterritorial Immigration Control, Preventive Justice and the Rule of Law in Turbulent Times: Lessons from the Anti-Smuggling Crusade' in S Carrera, JS Vara and T Strik (eds), *Constitutionalising the External Dimensions of EU Migration Policies in Times of Crisis: Legality, Rule of Law and Fundamental Rights Reconsidered* (Cheltenham, Edward Elgar Publishing, 2019).
Mohan, SS, 'The Interrupting Island: Trinidad and Tobago and the Shifting Migration Trajectories of Venezuelans' in J Crush, A Chikanda and S Ramachandran (eds), *New Directions in South-South Migration* (Singapore, Springer Singapore, 2025).
Molinari, C, 'The EU and its Perilous Journey through the Migration Crisis: Informalisation of the EU Return Policy and Rule of Law Concerns' (2019) 44 *European Law Review* 824.
Moraru, M, 'The EU Fundamental Right to Asylum: In Search of Its Legal Meaning and Effects' in S Iglesias Sánchez and M González Pascual (eds), *Fundamental Rights in the EU Area of Freedom, Security and Justice* (Cambridge, CUP, 2021).
Moreno-Lax, V, 'Must EU Borders have Doors for Refugees? On the Compatibility of Schengen Visas and Carriers' Sanctions with EU Member States' Obligations to Provide International Protection to Refugees' (2008) 10 *European Journal of International Law* 315.
Moreno-Lax, V, 'Seeking Asylum in the Mediterranean: Against a Fragmentary Reading of EU Member States' Obligations Accruing at Sea' (2011) 23 *International Journal of Refugee Law* 174.
Moreno-Lax, V, 'The Legality of the "Safe Third Country" Notion Contested: Insights from the Law of Treaties' in GS Goodwin-Gill and P Weckel (eds), *Migration & Refugee Protection in the 21st Century: Legal Aspects – The Hague Academy of International Law Centre for Research* (The Hague, Martinus Nijhoff, 2015).

Moreno-Lax, V, *Accessing Asylum in Europe: Extraterritorial Border Controls and Refugee Rights under EU Law* (Oxford, OUP, 2017).
Moreno-Lax, V, *The Interdiction of Asylum Seekers at Sea: Law and (Mal)practice in Europe and Australia* (Policy Brief 4, Kaldor Centre for International Refugee Law, 2017).
Moreno-Lax, V, 'The Architecture of Functional Jurisdiction: Unpacking Contactless Control – On Public Powers, *SS and Others v Italy*, and the "Operational Model"' (2020) 21 *German Law Journal* 385.
Moreno-Lax, V, 'Intersectionality, Forced Migration, and the Jus-Generation of the Right to Flee: Theorising a Composite Entitlement to Leave to Escape Irreversible Harm' in B Çalı, L Bianku and I Motoc (eds), *Migration and the European Convention on Human Rights* (Oxford, OUP, 2021).
Moreno-Lax, V, 'Protection at Sea and the Denial of Asylum' in C Costello, M Foster and J McAdam (eds), *The Oxford Handbook of International Refugee Law* (Oxford, OUP, 2021).
Moreno-Lax, V, 'The "Crisification" of Migration Law: Insights from the EU External Border' in SB Elias, K Cope and J Goldenziel (eds) *The Oxford Handbook of Comparative Immigration Law* (Oxford, OUP, 2023).
Moreno-Lax, V and Papastavridis, E, *'Boat Refugees' and Migrants at Sea: A Comprehensive Approach: Integrating Maritime Security with Human Rights* (Dordrecht, Brill Nijhoff, 2016).
Morris, JC, *Asylum and Extraction in the Republic of Nauru* (New York, Cornell University Press, 2023).
Mungianu, R, *Frontex and Non-Refoulement: The International Responsibility of the EU* (Cambridge, CUP, 2016).
Mussi, F and Tan, F, 'Comparing Cooperation on Migration Control: Italy–Libya and Australia–Indonesia' in F de Londras and S Mullaly (eds), *Irish Yearbook of International Law 2015* (Oxford, Hart Publishing, 2017).
Nafziger, JAR, 'The General Admission of Aliens under International Law' (1983) 77 *American Journal of International Law* 804.
Natter, K, 'Tunisia's Migration Politics Throughout the 2011 Revolution: Revisiting the Democratisation–Migrant Rights Nexus' (2022) 43 *Third World Quarterly* 1551.
Nessel, LA, 'Externalized Borders and the Invisible Refugee' (2009) 40 *Columbia Human Rights Law Review* 625.
Nethery, A, Rafferty-Brown, B and Taylor, S, 'Exporting Detention: Australia-Funded Immigration Detention in Indonesia' (2013) 26 *Journal of Refugee Studies* 88.
Nethery, A and Gordyn, C, 'Australia-Indonesia Cooperation on Asylum-Seekers: A Case of "Incentivised Policy Transfer"' (2014) 68 *Australian Journal of International Affairs* 177.
Neumayer, E, 'Unequal Access to Foreign Spaces: How States Use Visa Restrictions to Regulate Mobility in a Globalised World' (2006) 31 *Transactions of the Institute of British Geographers* 72.
Nicolosi, SF, 'Going Unnoticed? Diagnosing the Right to Asylum in the Charter of Fundamental Rights of the European Union' (2017) 23 *European Law Journal* 94.
Noll, G, *Negotiating Asylum: the EU Acquis, Extraterritorial Protection and the Common Market of Deflection* (The Hague, Martinus Nijhoff, 2000).
Noll, G, 'Seeking Asylum at Embassies: A Right to Entry under International Law?' (2005) 17 *International Journal of Refugee Law* 542.
Noll, G, Fagerlund, J and Liebaut, F, *Study on the Feasibility of Processing Asylum Claims outside the EU Against the Background of the Common European Asylum System and the Goal of a Common Asylum Procedure* (Copenhagen, Danish Centre for Human Rights and European Commission, 2003).
Nollkaemper, A and Plakokefalos, I, *Principles of Shared Responsibility in International Law: An Appraisal of the State of the Art* (Cambridge, CUP, 2014).
Nollkaemper, A and others, *The Practice of Shared Responsibility in International Law* (Cambridge, CUP, 2017).
Nollkaemper, A and others, 'Guiding Principles on Shared Responsibility in International Law' (2020) 31 *European Journal of International Law* 15.

Nowak, M, *UN Covenant on Civil and Political Rights: CCPR Commentary*, 2nd edn (Kehl, NP Engel, 2005).

Ogg, K, 'Protection Closer to Home? A Legal Case for Claiming Asylum at Embassies and Consulates' (2014) 33 *Refugee Survey Quarterly* 81.

Oloo, A and Vanderhole, W, 'Enforcement of Extraterritorial Human Rights Obligations in the African Human Rights System' in M Gibney and others (eds), *The Routledge Handbook on Extraterritorial Human Rights Obligations* (Abingdon/New York, Routledge, 2021).

Opi, B, 'Borders Recolonised – The Impacts of the EU Externalisation Policy in Africa' (2021) 3 *Journal of Decolonising Disciplines* 1.

Oppenheim, L and Lauterpacht, H, *International Law: A Treatise*, 8th edn (New York, Longmans, 1955).

Osso, BN, 'Unpacking the Safe Third Country Concept in the European Union: B/orders, Legal Spaces, and Asylum in the Shadow of Externalization' (2023) 35 *International Journal of Refugee Law* 272.

Ostrand, N, 'Overseas Immigration Liaison Officers: "Knowledge Brokers" and Transnational Spaces of Mid-Level Negotiations Shaping Extraterritorial Migration Control Practices' (2022) 10 *Migration Studies* 41.

Owen, D, 'Migration, Structural Injustice and Domination on "Race", Mobility and Transnational Positional Difference' (2020) 46 *Journal of Ethnic and Migration Studies* 2585.

Owen, D, 'Global Justice and the Governance of Transnational Migration' in L Weber and C Tazreiter, *Handbook of Migration and Global Justice* (Cheltenham, Edward Elgar Publishing, 2021).

Papastavridis, E, '"Fortress Europe" and FRONTEX: Within or Without International Law?' (2010) 79 *Nordic Journal of International Law* 75.

Papastavridis, E, *The Interception of Vessels on the High Seas: Contemporary Challenges to the Legal Order of the Oceans* (London, Hart Publishing, 2013).

Papastavridis, E, 'The Interplay Between Maritime Interdiction Operations and Human Rights Law' (2014) 1 *Acta Criminologica: Southern African Journal of Criminology* 36.

Papastavridis, E, 'EUNAVFOR MED Operation Sophia and the Question of Jurisdiction over Transnational Organized Crime at Sea' (2016) 30 *QIL Zoom-in* 19.

Papastavridis, E, 'The European Convention of Human Rights and Migration at Sea: Reading the "Jurisdictional Threshold" of the Convention Under the Law of the Sea Paradigm' (2020) 21 *German Law Journal* 417.

Paz, M, 'The Incomplete Right to Freedom of Movement' (2017) 111 *American Journal of International Law* 514.

Paz, M, 'The Law of Walls' (2017) 28 *European Journal of International Law* 601.

Paz, M, 'The Legal Reconstruction of Walls: *ND & NT. v Spain*, 2017, 2020' (2020) 22 *NYU Journal of Legislation & Public Policy* 693.

Pellet, A, 'Decisions of the ICJ as Sources of International Law?' in E Cannizzaro and others (eds), *Gaetano Morelli Lectures Series: Decisions of the ICJ as Sources of International Law?*, vol 2 (Rome, International and European Papers Publishing, 2018).

Perrin, D, 'Regulating Migration and Asylum in the Maghreb: What Inspirations for an Accelerated Legal Development?' in F Ippolito and S Trevisanut (eds), *Migration in the Mediterranean – Mechanisms of International Cooperation* (Cambridge, CUP, 2016).

Peters, A, 'Humanity as the A and Ω of Sovereignty' (2009) 20 *European Journal of International Law* 513.

Pijnenburg, A, 'From Italian Pushbacks to Libyan Pullbacks: Is *Hirsi 2.0* in the Making in Strasbourg?' (2018) 20 *European Journal of Migration and Law* 396.

Pijnenburg, A, 'Containment Instead of *Refoulement*: Shifting State Responsibility in the Age of Cooperative Migration Control?' (2020) 20 *Human Rights Law Review* 306.

Pirjola, J, 'Hostile Instrumentalized Migration and the Right to Seek Asylum: Reflecting the European Legal Framework' (2025) 27 *European Journal of Migration and Law* 1.

Provera, M, *The Detention of Asylum Seekers in the European Union and Australia: A Comparative Analysis* (Nijmegen, Wolf Legal Publishers, 2013).
Rachovitsa, A, 'The Principle of Systemic Integration in Human Rights Law' (2017) 66 *International & Comparative Law Quarterly* 557.
Raty, T and Shilhav, R, *The EU Trust Fund for Africa: Trapped between Aid Policy and Migration Politics* (Briefing Paper, Oxfam 2020).
Rayp, G, Ruyssen, I and Marchand, K (eds), *Regional Integration and Migration Governance in the Global South* (Cham, Springer, 2020).
Reardon-Smith, S, 'Linking Land and Sea: Intersections between Indigenous Peoples' Dispossession and Asylum Seekers' Containment by Australia' (2024) 7 *Migration and Society* 153.
Refugee Law Initiative, 'Declaration on Externalisation and Asylum' (2022) 34 *International Journal of Refugee Law* 114.
Reinisch, A, 'Securing the Accountability of International Organizations' in J Klabbers (ed), *International Organizations* (Abingdon/New York, Routledge, 2016).
Rietiker, D, 'The Principle of "Effectiveness" in the Recent Jurisprudence of the European Court of Human Rights: Its Different Dimensions and Its Consistency with Public International Law – No Need for the Concept of Treaty *Sui Generis*' (2010) 79 *Nordic Journal of International Law* 245.
Rijpma, JJ, 'External Migration and Asylum Management: Accountability for Executive Action Outside EU-territory' (2017) 2 *European Papers* 571.
Rinaldi, A and Teo, SA, 'The Use of Artificial Intelligence Technologies in Border and Migration Control and the Subtle Erosion of Human Rights' (2025) 74 *International & Comparative Law Quarterly* 61.
Robinson, WC, 'The Comprehensive Plan of Action for Indochinese Refugees, 1989–1997: Sharing the Burden and Passing the Buck' (2004) 17 *Journal of Refugee Studies* 319.
Rodenhäuser, T, 'Another Brick in the Wall: Carrier Sanctions and the Privatisation of Immigration Control' (2014) 26 *International Journal of Refugee Law* 223.
Rugunanan, P and Nomkhosi, XG (eds), *Migration in Southern Africa: IMISCOE Regional Reader* (Cham, Springer, 2022).
Ryan, B, 'Extraterritorial Immigration Control: What Role for Legal Guarantees?' in B Ryan and V Mitsilegas (eds), *Extraterritorial Immigration Control: Legal Challenges* (Leiden, Martinus Nijhoff, 2010).
Saddiki, S, *World of Walls: The Structure, Roles and Effectiveness of Separation Barriers* (Camdrige, Open Book Publishers, 2017).
Salter, MB, 'The Global Visa Regime and the Political Technologies of the International Self: Borders, Bodies, Biopolitics' (2006) 31 *Alternatives* 167.
Sassen, S, *Territory, Authority, Rights: From Medieval to Global Assemblages* (Princeton, Princeton University Press, 2008).
Sassen, S, *Losing Control? Sovereignty in an Age of Globalisation* (New York, Columbia University Press, 2015).
Schermers, HG and Blokker, NM, *International Institutional Law: Unity within Diversity*, 6th edn (Boston, Brill Nijhoff, 2018).
Scholten, S, *The Privatisation of Immigration Control through Carrier Sanctions: The Role of Private Transport Companies in Dutch and British Immigration Control* (Leiden, Brill Nijhoff, 2015).
Scholten, S and Minderhoud, P, 'Regulating Immigration Control: Carrier Sanctions in the Netherlands' (2008) 10 *European Journal of Migration and Law* 123.
Shachar, A, *The Birthright Lottery: Citizenship and Global Inequality* (Cambridge, HUP, 2009).
Shachar, A, *The Shifting Border: Legal Cartographies of Migration and Mobility. Ayelet Shachar in Dialogue* (Manchester, Manchester University Press, 2020).

Shachar, A and Ghezelbash, D, 'How and Why "Ideas Travel" in Migration Law and Policy' in K Cope, S Burch Elias and J Goldenziel (eds), *The Oxford Handbook of Comparative Immigration Law* (Oxford, OUP, forthcoming).

Shachar, A and Ramji-Nogales, J (eds), 'Unsettling the Sovereign "Right to Exclude"' (2024) 118 *American Journal of International Law* 187.

Shany, Y, 'Taking Universality Seriously: A Functional Approach to Extraterritoriality in International Human Rights Law' (2013) 7 *Law & Ethics of Human Rights* 47.

Sherwood, A, Lemay, I and Costello, C, 'IOM's Immigration Detention Practices and Policies: Human Rights, Positive Obligations and Humanitarian Duties' in M Bradley, C Costello and A Sherwood (eds), *IOM Unbound?: Obligations and Accountability of the International Organization for Migration in an Era of Expansion* (Cambridge, CUP, 2023).

Simma, B, 'From Bilateralism to Community Interest in International Law' (1994) 250 Recueil des Cours (Collected Courses of the Hague Academy of International Law) 217.

Soboka, BT and Chenwi, L, *Extraterritoriality in the African Regional Human Rights System from a Comparative Perspective* (Cambridge, Intersentia, 2018).

Sohn, LB and Buergenthal, T, *The Movement of Persons Across Borders* (Washington DC, American Society of International Law, 1992).

Somin, I, *Free to Move: Foot Voting, Migration, and Political Freedom* (Oxford, OUP, 2020).

Spijkerboer, T, 'Moving Migrants, States, and Rights: Human Rights and Border Deaths' (2013) 7 *Law & Ethics of Human Rights* 213.

Spijkerboer, T, 'Wasted Lives. Borders and the Right to Life of People Crossing Them' (2017) 86 *Nordic Journal of International Law* 1.

Spijkerboer, T, 'Bifurcation of People, Bifurcation of Law: Externalisation of Migration Policy before the EU Court of Justice' (2018) 31 *Journal of Refugee Studies* 216.

Spijkerboer, T, 'The Global Mobility Infrastructure: Reconceptualising the Externalisation of Migration Control' (2018) 20 *European Journal of Migration and Law* 452.

Spijkerboer, T and Steyger, E, 'European External Migration Funds and Public Procurement Law' (2019) 4 *European Papers* 493.

Staples, H, 'Adjudicating the External Schengen Border' in K Groenendijk, E Guild and P Minderhoud (eds), *In Search of Europe's Borders* (The Hague, Kluwer Law International, 2003).

Stats NZ, *Algorithm Assessment Report* (Wellington, Te Tari Taiwhenua Internal Affairs, 2018).

Stock, I, Üstübici, A and Schultz, SU, 'Externalization at Work: Responses to Migration Policies from the Global South' (2019) 7 *Comparative Migration Studies* 48.

Stoyanova, V, 'The Principle of *Non-Refoulement* and the Right of Asylum-Seekers to Enter State Territory' (2008) 3 *Interdisciplinary Journal of Human Rights Law* 1.

Stoyanova, V, 'Dancing on the Borders of Article 4: Human Trafficking and the European Court of Human Rights in the *Rantsev* Case' (2012) 30 *Netherlands Quarterly of Human Rights* 163.

Stoyanova, V, 'Causation between State Omission and Harm within the Framework of Positive Obligations under the European Convention on Human Rights' (2018) 18 *Human Rights Law Review* 309.

Stoyanova, V, 'The Right to Leave Any Country and the Interplay between Jurisdiction and Proportionality in Human Rights Law' (2020) 32 *International Journal of Refugee Law* 403.

Stoyanova, V, 'The Right to Life Under the EU Charter and Cooperation with Third States to Combat Human Smuggling' (2020) 21 *German Law Journal* 436.

Stoyanova, V, *Positive Obligations under the European Convention on Human Rights: Within and Beyond Boundaries* (Oxford, OUP, 2023).

Strik, T, 'The Global Approach to Migration and Mobility' (2017) 5 *Groningen Journal of International Law* 310.

Strik, T, 'Frontex's Expanding Mandate: Has Democratic Control Caught Up?' (2024) 30 *European Law Journal* 217.

Takele Soboka, B and Chenwi, L, *Extraterritoriality in the African Regional Human Rights System from a Comparative Perspective* (Cambridge, Intersentia, 2018).

Talbot, A, Vogl, A and Dehm, S, 'The Gender- and Sexuality-Based Harms of Refugee Externalization: A Role for Human Rights Due Diligence' (2024) 23 *International Journal of Refugee Law* 60.

Tan, NF, 'State Responsibility and Migration Control: Australia's International Deterrence Model' in T Gammeltoft-Hansen and J Vedsted-Hansen (eds), *Human Rights and the Dark Side of Globalisation: Transnational Law Enforcement and Migration Control* (Abingdon/New York, Routledge, 2017).

Tan, NF, 'The Manus Island Regional Processing Centre: A Legal Taxonomy' (2018) 20 *European Journal of Migration and Law* 427.

Tan, NF, 'International Models of Deterrence and the Future of Access to Asylum' in SS Juss (ed), *Research Handbook on International Refugee Law* (Cheltenham, Edward Elgar Publishing, 2019).

Tan, NF, 'Conceptualising Externalisation: Still Fit for Purpose?' (2021) 68 *Forced Migration Review* 8.

Tan, NF and Gammeltoft-Hansen, T, 'Topographical Approach to Accountability for Human Rights Violations in Migration Control' (2020) 21 *German Law Journal* 335.

Taylor, S, 'Offshore Barriers to Asylum Seeker Movement: The Exercise of Power without Responsibility?' in J McAdam (ed), *Forced Migration, Human Rights and Security* (Oxford, Hart Publishing, 2008).

Tennis, KH, *Outsourcing Control: The Politics of International Migration Cooperation* (Montreal, McGill-Queen's University Press, 2020).

Theilen, JT, 'Framing Migration in Human Rights: How the Reasoning of the European Court of Human Rights Legitimises Border Regimes' (2025) 27 *European Journal of Migration and Law* 66.

Thomas, C, 'What Does the Emerging International Law of Migration Mean for Sovereignty' (2013) 14 *Melbourne Journal of International Law* 392.

Tian, GY, McFarland, T and Guo, S, 'Automated Decision Making and Deportation: Legal Concerns and Regulation' (2025) *Griffith Law Review* 1.

Tinti, P and Reitano, T, *Migrant, Refugee, Smuggler, Savior* (Oxford, OUP, 2017).

Tonkin, H, *State Control Over Private Military and Security Companies in Armed Conflict* (Cambridge, CUP, 2011).

Torpey, J, *The Invention of the Passport: Surveillance, Citizenship, and the State*, 2nd edn (Cambridge, CUP, 2018).

Trauner, F and Manigrassi, E, 'When Visa-free Travel Becomes Difficult to Achieve and Easy to Lose: The EU Visa Free Dialogues after the EU's Experience with the Western Balkans' (2014) 16 *European Journal of Migration and Law* 125.

Trevisanut, S, 'The Principle of *Non-Refoulement* and the De-Territorialization of Border Control at Sea' (2014) 27 *Leiden Journal of International Law* 661.

Tsoukala, A, 'Looking at Migrants as Enemies' in D Bigo and E Guild (eds), *Controlling Frontiers: Free Movement Into and Within Europe* (Cardiff, Ashgate, 2005).

Tsourapas, G, 'The Refugee Rentier State and Norm Manipulation in the Arab World' in T Fakhoury and D Chatty (eds), *Refugee Governance in the Arab World: The International Refugee Regime and Global Politics* (London, Bloomsbury, 2025).

Tsourdi, E and Zardo, F, 'Migration Governance Through Funding: Theoretical, Normative, and Empirical Perspectives' (2025) 23 *Journal of Immigrant & Refugee Studies* 1.

Tyszler, E, 'From Controlling Mobilities to Control Over Women's Bodies: Gendered Effects of EU Border Externalization in Morocco' (2019) 7 *Comparative Migration Studies* 25.

Tzanakopoulos, A, *Disobeying the Security Council: Countermeasures Against Wrongful Sanctions* (Oxford, OUP, 2011).

Tzevelekos, VP, 'Reconstructing the Effective Control Criterion in Extraterritorial Human Rights Breaches: Direct Attribution of Wrongfulness, Due Diligence, and Concurrent Responsibility' (2014) 36 *Michigan Journal of International Law* 129.

University of Michigan, 'The Michigan Guidelines on Refugee Freedom of Movement' (2018) 39 *Michigan Journal of International Law* 5.

Üstübici, A, 'The Impact of Externalized Migration Governance on Turkey: Technocratic Migration Governance and the Production of Differentiated Legal Status' (2019) 7 *Comparative Migration Studies* 1.

Vallet, E (ed), *Borders, Fences and Walls: State of Insecurity?* (Abingdon/New York, Routledge, 2016).

Vammen, IMS, 'New Contested Borderlands: Senegalese Migrants En Route to Argentina' (2019) 7 *Comparative Migration Studies* 8.

Vammen, IMS, 'The Struggle Over Mobility Narratives: How Senegalese Activists Use Alternative Information Campaigns to Contest EU Externalization' (2024) *International Migration Review* 1.

Vammen, IMS, Signe, CR and Lucht, H, 'Borderwork in the Expanded EU-African Borderlands' (2022) 27 *Geopolitics* 1317.

Vari, E, 'Italy-Libya Memorandum of Understanding: Italy's International Obligations' (2020) 43 *Hastings International and Comparative Law Review* 105.

Vasak, K and Liskofsky, S (eds), *The Right to Leave and to Return: Papers and Recommendations of the International Colloquium Held in Uppsala, Sweden, 19-20 June 1972* (New York, The American Jewish Committee, 1976).

Vavoula, N, 'Artificial Intelligence (AI) at Schengen Borders: Automated Processing, Algorithmic Profiling and Facial Recognition in the Era of Techno-Solutionism' (2021) 23 *European Journal of Migration and Law* 457.

Vavoula, N, *Immigration and Privacy in the Law of the European Union: The Case of Information Systems* (Leiden, Brill Nijhoff, 2022).

Vedsted-Hansen, J, 'Article 28/Schedule' in A Zimmermann, J Dörschner and F Machts (eds), *The 1951 Convention Relating to the Status of Refugees and its 1967 Protocol: A Commentary* (Oxford, OUP, 2011).

Verdirame, G, *The UN and Human Rights: Who Guards the Guardians?* (Cambridge, CUP, 2011).

Vogt, W, 'Dirty Work, Dangerous Others: The Politics of Outsourced Immigration Enforcement in Mexico' (2020) 3 *Migration and Society* 50.

Waldron, J, 'Rights in Conflict' (1989) 99 *Ethics* 503.

Weinzierl, R and Lisson, U, *Border Management and Human Rights: A Study of EU Law and the Law of the Sea* (Berlin, German Institute for Human Rights, 2007).

Weis, P, 'The Right of Asylum in the Context of the Protection of Human Rights in Regional and Municipal Law' (1966) 6 *International Review of the Red Cross* 470.

Wellman, CH and Cole, P, *Debating the Ethics of Immigration: Is There a Right to Exclude?* (Oxford, OUP, 2011).

Whyte, B, 'Visa-Free Travel Privileges: An Exploratory Geographical Analysis' (2008) 10 *Tourism Geographies* 127.

Williams, K and Mountz, A, 'Between Enforcement and Precarity: Externalization and Migrant Deaths at Sea' (2018) 56 *International Migration* 74.

Winters, N and Mora Izaguirre, C, '*Es Cosa Suya*: Entanglements of Border Externalization and African Transit Migration in Northern Costa Rica' (2019) 7 *Comparative Migration Studies* 27.

Wolman, A, 'The Role of Departure States in Combating Irregular Emigration in International Law: An Historical Perspective' (2019) 31 *International Journal of Refugee Law* 30.

Wouters, J and others, 'Accountability for Human Rights Violations by International Organisations: Introductory Remarks' in J Wouters and others (eds), *Accountability for Human Rights Violations by International Organisations* (Plymouth, Intersentia, 2010).

Zampagni, F, 'Unpacking the Schengen Visa Regime. A Study on Bureaucrats and Discretion in an Italian Consulate' (2016) 31 *Journal of Borderlands Studies* 251.

Zanker, F, '"When There Is No Migration, the Whole Region Has a Problem": The Political Priorities of Migration Policies in West Africa' (2024) 10 *African Human Mobility Review* 9.

Zieck, M, 'Refugees and the Right to Freedom of Movement: From Flight to Return' (2018) 39 *Michigan Journal of International Law* 21.

Zolberg, AR, 'The Archaeology of "Remote Control"' in A Fahrmeir, O Faron and P Weil (eds), *Migration Control in the North Atlantic World: The Evolution of State Practices in Europe and the United States from the French Revolution to the Inter-War Period* (New York, Berghahn Books, 2003).

Zolberg, AR, 'Managing a World on the Move' (2006) 32 *Population and Development Review* 222.

Zolberg, AR, 'The Exit Revolution' in NL Green and F Weil (eds), *Citizenship and Those Who Leave : The Politics of Emigration and Expatriation* (Urbana, University of Illinois Press, 2007).

Zolberg, AR, 'Global Movements, Global Walls: Responses to Migration, 1885–1925' in G Wang (ed), *Global History and Migrations* (Abingdon/New York, Routledge, 2018).

Index

www.ingramcontent.com/pod-product-compliance
Ingram Content Group UK Ltd.
Pitfield, Milton Keynes, MK11 3LW, UK
UKHW020845290926
15470UKWH00004B/1563